19TH-CENTURY AMERICA
FURNITURE AND
OTHER DECORATIVE ARTS

Introduction by
BERRY B. TRACY
Curator, The American Wing

Furniture texts by
MARILYNN JOHNSON

Other decorative arts texts by
MARVIN D. SCHWARTZ
and SUZANNE BOORSCH

19TH-CENTURY AMERICA

FURNITURE AND
OTHER DECORATIVE ARTS

AN EXHIBITION IN CELEBRATION OF

THE HUNDREDTH ANNIVERSARY OF

THE METROPOLITAN MUSEUM OF ART

APRIL 16 THROUGH SEPTEMBER 7, 1970

New York (City).

THE METROPOLITAN MUSEUM OF ART.

Distributed by NEW YORK GRAPHIC SOCIETY LTD.

All photographs supplied by the lenders or Helga Photo Studio, Inc., except: Lee Boltin, 47, 92; Earl Colter Studio, 219; Andrew N. Foster, 68; H. Pearl, 185; The Holmes I. Mettee Studio, 6; Marvin Rand, 242, 294-298; Isreal Sack, Inc., 4, 24 (lower); John C. Sinclair, 198; Robert C. Smith, 34; Thurman C. Smith, 221; Taylor and Dull, 8, 120, 144.

ON THE COVER:

Art, Industry, and Science, detail of the chandelier NO. 135. Background: silk lampas reproduced from original upholstery fabric for a rococo parlor of Camden, a house built from 1856 to 1859 near Port Royal, Virginia, for William Carter Pratt. Gift of Mr. and Mrs. Richard Turner Pratt

Designed by Peter Oldenburg
Drawings by Donald McKay
Composition by Harlowe Typography, Inc. and Haber Typographers, Inc.
Printed in Great Britain by The Curwen Press Ltd.
All rights reserved
Library of Congress catalog card number 70-109965
Cloth binding: Standard Book Number 87099-004-7
Paperbound: Standard Book Number 87009-005-5

PREFACE

AMERICA IN 1870 was just beginning to emerge as the country she is today. It was her adolescence, and she was on her way to maturity. She still held to the security of some earlier habits. Nonetheless she revealed now and then glimpses of sophistication and even wisdom. At that time the scars of a brutal war were still raw; the young men who had survived looked around in bewilderment at still being there when so many of their generation had gone. The assassination of a beloved president had come on the heels of the war, and the succeeding president faced impeachment proceedings. But America has never been a country to dwell upon the past, and in 1870, thirty-seven states strong, she exhibited all the brashness of adolescence as she plunged into the final decades of the nineteenth century.

It was in such a bold and optimistic spirit that The Metropolitan Museum of Art was founded. A hundred years later, as we celebrate the accomplishments of the Museum's first century, it is fitting that we re-examine the artistic production—and in so doing see reflections of the breadth of national life—of nineteenth-century America.

Since 1924 the Museum has had an American Wing, thirty-five rooms in which the arts of this country could be seen in their own setting. But until now the Wing has extended only through the Federal period—just barely into the nineteenth century. As we begin our second hundred years, we are proud to announce our intention to add to the Wing an appropriate area to house the arts of the turbulent and fertile century that brought the Museum into being, and those of the twentieth century. We hope, with the addition to the Wing, that many more in the city and the nation will join those of us who believe in our past—who are excited by the American achievement—and will want to work toward saving and enhancing our heritage for the country as a whole.

This exhibition, beginning exactly one hundred years after the Museum first opened its doors, and seen as a preview of a new section of the Wing, is an exciting augury. The grand design is that of Berry B. Tracy, Curator of the American Wing. With the assistance of his able staff, Mr. Tracy selected the more than 350 objects—a good half of which were acquired by the Museum expressly for this occasion—and arranged them in period settings, many complete with rugs, draperies, and woodwork. The paintings and sculptures in the period settings, or in alternating galleries, were chosen by John K. Howat, Associate Curator in Charge of American Paintings and Sculpture; they are catalogued in a companion volume.

Simply to bring so much together would be in any circumstances a laborious undertaking, and it was made more so by the fact that relatively little study has been done on American decorative arts after about 1840. In getting each detail just right unexpected problems arose—a remnant of a rich Victorian drapery was chosen for the rococo parlor, but it was discovered that most modern looms could not reproduce the fabric with the proper depth and shine; special old looms were finally found. An immense amount of work has gone into the renovation of the objects—cabinetmaking, reupholstery, regilding, repainting—to make them as close to their original condition as possible—and also as beautiful, for we must not forget that beauty is one of the things that art is about.

But if the assembly has been laborious, it has been a labor of love, and the beauty justifies and rewards the efforts. There is beauty in the objects, and in the order created from their great variety; and finally there is the beauty of something perhaps best described as surprise—the special delight felt in walking through this exhibition in rediscovery of our very own past, of things that stir vague memories, of things that remind us that although we have changed we are still the same; for preserved in these objects is an intimate and basic connection with our present selves.

Now for the first time the major arts and styles of nineteenth-century America are brought together chronologically. The exhibition opens with a chest on chest from Salem, Massachusetts, in the sedate Federal style of the turn of the nineteenth century. It proceeds through the successive revivals that carried the century well beyond its midpoint—Gothic, rococo, Renaissance. By 1876 American artistic output seemed to be, to paraphrase Stephen Leacock, on its horse and riding madly off in all directions. But finally the direction that truly led to the twentieth century became clear, and the exhibition ends with the striking furniture by the California architects Charles and Henry Greene, made sixty-two years ago and still looking up to date today.

This book is more than just a record of the exhibition. By incorporating all the decorative arts chronologically, in visually related groups, the book is a pictorial summary of the century. It also embodies a comprehensive introduction, and an analysis of each object. Since three quarters of the material shown was acquired during the past few years, or lent for the exhibition, there was little research on it in the Museum's files; thus much of the scholarship—both research and interpretation—is entirely new.

The Trustees and I want to thank all of those who through their gifts to the Museum have got us off to this splendid start in collecting the arts of our own nineteenth century. In particular, we are indebted to Edgar J. Kaufmann, Jr., who through his interest and generosity made available to the American Wing funds from the Edgar J. Kaufmann Charitable Foundation, for the ready purchase of nineteenth-century decorative objects. The exhibition would not have been possible without the generosity of our Trustee, Mrs. Charles S. Payson, whose gifts to this museum over the years have enriched it enormously. We also thank those individuals and institutions who have lent objects, so that although we are only beginning to collect in this era, the exhibition will be a full presentation. Edward Vason Jones of Albany, Georgia, freely donated his time and labor in both the preparation of drawings and installation of the period rooms; and the W. E. Browne Decorating Company most generously made draperies for the room settings in the exhibition. Finally, to Berry Tracy and all his colleagues in the American Wing, as a complement to the satisfaction they can take in exacting work well accomplished, we give our warmest thanks.

THOMAS P. F. HOVING
Director

ACKNOWLEDGMENTS

For the production of this catalogue we are deeply indebted to many people who worked willingly and wholeheartedly giving their time, their talent, and their suggestions that produced this final result. We are especially grateful to Mary C. Glaze, Associate Curator of the American Wing, not only for her reading of the manuscripts and making certain revisions and corrections but for carrying the day-to-day responsibilities of the American Wing through this unusually busy period of preparation. We are equally grateful to Frances Gruber, Curatorial Assistant, for her always competent execution of departmental matters, but more especially for her thorough research on classical furniture and painstaking reading of the manuscripts and galleys, checking each and every fact for accuracy. We are much obliged to Morrison Heckscher, our new Assistant Curator, for identification of some sources and for writing ten of the object captions. All of us in turn are especially grateful to our Departmental Secretary, Mrs. John C. Reese, who, ever faithful and with good humor, carried much of the load of typing not only for the catalogue but particularly for the department's extensive paperwork.

One of the most difficult and trying tasks was in the accomplishment of ideal photographs for publication, which was entirely the good work of Catherine Struse-Springer, our special Centennial photography coordinator for this catalogue. In addition to her tremendous task of scheduling the photographers and the moving of furniture, she handled all the technicalities of the loan correspondence and brought the answers to many questions concerning the objects. It was the diligent and careful research of Mrs. William C. Flannery, who spent many hours in the libraries and records of New York for the authors of this catalogue, that made possible the inclusion of much of the specific information on nineteenth-century craftsmen and companies. We were fortunate indeed to have the aid of two very able volunteers, the first of whom, Mary Heming, spent many days organizing the initial files for the catalogue but more especially researched and located appropriate upholstery fabrics for the restoration of the furniture. The second volunteer was Mrs. Leo D. Bretter, formerly secretary to the Department of American Art, who gave from her busy family life her time in errands and research problems.

The most noble job well done was that of Joan Foley, who, as editorial producer, oversaw with infinite patience and brilliant perception the writing of every word in these texts. We are as well grateful to Anne S. Davidson for her immediate empathy in the enormous task of organizing a very useful bibliography.

Much of the credit for the success of the exhibition goes to Peter Zellner and the hardworking and creative staff of the Exhibition Design Department. It would have been physically impossible to move, clean, and prepare the great number of new acquisitions without the expert work of our faithful Senior Departmental Assistant Patrick Farry. In addition our Senior Housekeeper, Ruth Gottlieb, not only did emergency cleaning for photography but has made all the new covers for the freshly restored furniture. For the excellent restoration of the furniture and objects themselves—a seemingly endless task that has taken nearly two years—we are grateful to the Museum's Conservator, Kate C. Lefferts, and especially to those of her skilled staff listed here: Charles J. Anello, John Canonico, Rudolph Colban, Bruce Colvin, Kenneth Deveney, Shinichi Doi, Douglas Gallik, William Goldner, Frances Griffiths, Nobuko Kajitani, Knud Nielsen, Walter E. Rowe, Stephen Spaulding, Patrick Staunton, José A. Vega, Robert Wilkinson, Henry F. Wolcott.

For the restoration of furniture done outside the Museum we are grateful for the good work of the firms of Veleba and Hruban, Thorp Brothers, and Joseph LiVolsi.

We are grateful for the invaluable aid in specific research and direction to sources that came from the staff of many other departments within the Museum. We give special mention to Janet S. Byrne, Associate Curator of the Department of Prints and Photographs, whose great knowledge of their vast holdings was a boon to our search for knowledge. We will always be indebted to Mrs. James Pilgrim, who, within this department as a research fellow, compiled a biographical index on nineteenth-century American cabinetmakers and their known works. William D. Wilkinson, the Registrar, worked long and hard on behalf of this exhibition, as did members of his staff, particularly David Hudson, Nancy McGary, and David Mash.

Outside the Museum these people provided

specific information essential to the catalogue: Kathryn C. Buhler, Brookline, Massachusetts; E. Ann Coleman, The Brooklyn Museum; Marshall B. Davidson, American Heritage, New York; Maude B. Feld, New York; Stuart P. Feld, New York; David A. Hanks, The Art Institute of Chicago; Calvin S. Hathaway, Philadelphia Museum of Art; Lowell Innes, Saco, Maine; J. Stewart Johnson, The Brooklyn Museum; William R. Johnston, The Walters Art Gallery, Baltimore; Dorothy-Lee Jones, Wellesley, Massachusetts; John Keefe, The Toledo Museum of Art; Mary V. Kernan, Park District of Oak Park, Illinois; Robert Koch, South Norwalk, Connecticut; Mr. and Mrs. Terence Leichti, Los Angeles; Martin Leifer,

The New-York Historical Society; John McClean, Tiffany and Company; Randell L. Makinson, Gamble House, Pasadena, California; James R. Mitchell, The New Jersey State Museum, Trenton; Hester Rich, The Maryland Historical Society, Baltimore; Anna B. Sands, Meriden Historical Society; Margaret Stearns, Museum of the City of New York; Mrs. Douglas Williams, New York; Kenneth M. Wilson, The Corning Museum of Glass; Edwin Wolf, 2nd, Library Company of Philadelphia.

To all the lenders, both public and private, without whom this exhibition would not have been possible, we express our warmest thanks and deepest appreciation.

B.B.T. – M.J. – M.D.S. – S.B.

LENDERS TO THE EXHIBITION

Albany Institute of History and Art, Albany, New York

The Family of Richard C. Aldrich, Barrytown, New York

Amherst College Art Museum

Mr. and Mrs. James G. Balling, Albany, Georgia

The Brooklyn Museum

Fenton L. B. Brown, New York

Mrs. T. Wistar Brown, Ardmore, Pennsylvania

Jay E. Cantor, New York

The Cathedral Church of St. John the Divine, New York

Ronald R. Chitwood, Los Angeles

Chrysler Art Museum, Provincetown, Massachusetts

Mr. and Mrs. Walter P. Chrysler, Jr., Provincetown, Massachusetts

The City Art Museum, St. Louis

The Corning Museum of Glass

Court of Appeals of the State of New York, Albany

Mrs. Pietro Crespi, Cloverdale, California

Daughters of the American Revolution Museum, Washington

Diplomatic Reception Rooms, Department of State, Washington

Mr. and Mrs. William K. Dunn, Pasadena, California

Dr. and Mrs. Gerald L. Eastman, Huntington, New York

Essex Institute, Salem, Massachusetts

Dr. and Mrs. Alan W. Feld, Las Vegas, Nevada

Mr. and Mrs. Samuel B. Feld, New York

Stuart P. Feld, New York

Daniel N. Flavin, Jr., Cold Spring, New York

The Fogg Art Museum, Harvard University, Cambridge, Massachusetts

Gamble House, Greene and Greene Museum and Library, Pasadena, California

Dr. and Mrs. Roger G. Gerry, Roslyn, New York

Mrs. Benjamin Ginsburg, New York

Grand Rapids Public Museum

Mrs. John B. Greer, Shreveport, Louisiana

Mr. and Mrs. James Halpin, Bronxville, New York

Philip Hammerslough, West Hartford, Connecticut

Mr. and Mrs. C. Edward Hansell, Roswell, Georgia

Henry Ford Museum, Dearborn, Michigan

Lowell Innes, Saco, Maine

Mr. and Mrs. Edward Vason Jones, Albany, Georgia

Ronald S. Kane, New York

Edgar J. Kaufmann, Jr., New York

Alfred M. F. Kiddle, New York

Dr. and Mrs. Robert Koch, South Norwalk, Connecticut

John David Lannon, Jr., New York

Mr. and Mrs. Terence Leichti, Los Angeles

Mrs. Edwin A. S. Lewis, Baltimore

Randell L. Makinson, Los Angeles

The Maryland Historical Society, Baltimore

Mr. and Mrs. Robert Mattison, Berkeley

Mr. and Mrs. Hugh F. McKean, Winter Park, Florida

Mr. and Mrs. Richard P. Mellon, Ligonier, Pennsylvania

Dr. and Mrs. Joseph D. Messler, Pasadena, California

Virginia Watkins Mitchell, Boyce, Virginia

Munson-Williams-Proctor Institute, Utica

Museum of the City of New York

National Trust for Historic Preservation, Lyndhurst in Tarrytown, New York

Mrs. Cyril A. Nelson, Port Haywood, Virginia

Museum of Fine Arts, Boston

The Newark Museum

The New Jersey State Museum, Trenton

The New-York Historical Society

New York Yacht Club

Mr. and Mrs. Edward Nygren, New Haven

Mr. and Mrs. William G. Osofsky, Oyster Bay, New York

Park District of Oak Park, Illinois

Philadelphia Museum of Art

Portland Museum of Art, Portland, Maine

Mr. and Mrs. Douglas Richardson, Northampton, Massachusetts

Mrs. Walter B. Robb, Buffalo

Roosevelt Hospital, New York

Eric M. Schindler, Los Angeles

Patricia E. Smith, New Canaan, Connecticut

Smithsonian Institution, Washington

Joseph Sorger, Philadelphia

Chauncey Stillman, New York

Mrs. John V. Taggart, New York

The Toledo Museum of Art

Trinity Church, New York

Valley Forge Historical Society

William Bell Watkins, Jr., Boyce, Virginia

West Point Museum

Mrs. Frances Whitney, New York

Robert F. Woolworth, New York

Yale University Art Gallery, New Haven

Anonymous (5)

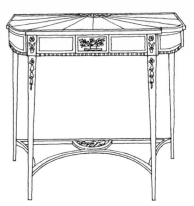

Light forms, geometric lines

Square back Shield back

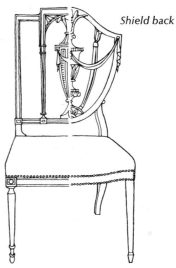

Fields, crossbanding

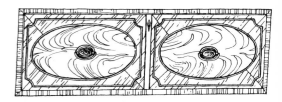

INTRODUCTION

1795-1845   IN THE NINETEENTH CENTURY, until the 1880s, high-style American decorative arts were basically a provincial, if rich, reflection of international styles. The creative artisans of English and French fashions were the arbiters of taste. The disseminators of style were both the European publishers of the design books and fashion periodicals and the immigrant craftsmen and "practical men" who interpreted and adapted the foreign conceits to the needs of Americans. The artful simplicity and masterful elaboration of their work often exceeded, in color and appeal, European prototypes.

The first four decades of the century were characterized by neoclassicism. Within this time, three separate but overlapping periods can be identified. Neoclassicism itself was born of archaeological discovery and a reaction to the eighteenth-century rococo fashion in Europe. The first two neoclassical styles in the United States were concomitant with the politically and socially formative era following the Revolution known as the Federal period. Early Federal design, between 1795 and 1815, grew out of French Louis XVI taste as absorbed into the English concepts of neoclassicism promulgated by the architect-designers Robert and James Adam in their *Works in Architecture* (1773-1779). The ideas of the Adam brothers were embodied in the plates of the furniture design books of Thomas Shearer (1788), George Hepplewhite (1788), and Thomas Sheraton (1793-1794 and 1803). The furniture of all three, in the neoclassical fashion, was distinguished by light—even delicate—forms and geometric lines—straight, or when curved, semicircular or elliptical. Shearer's greatest contribution is his ingenuity in mechanical devices for folding furniture, sliding shelves, drawers, and the like, but his name has been the least known of the three. As a result the two early Federal styles are often referred to as Hepplewhite or Sheraton. In both time and treatment, they overlap so subtly that a distinction is often difficult. Sheraton favored the turned leg and square backs on chairs and sofas, yet illustrated many square tapered legs, as did Hepplewhite, who, although known for his shield- and heart-shaped backs for chairs, also showed square-back chairs. The keynote of both styles is the emphasis on color and surface as opposed to the emphasis on form in the eighteenth-century taste typified by the work of designers like Thomas Chippendale. Generally in American cabinetwork "Hepplewhite" is used when the ornament is light wood stringings and inlays and small panels, or paterae, of marquetry on a dark ground. "Sheraton" connotes color in fields and crossbandings of richly contrasting grains of light and dark woods. Occasionally the elements of both tastes are so equal that the style can be called only early Federal.

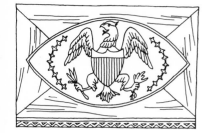

Inlay

Paterae

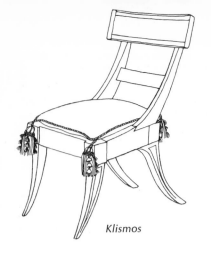

Klismos

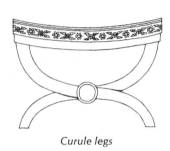

Curule legs

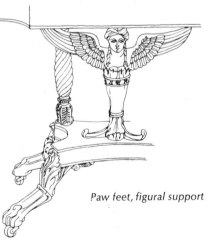

Paw feet, figural support

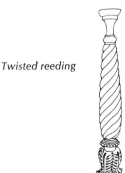

Twisted reeding

Late Federal (1815-1825) showed the influence of Sheraton's later designs published in 1812, which, like the designs of Thomas Hope of 1807 and George Smith of 1808, were characterized by Greco-Roman archaeological forms—klismos and curule chairs and animal supports. Hope, Smith, Sheraton, and other designers who formulated the tastes of the English Regency (1811-1820) had absorbed not only the knowledge of archaeological discoveries of the eighteenth century, but also the early nineteenth-century adaptations embodied in *le style antique*. This was the French term for the shapes and ornament evolving from Greco-Roman and Egyptian influences during the Directoire and Consulat (1795-1804) and the Empire (1804-1815). Late Federal furniture, therefore, is referred to in style as either Regency or Empire, depending upon the predominance of characteristics from English or French sources. Both concepts found expression in periodicals that were known in America although published abroad: in England, Rudolph Ackermann's *The Repository of Arts . . .* (1809-1828); in France, Pierre de la Mésangère's *Collection de Meubles et Objets de Goût* (1802-1835).

The third and final phase (1825-1845) of the neoclassical style in American furniture was related in its bold forms and monumental character to the prevailing architectural style now known as the Greek revival. Both English and French taste continued to be the arbiters of shape and ornament. The heavy architectonic style of the post-Regency was illustrated by Peter and Michael Angelo Nicholson (1826), and the continuing formulations of the French Empire taste of the Restauration, by George Smith, also of London, in his *Cabinet-Maker and Upholsterer's Guide* (1826). Furniture of the 1820s, however, showed a distinctly American divergence from the English tradition in a variety of baroque classicisms, particularly a profusion of heavy, deep carving of twisted reeding, acanthus leaves and plumes, diamond-patterned pineapple motifs, and large animal-paw feet with hairy shanks.

The carved style was superseded in the late 1830s by the simple lines and plain surfaces of the French Restauration in what is known as pillar and scroll. This was first illustrated in America in designs taken directly from Smith (1826) in an advertisement of 1833 by Joseph Meeks and Sons, cabinetmakers of New York, and finally published for manufacturers everywhere by the architect-designer John Hall of Baltimore in *The Cabinet Makers Assistant* (1840). It was to furniture in these styles, now collectively termed Greek revival or American Empire, that Professor Benjamin Silliman, Jr., of Yale referred when he condemned the "ponderous and frigid monstrosities," in reviewing the history of furniture in connection with the New York Crystal Palace exhibition of 1853.

These late neoclassical styles, like the two phases of the Federal style, were dependent on color rather than form. The Yankee plunder of readily available ancient forests of West Indian mahogany and satinwood gave an extraordinarily rich cast to the American cabinetwork that more remote provincial areas did not enjoy. The skillful selection and "laying on" of highly figured veneers became a nationwide aspect of standardization in American nineteenth-century cabinetmaking, yet the various urban centers within the new Republic developed individual stylistic characteristics. The key to their regional placement is generally found in the favored design sources and elements of ornament, particularly inlays, carving, or painted decoration.

In quantity, New York City was from the very beginning of the nineteenth century the leader of high-style cabinetmaking. In 1805 William Johnson of Newton, New Jersey, looking for a new business location, concluded that New York was "the London of America" and would "take the lead of business to any

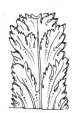

Acanthus leaves

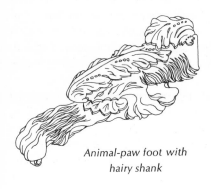

Animal-paw foot with hairy shank

Pillar

Scrolls

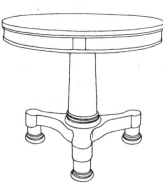

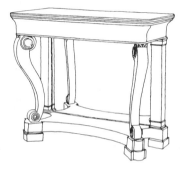

other place in the United States." In 1805/06 for the first time the New York directory listed the city's cabinetmakers in a separate body. By way of introduction to the profession the editor remarked: "This curious and useful mechanical art, is brought to a very great perfection in this city. The furniture daily offered for sale, equals, in point of elegance, any ever imported from Europe, and is scarcely equaled in any other city in America."

Although New York boasted many fine cabinetmakers, the most famous name was that of Duncan Phyfe. In 1816, Sarah Huger of New York wrote to relatives in Charleston of her difficulties in getting furniture executed for them by the busy Phyfe, stating that "Mr. Phyfe is so much the United States rage." Phyfe's workmanship and his interpretation of English Regency forms had become the envy and thus the model for many of his competitors. One of them was John Hewitt, who in 1811 noted in his ledger the measurements of ornamental wood columns by Duncan Phyfe and as well those of New York's Parisian immigrant cabinetmaker Charles-Honoré Lannuier.

Lannuier's cabinetry was the epitome of the finest French Empire work, but he also made furniture in the Anglo-American style. The roster of patrons enjoyed by both men reads like an early nineteenth-century social register, stretching from the home of Stephen Van Rensselaer in Albany to Sans Souci, the palace of Henri Christophe, the self-styled Emperor of Haiti. The brilliant Lannuier died an untimely death at age forty in 1819, but Phyfe, his neighbor Michael Allison, and other titans like Joseph Meeks carried on with superior interpretations of successive fashions until the mid-century. Meeks cabinetwares were shipped all over the nation through the firm's "American and Foreign Agency," and by 1835 the company had showrooms in New Orleans as well as in New York.

Despite the dominance of New York artisans, distinctive achievements came from highly skilled workmen in other cities. In Salem there was the masterful carving, on furniture and architecture, of the local architect-designer Samuel McIntire. The richest interpretations of Sheraton came from the Boston Cabinet Manufactory of Thomas Seymour, followed by the work of contemporaries like Lemuel Churchill, whose Regency furniture was of the tightest plan and best proportions, emulating a prominent English manufacturer, Gillow of Lancaster. Following Churchill were the Hancock brothers. Henry and more certainly William dominated the scene in the late twenties and early thirties with finely carved and inventive furniture essentially English in form.

In Philadelphia the Sheraton style of Henry Connelly and Ephraim Haines was supplanted by the work of the Dublin-born and London-trained Joseph B. Barry, who, with his son, advertised in 1810 furniture "finished in the rich Egyptian and Gothic style," belying his Sheraton and Regency background. Joseph B. Barry and Son in turn were superseded by Philadelphia's most successful immigrant cabinetmaker of the Greek revival era, Antoine-Gabriel Quervelle, who by 1829 was making furniture for the White House and in 1830 advertised in the *United States Gazette* that "orders from any part of the Union will be promptly executed."

From Federal Baltimore came the richest interpretations of London fashions, in caned and painted seating furniture and highly inlaid cabinetwork. John and Hugh Findlay made a suite of painted Grecian furniture for the White House in 1809, from designs by the architect Benjamin Latrobe. The most distinctive element of Baltimore's Federal style, however, was the extensive use of reverse-painted glass, or églomisé, panels, inset in bookcases, desks, and tables. A richly ornamented group survives today, undocumented to a particular shop but variously attributed to William Camp and to Baltimore's branch of the Philadelphia firm of Joseph B. Barry and Son. The later Greek revival work of Baltimore's John Needles was distinguished by its chaste architectural designs executed in "curled maple."

The chronology of styles within the neoclassical periods can be best understood in the visualization of the forms and parts described in the cabinetmakers' price books, particularly in those of New York from 1796 to 1834. Lists within the successive books—in effect composite parts of contracts for work done by journeymen for the masters—reflect changing styles and costs. The books, a product of the gradual unionization of the cabinetmakers' societies, aided in the execution of ready-made parts and the process of American industrialization. By 1840, with a rapidly expanding market, there had been a definite change from individual assembly of furniture to the mass production of parts, which were shaped with the aid of lathes and scroll saws powered by steam-driven machines.

Of the other crafts of the neoclassical periods, silver followed closely the development and changing fashions in furniture. The respected position and high standards of the gold- and silversmiths had been established in Colonial times, and their products continued to be a form of investment for the patron as well as useful and beautiful objects. In the early Federal period, elaborate rococo forms and decoration gave way to the symmetrical designs and neoclassical ornament of the Adam style. The shapes of hollow ware were now those of elongated ovoids, rounded urns, and helmets, frequently fluted and embellished with "bright-cut" decoration of garlands and geometric bands. In Boston, the silver of Paul Revere, Jr., conveyed Adamesque elegance and simplicity, as did the work of the Richardsons, Abraham Dubois, and Christian Wiltberger of Philadelphia.

By 1815 the English Regency and the French Empire styles had become firmly established. In Boston the partners Jesse Churchill and Daniel Treadwell emulated Regency forms in their hollow ware, to be succeeded in style by the more robust American Empire silver of Obadiah Rich. In New York the work of the leading silversmiths John W. Forbes, John Targee, William Thomson, Garret Eoff, William Gale, and William Adams followed the helmet-shaped and round bulbous melon-reeded forms of English prototypes. Forbes was evidently the major figure of the 1820s, since he was selected by the citizens of the state of New York in 1824 to

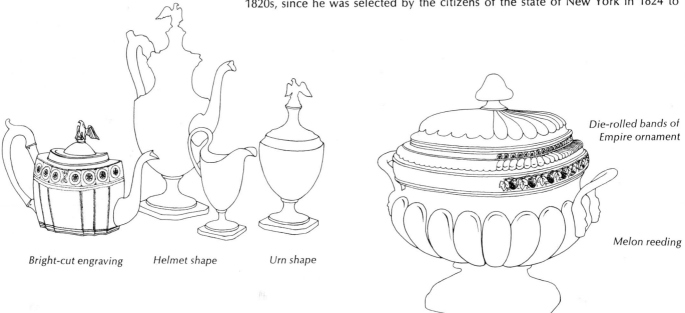

Bright-cut engraving Helmet shape Urn shape

Die-rolled bands of Empire ornament

Melon reeding

fabricate a monumental silver plateau for presentation to Governor DeWitt Clinton for his promotion of the Erie Canal project.

In Philadelphia the French and English strains were equally influential. The immigrants from Paris Simon Chaudron and Anthony Rasch had a distinct French influence on the work of their most outstanding Philadelphia contemporaries, Harvey Lewis and Thomas Fletcher. Tea sets made up of tall footed pieces were decorated with pre-cast and die-rolled bands of Empire ornament and beading not unlike French prototypes. A collection of designs and working drawings (now in the Metropolitan Museum) by Fletcher includes a plan for a presentation urn annotated by Fletcher as "Chaudron's vase"; yet Fletcher, an astute merchant and promoter as well, had made trips to London and much of his elaborate presentation work resembled in design and quality the work of leading London silversmiths like Benjamin Smith and Paul Storr. Fletcher and his partner Sidney Gardiner created silver for presentation to nearly every American hero of the War of 1812. In 1824 they made two monumental urns based on the Warwick Vase for the merchants of Pearl Street, New York, to present to DeWitt Clinton. As late as 1838 the Philadelphia firm was still flourishing, and Philip Hone of New York stated in his diary that "Nobody in this 'world' of ours hereabouts can compete with them in their kind of work."

By the 1820s American Empire silver had an essentially national style of ornament, including a profusion of cast and chased leafage, sheaves of wheat, or fruit clusters, in a kind of baroque classicism related in concept to the highly carved furniture of the time. In the late twenties repoussé decoration replaced the cast and chased ornament, and by the mid-thirties plain and paneled surfaces on pyriform shapes with rococo handles and spouts bespoke the late classical style of the Restauration and marked the beginning of the rococo revival of the mid-century.

Elegant glassware of American manufacture gave little rivalry to the refinement of English imports until the 1820s. Windowpanes, milk bowls, demijohns, and whiskey flasks of a common green soda metal were the principal products of the glasshouses throughout the first half of the nineteenth century, as they had been in the eighteenth. Most of the glass produced was purely utilitarian. A few high-style pieces from the end of the eighteenth century survive, some attributable to John Frederick Amelung, who along with fellow Germans set up operations at New Bremen, Maryland, in 1784. Four major examples of their earliest work, two of which are in the American Wing, are highly engraved presentation pieces, more rococo than classical—indicative of a tradition that had begun earlier, in the eighteenth century. Several disastrous fires and financial difficulties caused Amelung's failure, but his son and some of his workmen are reputed to have carried on their work in the early nineteenth century in south Jersey under the corporate names of Philadelphia investors.

The first successful venture in competition with fine imports was that of Benjamin Bakewell at Pittsburgh in 1808. He produced clear, dense lead glass, deeply and brilliantly cut in the English classical manner. President Monroe was so impressed by his work that in 1817 he ordered a large service engraved with the arms of the United States for the White House. In 1818 Deming Jarves of the New England Glass Company commenced similar productions, which were followed by those of the Boston and Sandwich Glass Company he founded in 1825. By that year the glasshouses of George H. Bergen near Philadelphia and George Dummer at Jersey City were also in operation.

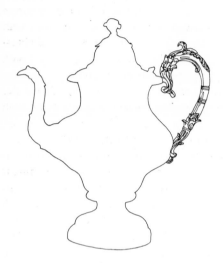

Pyriform shape, rococo handle

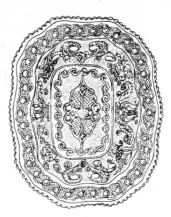

Lacy pressed glass

In 1827 Dummer submitted patents for the pressing of glass drawer knobs, and about the same time Jarves's men are reputed to have perfected a pressing process for hollow ware. In 1829 an English observer remarked that pressed glass he saw in New York "was far superior, both in design and execution, to anything of the kind I had ever seen either in London or elsewhere. The merit of this invention is due to the Americans; and it is likely to prove one of great national importance."

Although the aim of pressed glass was at first to imitate high-style cut glass, the manufacturers did not follow its patterns closely, and the combined rococo and classical motifs of so-called lacy pressed glass of the 1830s and 40s have highly original combinations of eagles, shields, portrait busts, and other symbols of American nationalism. The sources of the rococo elements are unrecorded, yet very definite stylistic analogies can be drawn with Continental porcelains of the 1820s and 30s, and similar glass designs of the early Baccarat factory in France. By the 1830s enormous quantities of glasswares were exported to Europe, and in 1836 a Bohemian manufacturer complained that cheap pressed glass from America and France threatened "to eclipse our glass manufacture."

Sophisticated pottery and porcelain was a rare achievement in nineteenth-century America until the decade following the Civil War. A number of unsuccessful factories began in New Jersey and Philadelphia in the Federal era. The low prices and high quality of Chinese export and English Staffordshire products along with local production problems and lack of financial support caused most efforts to fail both technically and commercially. The major survivor was the firm of William Ellis Tucker, which in Philadelphia produced handsomely decorated urns and tablewares of a vitreous white porcelain in French classical forms for about thirteen years. But the Tuckers became discouraged by the financial panic of 1837, and in 1838 they began importing from Europe.

1845–1876

By mid-century a number of factors of the furniture trade were changing. Geographically the trade was still centered in the major cities of the Eastern seaboard, with their orientation to Europe and particularly France and England. At the time of the Crystal Palace exhibition of 1853, New York was still the leader in both style and production; during the rest of the century it remained the leader in style, but increased mechanization and the westward movement of the population created new furniture centers, particularly on the Mississippi River and her tributaries. Styles continued to be strongly dictated by European, and particularly French, fashion and to be known in this country through both foreign pattern books (or American interpretations of them) and immigrant craftsmen who brought with them European tastes and skills. To these influences were added the great international exhibitions, beginning with the London Crystal Palace in 1851 and held every few years in one of the major capitals of Europe. The most important of these were the Paris exhibitions of 1855 and 1867 and the London exhibition of 1862.

A change in the ethnic character of the furniture artisans in America began in the 1840s, with a large influx of German carvers and cabinetmakers. At this time a number of French cabinetmakers also came as immigrants or set up branches of their Paris establishments. These Frenchmen, though far outnumbered by the Germans, dominated the fine furniture trade of the fifties and set the style for several decades. The French influence of this period was thus of a similar nature to that of the neoclassical period but more direct, less filtered through Anglo-American interpretations. British influence continued, however, most strongly in the romantic revivals, particularly the Gothic and Elizabethan, which had a literary basis and were in the English tradition of the picturesque.

A variety of romantic revivals had begun in England and on the Continent in the late twenties. In 1833 Loudon's *Encyclopaedia* defined the dominant styles as "the Grecian or modern style, which is by far the most prevalent; the Gothic or perpendicular style . . . the Elizabethan . . . , and the style of the age of Louis XIV . . . which is characterized by curved lines and an excess of curvilinear ornaments." By 1849 England's *Journal of Design* commented upon the eclecticism of the era:

> Every one elects his own style of art, and the choice rests usually on the shallowest individualism. Some few take refuge in a liking for "pure Greek," and are rigidly "classical;" other[s] find safety in the "antique," others believe only in Pugin; . . . and some extol the *Renaissance*. We all agree only in being wretched imitators.

This imitation of the styles of the past continued in various forms throughout the century in America as in Europe; however, the period of the late forties to the Philadelphia Centennial of 1876 was particularly characterized by the emergence of a range of styles, labeled variously as Grecian, modern, Gothic, rococo, Elizabethan, Louis XIV, Louis XV, Renaissance, Louis XVI, and "neo grec."

One of the first revivals emerging in England was the Gothic, which had been in continual though minimal application since the eighteenth-century vagaries of Horace Walpole's Strawberry Hill. A resurgence of the style was consolidated in the 1830s by designers like A. W. N. Pugin, but inspiration conformed with romantic literary preoccupations of the time, as found particularly in the novels of Sir Walter Scott. The Elizabethan and Gothic settings of novels like *Kenilworth* and *The Talisman* captured the public imagination, and a literal borrowing of Elizabethan and Gothic stylistic elements began. Between 1828 and 1838 at Snelston Hall in Derbyshire the architect Lewis N. Cottingham designed carved and painted Gothic furniture from "ancient material," salvaged from old buildings and furniture.

Such a romantic composite was impossible in America, where there were no ancient buildings or ruins. As Nathaniel Hawthorne lamented, here was "no shadow, no antiquity, no mystery, no picturesque and gloomy wrong. . . ." Designers and furniture makers were forced to contrive upon European, and particularly English and French, precedent, their own enchantments in new material. In America as in Europe the Gothic revival furniture of the forties and fifties bore no relation to actual prototypes of the Gothic age but was an adaptation and application of Gothic architectural form and ornament to early nineteenth-century furniture forms. The first published evidence of the Gothic style in American cabinetwork was a sideboard illustrated as the frontispiece of *The Cabinet Maker's Assistant*, designed and drawn by Robert Conner of New York in 1842. Conner prefaced the book by describing the current color and arrangement of various rooms, and saying: ". . . it might be of some service to such of our Cabinet friends as have not been in Europe, to state the manner in which the various rooms are now furnishing, as it will enable them to unite the European style with the American, which will at once give the desired effect."

In this country the Gothic style of Europe was best united with the styles of America by the architect Alexander Jackson Davis and his associate, the land-

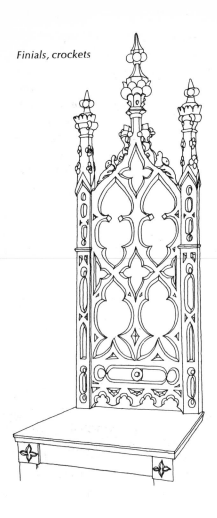

Finials, crockets

scapist and aesthete Andrew Jackson Downing. Davis, who worked in a wide range of architectural styles, particularly in the Grecian, saw no reason why his patrons should be "foolishly frightened at a few *crockets & finials.*" His first notable residential design in the Gothic style was Glen Ellen, built for the Gilmors of Baltimore in 1832. His second great domestic work was the country seat of New York Mayor William Paulding, completed near Tarrytown in 1841, now known as Lyndhurst. Davis designed some of the furniture in Gothic style (for which drawings survive), and his collaborator, Downing, conceived the surrounding landscape of nature refined and softened by art. Downing, as editor of *The Horticulturist,* was a prolific author on the taste of his time, and he devoted an extensive chapter to fashionable furniture by approved manufactories in his often reprinted work *The Architecture of Country Houses* (1850). Influenced by English designers like J. C. Loudon, he illustrated and extolled the appropriateness of certain styles for particular rooms: Gothic for libraries, halls, and bedrooms; Elizabethan and rococo for parlors and sitting rooms.

The dominant taste of mid-century America was the rococo of Louis Philippe. It was sometimes called "French modern" because it was the latest style, sometimes "French antique" because it was a regeneration of the eighteenth-century cabriole leg, C- and S-scrolls, and naturalistic carving of the Louis XIV and Louis XV styles. Rococo furniture was prominent among the displays in the Crystal Palaces of London (1851) and New York (1853) and again in the Paris exhibition of 1855, when French influence on American design was at its height. Such displays filled various needs. Sir Henry Cole, a leading reform designer and editor of *The Journal of Design,* felt that "one great advantage of exhibitions is that it teaches the public and people who are not otherwise taught at all." The greater advantage, however, was taken by American manufacturers who, inspired by the pretentious displays of their European tastemakers, tried new styles and ornament in meeting the demands of a rapidly growing mercantile class.

Concurrent with Gothic and rococo was a new concept called "Renaissance," typified by massive forms and deeply carved ornament, often of cabochons, portrait medallions, and seventeenth-century strapwork terminating in high volutes. By the sixties this style in its varied manifestations surpassed the rococo. The designations "Elizabethan" or "Jacobean" referred to another though related development used primarily for chairs and cabinet pieces and characterized by spiral- or spool-turned legs and stiles derived directly from the style of Charles II and contemporary seventeenth-century Flemish work. As with other styles of the period, the demarcation lines here were unclear, and individual pieces could be as eclectic as the wide-ranging terminology. All three styles—rococo, Elizabethan, and Renaissance—often had naturalistic carving of leaf scrolls, shells, fruit, flowers, winged creatures, putti, and portrait busts.

Distinct from these revivals at its inception, but subsequently merging into the Renaissance revival style, was the regeneration of Louis XVI neoclassical furniture. The Paris-New York firm of Ringuet LePrince and Marcotte was instrumental in the American introduction of this style, which in their work followed late eighteenth-century precedents in form and ornament. Generally finished in black and gilt, their chairs and sofas with turned, fluted legs, square molded backs, and bright ormolu appliqués were concurrent with, although the complete antithesis of, the highly carved forms and curving lines of the more popular rococo and Renaissance styles.

Out of this *bon goût* Louis XVI style, at its height about 1860, evolved a new

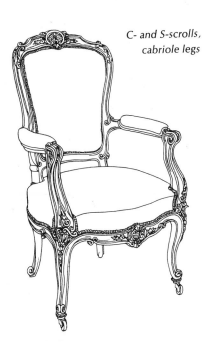

C- and S-scrolls, cabriole legs

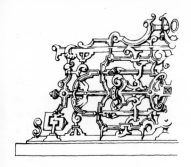

Strapwork

taste of the late sixties and early seventies, sometimes referred to by the French design books as "neo grec." Stylistically it was still another composite, today generally referred to as Victorian Renaissance. Different in aspect from the earlier Renaissance revival style, it had a squared, geometric, architectonic look with heavy turned legs, classical entablatures, and ornament of oval or round bronze, porcelain, terracotta, or mother-of-pearl plaques and incised gilt lines often separating a variety of richly contrasting light and dark woods and marquetry panels. Case pieces were invariably pedimented with a straight or rounded broken arch and finished by heavily turned finials, carved symbols, busts, or stylized anthemia. In its final form in the 1870s this style of furniture—influenced by machine production and current English reform—became increasingly flat. Its more sophisticated versions, emanating from New York, often had intricate marquetry as did some of the art furniture of the period; and its factory interpretations, usually from the Midwest, exhibited fields of burl walnut set off by incised lines, with a minimum of carved or applied ornament.

All through the third quarter of the nineteenth century, New York, by its rapid growth and cosmopolitan character, continued to be the leader of style in furniture fashions. As in other American cities designs, joinery, carving, and upholstery of the best furniture were almost entirely executed by visiting or immigrant French

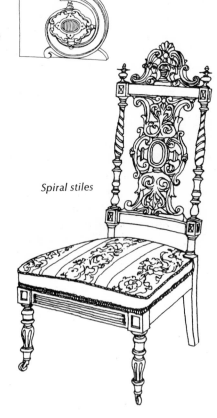

Cabochon
with volute
terminal

Spiral stiles

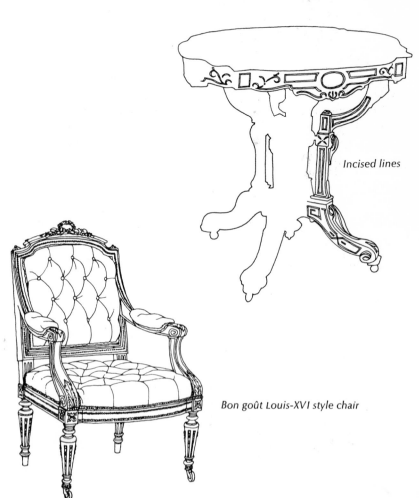

Incised lines

Bon goût Louis-XVI style chair

Stylized anthemion

and German craftsmen. In 1854/55 *Trow's New York City Directory* listed 193 cabinetmakers and furniture dealers of whom 131 had German names. Although French names were smaller in percentage, the influence of these Frenchmen was tremendous. Most of the fine furniture of this period was in the French taste.

Many of the French immigrants had close ties with their native land. Ringuet LePrince, father-in-law of Leon Marcotte, was one of Paris's leading decorators when he founded the New York branch of his firm. By 1846 Alexander Roux, born in the French Alps, was in New York as "an extensive Manufacturer of Cabinet Work of the finer and generally fashionable description." In the following year, 1847/48, Roux's firm was listed as Roux and Brother, and the name Frederick Roux appeared for the same address. This listing occurred for only two years, and Frederick apparently returned to Paris. A decade later an advertisement in the *New York Evening Post,* headed "Alexander Roux & Co.," stated that the firm was offering at reduced prices "their large stock of Plain and Rich furniture, in Rosewood, Oak, Black Walnut and Ebony; also, their large assortment of Black & Gilt Furniture, manufactured by F. Roux, of Paris, expressly for this market."

The New York Crystal Palace exhibition of 1853 saw prominent displays by many of the great French cabinetmakers in New York. Among them, in addition to Roux and Ringuet LePrince and Marcotte, were Julius Dessoir, who made the bedroom furniture for the new marble house of John Taylor Johnston in 1855, and the business establishment of Rochefort and Skarren, whose foremen in the fifties, Auguste Pottier and William Stymus, were to take over the company on Rochefort's death and make it one of the most important decorating firms in New York in the 1870s and 80s.

Another partnership in the fifties was that of Anthony Bembe and Anthony Kimbel, whose known surviving work is the furniture they made for the United States House of Representatives in 1857. On November 11, 1854, the editors of *Gleason's Pictorial Drawing-Room Companion* illustrated a New York parlor and praised the furnishings by "the French house of Bembe & Kimbel," as a "true and classic idea of the beautiful in decorative art." The editors noted that "although manufactured by the French house," the furniture "is not altogether French in design. Mr. Kimbel was for several years principal designer in Mr. Badouine's [sic] well known furniture establishment in Broadway, and his unique styles appear to be American modifications of those now in vogue abroad."

Charles Baudouine, for whom Kimbel had worked, was born in New York of French descent. According to the reminiscences of nineteenth-century cabinetmaker Ernest Hagen, "he went to France every year and imported a great deal of French furniture and upholstery coverings, French hardware, trimmings, and other material used in his shop." Today Baudouine is primarily remembered for his ornate rococo furniture in the style of his contemporary John Henry Belter and his infringement on Belter's patent for laminated rosewood.

Just as the name Phyfe stands out among early nineteenth-century cabinetmakers, so John Henry Belter has become the best known of America's midcentury cabinetmakers. One of many German-born craftsmen working in New York, he was and is renowned for his laminated and carved rococo revival rosewood parlor and bedroom suites. Although the principle of lamination was not a new one, Belter's method of steaming layers of wood in "cawls," or molds, so that they could be bent into graceful shapes created a distinctive style. According to Hagen, even in Belter's own era this type of furniture was designated, as it is today, "Belter furniture."

The period of the 1840s, when Belter came to New York, witnessed the immigration of many German as well as French craftsmen. Hagen, himself German-born and -trained, wrote of the early days in his neighborhood of Rivington and Norfolk Streets, where all "old residents moved away and a Colony of German mechanics took their place. There were cabinet makers shops, saw mills and marble mills everywhere." Hagen further noted that "the hardware, locks, hinges, bolts and etc. was [sic] mostly imported from Germany."

Hagen's choice of the word "mechanics" was appropriate, for despite the fact that these German craftsmen formed the majority of the carver-cabinetmaker population, their influence on style was negligible. John Henry Belter and Gustave Herter were exceptions. The presence of a New York German-language newspaper of 1866 behind one of the porcelain plaques on a cabinet labeled by Alexander Roux suggests that even in a French shop the workmen might be German. The style, however, remained French. In the sixties and seventies, when the Germans began to have a greater effect upon high-style furniture, the best designers still turned to France for inspiration. Christian Herter, half brother of Gustave, returned to Europe to study in the late 1860s before taking over the firm of Herter Brothers in 1870. It seems significant that he did not go to Germany for the training that was to help him make Herter Brothers one of the greatest New York decorating firms. Rather, he went to the Paris atelier of Pierre Victor Galland.

In other cities also the French and German cabinet manufacturers were the most prominent. Downing had recommended "Paul, in Boston" as having "The best specimens of Elizabethan and Renaissance furniture to be seen for sale in this country," and Professor Silliman praised the work of Boston's French-born Auguste Eliaers, who exhibited at the New York Crystal Palace a sideboard and a pier table "with a richly carved rose-wood frame and white marble top." Eliaers was in another respect typical of immigrant craftsmen. Having begun and advertised himself in Boston as a "Stair Builder" from Paris, he eventually emerged as Boston's principal manufacturer of fine furniture.

The South, which received much of its best furniture from northern manufacturers, also had its craftsmen of foreign birth. In New Orleans the two greatest cabinetmakers both had French names: François Seignouret and Prudent Mallard. The latter, younger than Seignouret, became known for his large-scale richly carved rococo and Renaissance furniture suited to the cavernous splendor of ante-bellum mansions.

By the 1870s midwestern manufacturers, mostly German craftsmen, had eclipsed, in fact "wiped out," as Hagen put it, the smaller cabinetmakers. The Stein Brothers of Muscatine, Iowa, had been since 1854 one of the principal sources for furniture in the upper Mississippi Valley and the Great Plains. Grand Rapids, Michigan, and Cincinnati, Ohio, had become major centers of the cabinet-making trade, shipping their goods in all directions. The Philadelphia Centennial Exhibition of 1876 was richly represented by the major figures of these cities, Berkey and Gay of Grand Rapids and Mitchell and Rammelsberg of Cincinnati.

A new material in furniture became important during the middle years of the century—cast iron. Although its role was to reflect, rather than to set, high style, its diverse applications and rapid adoption give it a place in a discussion of nineteenth-century decorative art. Early in the century cast iron was made into stoves and other prosaic items and in England was known for garden furniture; but its use as the skeleton for the immense "crystal palaces" housing the international exhibitions, first in London and then in New York, established its glamor and

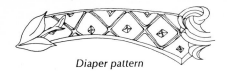

Diaper pattern

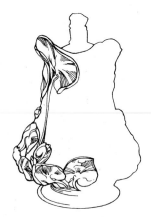

Naturalistic repoussé ornament

Beading

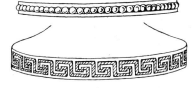

Greek key

popularity in America. The Boston Ornamental Iron Works, founded in 1850, took three pages in *Bigelow's Annual,* a book of advertising published in Boston in 1857. In a panegyric to the material, they wrote: "Until quite recently the multiform uses of Iron have been unknown to the American people. . . . Its use has followed the progress of civilization into the world, and the amount of it consumed by any nation at the present day indicates very truly the degree of its advancement in the arts and sciences." Cast iron was employed throughout the remainder of the century, and the chairs and settees made from it followed—if sometimes at quite a distance—the styles of parlor furniture. Because of the nature of the material and the method of manufacture, models were widely re-duplicated and persisted long after the creation of the original design.

As in cabinetwork, designs in silver and gold from the 1840s through the next few decades were derived from European revivalism. Hollow ware and flat-ware were now being factory produced. The discovery of American silver de-posits established a supply to meet a growing demand for silver created by middle class and newly rich buying power. Although the editors of *Harper's Monthly,* writing of the Crystal Palace exhibition in 1853, said, "the time is not far off, we feel sure, when we shall have no need of foreign designers of our plate and jewelry," the best American manufactories depended almost entirely for the next twenty-five years upon immigrant masters. The great Tiffany and Company relied upon creative artisans like Gustave Herter, who came from the atelier of a German architect in 1848; it was not until the late 1870s that the American Edward C. Moore is said to have won recognition from the Parisian dealer and critic Siegfried Bing for his original silver designs. The other major producer of silver was the Gorham Manufacturing Company, in Providence, whose chief designer, Thomas Pairpoint, came about 1868 from the important London company of Lambert and Rawlings after an apprenticeship in Paris.

Although minor elements of neoclassicism persisted in the designs of the third quarter of the century, the dominant tastes in silver were the current rococo and Renaissance fashions. The Gothic style was occasionally evident in engraved or repoussé vignettes of picturesque ruins or castellated monuments on rococo hollow ware. It appeared, but rarely, in approximations of actual medieval forms in the communion vessels of the most affluent churches. Rococo applications to hollow ware, having begun in the late 1820s, reached their full flowering in the 1850s, and silver characteristically bore heavy chased C- and S-scrolls and diapers combined with bold repoussé of naturalistic flora, raised on inverted or upright pyriforms. The concurrent Renaissance taste, applied to the same forms, showed repoussé strapwork and cabochons. The angular, geometric elements of strap-work reappeared in handles, pedestals, and feet on kettles, pots, and compotes.

By the late 1860s, after the rococo had subsided, the Renaissance fashion known as "neo grec" in furniture made its appearance in silver, especially in beading, anthemia, arabesques, Greek key borders, portrait medallions, and ani-mal heads and feet all applied to classical shapes, now returning in modified form. The Victorian predilection for symbol and allusion brought a common element of decoration to the rococo and the Renaissance styles in the appearance of sculptured allegorical figures, particularly on presentation pieces.

Technological advances in the mechanized casting, rolling, and electroplating of metal brought into being numerous manufactories of plated ware, of which the two major ones were Reed and Barton of Taunton, Massachusetts, established in 1840, and Meriden Britannia Company of Connecticut, begun in 1852. These firms, an outgrowth of the whitesmiths' shops that had produced Britannia metal, manufactured a cheaper product for a more popular market. In sterling Tiffany and Gorham were the leaders, and yet there were a dozen or more major manufacturers in cities over the nation. Among the outstanding ones in New York were Cooper and Fisher, Wood and Hughes, William Gale and Son, and Ball, Tompkins and Black, which became Ball, Black and Company in 1851 and Black, Starr and Frost in 1876. Prominent in Boston were Jones, Ball and Poor, which in 1869 became Shreve, Crump and Low Company, and the Laforme brothers; in Philadelphia, R. and W. Wilson during the 1840s, Bailey and Kitchen, and the still extant J. E. Caldwell and Company; in Baltimore, Andrew E. Warner and the still flourishing and prolific firm of S. Kirk and Son. In Charleston, Hayden and Whilden produced enormous dinner services for plantation society from about 1855 to 1863, and in San Francisco, the companies of W. K. Vanderslice and the Shreve brothers satisfied new appetites for rich living after the discovery of gold at Sutter's Mill and both gold and silver at the Comstock Lode.

In the middle period American glass tablewares and ornaments were extensively developed, as a result of protective import tariffs, an ever expanding market, and technical achievements in color, frosting, and engraving. Throughout the period, however, as indeed throughout the century, the highest style in glass remained that of the fine cut products. According to the census of 1840, there were then eighty-one glasshouses, and thirty-four cutting shops engaged in the manufacture of fine cut ware; but by 1865 it was reported that keen competition and the exigencies of the Civil War had reduced the producers of luxurious cut glassware to eight major companies. Between 1840 and 1855 there were more than a thousand men cutting and engraving glass; by 1860 there were only 225 cutters and engravers, working chiefly in Eastern glasshouses, where the best metal of the furnaces was a dense, clear lead of high quality. Most of the glasshouses of Wheeling, West Virginia, and Pittsburgh had converted completely by the sixties to the manufacture of pressed glass of cheaper soda ash or lime metal, which seldom had the clarity and never the brilliance of lead glass.

Stylistically the fine cut and engraved wares had a limited range of ornament. The principal decoration of tablewares was the traditional flute-cut panels, which became popular in the 1830s and remained standard until about 1860. Engraved decoration of landscapes and naturalistic forms of flora and fauna were analogous to the rococo carving on furniture. The shapes of pitchers, vases, and bowls continued to be modifications of classical models well into the linear Renaissance style of the 1870s. The finest examples had elaborate engraving and/or deep cutting leaving projecting panels of fine-line cutting. The richest achievement of the era was the application of color by flashing and casing one or two layers of colored glass and cutting through in geometric arrangements of diamonds, thumbprints, stars and prisms, or engraving in figural designs. This elegant technique, creating wares in the so-called Bohemian style, was usually lavished on toilet bottles, ornamental garnitures, stemware, paperweights, and, most frequently, the oil fonts of lamps. As earlier, however, the most typical and uniquely American products were the scores of novel and commemorative patterns in pressed glass, which reached all the markets of the nation as well as those abroad.

At the Philadelphia Centennial Exhibition of 1876 the major glass manufacturers of the middle period were well represented. The venerable and prestigious New England Glass Company displayed chandeliers and other wares, which doubtless were of a high quality consistent with that of Crystal Palace days. The firm had the advantage of one of the finest glass engravers of his time, Louis Vaupel, who came from Germany in 1856. Two neighboring competitors, the Boston and Sandwich and the Mt. Washington companies, were at the exhibition as well. One of the most colorful and distinguished manufacturers was Christian Dorflinger. Dorflinger, born in Alsace and trained in Saint-Louis, Lorraine, had by 1852 established the Long Island Flint Glass Works in Brooklyn and by 1860 was operating three glasshouses. In 1861 Mrs. Lincoln ordered the tableware for the White House from Dorflinger. Also represented was the leading crystal chandelier company of the time, William Gillinder and Sons of Philadelphia and Greensburg, Pennsylvania. Distinguished for their brilliant frosted and cut "gasoliers," they set up a complete production exhibit, showing cutting methods and selling small souvenirs of cut pieces and pressed Liberty Bell cups. Last, yet internationally known, was the Wheeling, West Virginia, firm of Hobbs, Brockunier, whose pressed-glass tablewares were to be found the world over.

Notable achievements in sophisticated porcelain manufactures after the demise of the Tucker factory in 1838 were not evident again until the years following the Crystal Palace exhibition of 1853. The 1840s and early 50s witnessed innumerable failures of kilns built mostly in the middle states. The major producers of a variety of earthenware table articles were D. and J. Henderson's American Pottery Company, which operated from 1828 to 1845 in Jersey City, New Jersey, and the later kilns of Christopher Webber Fenton in Bennington, Vermont, called by 1853 the United States Pottery Company. The Hendersons' firm produced pitchers, Toby jugs, tea sets, and transfer-printed dinnerware in the English Staffordshire manner, having the advantage in the 1840s of an English-trained modeler, Daniel Greatbach, who by 1852 was working for Fenton at Bennington. Both potteries used the traditional Empire paneled or rounded jug forms, molded with stylized flora, Gothic ornament, and hunt scenes; these motifs appeared upon pitchers, spittoons, and water coolers, all finished in a Rockingham glaze varying from a creamy buff color to dark brown. Fenton's pottery works were particularly well known in the 1850s for the ornamental flint-enamel glazed figures of the imperial lion, the reclining stag and doe, and the standing poodle carrying a basket of flowers in its teeth.

Although Fenton is credited with the first attempts to make rococo revival porcelain, his Parian wares of the 1850s were rivaled by two other Crystal Palace exhibitors, from Greenpoint, Long Island. Both Charles Cartlidge and Company and the works of William Boch and Brother, established respectively in 1848 and about 1850, are credited with the first successful pitchers and tea sets finished in a high-glazed porcelain, of rococo pyriforms with naturalistic handles. One of the best known today is Boch and Brother's pitcher ornamented with a molded relief of rococo leafage and a vignette of the infant Bacchus ensconced among the grapevines. Cartlidge closed in 1856 and Fenton in 1858, but Boch carried on in Greenpoint until about 1862, when Thomas C. Smith took over his Union Porcelain Works.

The disturbances of the Civil War caused, as they did in other industries, the failure of some potteries and the interruption of work at others. However, in 1863, the Trenton, New Jersey, partnership of Bloor, Ott and Booth was formed, and they produced chiefly a high-fired earthenware until 1871, when the firm became Ott and Brewer and began to make porcelain and Parian ware, particularly in readiness for the Philadelphia exhibition. Both this major Trenton firm and Smith's Union Porcelain Works in Greenpoint subscribed the services of professional sculptors for exhibition pieces. Stylistically all their works reflected the forms of the Victorian Renaissance, embellished, appropriately enough, with nationalistic themes and classical allusion. Isaac Broome, a sculptor of some repute working for Ott and Brewer, modeled among other objects a baseball commemorative vase and a Parian bust of Cleopatra. The Union Porcelain Works, however, must have made the greater showing with their colorfully decorated and highly glazed porcelain wonders like the Century Vase, especially designed, along with other smaller marvels, by the German-born Karl Mueller. The original exhibition version of the Century Vase, the feature of the Union Porcelain Works exhibit, was reportedly over seven feet in height, the size alone being a major technical feat in ceramics.

1876–1910

The decorative arts exhibits shown by American manufacturers at Philadelphia's International Centennial Exhibition of 1876 were generally condemned by the critics as "vulgar renditions of the French Renaissance," some hoping in particular that those pieces of furniture "as emanated from the thriving city of Grand Rapids will never again bring disgrace upon the American name at an international exhibition." Nevertheless, one of every twenty exhibits, native and foreign, revealed to the critics and producers new ideas for exotic departures from the tenets of the past or presented three-dimensional evidences of reform that bespoke the influence of a totally new and English philosophy.

For nearly thirty years before the Centennial, while America, like England, explored the super-ornamented rococo and Renaissance formulations of Continental craftsmen, English philosophers like John Ruskin urged reform. By the 1860s the English designers William Morris and Bruce J. Talbert and their followers were pioneering the Arts and Crafts movement in a reaction to the excesses of mid-century revivals and the mechanically induced decline in the quality of ornament. Their chief apostle in England and America was Charles Lock Eastlake. His *Hints on Household Taste* of 1868 (with eight American editions from 1872 to 1890) was as influential in matters of household furnishing as Sheraton or Hepplewhite had been at the start of the century. His was not a design book, however, but a theory book for American furniture manufacturers. Eastlake's objection to excessive curves and his doctrine of rectangular lines and simple and honest construction were taken by the makers of mediocre furniture—emphatically bearing the impress of the machine—as license to assign to it the approved and demanded name of "Eastlake." Eastlake's concepts, however, were interpreted with competence and elegance by the more expensive American shops. In a sense, such interpretations defeated his idea of simplicity affording economy.

In 1877 *Gems of the Centennial Exhibition* illustrated a sideboard and hall stand of plain oak with burnished steel hinges made in Cincinnati by the firm of Mitchell and Rammelsberg. Their designs supported the revival of "medieval principles of construction" sought by men like Morris and Ruskin and interpreted by Talbert in his *Gothic Forms Applied to Furniture* (1867). The furniture had little relation to the earlier revival of applied Gothic architectural ornament but rather was composed upon the angular bracket, trestle, and spindle forms derived from medieval woodwork. Photographs and engravings of the 1870s from the New

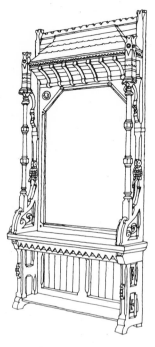

Bracket, trestle, and spindle ornament

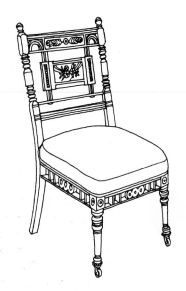

Eastlake-style chair

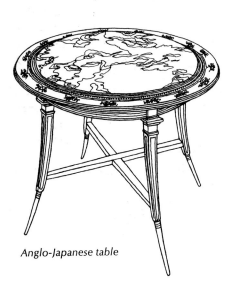

Anglo-Japanese table

York firm of Kimbel and Cabus indicate that by 1877 they had a ready stock of what could be honestly called Eastlake. Their exhibit of a drawing room in the new aesthetic at Philadelphia in 1876 was illustrated and reported as ranking "among the very best of the American exhibits in household art."

At the same time, the reform movement in England had resulted in "art furniture," a designation implying "useful" furniture to which ornamental art was added. In spite of his plea for simplicity and sincerity of design, Eastlake recommended the use of marquetry, inlay, and shallow carving to achieve "an effect of greater richness." Showing an increasing flatness and angularity, the most popular interpretations of art cabinetwork were finished in black or ebonized hardwood. The stiles, rails, and spindles of chairs and cabinets were strung with light woods or picked out in gold incised lines and frequently centered by panels of painting or marquetry. The New York firm of Christian Herter interpreted very well in the 1880s the richer schemes of ebonized art furniture for the new fortunes of America. The Centennial furniture of Kimbel and Cabus was ebonized cherry, and Henry James in 1884 in his story *A New England Winter* revealed that Miss Daintry's sister-in-law "was a votary of the newer school, and had made sacrifices to everything in black and gilt."

Whereas the earlier Renaissance revival style occasionally displayed motifs of ancient Egypt inspired by archaeological discovery and the opening of the Suez Canal, the new art furniture showed in its decoration the craze for all types of exotica, especially Japanese, but also Egyptian and Moorish. The interest in Japan originated in the displays of the Japanese Court at the London International Exhibition in 1862 and was disseminated by the influential English architect Edward W. Godwin, whose comprehensive catalogue of designs for art furniture, issued in 1877 by William Watt, was a prime source of inspiration for American manufacturers. Godwin's simple, light Anglo-Japanese designs, with shelves, brackets, and geometric latticework, were a perfect complement to the "cloisonné enamel display . . . lacquered furniture ornamented with incrusted mother-of-pearl shell . . . pictures on silks and painted screens" that so excited visitors to the Japanese bazaar at the Philadelphia Centennial. By 1880 Bruce Talbert's advocacy of the use of ceramic tiles to ornament furniture manifested itself in tiles of Japanese decoration on the furniture of Christian Herter.

At the Centennial, it was already evident that exotic displays of other countries in previous exhibitions, such as that of Paris in 1867, had induced a new attitude toward collecting. In 1868 Eastlake had written that "the smallest example . . . of anything which illustrates good design and skilful workmanship, should be acquired whenever possible, and treasured with the greatest of care . . . [that they] may each become in turn a valuable lesson in decorative form and color." It was this notion of gathering objects for domestic lessons in art that brought about in the seventies and eighties the founding of art museums, private collections, and the concept of artful clutter. This clutter, characterizing the drawing rooms of the best American homes for three decades to follow, brought into being the typical hanging and standing "art" cabinets, with studied arrangements of open shelves and mirrored and beveled glass closets for objects.

The wave of Orientalia had already hit when the prestigious firm of Pottier and Stymus conceived the richly ornamented Moorish smoking room of John D. Rockefeller, now in the Brooklyn Museum—the firm had redecorated the house shortly before 1884 for its former owner, Mrs. John Worsham. Louis C. Tiffany's

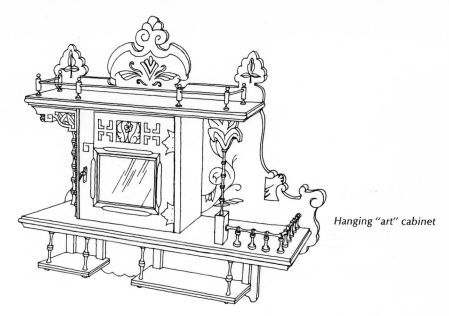

Hanging "art" cabinet

friend and associate Lockwood de Forest, recognizing the value of artistic creations in carved and mosaic wood, established a shop in Ahmadabad, India, to produce for his decorating studio in New York ornament of ambience and furniture in an exotic mode. The American tastemaker Clarence Cook expounded in the eighties the charm of bamboo furniture, which had been popular for a decade in England and France. Pieces in real bamboo were made in America particularly by Nimura and Sato of Brooklyn, but a more substantial quality was lathe-turned in imitation of bamboo from natural light maple, the flat case parts of the furniture being finished in bird's-eye maple.

Concurrent with the studied clutter of exotica and art furniture were other stylistic forces. Two of them, unabated even today, were the Colonial revival, beginning in the eighties, and the revival of "Old World" styles, evident in the nineties. Because of our concern here with new concepts in furniture design evolving in the last two decades as a result of American architectural reform, we have omitted representation of these two revivals. Historically both are important in their resultant formation of private collections of antique furniture, one of which, the American Wing's Bolles Collection, was shown here at the Hudson-Fulton Exhibition of 1909 and purchased for the Metropolitan by Mrs. Russell Sage the same year. The quest for Colonial, which emerged from antiquarian circles of New England in the 1870s, provided for some a comforting return to the past and a respite from the raw furniture of new manufacture and the imposition of foreign fashions. For others, the three Louis styles of eighteenth-century France and the Renaissance styles of seventeenth-century Italy were the perfect complements to their Beaux-Arts châteaux and villas in Newport and their new French classical and Gothic town houses in New York. Although some convincing copies were handmade, both the Colonial enthusiasms and the *bon goût* identifications with "Old World" styles resulted largely in a wave of misunderstood commercial hybrids, which ever since have pervaded the American scene.

The trend toward architectural reform evident in the work of Boston's Henry Hobson Richardson in the early eighties marked the beginnings of new precepts in decorative form and ornament, epitomized in the furniture he designed for public buildings. His early chairs and benches for the Woburn Library in Massa-

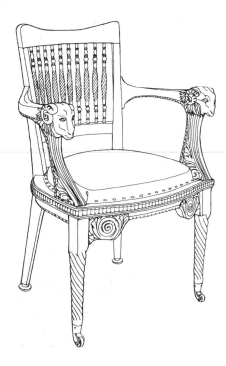

Richardson chair

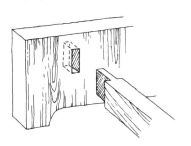

Mortise and tenon joint

chusetts reflected the theories of Eastlake and the neomedieval designs of Talbert in their "honest" mortise construction and rows of spindle ornament. By 1884 his own monumental Romanesque style, at its best in the interior of the chamber of the Albany Court of Appeals, showed the full development of his spindle armchairs with organic, carved ornament of Byzantine inspiration. His rugged designs for tables with spiral-turned legs and pedestals and the high-back spindle chairs of a basically Windsor form were executed in the Boston shop of Irving and Casson and Davenport. It is this firm that we credit with the promulgation in the eighties and nineties of the Richardson style, particularly in oak dining chairs with high backs of full-length spindles and cane or plank seats. To one of the members, Davenport, is attributed the original design for the turn-of-the-century boxy sofas that to this day bear his name.

Richardson passed from the scene in 1886, but a brilliant minority of architect-designers in Chicago and on the Pacific coast during the eighties and nineties were developing a national style. This style was the antithesis of the pretentious classical and Renaissance creations of the World's Columbian Exposition at Chicago. The fair of 1893 was aptly described by Henry Adams as a "product of the Beaux-Arts artistically induced to pass the summer on the shore of Lake Michigan." The architectural scheme, supporting great domes, porticos, and classical entablatures, was acidly criticized by the progressive architect Louis Sullivan as "a naked exhibitionism of charlatanry in the higher feudal and domineering culture, conjoined with expert salesmanship of the materials of decay." He further predicted that "the damage wrought by the World's Fair will last for half a century." The Beaux-Arts style did reign supreme, and the principal architect of the fair, Richard Morris Hunt, was commissioned shortly after the exposition to design the new Fifth Avenue façade of The Metropolitan Museum of Art. The majority of the furniture exhibits at the fair, especially those of the large manufactories of Grand Rapids, reflected in their peculiar eclecticism all the elements of the revivals of the Colonial and "Old World" styles, combined with degenerated forms of an earlier Eastlake conception.

At the same time, however, the Chicago school architects like Sullivan and Frank Lloyd Wright, with their concepts of simple masses enhanced by a modicum of integrated organic ornament, had a profound influence on the salient points of the custom-made furniture from Chicago's leading makers, the Tobey Furniture Company. Wright designed his own furniture in the nineties, anticipating the squared simplicity of the Craftsman style that followed. He recounted years later that the houses of his Oak Park days were "painful" to him because the clients, not entrusting the furnishings to his design, "helplessly dragged the horrors of the old order along after them."

By 1900 an independent furniture maker, Gustav Stickley of Eastwood, New York, had formulated his own style in his Craftsman furniture. Its squared elements of solid oak were joined by hand with visible mortise joints. The upholstery and table tops were of a natural green canvas or brown leather. *The House Beautiful,* enthusiastic over Stickley's exhibition at Grand Rapids in 1900, exclaimed: "The day of cheap veneer, of jig-saw ornament, or poor imitations of French periods, is happily over." Stickley's truly functional forms, which later became known as the Mission style, were widely imitated by Elbert Hubbard and others; yet none of the imitations ever attempted the quality of Stickley's construction.

In correspondence with Stickley were the Pasadena, California, architects Charles and Henry Greene, who recommended Stickley's furniture to those who could not afford their own more costly custom-made designs. The Greene brothers graduated in the Beaux-Arts tradition from the Massachusetts Institute of Technology School of Architecture in 1892, and like Wright, they were inspired by the simple truths of construction that distinguished the Japanese Pavilion at the World's Fair of 1893.

Silver produced in the mid-1870s by the most prominent makers was still chiefly in the Renaissance revival style. In 1875 Tiffany and Company made the famous testimonial vase for William Cullen Bryant in a classical form with a full repertory of Renaissance decoration and allegorical motifs. By that same year, however, Tiffany, under the aegis of Edward C. Moore, was exhibiting a completely new concept in hollow ware, showing Moore's talent for adapting and mingling all kinds of Eastern designs—of Japanese, Indian, Moorish, and Egyptian flavor. Moore had a splendid collection of Eastern and Near Eastern artifacts in metal and glass (now in the Metropolitan Museum), which inspired much of his work. Soon all of the elements of exotica seen in art furniture and decorations of the eighties were to be found in profusion on the work of leading manufacturers of sterling and silver plate. The increasing elaboration of electroplated silver, with its variety of easily cast and stamped designs, inspired more elaboration on sterling.

By 1893, under the influence of the Beaux-Arts, silver flatware and hollow ware were exhibiting new interpretations of rococo scrolls and classical elements concurring with the interest in "Old World" styles of furniture and architecture. Of this period, the work of Tiffany and Company was exemplary in the fantastic Adams gold vase designed by Paulding Farnham, and the special exhibition pieces made for the Chicago World's Columbian Exposition.

By 1900 the sinuous flowing lines of the European art nouveau style were being reflected in American silver. Perhaps the largest amount of richly conceived art nouveau silver was made by Gorham. Under the guidance of William Codman, their English-born and -trained chief designer, this company produced enormous numbers of handwrought forms in soft silver decorated with floating long-haired female figures and waves, sea plants, and flowers. Each of these pieces, identified by the trade name Martelé, was unique and costly. Gorham also made a fine silver deposit, which was applied in traditional and art nouveau profiles on glass and on the deep glazes of Rookwood pottery. Smaller companies like the Alvin Manufacturing Company of Providence produced silver-deposit ware using colored as well as clear glass. A variety of objects were decorated with gold or silver mounts, frames, or rims. Silver novelties and personal objects, many of them in art nouveau patterns, were the stock-in-trade of firms like Unger Brothers of Newark, New Jersey, who until 1910 were the most prolific manufacturers of items such as brooches, buckles, comb and brush sets, and letter openers.

The last quarter of the nineteenth century might aptly be called The Great Age of Glass. At no time before was glass manufactured in such a variety of colors and decorative techniques and so widely adapted to so many uses. Leaded windows in geometric or figural designs were used in the vestibules, salons, libraries, and stairwells of "artistic" houses. Some of the best were designed by men like John La Farge and the company of artisans working with Louis C. Tiffany, who also used glass mosaics around fireplaces, on columns, and in other archi-

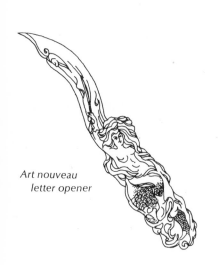

Art nouveau letter opener

tectural treatments. The affluence of the eighties and nineties created a great demand for artistic decorating, and the great firms of Christian Herter, Auguste Pottier, and Louis C. Tiffany all created multicolored glass screens—movable or stationary—for fireplaces, alcoves, transoms, and partitions. The earliest were leaded in flat geometric patterns symmetrically interspersed with bull's-eye roundels for light refraction and variety. Those of the late eighties and the nineties were more often figural, reflecting either the conventional forms of the Beaux-Arts or the rich floral motifs of La Farge and Tiffany.

In the 1880s, to the domestic table glass production of pressed and cut wares was added a whole new series of "novelties" in art glass generated by the rapidly growing concern with art as opposed to mere utility. The old and experienced glasshouses of the mid-century—New England Glass, Mt. Washington Glass, and Hobbs, Brockunier—became the leaders of experimentation in colored and decorated ornaments that led to such intriguing patented names as Burmese, Peachblow, Pomona, Amberina, Agata, Crown Milano, and Royal Flemish. Although the different wares were sometimes made in many forms, both useful and ornamental, their production was often short-lived, as manufacturers could only find new markets by constant innovation.

By the 1890s an enormous variety of patterns in high-quality deeply cut glass of the so-called Brilliant period had reached what *The Decorator and Furnisher* called "the acme of elegance." The Libbey Glass Company of Toledo, Ohio, Christian Dorflinger and Sons of White Mills, Pennsylvania, and T. G. Hawkes and Company of Corning, New York, were the most prominent makers of this cut glass at the turn of the century. Hawkes was renowned for his Russian pattern tableware, bought for the White House in 1885 and used there until 1938.

Hawkes's Corning neighbor, Frederick Carder of Steuben Glass Works, was known for his iridescent glass in traditional shapes with a special finish he called Aurene because of its golden luster. The grand master of iridescence, however, was Louis Comfort Tiffany, who, through his search for beauty and dramatic business acumen, had by 1898 created an estimated five thousand colors and varieties of his world-famous Favrile glass. Tiffany's contribution was by far the most original, and his is the greatest creative expression in glass American art has known.

In late nineteenth-century American ceramics, the manufacture of art porcelain was for the most part an attempt to imitate the English Royal Doulton work and the eggshell translucence of Irish Belleek. Knowles, Taylor and Knowles of East Liverpool, Ohio, produced after 1889 a variant of Belleek, which they called Lotusware. One of its most distinguished technical achievements was the decorative use of fine reticulated bosses of an Oriental character. In the East, the Union Porcelain Works at Greenpoint perfected another variant of Belleek in tea wares, which they called Blanc de Chine. Their neighboring competitor, Edward Lycett of the Faience Manufacturing Company, emulated in his rich blue glazes and satiny cream-colored finishes the highly decorated Oriental character of the best English work. By 1900 Trenton, New Jersey, had become, as it is today, the center of American porcelain manufacture. One of the major firms, the Ceramic Art Company, produced mostly porcelains in the rococo spirit, under the guidance of Walter Scott Lenox, formerly of the prestigious firm of Ott and Brewer, which in 1882 had made the first true Belleek porcelain in America.

In the 1880s and 90s the more distinctive achievements in American ceramics were those of the artist-potters whose commercially produced work was an individual reflection of the current English Arts and Crafts movement. The earliest and greatest of them was the group at the Rookwood Pottery, established in Cincinnati, Ohio, in 1880. Their deep brown and green glazes on essentially Oriental and Near Eastern shapes were imitated by other leading Ohio potters, particularly in Zanesville, by the J. B. Owens Pottery Company and the larger firm of S. A. Weller. The latter, with the French artist J. Sicard in its employ, was distinguished after 1900 for rich iridescent glazes, emulating the colors and character of Tiffany glass.

The Boston area was the other center of art pottery, growing out of the ceramic tile and architectural pottery industries. The Chelsea Keramic Art Works of the Robertson family—Alexander, Hugh, and later James—produced pottery that was essentially Oriental in inspiration. They are best remembered for their recreation of the rich, red Chinese *sang de boeuf* glaze after 1884 and their crackleware of the 90s. The Art Tile Works of John G. Low, also in Chelsea, beginning in 1879 made decorative architectural tiles for fireplaces and dados, which, like the tiles manufactured in Trenton, New Jersey, displayed all the motifs of the era as well as portrait busts of famous men. More serious endeavors in hollow ware were made by South Boston's Grueby Faience Company, organized in 1897. William H. Grueby's work, distinguished by its matte green or tan glazes, was awarded prizes in exhibitions at home and abroad.

Other potters of the crafts movement were scattered over the nation by 1900. One of the best known was Artus van Briggle, who began at Rookwood, studied in Paris, and in 1899 opened a pottery in Denver, Colorado, where the firm is still flourishing on a wholly commercial level. At the turn of the century a number of art schools produced works of an honest, functional sort different from the commercial wares of the day. The most successful of these were the Newcomb College potters at New Orleans, whose pottery—much of it experimental—was particularly sympathetic to the simple craftsmanlike designs of Gustav Stickley, Frank Lloyd Wright, or Charles and Henry Greene. Their work, like the work of these men, supremely utilitarian but giving beauty beyond its immediate function, foreshadowed the finest artistic concepts of the twentieth century.

REFERENCES CITED

Silliman, Benjamin, Jr., and Goodrich, C. R., eds. *The World of Science, Art and Industry from Examples in The New-York Exhibition, 1853-54*, New York, 1854, p. 185 for quotation on "frigid monstrosities"; pp. 114, 164 for quotations on Augustus Eliaers

Johnson, William. "A Young Man's Journal of 1800-1813 [William Johnson of Newton, N.J.]," in *New Jersey Historical Society, Proceedings*, n.s., vol. 8 (1923), as quoted in Still, Bayrd. *Mirror for Gotham, New York as seen by Contemporaries from Dutch Days to the Present*, New York, 1956, p. 56

[Longworth, David, ed.] *American Almanack. New-York Register, and City Directory for the Thirtieth Year of American Independence*, New York, 1805-1806, p. 111

Letter, Sarah Huger to Mrs. Daniel Horry, Tradd Street, Charleston, South Carolina (New York, Jan. 4, 1816), copy in the American Wing Archives, The Metropolitan Museum of Art

Johnson, Marilynn A. "John Hewitt, Cabinetmaker," *Winterthur Portfolio IV* (1968), pp. 185-205 for information on John Hewitt's ledger

Pearce, Lorraine W., Pearce, John N., and Smith, Robert C. "The Meeks family of cabinetmakers," *Antiques*, vol. 85, no. 4 (Apr. 1964), pp. 414-419

Relf's Philadelphia Gazette and Daily Advertiser (Jan. 19, 1810), Joseph B. Barry and Son advertisement

Smith, Robert C. "Philadelphia Empire furniture by Antoine Gabriel Quervelle," *Antiques*, vol. 86, no. 3 (Sept. 1964), pp. 304-309, Quervelle advertisement p. 305

The White House Association. *The White House, An Historic Guide*, 4th ed., by Lorraine W. Pearce, rev. and enl. by William V. Elder, III, Washington, 1963, pp. 95-96

Montgomery, Charles F. "John Needles—Baltimore cabinetmaker," *Antiques*, vol. 65, no. 4 (Apr. 1954), pp. 292-295; term "curled maple" used in *The Cincinnati Cabinet-Makers' Book of Prices for Manufacturing Cabinet-Ware*, printed for the Cabinet Makers by Whetstone and Buxton Rule, 1830

[Hone, Philip]. *The Diary of Philip Hone 1828-1851*, ed. with introd. by Allan Nevins, enl. ed., New York, 1936, pp. 301-302

Davidson, Marshall B., ed. *The American Heritage History of American Antiques from the Revolution to the Civil War*, New York, 1968, p. 206 for quotation from an English observer of 1829, 252 for quotation from a Bohemian manufacturer in 1836; p. 174 for quotation from *Harper's New Monthly Magazine* on "foreign designers"

Loudon, J. C. *An Encyclopaedia of Cottage, Farm, and Villa Architecture and Furniture; . . .*, 1st ed., 1833; new ed., London, 1835, p. 1039, no. 2072

"Hints for the Decoration and Furnishing of Dwellings," *The Journal of Design and Manufactures . . .*, vol. 2, no. 7 (Sept. 1849), p. 17

Aslin, Elizabeth. *Nineteenth Century English Furniture*, Faber Monographs on Furniture, New York, 1962, p. 30 for information on Cottingham's use of "ancient material"; p. 36 for quotation from Sir Henry Cole on exhibitions

Hawthorne, Nathaniel. *The Marble Faun*, New York, 1902, preface, p. xxv

Conner, Robert. *The Cabinet Makers' Assistant, Designed and Drawn by Robert Conner*, New York, 1842, frontispiece and preface

Donnell, Edna. "A. J. Davis and the Gothic Revival," *Metropolitan Museum Studies*, vol. 5 (1934-1936), p. 200

Hauserman, Dianne D. "Alexander Roux and His 'Plain and Artistic Furniture'," *Antiques*, vol. 93, no. 2 (Feb. 1968), pp. 210-217

New York Evening Post (Sept. 28, 1859), advertisment for "Alexander Roux & Co., 479 B'way"

"A Parlor View," *Gleason's Pictorial Drawing-room Companion*, vol. 7, no. 19 (Nov. 11, 1854), p. 300

Ingerman, Elizabeth A. "Personal experiences of an old New York cabinetmaker," *Antiques*, vol. 84, no. 5 (Nov. 1963), pp. 576-580 for quotations from Hagen

Downing, Andrew Jackson. *The Architecture of Country Houses . . .*, New York and Philadelphia, 1850, p. 451

Drepperd, Carl W. *Victorian The Cinderella of Antiques*, New York, 1950, p. 37, advertisement for Eliaers

Bigelow, David. *History of Prominent Mercantile and Manufacturing Firms in the United States . . .*, (annual), vol. 6, Boston, 1857, p. 214

"Decorative Fine-Art Work at Philadelphia. American Furniture," *The American Architect and Building News*, vol. 1 (Dec. 23, 1876), p. 412; vol. 2 (Jan. 13, 1877), p. 13

Gems of the Centennial Exhibition: Consisting of Illustrated Descriptions of Objects of an Antique Character . . . at the Philadelphia International Exhibition of 1876, New York, 1877, pp. 140, 141

Eastlake, Charles L[ock]. *Hints on Household Taste in Furniture, Upholstery, and Other Details*, Boston, 1872, p. 183 for information on the use of decoration; pp. 136-137 for quotation on collecting

James, Henry. "A New England Winter," in *Henry James' American Novels and Stories*, ed. with introd. by F. O. Matthiessen, New York, 1947, p. 339

Norton, Frank H[enry]. *Illustrated Historical Register of the Centennial Exhibition Philadelphia, 1876; . . .*, New York, 1879, p. 249

Adams, Henry. *The Education of Henry Adams*, New York, 1931, p. 340

Sullivan, Louis H. *The Autobiography of an Idea*, New York, 1956, pp. 322, 325 for quotations on Chicago Columbian Exhibition

Wright, Frank Lloyd. "Prairie Architecture," in *Frank Lloyd Wright: Writings and Buildings*, selected by Edgar Kaufmann and Ben Raeburn, Cleveland, 1960, p. 49

Edgewood, Margaret. "Some Sensible Furniture," *The House Beautiful*, vol. 8, no. 5, (Oct. 1900), pp. 653-655

Poole, Hester M. "Pottery Porcelain and Glass," "Cut Glass and Crystal—II," *The Decorator and Furnisher*, vol. 27, no. 1 (Apr. 1896), p. 14

19TH-CENTURY AMERICA
FURNITURE AND
OTHER DECORATIVE ARTS

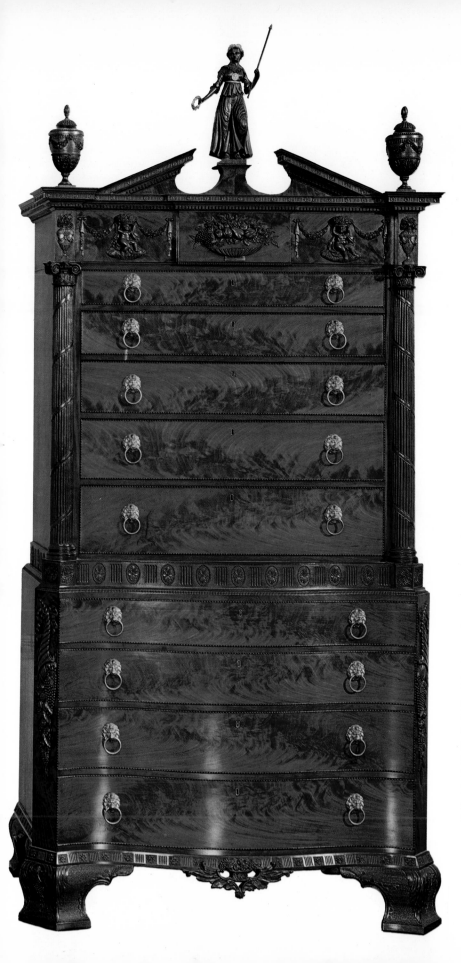

1

Considered the masterpiece of Salem furniture, this mahogany double chest of drawers is attributed to William Lemon. The chest descended in the Derby family of Salem and the Curtis family of Boston; there is reason to believe it is the "case of drawers made by Mr. Lemon" and carved by Samuel McIntire for which McIntire billed Elizabeth Derby on October 22, 1796. Few, if any, pieces can better show the transition from the craftsmanship of the Colonies to the craftsmanship of Federal America. The structure itself—sturdy bracket feet, basic form of chest on chest with canted corners, carved classical frieze, and broken pediment—looks to the eighteenth century; the decorative elements—brass lion's-head pulls, carved cornucopias, urns, baskets, and putti with swags, and punchwork background—look to the nineteenth century. The carving makes this chest not only one of the greatest productions of Salem's master carver, but also the first example of the Salem Federal style. How much tastes and values can change is shown by the history of the chest. When first seen by Maxim Karolik, who subsequently purchased it for the Museum of Fine Arts in 1941, the chest was in a house on the Massachusetts North Shore, where its drawers were being used for ripening pears.

H. 102¹/₂ inches
Museum of Fine Arts, Boston, M. and M.
Karolik Collection

2

Although this press cupboard on chest owes much to the pattern books of Hepplewhite and Sheraton, it is a distinctly New York interpretation of the English neoclassical style. Made about 1800 to 1810, it is attributed to Michael Allison, who worked from 1800 to 1845 in New York City. The shape of the apron and line of the French foot are found on numerous New York bureaus, some of them labeled by Allison. Typical, too, of New York Federal furniture is the large expanse of highly figured mahogany veneer, its rich but restrained appearance relieved by stringing and by two light ovals of inlay with eagles. Such inlay designs, which appear often upon documented New York furniture of the period, were either made by the individual cabinetmaker or purchased from specialists. The most decorative part of this wardrobe, the broken scroll pediment, was not taken from contemporary pattern books but is a holdover from earlier designs. The unusually open and free pierced leaf design is virtually identical to the pattern of a closed pediment on a similar piece in the Winterthur collection. The Winterthur example, also attributed to Allison, has, like this chest, a brass eagle finial upon a plinth with Prince of Wales feather inlay.

H. 96¹/₂ inches
Diplomatic Reception Rooms, Department of State, Washington

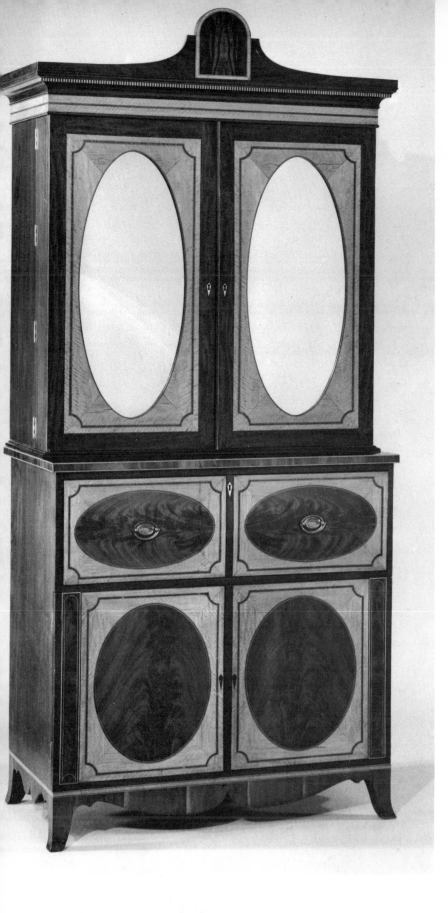

3

In contrast to the sober darkness of the Allison press cupboard (no. 2) is the striking use of light and dark woods on this secretary made in Philadelphia about 1805 to 1810. With large fields of satinwood and mahogany veneers, the cabinetmaker, John Davey, created a design that places all visual emphasis on the arrangement of inlaid ovals upon mitered panels, behind which are concealed the workings of the piece. The doors of the lower section open to tiers of three drawers on each side; the drawer above, with its single ivory escutcheon, pulls out and the front falls to form a writing surface, above which is a satinwood interior of drawers and pigeonholes. The bookcase doors, with their unusual mirrored ovals, open to show spaces for books built into their backs, as well as the bookshelves of the case. The maker was justifiably proud of his work, for in various locations, and apparently by the same hand, "John Davey" is inscribed no less than seven times and "John Davey Junr" twice. Davey is listed in the Philadelphia directories as a cabinetmaker for most of the period from 1797 to 1822. To date this secretary is the only known documented example of his work.

H. 95⁷/₈ inches

The Metropolitan Museum of Art, Fletcher Fund; Rogers Fund; Gift of Mrs. Russell Sage; The Sylmaris Collection, Gift of George Coe Graves, 62.9

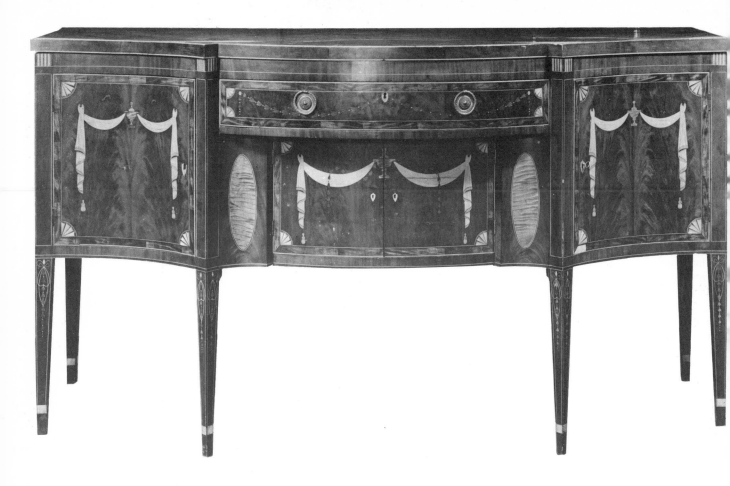

4 Sideboards appeared only toward the end of the eighteenth century. English furniture makers had produced them for about a dozen years when the 1788 London book of prices, featuring sideboards, was published, and Hepplewhite's *Guide* of that year commented: "The great utility of this piece...has procured it a very general reception; and the conveniencies it affords render a dining-room incomplete without a sideboard." Based somewhat on Hepplewhite's designs, this mahogany sideboard was made by William Mills and Simeon Deming, partners from 1793 to 1798, for Governor Oliver Wolcott of Connecticut. It bears their label: "Mills & Deming,/No. 374 Queen Street, two doors above the Friends Meeting,/NEW-YORK,/Makes and sells, all kinds of Cabinet Furni-/ture and Chairs, after the most modern fashions/ . . . on reasonable terms." Since Queen Street was joined to and given the name of Pearl ·Street in February 1794, the sideboard was presumably made by that date. It has canted legs typical of New York and many touches of veneer and inlay that would have been extras in a cabinetmaker's price book: triple stringing outlining the oval panels; quarter fan corners and flutes, a common motif for New York furniture, above the legs; bellflowers, or "husks," on the legs and across the drawer; and swags with urns on the doors, perhaps unique on American sideboards of the Federal period.

L. 76 inches
Mrs. Walter B. Robb, Buffalo

5

This superb square-back mahogany armchair was made in New York about 1800. Highly favored by New York cabinetmakers and chairmakers, this type of chair was listed in the 1802 New York price book at nineteen shillings and six pence for the cheapest version. The source for the design was plate 36, no. 1, of the 1794 edition of Sheraton's *Drawing Book*. The primary difference between this chair and the Sheraton design is the use of inlay in place of carved decoration. As on the majority of New York chairs of this kind, the vase-shaped center baluster is pierced rather than solid, and the arms, or "elbows," are fastened into the side seat rails. The swag of satinwood, which is analogous to the swags on the Mills and Deming sideboard (no. 4), the Prince of Wales feathers, and the fans are all interpretations in veneer of the carved ornament shown in pattern books. Lines of stringing on stiles, rails, arms, and legs replace the beaded edging that would have appeared on the finest carved versions, and inlaid stars on the front of each arm replace the carved rosettes.

H. 36 inches
Mrs. Pietro Crespi, on loan to the Museum of the City of New York

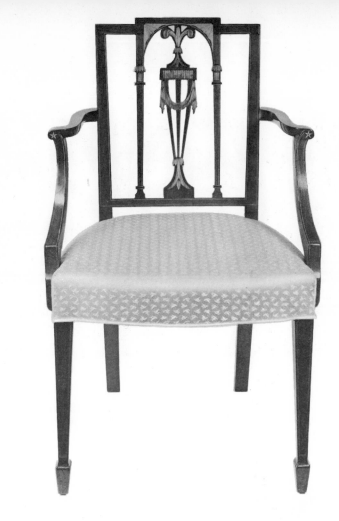

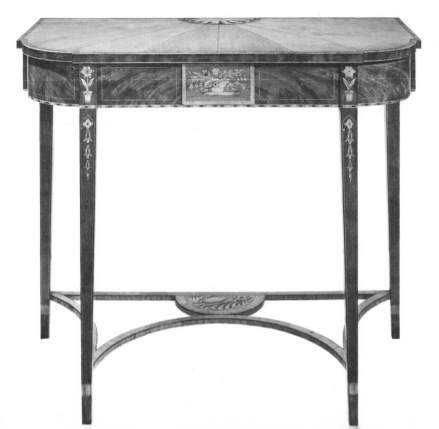

6

In Baltimore inlaid and painted adaptations of Sheraton designs reached their highest degree of elaboration. This side, or pier, table made of mahogany and satinwood about 1790 to 1800 in Baltimore is patterned after plate 4 in the appendix to the *Drawing Book* of 1793. Although the original design had turned legs and feet rather than the straight tapering ones found here, the shape of the stretcher is identical, even to the small, semicircular shelf that joins front and back. Details of the inlay, however, are totally in the Baltimore style, with flower pots and blossoms above pendent bellflowers on the legs. On the top of the table panels of satinwood radiate from an inlaid semicircle with a shaded petal or shell pattern (compare no. 15). The edge of the top is crossbanded with mahogany.

H. 39 1/2 inches
Lent anonymously

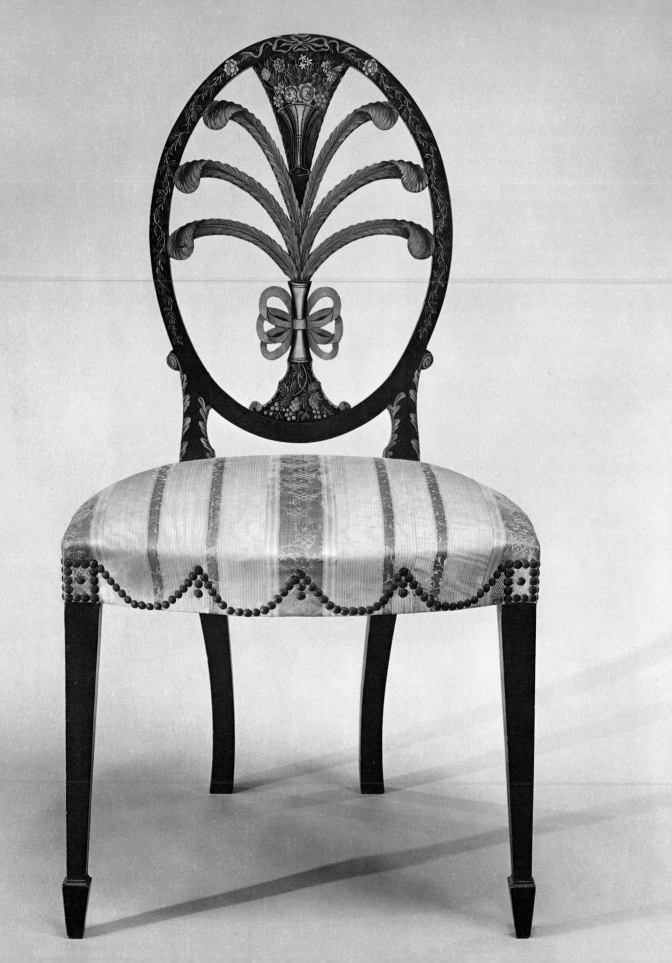

7

In 1796 the wealthy Salem merchant Elias Hasket Derby ordered twenty-four oval-back chairs from Philadelphia. Traditionally this maple chair and its mate, painted black, have been ascribed to that group, although all the examples known with certainty to have come from the Derby family were painted white. Patterned after designs in Hepplewhite's *Guide* of 1788, these chairs, and similar ones at Winterthur and the Museum of Fine Arts, Boston, differ from the white ones in having three feathers on either side of the back instead of two. Carved mahogany versions of this oval-back chair, following Hepplewhite very closely and attributed to the Salem area, are known. The painted chairs, a freer interpretation of the original design, achieve their effect through color, well-delineated curves of the plumes, delicate painting of flowers, ribbons, and grapes, and touches of fine detailing such as the foliate and scroll borders of the stiles.

H. 38¹/₂ inches

The Metropolitan Museum of Art, Gift of Mrs. J. Insley Blair, 47.103.1

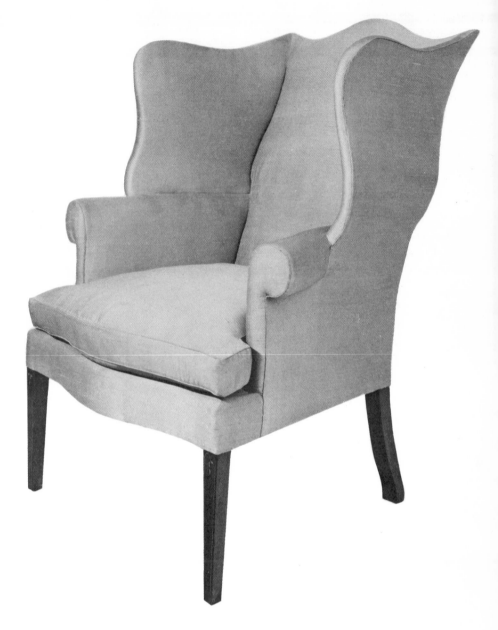

8

The sinuous lines of sides and cresting, the subtle curve of front rail and rear legs, and the excellent proportions of this mahogany easy chair proclaim it the best of its era. Made about 1800 to 1810 in Salem, it is an adaptation of plate 15 in Hepplewhite's *Guide* of 1788. Unlike the original design, which has plain tapered legs with stretchers and spade feet, this version has tapered front legs outlined in stringing, which curves in at the top to one pendent husk and drop.

H. 46 inches

Fenton L. B. Brown, New York

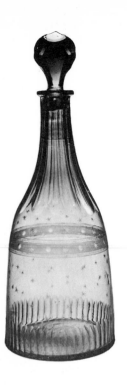

9

The first glasshouse to be established after the Revolution was the New Bremen Glass Manufactory, founded by John Frederick Amelung near Fredericktown, Maryland. At its height between 1788 and 1792 it employed about a hundred people, who made bottle, window, and flint glass; the factory closed in 1795. The production of decanters is mentioned in the company's advertisements in the Maryland *Journal* and Baltimore *Advertiser* from 1785 to 1795. This decanter of simple, light proportions with engraved ornament is typical of a group that has been associated with this glasshouse even though it does not bear any mark. The glass of the Amelung works was often the smoky gray of this decanter or a pale green, because of impurities in the metal. The star motif, fashionable in the post-Revolutionary era, came from the neoclassical models that were an almost universal source of inspiration at the time. The slight touch of color and the schematic quality of the decoration are characteristic of American work.

H. 8 inches
The Corning Museum of Glass

10

The simplicity of the silversmith's interpretation of the classical style gives this pair of early nineteenth-century candlesticks a contemporary look. They were made between 1800 and about 1815 by Isaac Hutton of Albany, and one bears on the side of the square plinth the mark "HUTTON" in a rectangle.

H. pair 8¹/₂ inches
The Metropolitan Museum of Art, Bequest of A. T. Clearwater, 33.120.204, 205

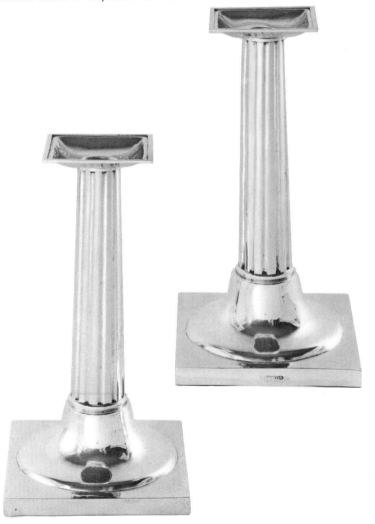

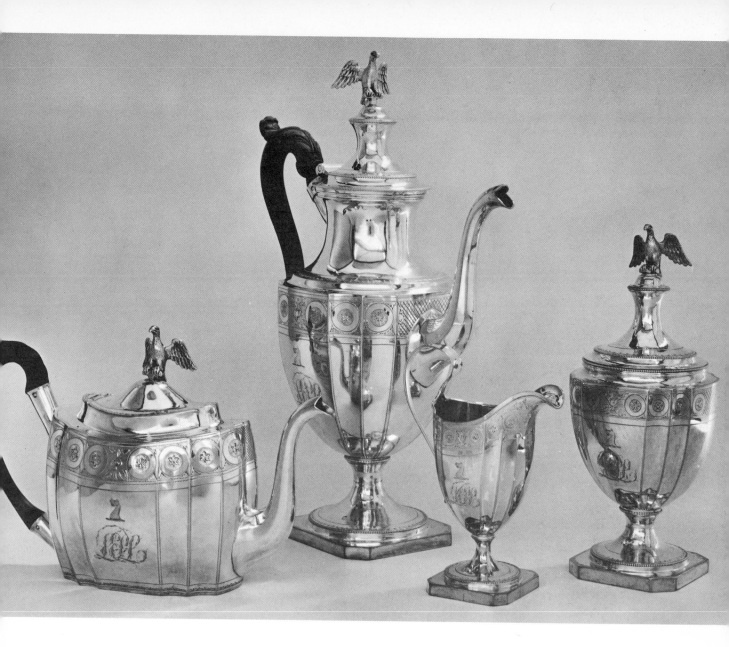

11 Unmarked but attributed to Philadelphia silversmith Christian Wiltberger, this four-piece tea service of the late eighteenth century is important for both its artistic qualities and its historic associations. As an impressive example of the Federal style in silver, the set uses classic forms; urn-shaped coffeepot and sugar bowl and helmet-shaped cream pitcher. Like much furniture of the period, this silver shows the craftsman's interest in modifying form by varying surface. Here, as on elaborately veneered and inlaid case pieces, there are no large plain areas; the surfaces are broken up by convex and concave panels and by bright-cut engraving, that is, with designs lightly cut so as to make a highly reflective surface. Even the spouts are paneled. The tea set descended in the Lewis family of Virginia and bears the Lewis crest and monogram. According to family tradition, the set was the gift of George Washington to his stepdaughter Eleanor (Nellie) Parke Custis on the occasion of her marriage to Lawrence E. P. Lewis, February 22, 1799.

H. coffeepot 14¹/₂ inches

Mrs. Edwin A. S. Lewis, on loan to The Metropolitan Museum of Art since 1927, L.2641.1-4

12

A comparison of this mahogany sideboard, made about 1800 to 1810 and attributed to the Boston workshop of John and Thomas Seymour, with the Mills and Deming sideboard (no. 4) reveals both similarities and differences. Both show unusual skill of design and execution and the use of classical motifs. Here, however, the patterns of inlay are more restrained and thus subordinate to the overall concept, and carving is an important part of the decoration. The most striking feature of the sideboard is the veneering of the tambour doors, in which flat strips of dark-stained wood alternate with light strips of birch, with cherry stringing between. At the sides and in the center are simulated pilasters of shaded stringing. A lunette banding appears around three edges of the top and along the arched skirt and bottom edge. Reeding and carving on posts and legs, ivory neoclassical urn escutcheons, and brass lion's-head drawer pulls complete the decorative details. The high quality of this sideboard brings to mind a comment by the English architect-designer Robert Adam: "The eating rooms are considered as the apartments of conversation . . . it [is] desirable to have them fitted up with elegance and splendor. . . ."

L. 73 inches
The Metropolitan Museum of Art, Gift of the family of Mr. and Mrs. Andrew Varick Stout, in their memory, 65.188.1

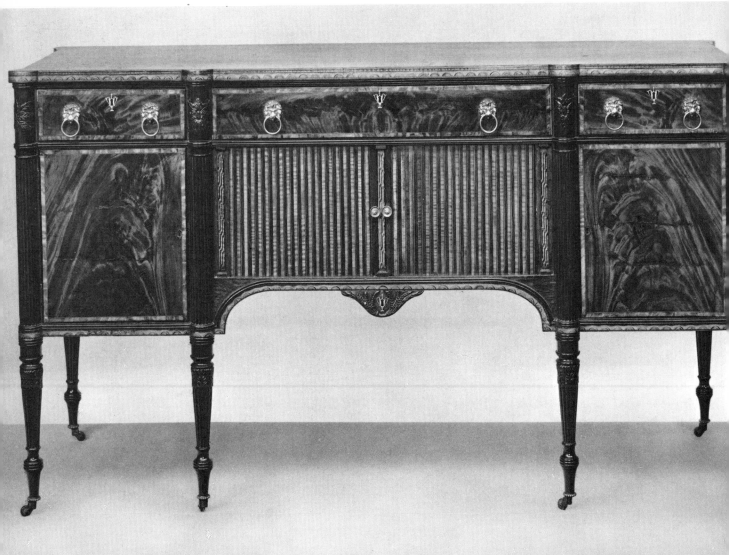

13

Transitional in style between Federal veneered furniture based on Sheraton or Hepplewhite and the Boston interpretation of the English Regency, this small table was made about 1810 to 1815. Using a pleasing circular shape rather than the conventional square or rectangle, the unknown maker has achieved success through repetition with variation: the circle of the top is repeated in the smaller roundel; ring turnings at the top of the legs occur again below. The brass of the paw feet and ball pulls is picked up in the decorative bands on the legs and the button in the center of the roundel. The heavy reeding of the legs is typical of the Boston area. The use of repetition and contrast—light maple veneer against dark mahogany, flat surfaces against reeded or molded ones—gives a feeling of harmony and energy. The feeling of movement is most apparent at the base, where the three bands of the stretcher joining the slender ankles spring upward to support the turned roundel, completing a design that is both self-contained and lively.

H. 30 inches
Essex Institute, Salem, Massachusetts

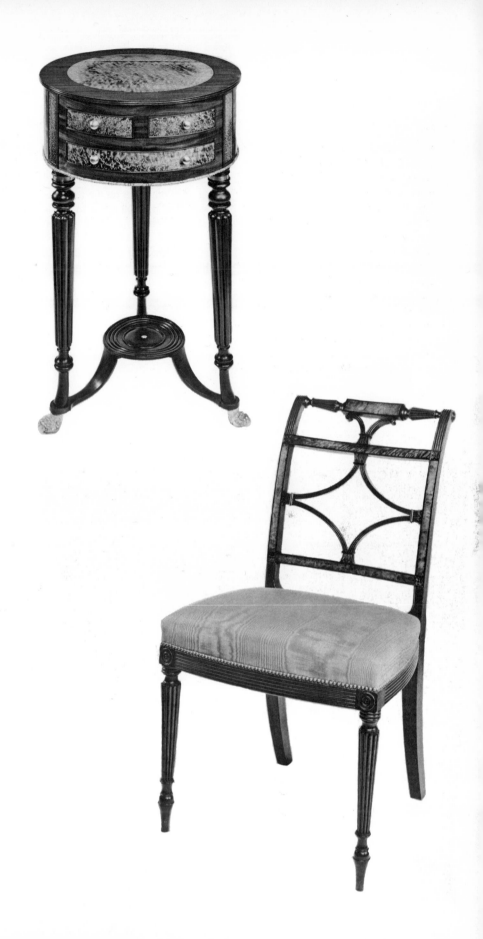

14

This chair, attributed to the workshop of John and Thomas Seymour, is a variation on a design shown in the 1802 edition of *The London Chair-Makers' and Carvers' Book of Prices for Workmanship*; the embellishments available for the design are listed under "side chair with scroll back." Primarily of mahogany, the chair is paneled with figured birch on the stiles and lower rail of the back and the tablet of its reeded top rail, or roller. Other versions of the chair are known, also attributed to the Seymours. At Winterthur there is a related set of furniture, with the same scroll back, including a five-chair-back settee and a double-chair-back settee. These differ in having straight front legs that turn outward and more veneering in light wood.

H. 36 inches
The Metropolitan Museum of Art, Gift of Mrs. Russell Sage, 10.125.312

15 Based upon English design books, and particularly Hepplewhite's *Guide* of 1788, this demilune commode was made by the Seymours of Boston. A bill for it from Thomas Seymour to Mrs. Elizabeth Derby, daughter of Elias Hasket Derby of Salem, was rendered in 1809. With its light and dark veneer, inlay, carving, and painted decoration, the commode is equal in sophistication to almost any furniture of its period, here or abroad. The radiating strips of veneer on the top, alternately satinwood and mahogany, are found on other pieces of furniture from the Boston-Salem area. The strips converge on a semicircle of rosewood containing painted decoration of sea shells. According to the 1809 invoice, the painter was the Boston artist John Penniman, who often worked for the Seymours. Bordering the semicircle of rosewood is a rope inlay frequently used by the Seymours. Dart inlay, also found on many Seymour pieces, trims the top edge. The drawers and the swinging side panels made to simulate drawers are veneered with bird's-eye maple and banded with cross-grained rosewood. Four ovolo mahogany posts, with carving probably by Thomas Whitman, continue to turned legs, which terminate in the type of brass paw feet more often used by Phyfe and other New York cabinetmakers.
H. 42¹/₂ inches
Museum of Fine Arts, Boston, M. and M. Karolik Collection

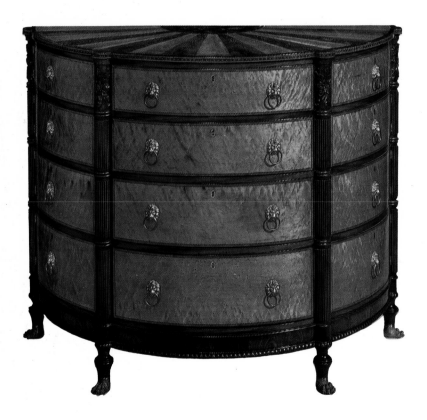

16

Modeled upon the *"Sister's Cylinder Bookcase,"* plate 38 in Sheraton's *Cabinet Dictionary* of 1803, this mahogany desk and bookcase was made in Baltimore or Philadelphia about 1811. From Sheraton comes the overall design, but there is some visual awkwardness in the original concept, and this desk seems in some ways an improvement. The American cabinetmaker substituted a straight dropfront desk for the cylinder roll top and replaced the fretted gallery and globe surmounting the Sheraton version with a graceful pediment echoing the pyramid of the base. He relieved the top-heavy quality of the original arcaded Gothic form by substituting neoclassical painted decoration, a typical Baltimore device, which breaks up the surface and gives a feeling of lightness. The midsections are veneered and inlaid with satinwood ovals and banding in the Baltimore manner. The long center drawer pulls out and falls open to a writing surface and satinwood drawers. A pencil inscription on the bottom of one drawer reads: "M Oliver Married the 5 of October 1811 Baltimore." The date is that of the wedding of Roswell Lyman Colt and Margaret Oliver, one of the four daughters of Robert Oliver, millionaire merchant of Baltimore.
H. 91 inches
The Metropolitan Museum of Art, Gift of Mrs. Russell Sage and Various Other Donors, 69.203

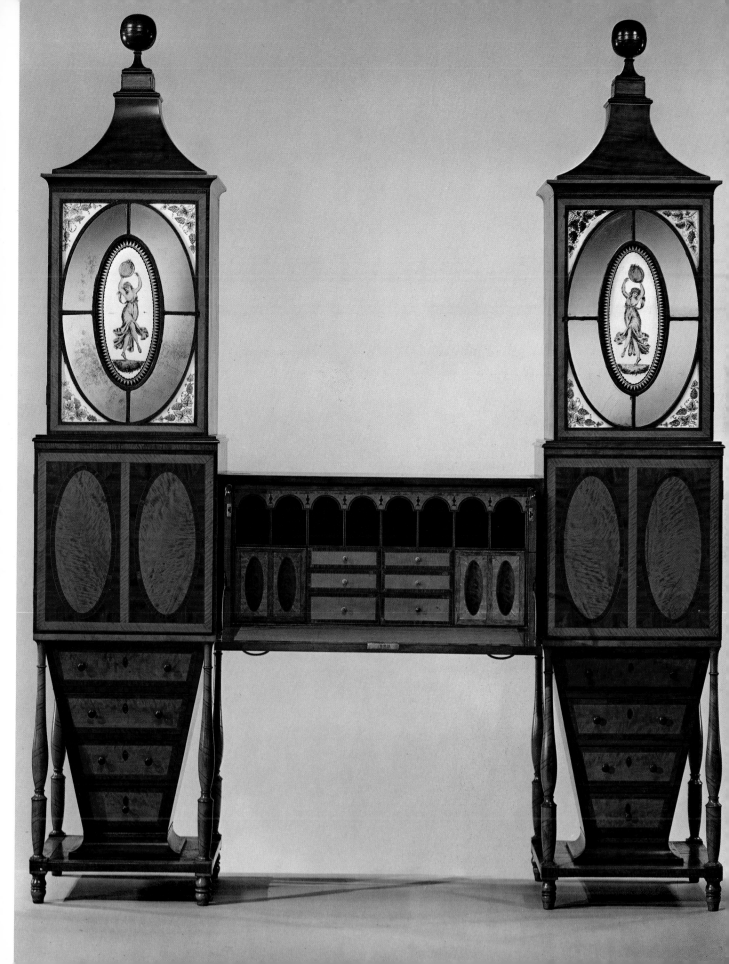

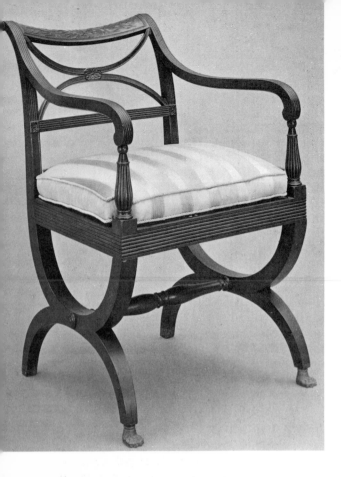

18

Large panels of flame-grained mahogany set off by contrasting borders of cross-cut veneer enrich the surface of this handsome and rather chaste small sideboard, made about 1812 and attributable to a major New York shop such as that of Phyfe or Charles-Honoré Lannuier. The crisp stop fluting on the columns and leaf carving on front legs and capitals suggest the work of both masters. The brass embellishments—paw feet, lion's-mask pulls with rings, and gallery of turned spindles—are based on English Regency prototypes; the contrast of these with the rich dark wood is typical of Regency and Empire furniture. Unusually compact in scale, this sideboard was well suited to a society that valued space. Sideboards, along with other case pieces such as armoires and bookcases, were meant to be stationary; consequently there are no casters on the paw feet, as there would have been on smaller, more mobile furniture of the period.

L. 58 inches
Ronald S. Kane, New York

17

Despite the span of his working career (1792-1847) and the wide range of the furniture he produced, Duncan Phyfe's name has been given specifically to American furniture in the Regency style. A superb example is this mahogany armchair with crossed legs at the sides, made by Phyfe, according to a family tradition, about 1810 as part of a set for Thomas Cornell Pearsall of 43 Wall Street. The attribution is strengthened by Phyfe's sketch, at Winterthur, of a chair with curved crossed legs at front and back. The curule shape, or Grecian cross as it was called in the price books, based on a Roman magistrate's folding chair, had precedents in first decade nineteenth-century design plates such as those of Pierre de la Mésangère, Thomas Sheraton, George Smith, and Thomas Hope, but all of these examples had the cross in front and back. The 1808 *Supplement to the London Chairmakers' and Carvers' Book of Prices for Workmanship* showed two stools, from which this design was probably taken, with the addition of a square back with "ogee splat." Phyfe's mastery is demonstrated by his successful combination of various elements. The curves of the leg are repeated in the curves of the back; the joining of the legs by a baluster stretcher appears solid as well as graceful. Reeding on the stiles, rails, and arms breaks up the surfaces of the upper chair and gives it a feeling of delicacy. Twelve of the Pearsall chairs are in the American Wing of the Metropolitan; a similar pair of side chairs is at Winterthur.

H. 32³/₄ inches
The Metropolitan Museum of Art, Gift of
C. Ruxton Love, 60.4.2

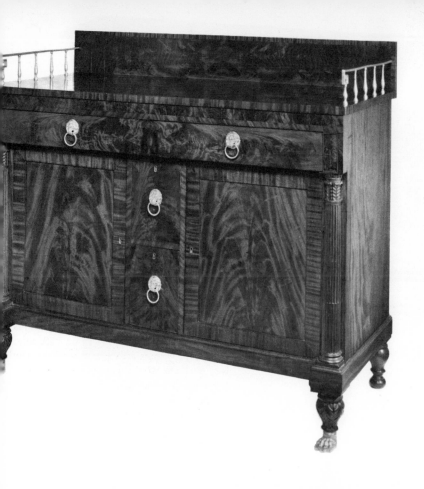

19

Showing marked characteristics of the New York Regency style, this mahogany extension dining table was made about 1815 in New York, perhaps in the shop of Duncan Phyfe. Slender columns with vase and ring turnings support the top; the lower turnings with twisted flutes with fillets—the terminology used in New York price books—are found on furniture attributed to Phyfe (see no. 20). The splayed reeded legs terminate in carved paw feet rather than the brass ones often found on New York furniture. Skill in mechanical contrivance is characteristic of the best work of the period. Here an understructure of hinged, accordion-like bracing permits the insertion of one to four leaves; when fully extended the table seats as many as fourteen people.

H. 30 inches

Mr. and Mrs. James G. Balling, Albany, Georgia

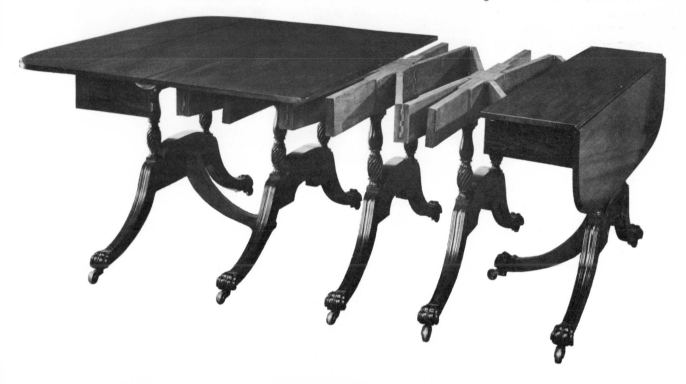

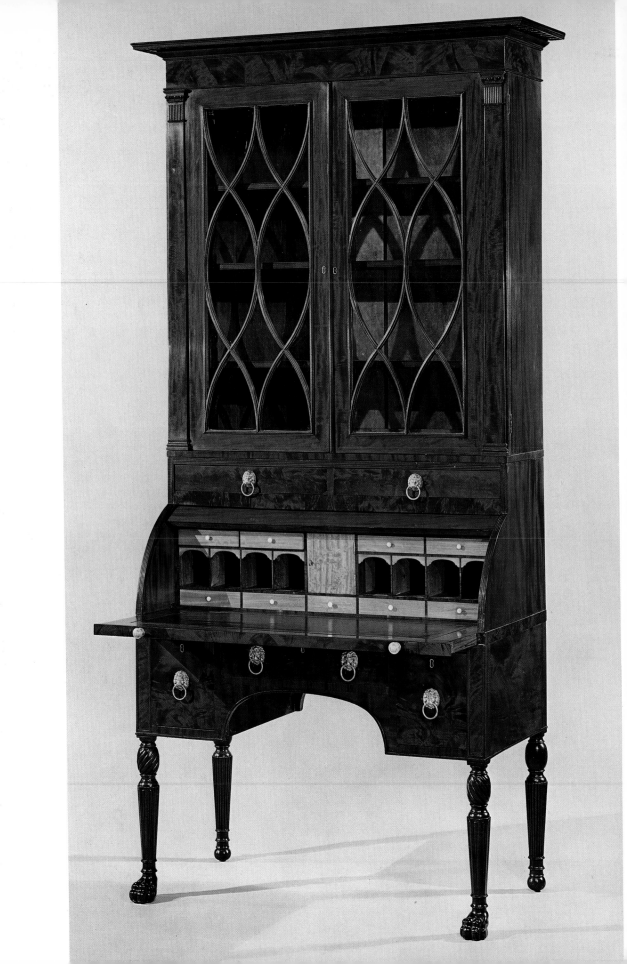

20 The workshop of Duncan Phyfe produced a number of case pieces of the quality of the better-known chairs, sofas, and tables, but few have been located or published. This strikingly handsome desk and bookcase, made in New York about 1815, bears the impress of the Phyfe style: well-figured mahogany veneers, moldings around drawers and edges, reeding on rear legs, above the top drawers, and on the sides of the cylinder desk, finely carved capitals on the flanking pilasters, a beautifully finished satinwood interior of drawers and pigeonholes, and a smooth mechanism. As the flat writing surface pulls out, the cylinder front slides up and disappears. The octagonal reeded front legs with twisted flutes with fillets are typical of Phyfe's work, as are the dog's-paw feet. Perhaps the finest detailing of the piece is on the paneled soffit under the cornice, where carved gilded rosettes repeat the gilding of the lion's-head pulls.

H. 95¹/₂ inches

Mr. and Mrs. Edward Vason Jones, Albany, Georgia

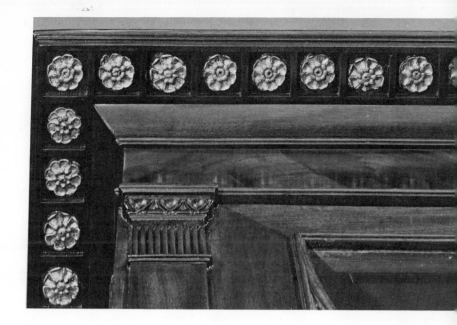

21 In the early nineteenth century this pier table and its mate graced the interior of one of the finest Federal houses in New York, the home of Moses Rogers at 7 State Street across from the Battery. Typical of the New York Regency style, this pair was made about 1815, perhaps in the workshop of Duncan Phyfe, and descended in the Verplanck family of New York. The reeding of the legs, tight leaf carving on their turned upper portions, and massive paw feet are all found on other New York furniture of the period. Additional refinements are ovolo front corners with deep fluting, which is repeated above the back leg, reeding on the edge of the marble top, and brass trim finishing the edge of the apron—brass moldings were included in the New York price book of 1810 and appeared regularly in subsequent editions. Viewed as a pair, these tables are particularly handsome. The cabinetmaker's sensitivity is apparent in the way he has used the highly figured mahogany veneer on the aprons, turning it in opposite directions on the two tables to enhance their effectiveness as a matched pair against the same wall.

H. 34 inches

The Metropolitan Museum of Art, Gift of John C. Cattus, 67.262.2

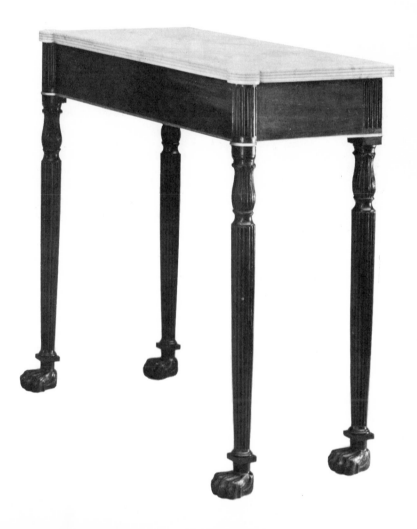

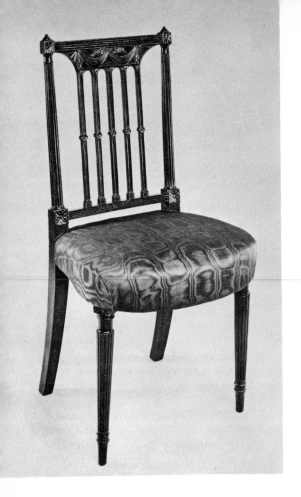

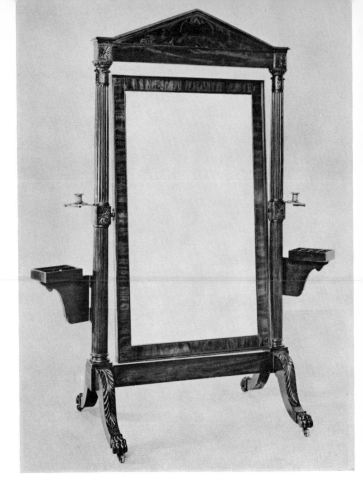

22

Following quite closely a design published by Hepplewhite in 1787 and appearing as plate 2 in his 1794 *Guide,* the unknown New York maker of this mahogany chair, working about 1805, changed some of the decorative details. As in the model, the rectangular back has five narrow banisters decorated with rosettes below a tablet with fanlike spandrels. Noticeable differences are the omission of the cresting and of the leaf motif at the top of the front legs seen in Hepplewhite's version, the addition of reeding on the front legs and the stiles and rails of the back and of foliate carving at the four corners of the back, and the substitution of ribbon and swags on the tablet for the hunting horns in the original design. Carving at the corners and drapery swags—not on the tablet but linking the banisters—appear on a chair back of similar outline in plate 49 of the 1802 Appendix to Sheraton's *Drawing Book.*

H. 36⅝ inches

Mr. and Mrs. James G. Balling, Albany, Georgia

23

This New York mahogany cheval glass of about 1815 is the richest American example known, and the high quality of execution of its reeding, fluting, and foliate carving is characteristic of the work of Phyfe or the French master cabinetmaker Charles-Honoré Lannuier. The form, with its pillars, squared legs, paw feet, and pedimented top is identical to that of the cheval glass framing the bilingual label engraved by Samuel Maverick for Lannuier and is included in the 1817 New York price book under the name "screen dressing glass." At the center of each column is an adjustable gilt-brass candle arm, and below are the trays on brackets, attached by hinges and called "swingers," for holding combs, pins, and other paraphernalia for dressing.

H. 75 inches

The Metropolitan Museum of Art, Gift of Ginsburg and Levy, Inc., in memory of John Ginsburg and Isaac Levy, 69.183

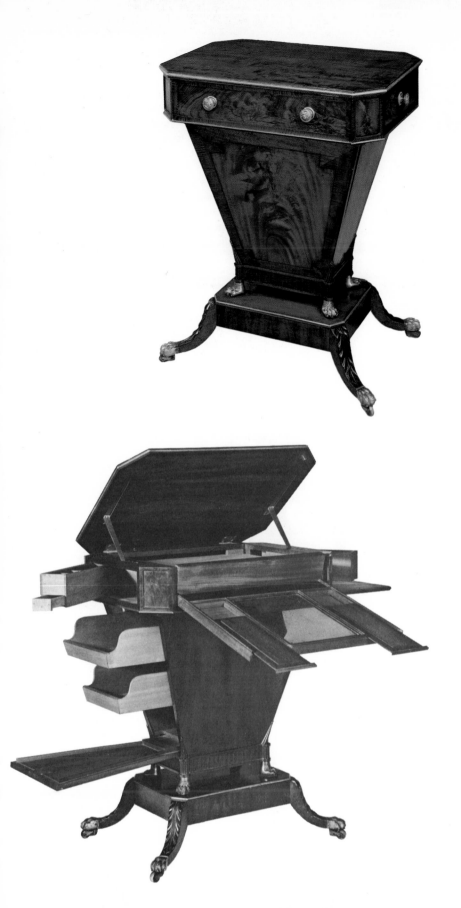

24

Perhaps unique in design and intricacy of interior compartments, this dressing or work table—one of two known—was made in New York, probably in Phyfe's shop, about 1810. The best features of the New York Regency style are seen in its shape and decoration. Basically modeled on a pedestal form, the table has a front of elaborately figured and cross-banded mahogany, with carefully matched but less spectacular surfaces on sides and back. Four curving legs with brass lion's-paw feet and leaf carving support the platform bearing the tapered pedestal, which has brass dog's-paw feet. The rectangular top with canted corners repeats the shape of the platform as well as its brass molding. The workings of the table's interior are even more unusual than its appearance. At the release of a hidden catch, the lid, hinged at the front, springs up, and two brass supports drop to one of several positions on brass ratchets. A plain panel is revealed that can be raised and flipped over to show a mirror flanked by trays with sliding tops. At each end of the top a tray pivots outward; below one is a candle slide. One side, hinged at the bottom, falls open to beautifully finished sliding drawers. It has been suggested that this piece was not made as a dressing table but for the convenience of a highly skilled artisan such as a miniaturist. Whether its compartments held a lady's scents and rouge or a painter's turpentine and umber, no artist could wish for a more ingenious work box.

H. 27⁷/₈ inches
The Metropolitan Museum of Art, Rogers Fund, 66.48.1

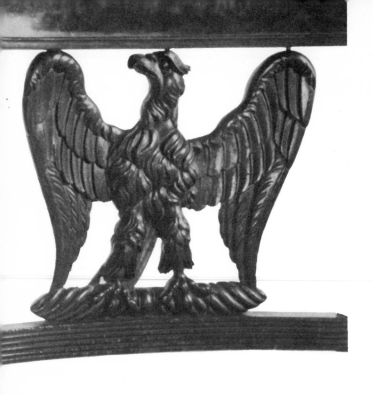

25

The eagle, symbol of the new Republic, is
used as a back splat on this Regency-style mahogany side chair made in New York about
1815. Duncan Phyfe is thought to have made
the chair and the set to which it belongs for
DeWitt Clinton, mayor of the city of New
York for most of the period 1803 to 1815 and
later governor of the state. Though many variations on the scroll-back chair are given in
New York price books of the early nineteenth
century, there is no mention of eagle backs.
A crouching spread eagle is fairly commonly
found as a back rail on New York chairs of
the period; this standing eagle, however, joining cresting rail and stay rail, is unusual.

    H. 31¹/₄ inches

    *Museum of the City of New York, Bequest
of Mrs. Henry O. Tallmadge*

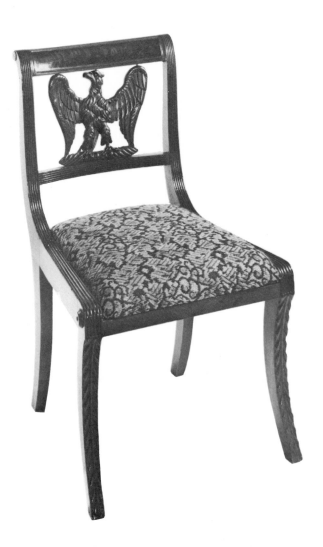

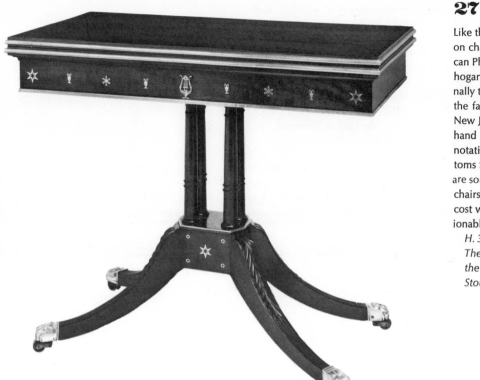

27

Like the Grecian cross-front legs, the lyre back on chairs is associated with the name of Duncan Phyfe in the period 1810 to 1820. This mahogany chair, one of a set of thirteen, originally twenty-four in all, was made by Phyfe for the family of William Livingston, governor of New Jersey. A sketch of about 1816 in Phyfe's hand shows this type of chair and gives price notations for different versions: "Cane bottoms $22 Cushions 3 Stuffed 23." These prices are somewhat higher than for other scroll-back chairs in the New York price book. The extra cost was for front paw feet, which were fashionable because of their antique connotations.

H. 32¹/₄ inches
The Metropolitan Museum of Art, Gift of the family of Mr. and Mrs. Andrew Varick Stout, in their memory, 65.188.2

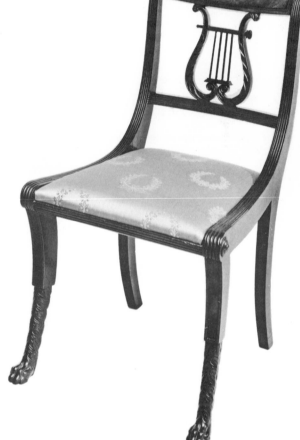

26

Both French and Anglo-American in style, this mahogany pedestal card table, one of a pair made in New York about 1810 to 1815, is attributed to French émigré cabinetmaker Charles-Honoré Lannuier. Two similar pairs of labeled tables are known. Although the legs, with their water-leaf carving, reeding, and brass paw feet, are based upon the Regency style as interpreted by Phyfe and his New York contemporaries, the top is closer to the French neoclassical style of the late eighteenth century. Brass inlay of center lyre, six-pointed stars, classical urns, and petaled form as well as the heavy brass molding around the apron and pedestal bear out Lannuier's first known advertisement in America, July 1803. At that time he stated that he made "all kinds of Furniture, Beds, Chairs, &c in the newest and latest French fashion," and that he brought "for that purpose gilt and brass frames, borders of ornaments, and handsome safe locks, as well as new patterns." This table was originally part of the furnishings of Point Breeze, the Bordentown, New Jersey, home of Napoleon's brother, Joseph Bonaparte.

H. 30¹/₂ inches
Lent anonymously

28

Reverse curves of leg and arm give grace to this Regency-style mahogany armchair made in Boston about 1810 to 1815. The sweeping line of its plain barrel back, the canting of the back legs, the subtle swell of the seat rails, and the bold curl of the arm terminals all contribute to give movement and rhythm to a shape that could, in a less skillful interpretation, be heavy and static. The basic shape of upper chair and legs can be seen in Sheraton's 1803 *Cabinet Dictionary* (plate 8, no. 1), where the chair is described as "a cabriole arm-chair stuffed all over." Wide bold reeding on the arms and seat rail is a Boston characteristic, as is the small flat panel of horizontal reeding above the leg, often seen on Boston card tables.

H. 41½ inches
Mr. and Mrs. Samuel B. Feld, New York

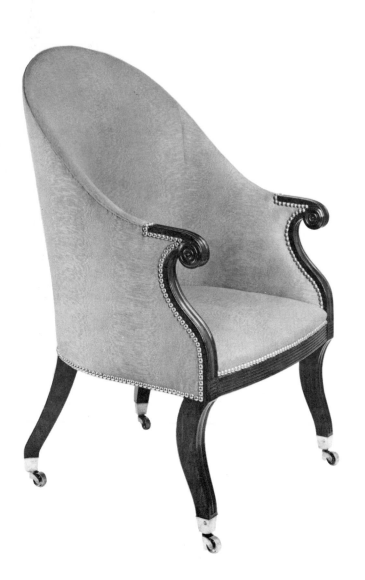

29

A masterpiece of the Boston Regency style, this mahogany lyre-base writing and sewing table was made about 1810 to 1815. By virtue of the name "Churchill" chalked on the underside, as well as the masterful proportions and skillful execution, it is attributed to the Boston cabinetmaker Lemuel Churchill, whose only known labeled piece is a "lolling chair" at Winterthur. The table incorporates many characteristics of the Boston interpretation of English designs, among them the ebonized turnings and inlay and the five brass rods in each of the lyres of the pedestal. The acanthus-leaf and scroll carving on the lyre is similar to carving by Thomas Whitman on other Boston furniture, including that on a bed in the Museum of Fine Arts. The ovolo corners with segmented reeding appear on numerous tables and case pieces of the Boston-Salem region, some of them documented works by John and Thomas Seymour.

H. 28½ inches
Lent anonymously

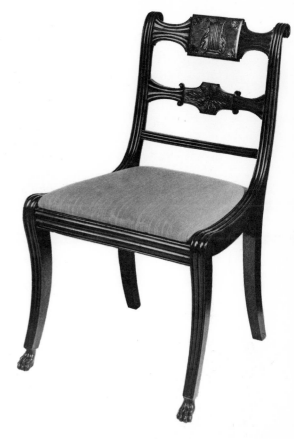

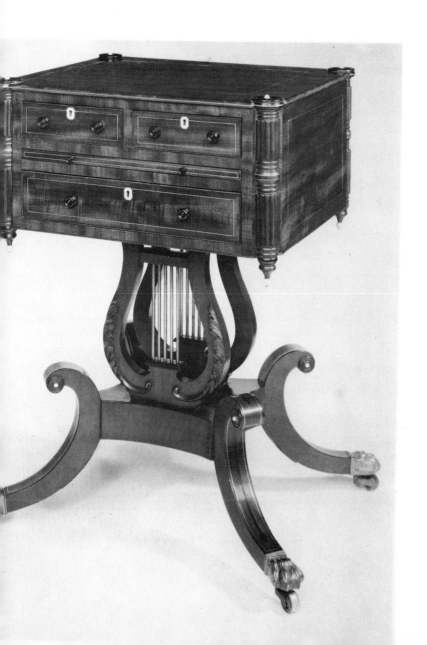

30

This mahogany side chair, a Boston version of the Greek, or klismos, type of the early nineteenth century, is one of numerous examples made about 1810 to 1815. Although the form is the same as that of many New York chairs of the period and is, like them, based upon examples in the London price book of 1802 and the supplement of 1808, there are differences. The "sweeped rails," which continue upward to form the square scrolled back and downward to form the front legs, are boldly reeded. Animal-paw front feet are tighter and more vertical-looking than their New York counterparts. Instead of a banister, the back has two rails below the top rail, with a lyre in relief on its center tablet. The lyre, with seven strings and tight scrolls in the English manner, displays the fine carving characteristic of Boston.

H. 33¹/₈ inches

Mr. and Mrs. Samuel B. Feld, New York

31

Before they dissolved their partnership in 1816, the silversmiths Jesse Churchill and Daniel Treadwell of Boston made this handsome wine cooler for presentation to Commodore Oliver Hazard Perry. It is marked, on the bottom, inside and outside, "CHURCHILL & TREADWELL" in a rectangle. On one side, beneath an engraved victor's wreath, is inscribed: "Sepr. 10th. 1813, Signalized our first triumph in squadron, A very superior BRITISH FORCE on LAKE ERIE, was entirely subdued by Com. O. H. PERRY, whose gallantry in action is equalled only by his humanity in victory." On the opposite side appears: "Presented in HONOUR of the VICTOR, by the Citizens of BOSTON." Although the cooler is classical in shape and decoration, it is the classicism of the early Empire rather than the classicism of the Federal period. The heaviness of the body, enlarged gadrooning at base and lip, and handles of eagles' heads bearing rings in their beaks all presage the more elaborate styles to come in the next two decades.

H. 9 inches
Amherst College Art Museum

32

Forms from the antique world have been Americanized on this inkstand in the French taste, marked twice "H. LEWIS" in a serrated rectangle for Philadelphia silversmith Harvey Lewis, who worked from 1811 until about 1828. The three winged sphinxlike monopodes supporting the urn-shaped well bear feathered American Indian headdresses. Philadelphia silversmiths predominated in making silver in the Empire style, typically with ornament as here, of cast flowers and die-rolled bands. The inkwell is inscribed on the top: "An evidence of the Cherished Love and Esteem of Elizth Powel for her favorite Sophia H. Olis."

H. 3 7/16 inches
Yale University Art Gallery, New Haven, The Mabel Brady Garvan Collection

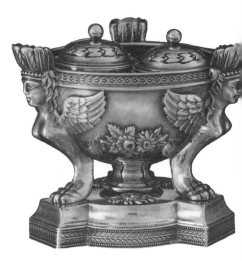

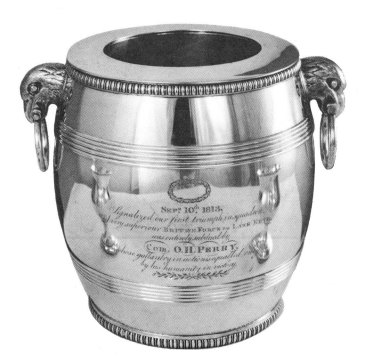

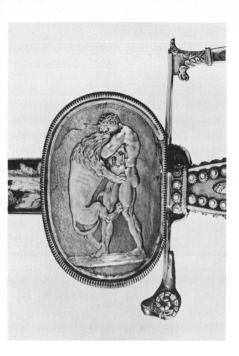

33

The contrast of the cast gold hilt with its eagle's-head pommel to the blue-steel blade bearing etched and gilded designs makes this one of the more colorful and dramatic presentation swords of the nineteenth century. Marked on the underside of the crossarm "I.T." for the New York silversmith John Targee, and also with two pseudo-hallmarks, it was given to Alfred Davis, eldest male heir of Brigadier General Daniel Davis, who was killed in the Battle of Erie, September 17, 1813. On knuckle guard, blade, and scabbard, symbols of the nation are mingled with those of battle and classical motifs. The eagle of the new Republic decorates the knuckle guard, and is engraved on an American shield on the blade. Also on the blade is a liberty cap on a pole encircled with leaves. The oval guard has a cast design of Hercules wrestling with the Nemean lion. This same design is found on an almost identical Targee presentation sword in the Metropolitan and on the cover of a silver snuffbox by Targee once owned by DeWitt Clinton, also at the Metropolitan. Proportions and details of the snuffbox cover indicate that it is from the same die as the oval sword guards.

L. 35 3/16 inches
The Metropolitan Museum of Art, Gift of Francis P. Garvan, 22.19

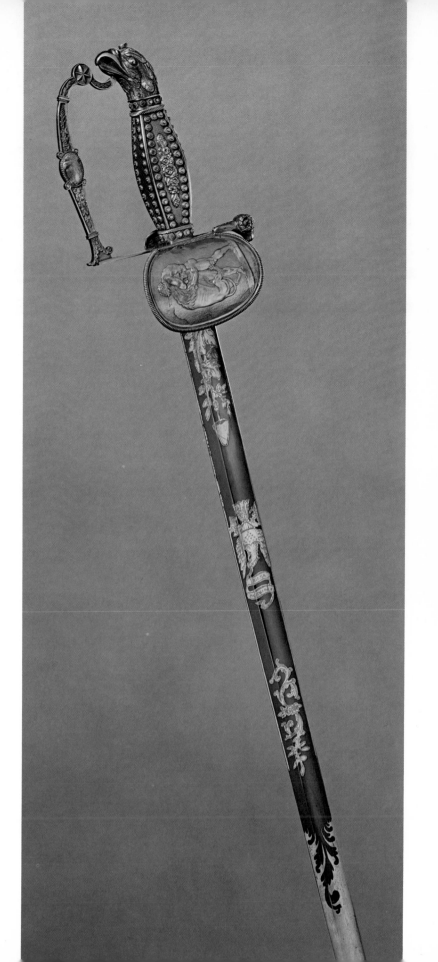

34 Much of the highly sophisticated furniture produced in America during the Federal period was made by immigrant cabinetmakers from England, Ireland, Scotland, and France. Such a craftsman was Joseph B. Barry, who was born in Dublin in 1757 and came to Philadelphia before 1790. His elaborate trade label, used after 1804, is made up of illustrations from the appendix to Sheraton's *Drawing Book*. The words "& Son" were added to the label about 1810, and they help to date this labeled mahogany pier table made for Louis Clapier as about 1810 to 1815. The table is an extraordinary creation that combines all the skillful cabinetmaker's methods of decoration: veneering, carving, gilding, and use of ormolu mounts. Its most prominent feature, the carved and pierced decoration in the back gallery, also depends upon Sheraton: the griffin panel is based closely upon the "Ornament for a Frieze or Tablet," published in the *Drawing Book* and dated October 1791. This design was popular in Baltimore and appears as both inlay and painted decoration on Baltimore Federal furniture. The garlands around the columns, although not found in Sheraton, are a French motif used on Sheraton forms by Philadelphia and Baltimore cabinetmakers. In 1810 Barry advertised furniture in the "rich Egyptian and Gothic style"; here the pierced quatrefoils in the railing are Gothic, and the griffins may have been thought to be Egyptian.

L. 54 inches
Mrs. T. Wistar Brown, Ardmore, Pennsylvania

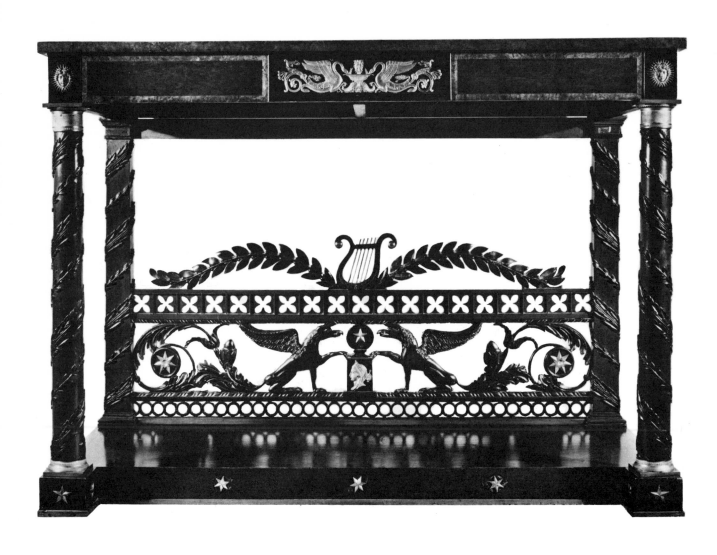

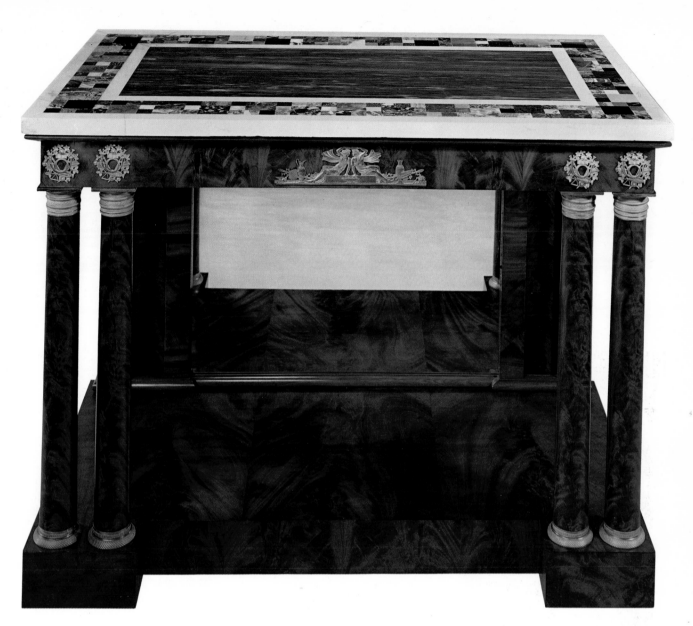

35 A Philadelphia version of a French-style pier
table, this example was made about 1815. Typical of these early Empire Philadelphia tables
are the massive mahogany platform resting
directly on the floor (see no. 34) and the
double columns on either side with ormolu
mounts above. This table, more ornate than
most, has an elaborate *pietra-dura* top centered with gray King of Prussia marble,
which was often used on Philadelphia furniture.

L. 52 inches
Stuart P. Feld, New York

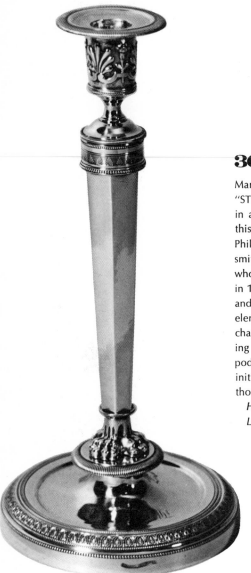

37

The classical style of the French Empire, which at its worst could be ponderous and dull, is shown at its best in this silver sauceboat, one of a pair by Anthony Rasch, who worked in Philadelphia between 1808 and 1819 (see also no. 36). It is marked "A. RASCH & Co.," in a rectangle, and, below, also in a rectangle, "PHILADELPHIA." Animal forms of the classical vocabulary are used here with flair and a sense of whimsey. On the traditional boat shape a sinuous serpent handle thrusts forward toward a ram's-head spout, which echoes this forward motion. Rather than being superfluous decoration, the serpent and ram's head are integral parts of a unified and graceful whole.

L. 11 3/16 inches
The Metropolitan Museum of Art, Fletcher Fund, 59.152.1

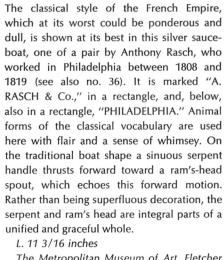

36

Marked "CHAUDRON'S & RASCH" and "STER[ling] AMERI[can] MAN[ufacture]," each in a ribbon on the side of its circular base, this candlestick, one of a pair, was made in Philadelphia by the French émigré silversmiths Simon Chaudron and Anthony Rasch, who are known to have advertised together in 1812. In addition to the often seen beading and bands of anthemia, it has other classical elements of the French Empire style in the chased anthemia and torch design ornamenting the bobêche and the three bold monopodes supporting the paneled baluster. The initials "UPL" in script on the base, probably those of an owner, are unidentified.

H. 12 inches
Lent anonymously

38

Animal heads, popular motifs throughout the Empire period, are used on this punch pot made in Philadelphia about 1805 to 1810 by Simon Chaudron (see also no. 36). It is marked "CHAUDRON" in a ribbon four times on the underside of the foot. The high cylindrical shape and rose finial are in the French style, as are the bands of ornament encircling the body—beading, leaves, and palmette— which appear on pieces by other silversmiths working in the French manner, including Anthony Rasch, Harvey Lewis, and Fletcher and Gardiner. The double spouts give the symmetry important to the classical taste; the chased leaves at their bases and heads are similar to the leaf carving found on Empire furniture. The monogram "EW" on the front is unidentified.

H. 8⁷/₈ inches
The Metropolitan Museum of Art, Purchase, Mr. and Mrs. Marshall P. Blankarn Gift, 66.103

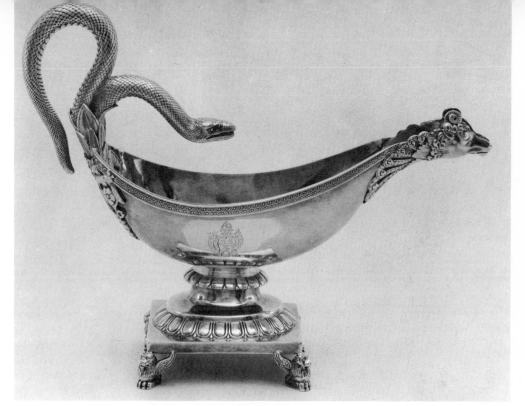

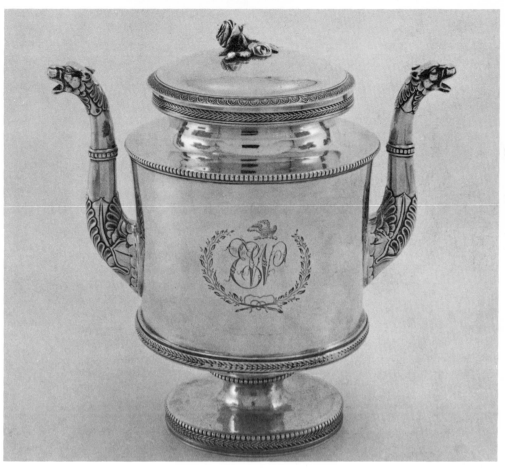

39 In 1817 one of America's wealthiest men, Stephen Van Rensselaer IV, built a house in Albany for his bride, Harriet Elizabeth Bayard. Designed by architect Philip Hooker, it was furnished in the current Empire fashion and included a number of pieces made by New York cabinetmaker Charles-Honoré Lannuier. This bed, one of the Lannuier pieces, is as elaborate as any produced in America during the nineteenth century. It was made to be placed lengthwise against a wall and is therefore ornamented on only one side. Gilded and painted dolphin feet of ash support the sleigh-shaped mahogany frame, which has crotch-cut veneer on the curved tops of both ends. Panels of amboina veneer outlined with bands of hand-sawed brass inlay decorate the side. Centered on the panels are fine French gilt ornaments of griffins, winged gods, and a classical head—possibly Hypnos, god of sleep—flanked by poppy sprays. Lannuier's bilingual label is affixed to the inside of the headboard and footboard. Engraved by Samuel Maverick of New York, it is in the shape of a cheval glass and is inscribed within the frame: "Hre. Lannuier,/Cabinet Maker from Paris/Kips is Whare house of/new fashion fourniture/Broad Steet, No. 60, New York./Hre. Lannuier,/Ebéniste de Paris/Tient Fabrique &/Magasin de Meubles/les plus à la Mode,/New-York."

L. 85 1/2 inches
Albany Institute of History and Art, Albany, New York

40

About 1815 Baltimore merchant James Bosley ordered a set of parlor furniture from Lannuier. The rather severe rectilinear character of this mahogany window seat from the set has been lightened by the addition of Directoire and Empire ornament: carved and gessoed dolphin feet with verd and gilt decorations and gilded winged-caryatid arm supports. The gold tones of these figures are picked up in rosettes at the ends of the arm rails and in the ormolu caps at base and top of the rear turned stiles, which are surmounted by highly polished ebonized ball finials.

L. 58 1/4 inches
The Maryland Historical Society, Baltimore

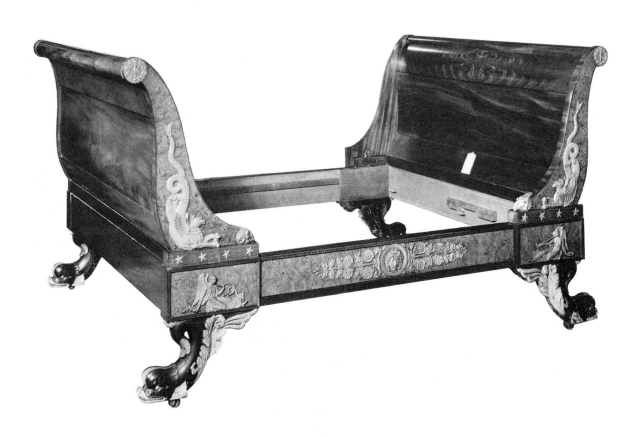

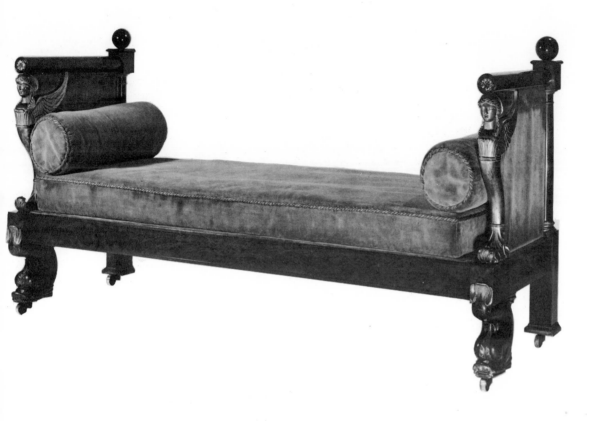

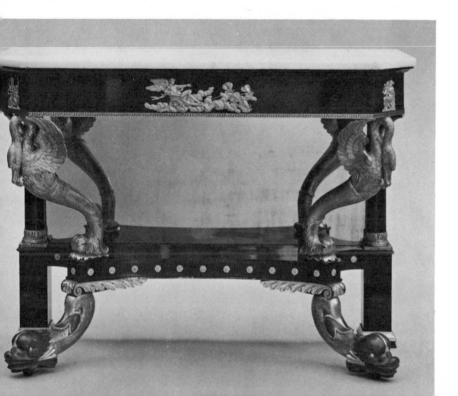

41

One of nine pier tables known to have been made by the shop of Lannuier, this example of about 1815 bears the remnants of three labels. As an American interpretation of the French Empire style, it follows closely the designs featured in La Mésangère and other pattern books, and uses the popular figural elements of dolphin feet and swan supports. Gilded terracotta rosettes and caps and bases for the columns, ormolu mounts depicting gods and goddesses, including a central figure of Apollo drawn by bees, and brass inlay in a Greek-key pattern further enhance the rosewood veneered surface.

H. 35 inches
The Metropolitan Museum of Art, The Friends of the American Wing Fund, 68.43

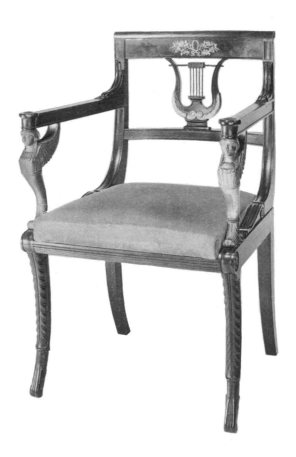

The American painter Henry Sargent may have owned this mahogany easel, which descended in the Sargent family. Made in New York or Boston about 1805 to 1815, it is related in style to Sargent's set of Empire furniture shown in The Tea Party, which he painted by 1825 (see paintings and sculpture volume, no. 26). The swan's-head terminals, carved separately and attached, are a common Empire motif that appeared in early nineteenth-century pattern books, including those of La Mésangère, Thomas Hope, George Smith, and Rudolph Ackermann. On the panel between the swan's heads is an ormolu mount of urn, cornucopias, insects, and flowers.

> H. 59³/₈ inches
> Museum of Fine Arts, Boston, Gift of the Misses Aimée and Rosamond Lamb

This mahogany armchair, part of a parlor set bought by James Bosley about 1815 (see no. 40), incorporates many of the elements found in other Lannuier furniture: winged and gilded caryatid arm supports, French gilt center ornament on the cresting rail, and water-leaf carving on the legs. Other fine details that are not so characteristic of this maker include the reeding of the front seat rail, paneling of cresting and stay rails, arms, and stiles, scrolled plantain leaf on foot and seat rails, and brackets that link back and arm delicately carved with bands of Egyptian lotus. The French lyre splat, with its gilded water leaf, is wider and more open than the compact English lyre used by Phyfe.

> H. 35¹/₂ inches
> The Maryland Historical Society, Baltimore

44

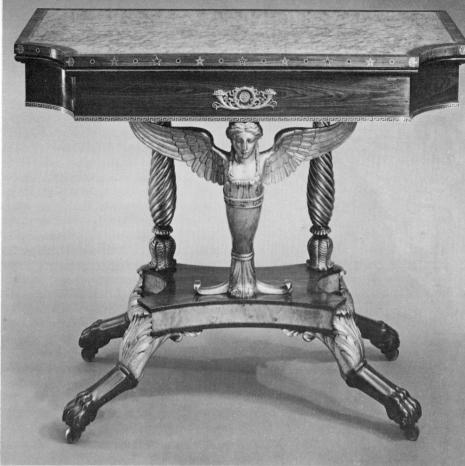

Prominent businessman, inveterate diarist, and mayor of New York during the year of 1826, Philip Hone was typical of the fashion-conscious society for whom Lannuier made furniture. This card table of about 1815 was probably purchased for the house Hone completed in 1813 at 44 Cortlandt Street, which was, in his own words, "one of the most genteel residences in the city." Created in the French fashion, the table shows Lannuier's skillful combination of Directoire, Consulat, and early Empire styles. In the lightness and simplification of these styles it is also akin to the furniture made by Phyfe and Michael Allison. The most distinctive elements of its design, the gilded and winged caryatid and hocked animal leg, were illustrated in 1802 in La Mésangère's *Les Meubles et Objets de*

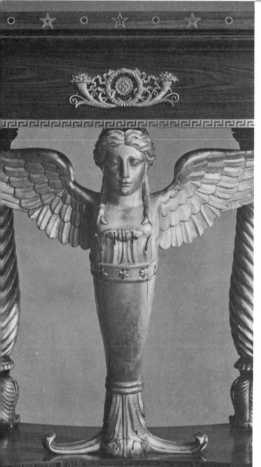

Goût. The table is not labeled, but three pairs of similar figural tables, differing only in minor details, are labeled or documented as Lannuier's work. Of all of them, this one has the most unusual use of decorative woods. Bird's-eye maple appears on the sides of the platform and on the top of the closed leaf, which is outlined in rosewood; satinwood veneer is used inside the top. There is twisted reeding on the gilded rear colonettes. The inlaid brass ornament of stars, circles, and anthemia around the outer edge of the folding leaf is not found on the others, which bear only cut-brass banding. Inlaid brass ornaments do appear on the aprons of three additional pairs of nonfigural Lannuier card tables, one of which is no. 26.

H. 31 inches
The Metropolitan Museum of Art, Funds from Various Donors, 66.170

45

American cabinetmaking in the Empire style reached its high point in the flowing line, skillful carving, and subtle color of this dolphin sofa. Numerous interpretations of couches and sofas with scrolling arms, called "Grecian," were given in the 1802 edition of the *London Chair-Makers' and Carvers' Book of Prices for Workmanship.* Made about 1820, this sofa shows a bold design in which each part is completely necessary to the whole. The gilt and verd-antique legs and feet are in the shape of a dolphin, which continues in the scaly sweep of the arm. Carved and gilded leaf sprays lead into the seat rail, strengthening the design as well as the structure. The inlaid brass Greek key of the seat rail visually links the two sides. The curves of leg and arm are repeated in the gentle curves of the mahogany back. Terminal brass rosettes on the scrolled ends echo the brass and gold tones on seat rail and leg. A smaller version, lacking the scrolled back and inlaid Greek key, but with virtually identical dolphin arms and feet, is in the White House.

L. 97³/₈ inches

The Metropolitan Museum of Art, Friends of the American Wing Fund, 65.58

46

One of a set of nine, each with a different design on the tablet, this side chair in the Empire style was made about 1815 to 1820 in Baltimore. A Roman version of the Greek klismos, with turned legs in place of the Grecian saber-shaped ones, it is painted gold with green and black decoration: a pair of winged dragons facing a shield on the tablet, a dart centered with crossed torches on the stay rail, anthemia on the side rails, fasces on the front rails, and fanlike palmettes above the draped swags of the turned legs. Greek chairs were popular in the new Republic. During the Madison administration (1809-1817), the architect Benjamin Latrobe designed for the White House a suite of furniture with low sofas and chairs based on Greek forms. Although the furniture was destroyed in the fire of 1814, drawings for it bearing Latrobe's instructions to the Baltimore cabinetmakers John and Hugh Findlay still exist. Possibly this chair and its set were also produced in the Findlay shop.

H. 34 inches

The Metropolitan Museum of Art, Purchase, Mrs. Paul Moore Gift, 65.167.6

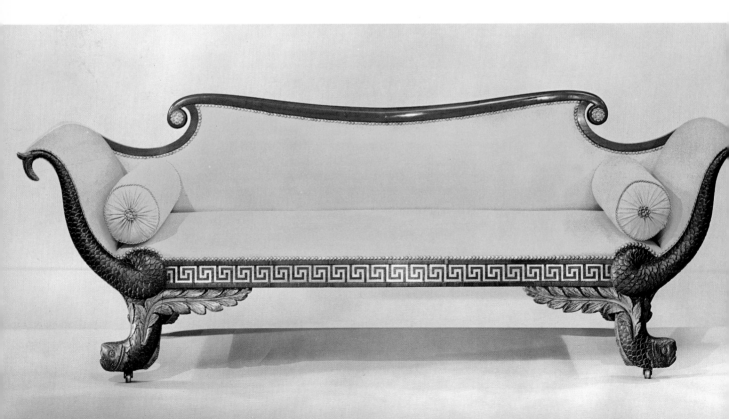

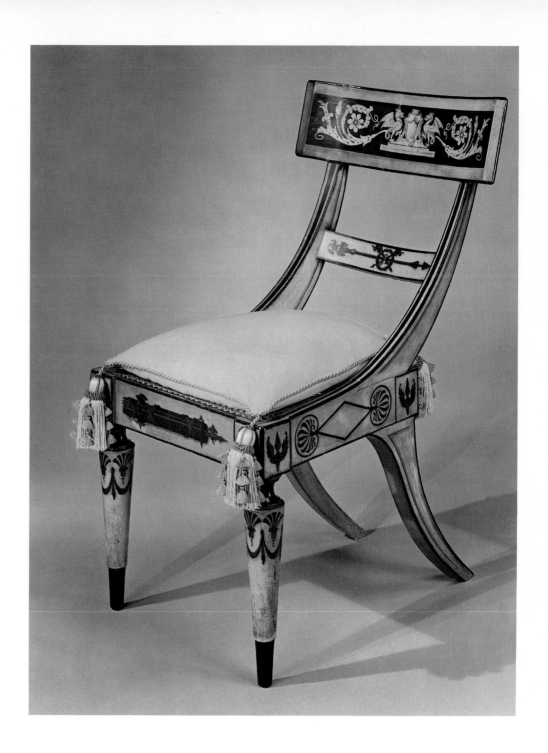

47

Greco-Roman designs of the Empire style also influenced the work of the southern New Jersey glasshouses specializing in utilitarian pieces. The greenish-blue cast indicates that this candlestick, one of a pair dating probably between 1820 and 1850, was made of window or bottle glass rather than the finer, colorless metal used at glasshouses producing decorative objects and tableware. The gadrooned ornament and double-baluster shaft are in the Empire style, even though most frequently the decorative products of the bottle and window glassworks were in traditional shapes, with ornament merely a device to show the skill of the glassblower rather than an element of fashion. This decorative work has been called end-of-the-day amusement for the workmen, but enough of it has survived to make it seem more likely that these glasshouses supplied their neighborhoods with decorative pieces while sending their utilitarian wares to a broader market.

H. 9¹/₈ inches

The Metropolitan Museum of Art, Rogers Fund, 35.124.1

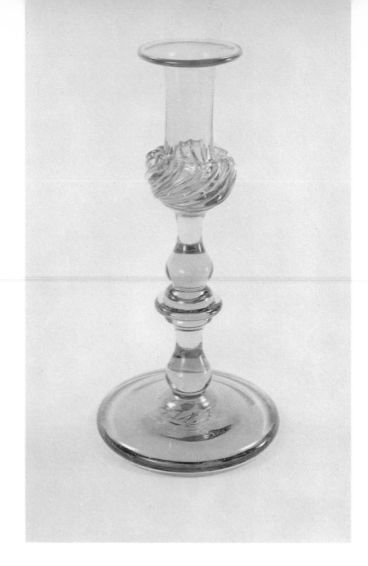

48

Although fashionable designs were usually executed in the most up-to-date ceramics, this coffeepot made about 1825 by Thomas Haig and Company of Philadelphia manifests the latest trends in a material generally considered too breakable for anything but the most inexpensive kitchen wares. By 1825 American potters were making stoneware and attempting to produce creamware, the high-fired earthenware Staffordshire potters were using to capture the world market in inexpensive pottery. Thomas Haig and Company, however, continued to specialize in red earthenware, which, in this coffeepot, is covered with a black glaze. The dome-shaped top and pyriform body are found in Empire-style porcelain and silver.

H. 10³/₄ inches

The Metropolitan Museum of Art, Rogers Fund, 22.26.3

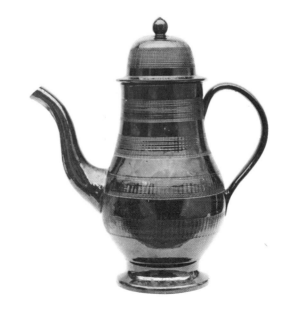

49

At the New England Glass Company, operating in Cambridge, Massachusetts, from 1818 to 1888, a fine, clear, colorless flint glass was blown into a variety of objects like this large sugar bowl of about 1840. The heavy classical shape with gadrooning on bowl and top is closely related to Empire objects in metal and wood.

H. 9³/₄ inches
The Toledo Museum of Art, Gift of Edward Drummond Libbey

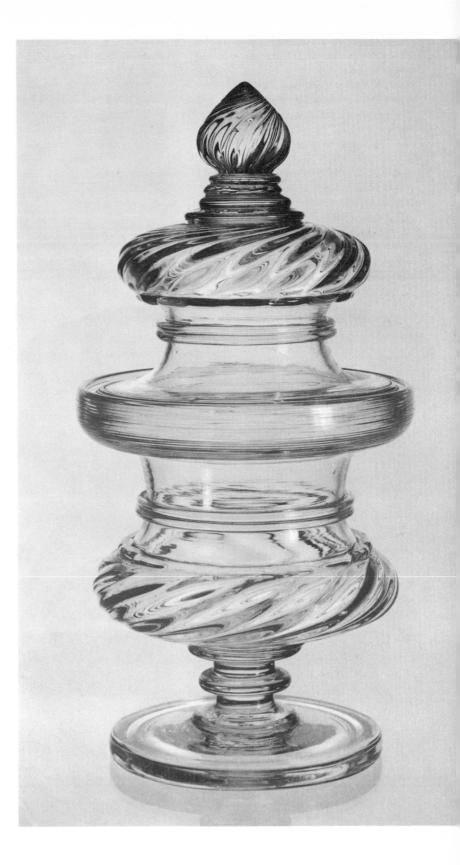

50

Made about 1830 in a heavy version of the Regency style, this circular mahogany pedestal table is from the workshop of Antoine-Gabriel Quervelle. Born in Paris in 1789, Quervelle was in Philadelphia by 1817 and worked there until his death in 1856. On the underside of its top are two printed labels with his name and his address for 1825 to 1849: "126/ANTHONY G. QUERVELLE'S/CABINET AND SOFA MANUFACTORY,/SOUTH SECOND STREET, A FEW DOORS BELOW DOCK,/PHILADELPHIA." Along with other pieces by Quervelle, the table is similar to designs in George Smith's *Cabinet-Maker and Upholsterer's Guide* (1826). It is also closely related to three circular tables made by Quervelle for the East Room of the White House in 1829, when Andrew Jackson was president. Like them it has an applied gilt-brass foliate band around the lower edge of the apron and a depressed marble inset center, a triangular base supported by boldly carved paw feet, and the large gadrooning characteristic of his work. This example is further enriched by intarsia marble, stenciled gilt patterns on top and chamfered edge of base, an ormolu collar at juncture of pedestal and base, and gilding on pedestal and verd-antique feet.

H. 29 13/16 inches
The Metropolitan Museum of Art, Edgar J. Kaufmann Charitable Foundation Fund, 68.96

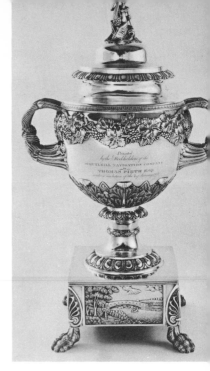

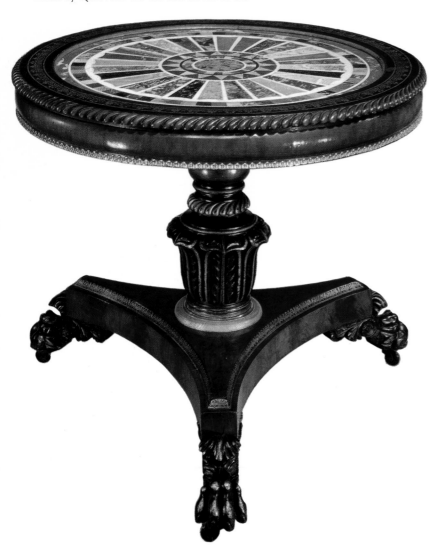

51

In 1833 the Schuylkill Navigation Company presented to each of five of its Philadelphia managers a piece of silver by the Philadelphia silversmith Thomas Fletcher. This vase is inscribed to Thomas Firth and marked "T. FLETCHER PHILAD," within the outer band of an oval on its underside. Fletcher was the partner of Sidney Gardiner from 1808 to 1827. In 1823/24 they made a pair of vases to be given to DeWitt Clinton for his support of the Erie Canal project. The Firth vase copies earlier works by Fletcher and Gardiner, particularly the Clinton vases, which were in turn based on a classical example excavated in 1771 from Hadrian's Villa, and later owned by the Duke of Warwick. Twisted handles and grapevine borders—here cast—appear on all these vases, but the shapes differ. The square base with large paw feet on this one is typical of Fletcher and Gardiner silver, as is the use of specific scenes, such as those of the Schuylkill chased on the base panels: shown here is a view taken from a George Lehman engraving, published in 1829, of the Upper Ferry Bridge. Also typical of their work is the interest in allegory; the finial's classical figure rests on an urn pouring out the river's waters and holds a cornucopia from which flows the plenty coming from distant places on the canal.

H. 20 1/8 inches
Joseph Sorger, Philadelphia

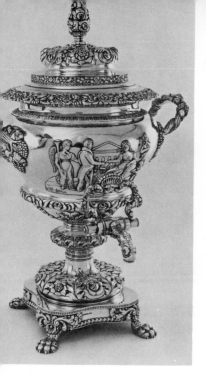

53

Like silversmiths, cabinetmakers of the major centers of the 1820s and 30s worked in distinct regional styles. While interpretation of decorative details varied from area to area, all craftsmen made use of the increasingly heavy late classical forms. In skillful hands these forms took on a kind of massive elegance. This New York mahogany center table bears on the underbrace of the top the remnants of a label of Thomas Astens, which originally read: "Thomas Astens, Cabinet and Warehouse, 20 Beaver St. All orders executed in a prompt and fashionable manner." Astens was first listed in the New York directories for 1820/21 and at the above address only in 1822/23. The firm Asten [*sic*] and Hyslop appeared as early as 1816. In the somewhat florid New York style of the era, Astens has employed extraordinary delineation of carving in hairy legs topped by bold acanthus. The crisp leaf carving is repeated on the pedestal below a faceted turning resembling a pineapple. Flame veneers on the roundel and apron provide further elaboration, as does the black and gold marble top.

H. 29 inches

Mr. and Mrs. James G. Balling, Albany, Georgia

52

New York firemen presented merchant John W. Degrauw with this silver urn upon his retirement in 1835 from their Board of Trustees. It is twice stamped "FORBES & SON" in rectangles on the sides of the base—thought to be the mark of Colin V.G. and John W. Forbes. The inscription to Degrauw is engraved on one side; a repoussé vignette, illustrated here, on the other. The scene shows Columbia, seated before a temple façade, honoring a worthy citizen. Excepting the dolphin spout, this urn has the same components as the Fletcher urn (no. 51), but the shape and decoration are different. Compare the almost severe classicism, the flat chased ornament of the Philadelphia example with the undulating shapes and bulging repoussé of the New York one. This urn, for all its restriction of decoration to tight-knit bands, is an early example of the rococo revival. The contrast found here between New York and Philadelphia silver is paralleled in furniture, as nos. 50 and 53 readily demonstrate.

H. 20 inches

Dr. and Mrs. Gerard L. Eastman, on loan to the Museum of the City of New York

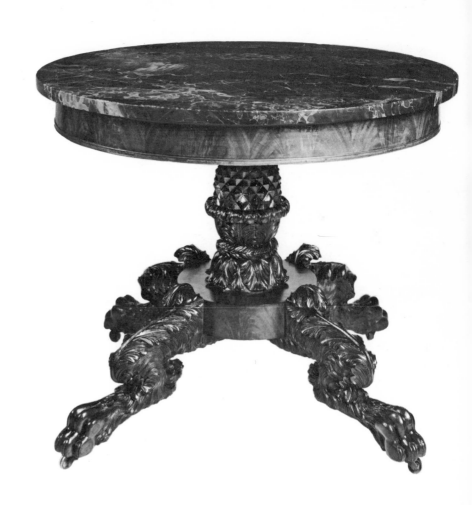

54 Pittsburgh, from 1810 on, was an important center for the manufacture of clear, heavy flint glass, the material best suited for the cutting that became fashionable with the Empire style. Cut-glass tumblers with portrait profiles in the bottoms were made in Pittsburgh during the 1820s. This profile is of DeWitt Clinton, governor of New York from 1817 to 1822 and 1825 until his death in 1828. The use of profiles on decorative objects became particularly popular with eighteenth-century English pottery medallions made by Josiah Wedgwood, and the interest continued into the nineteenth century. The medallion itself is a "sulfide," a ceramic cameo imbedded in the glass by a process patented in 1819 by the English glassmaker Apsley Pellatt. The delicate diamond pattern of the glass is a handsome example of American cutting.
H. 3³/₈ inches
The New-York Historical Society

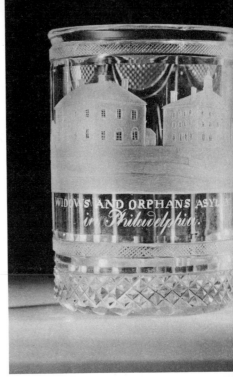

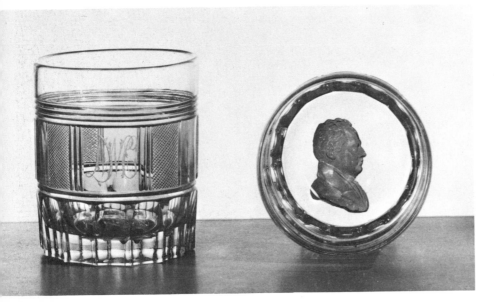

55

Another kind of commemorative decoration on glass is the engraving of a scene or portrait. This tumbler may well have been made in Philadelphia, since it is based on George Strickland's view, published in 1830, of the Orphans' Society Building and the Indigent Widows' and Single Women's Home, built by his architect brother William. The delicate and skillful cutting creates a highly reflective surface close in spirit to the bright surfaces of the ormolu decoration on Empire furniture.
H. 4³/₈ inches
The Corning Museum of Glass

56

The strawberry-diamond and fan pattern on this cut-glass punch bowl and cups was characteristic of Pittsburgh around 1820. It had been introduced by English glasscutters a few years earlier and is adapted from patterns on ancient molded glass. The foot is a heavy classical baluster in the spirit of the Empire style.
H. 8 inches
Henry Ford Museum, Dearborn, Michigan

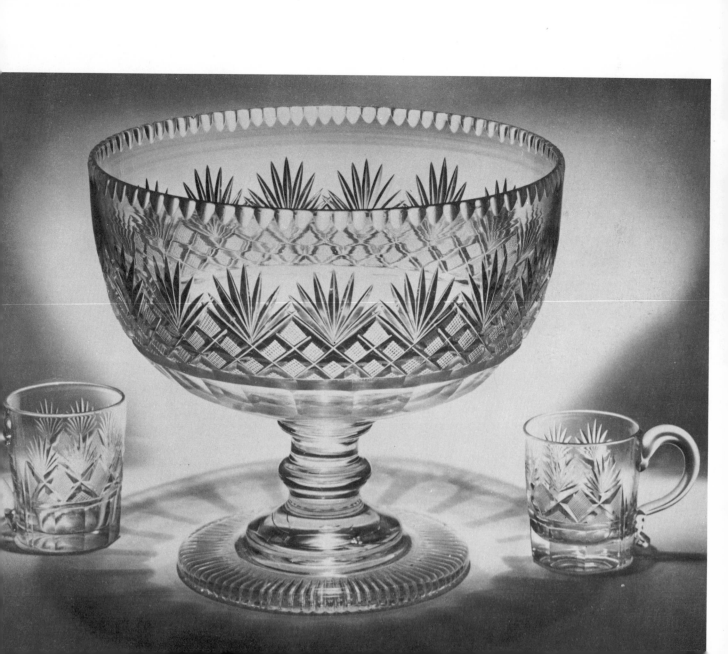

57 This pair of whale-oil lamps made at the Boston and Sandwich Glass Company in the 1830s is an ideal illustration of the range of skills employed there: the bases were made by pressing, an innovation of the 1820s; traditional glass-blowing was used to form the conical fonts and their supports; and cutting traced the intricate pattern and fluting on the fonts and bold facets of the supports. Many lamps combined pressed and blown glass, but few are so handsome as these.

H. pair 12³/₄ inches
Lent anonymously

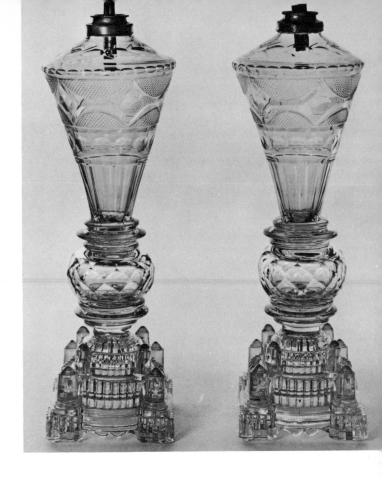

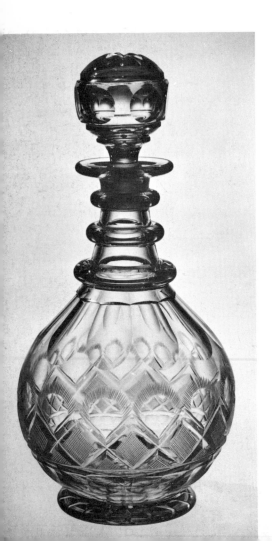

58 Benjamin Bakewell, head of Pittsburgh's foremost nineteenth-century glasshouse, gave this cut-glass decanter to Henry Clay Fry of the Fry Glass Company of Rochester, Pennsylvania, about 1820. Bakewell and Company, also known as Bakewell and Page, had begun producing flint glass about 1810, and by the following decade travelers' accounts described their fine cut glass. Decanters were turned out in great numbers by the Pittsburgh glasscutters. They kept up with the London fashions, but the American product was distinctive. Although the strawberry diamond of this decanter was a familiar motif on both English and American glass, in Pittsburgh it was used with a greater boldness and less detail than in the London glasshouses.

H. 10³/₄ inches
The Corning Museum of Glass

59 The technique of pressing glass was introduced to America in the late 1820s. Pressing had been used in England during the eighteenth century, but elaborate molds were more likely an American innovation. Pressed glass represented a radical change in technique. In the earlier blown-molded glass, the glass blower could manipulate the metal before it hardened; in pressed glass, the design depended entirely upon the moldmaker. The patterns used at first were meant to simulate cut glass, as is well exemplified by the bowl at the right, made in New England about 1825 to 1830, with its diamond, star, and fan patterns. The pressing technique made possible a greater variety of designs during the 1830s.

The covered dish, with a tray, has the pointed Gothic arch as its major motif, expressing the growing interest in the Gothic revival. It also has a heart motif, which is used, alternating with stars, on the tray. The casket shape is an innovation made possible by pressing. The overall stippling on the pieces—sometimes used to disguise imperfections in the pressing—is more intricate than the most delicate cutting and inspired the term "lacy" for pressed glass of 1830 to 1840.

Diam. bowl 12 1/16 inches
The Metropolitan Museum of Art, Gift of Mrs. Charles W. Green, in memory of Dr. Charles W. Green, 51.171.36,37,153

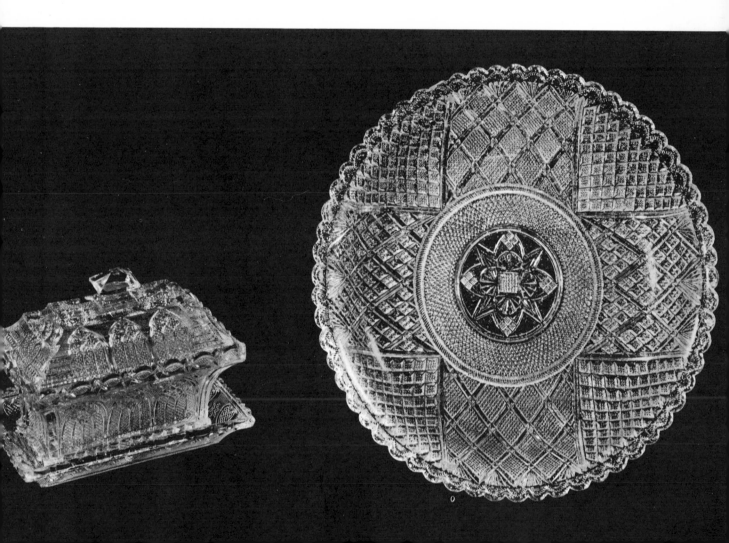

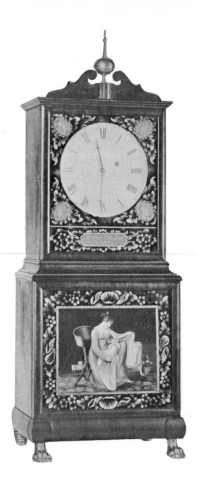

60

The shelf clock, made possible by the development of weight-driven movements that did not require a long pendulum, took various forms, among which the pillar and scroll and case on case, like this one, were popular. This example in a mahogany case, dated according to family tradition about 1817, bears the maker's name, "Aaron Willard," and "BOSTON" below the enameled face. Aaron Willard was the youngest of four clock-making brothers (see no. 62) in and around Boston in the late eighteenth and early nineteenth centuries. Both glass tablets are painted on the reverse, the lower one showing a woman seated in a Grecian chair (compare no. 46) with an infant on her lap, the source for which may have been an English print. This scene and the delicately painted flowers and shells, as well as the gilded paw feet below a torus molding, cavetto molding between the two cases, broken scroll pediment, and ball and spike finial, made the clock suitable for a room furnished in the Empire style.

H. 36 inches
Museum of Fine Arts, Boston, Gift of Mrs. Mary D. B. Wilson

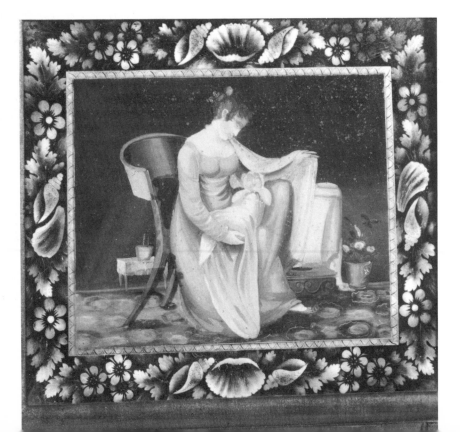

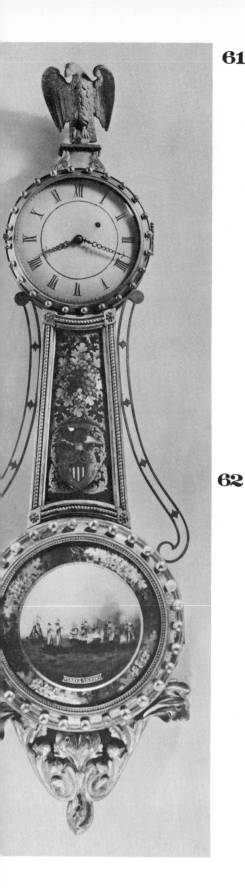

61 Lemuel Curtis, an apprentice of Aaron Willard (see no. 60) and nephew of Willard's wife, created the only truly American clock design, the girandole. Patented by Curtis in 1816, while he lived in Concord, Massachusetts, the clock has a working similar to the so-called banjo clock for which Simon Willard (see no. 62) received a patent in 1802. The design comprises certain invariable features, including the acanthus-leaf bracket, brass or gilded wood balls around the tablet and the clock face, brass scrolls at the sides, slightly convex iron dial face with Roman numerals, and eagle finial. The painted glass tablet shows one of several subjects, often mythological or patriotic; here it is the victory of Commodore Oliver Hazard Perry over the English on Lake Erie in September 1813, a scene sometimes painted for these clocks by Lemuel Curtis's brother Benjamin. The grace of the curves and boldness of gilding made such clocks well suited to accompany Empire furniture.

H. 45 inches

Mr. and Mrs. Richard P. Mellon, Ligonier, Pennsylvania

62 The lighthouse clock was a fancy of Simon Willard, best-known of the clockmaking family, said to have made over 5,000 timepieces between 1802 and 1840. He also made lighthouse mechanisms, so it is perhaps not surprising that he intended this clock to resemble the famous Eddystone light in the English Channel off Plymouth. Patented in 1822, the clock, according to the Willards' descendant and biographer, John Ware Willard, was "on the same plan" as a forty-day clock, with a very heavy weight; it never worked well and thus was never popular. All the lighthouse clocks had a removable glass dome; this one, original to the clock, has a knop with ruffled base and a folded rim. The words "SIMON" and "WILLARD" are on the face, and "PATENT" is in gilt stencil on the body. Bases of these clocks differed somewhat. This one is square, with accents of gilt lacquer on brass—animal-paw and rose front feet and an applied ornament of a winged putto reclining in a sort of goblet, surrounded by a laurel wreath.

H. 28³/₈ inches

Robert F. Woolworth, New York

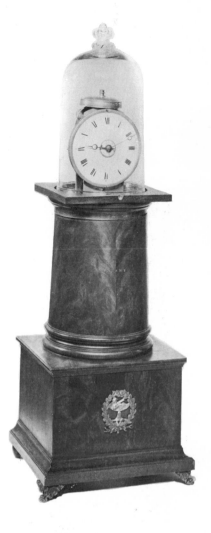

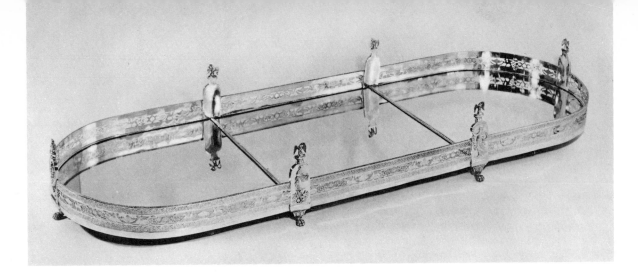

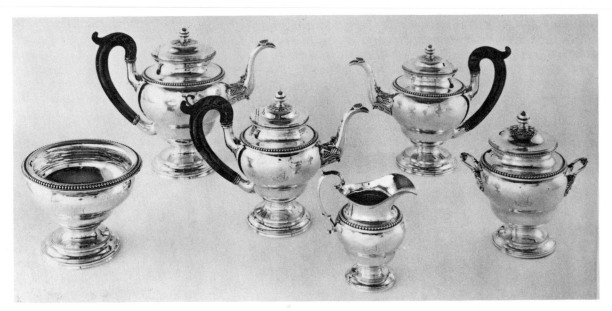

63 The silver plateau, which became popular in France during the Empire, was rare in America. This example, bearing the mark "I.W. FORBES" in a rectangle with four pseudo-hallmarks, is one of two known by John W. Forbes of New York. It was presented to De-Witt Clinton by the citizens of the state of New York after the completion of the Erie Canal in 1825. The other, virtually identical, was owned for many years by the Hunter family of New York and is now in the White House. Both are in three mirrored sections supported by paw-foot pedestals, and have pierced galleries formed by repeated motifs of garlands and winged lions flanking an urn. On the pedestals, which are surmounted by spread-eagle finials, are applied chased figures of Flora, goddess of flowers, Pomona, goddess of the orchard, and American trophies.

L. 64 inches
Virginia Watkins Mitchell and William Bell Watkins, Jr., on loan to The Metropolitan Museum of Art since 1964, L.64.85.1

64

In 1827 the silversmith Harvey Lewis of Philadelphia made this six-piece tea service. To rather plain bodies Lewis added discreet touches of classical ornament: bands of beading, water-leaf scrolls at the bases of the spouts and around the acorn finials, and molded shells at the pouring lips. Although these decorative elements and the chaste simplicity of the surfaces represent the Empire, or classical, style, the lightness of the bodies and the scrolled handles are evidence of the rococo revival, which was just beginning in America in the 1820s. The set bears the coat of arms, crest, and motto of a member of the Wheeler family. The teapots and waste bowl, inscribed 1827, are marked "HARVEY LEWIS" in a rectangle. The teapots also bear the mark "PHILA" in a rectangle, while the sugar and creamer are each stamped twice with "H. LEWIS" in a serrated rectangle.

H. tallest teapot 9 15/16 inches

The Metropolitan Museum of Art, Gift of Mrs. Arthur C. Steinbach, 68.130.1-6

65

In a style sometimes called American Empire, or Greek revival, this mahogany sofa was made in Boston about 1826 to 1828. The brass rosette pulls on the arms open cylindrical drawers, both labeled on the inside: "WIL-LIAM HANCOCK,/Upholsterer,/39 & 41 MARKET STREET,/BOSTON." Hancock, a prominent cabinetmaker (as was his brother Henry Kellam Hancock), was born in 1794 and listed intermittently as a cabinetmaker and/or upholsterer in the Boston directories from 1820 to 1849. To date the half-dozen known labeled pieces of his furniture are of the style and period of this sofa (see no. 66). Although no exact prototype is known for the design of this piece, a sofa with upholstered cylindrical arms resembling the fashionable cushions of the classical period of the early nineteenth century appeared in Sheraton's *Cabinet Encyclopaedia* (plate 2 of sofas) as early as 1805. Its foot is similar to that on a "Grecian Sofa" on plate 75 of the *Cabinet Dictionary*. A number of Hancock's advertisements and billheads of the late 1820s and early 30s bear the engraving of a fantastic Grecian couch, which has a single cylindrical arm with drawer like the two shown here.

L. 89¹/₂ inches

The Metropolitan Museum of Art, Gift of Mrs. William W. Hoppin, 48.164.1

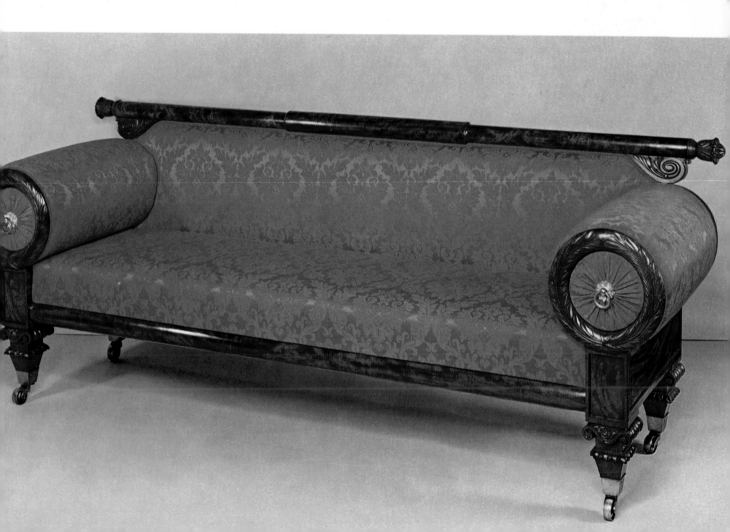

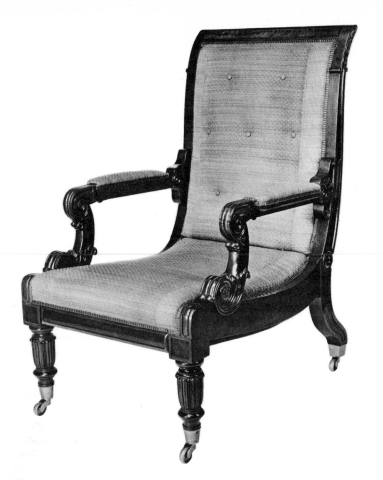

66

Unusually fine carving decorates this mahogany library chair, which bears remnants of the label of Boston cabinetmaker William Hancock underneath the pad of the footrest. Made about 1829 to 1831, in a late Regency style, with the kind of ornament seen in pattern books like those of George Smith, it is based upon models often called in English publications of the time "reading machines." An early mechanical prototype, designed by the architect William Pocock and called a "Reclining Patent Chair," appeared as no. 51 of Ackermann's *Repository of Arts,* published in March 1813. Here brass ratchets on the top of both side rails permit the arms to move and the hinged back to recline gradually. The paneled torus molding of the seat rail is the front of a drawer that pulls out to make a footrest. In any position the chair presents a pleasing flow of curves.

H. 41³/₄ inches
Dr. and Mrs. Roger G. Gerry, Roslyn, New York

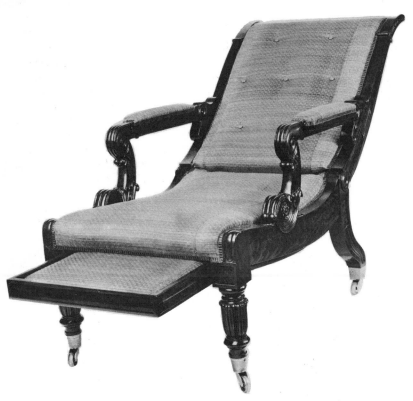

67

William Ellis Tucker, the first important manufacturer of porcelain in America, opened a factory in Philadelphia in 1826. In the dozen years before the factory closed, it produced tablewares adapting fashionable European designs to suit the simpler American taste. That products of the Tucker factory could also be elaborate is shown by these two porcelain vases with ormolu handles, each one of a pair. Their designs reflect the dominant influence of the Empire style during the 1830s. The shape and the handles with griffin's heads have classical prototypes; the flowers on the vase on the left are naturalistic clusters in the French manner; the gold borders on the other vase offer a Gothic counterpoint. The bright and realistically painted scene represents the Schuylkill waterworks at Fairmount and the Schuylkill Dam. Friedrich Sachse designed the bronze handles, which were cast by C. Cornelius and Son, the Philadelphia firm famous for lamps and chandeliers (see nos. 82, 111).

H. 22 inches
Philadelphia Museum of Art; Valley Forge Historical Society

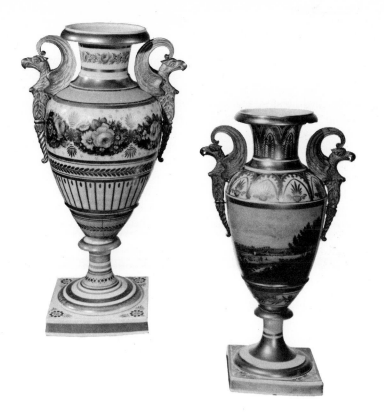

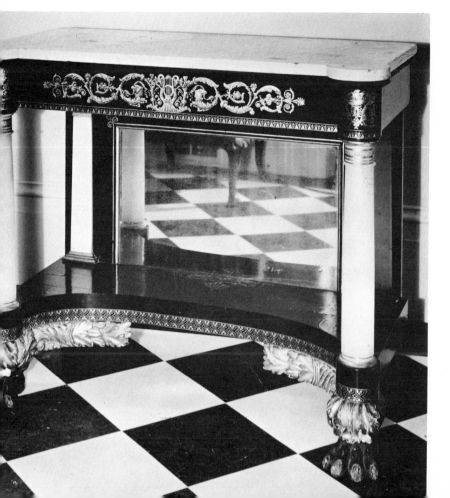

68

Among the firms that produced furniture in the late classical style of the 1820s to 40s, one of the most important was that of Joseph Meeks and Sons of New York, which existed from 1797 to 1868. On this mahogany pier table made between 1829 and 1835 appears the Meeks label, an engraving of their five-story factory with a sign reading: "MEEKS & SONS MANUFACTORY/of/CABINET-FURNITURE." Below the building is the address "Nos 43 & 45 Broad Street/NEW-YORK." The same address and engraved representation of the factory appear on the well-known broadside printed for the Meeks firm by Endicott and Swett of New York in 1833. This colored lithograph is one of the most important documents of American styles of the late classical period; it shows forty-one pieces of furniture, most of them, however, simpler than this table and more in the pillar and scroll style. Here the massive paw feet, gilded leaf brackets, elaborate pilasters, and columns are all typical of painted New York pier tables. Around the mirror at the back is a line of gilding resembling brass inlay, with anthemia at the corners; the tight stenciled gilding on shelf and apron edge also imitates brass inlay. Decorating the ovolo top front corners and center frieze is freehand gilding, skillfully executed and employing classical motifs taken from Sheraton. The gilded pattern at the back of the shelf is completed by its reflection in the glass.

L. 43 inches

Mr. and Mrs. C. Edward Hansell, Roswell, Georgia

69

Above the keyboard of this rosewood piano, made about 1825, is a gilded tablet with black script letters: "Loud & Brothers Philadelphia." Thomas Loud, Jr., was manufacturing pianos in Philadelphia by 1816, but the name "Loud Brothers" was not used until 1822; it continued until 1837. Even without the inscription, it would be possible to guess the origin of the case, for the partial anthemion that scrolls into a cornucopia and forms the bracket between leg and case is often found on Philadelphia sofas of the period. The stenciled decoration is also typical of Philadelphia, with wide flat areas and little of the shading characteristic of New York stenciling. Heavy turned legs, distinctive in their bold shape, are true to their classical prototypes.

L. 69 inches
The Metropolitan Museum of Art, The Crosby Brown Collection of Musical Instruments, 89.4.2812

70

Stenciled and painted New York furniture in the Empire style is epitomized by this secretary made about 1825, possibly by Joseph Meeks and Sons. In form and character the lower section, with massive paw feet below gilded cornucopia brackets, painted fretwork of interlocking circles imitating brass inlay, and columns with gilded composite capitals, is related to numerous New York pier tables. The upper section, divided glass doors with gilded mullions flanked by columns and surmounted by an upcurving architectural cornice, is related to New York wardrobes. The darkened mahogany background, liberal use of gilding and brass, and variation in style and scale of painted pattern —abstract linear patterns, tight Greek revival anthemia, large fruit and floral motifs like those on Hitchcock chairs—all contribute to the striking effect. Labeled examples of stenciled and painted pieces show that Haines and Holmes, C. and W. Miller, John Banks, Roswell A. Hubbard, Kinnan and Mead, and Williams and Dawson, all of New York, did similar work at this time.

H. 101 inches
The Metropolitan Museum of Art, Gift of Francis Hartman Markoe, 60.29.1

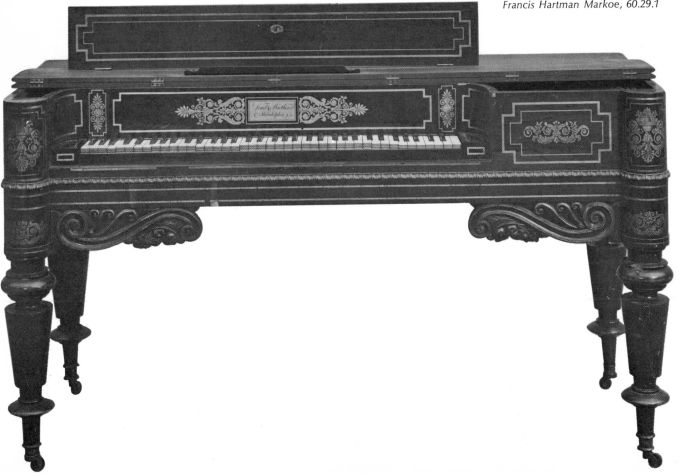

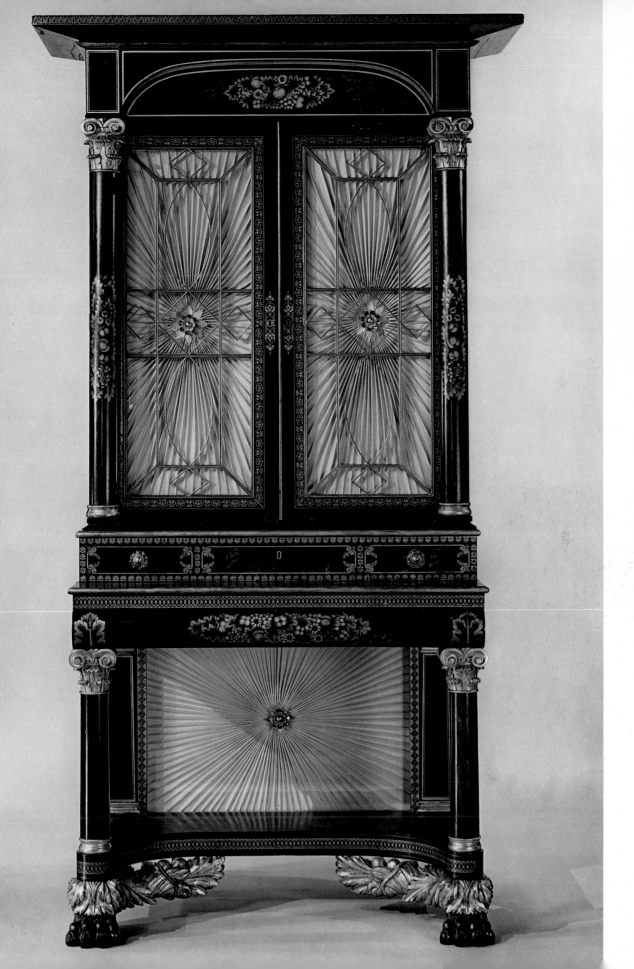

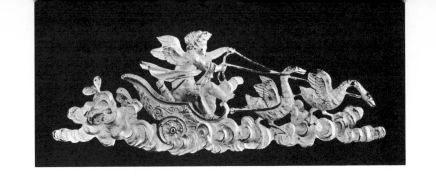

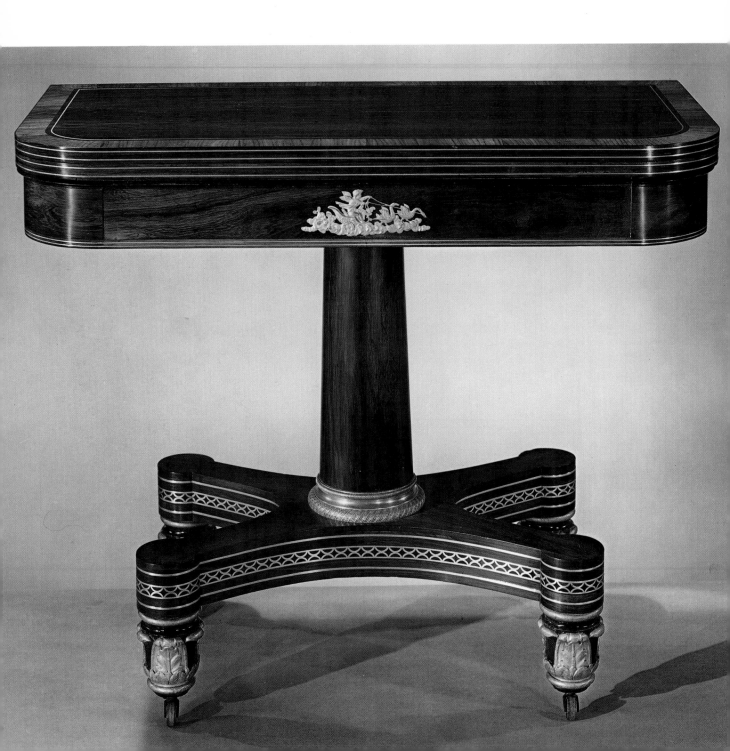

71

Simplicity of shape and a gleaming surface of rosewood inlaid with brass and accented with gilding make this card table, one of a pair, among the handsomest productions of its period. Made in New York about 1825, perhaps in the workshop of Duncan Phyfe, it is in the French Restauration style. In France this style, which derived its name from the restoration of the Bourbon monarchy, can be dated from 1814 to 1830. Its chief patroness was the Duchess of Berry, and one of its most important disseminators was Pierre de la Mésangère, in his periodical *Les Meubles et Objets de Goût,* published between 1802 and 1830. Here Restauration influence is evident in the pillared pedestal with gilded brass cap and base and the gilt and verd-antique feet. A single French gilt center ornament decorates the front. The shaped top flips over, creating a full-size gaming surface covered with baize; a marbleized paper covers the interior. The entire table top swivels on a carefully fitted edge cushion of velvet and centers over the pedestal when open.

H. 29¹/₂ inches
The Metropolitan Museum of Art, Edgar J. Kaufmann Charitable Foundation Fund, 68.94.2

72

In Boston the style of the French Restauration was interpreted with considerable éclat, as is shown by this sewing table made about 1825. Like other American furniture of this type, the table derives its effect from simple lines and highly figured mahogany veneers. Metallic accents are supplied by French ormolu capitals and bases for the legs, gilded brass floral pulls, and a row of brass beading around the ebonized ball feet, which are often found on Boston furniture of the Empire period.

H. 29¹/₂ inches
Mr. and Mrs. James Halpin, Bronxville, New York

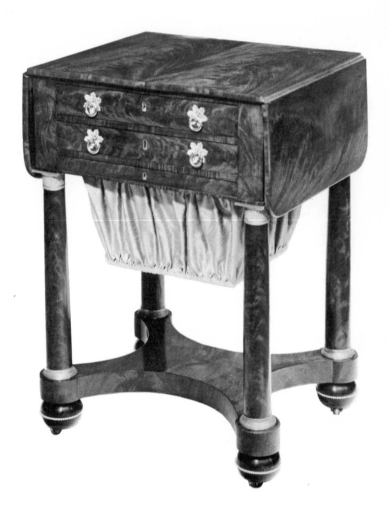

73 Called in contemporary price books a pedestal end sideboard, this form was popular during the Empire period. In this example, made in New York about 1825 or 1830, are elements of the New York Empire style: large panels of flame-grained mahogany, columns with ormolu caps and bases, crisp leaf carving, and a reeded edge on the white marble top. That characteristics of style carried over from one medium to another is evident in the boldly gadrooned feet, resembling melon-reeded silver of the period (see nos. 74, 76). Sideboards were an expression of the American love of ostentation and plenty, as observed by James Fenimore Cooper in 1828 in his *Notions of the Americans: Picked up by a Travelling Bachelor:*

> In one of the rooms . . . is a spacious, heavy, ill-looking side-board, in mahogany, groaning with plate, knife and spoon cases, all handsome enough, I allow, but sadly out of place where they are seen. Here is the first great defect that I find in the ordering of American domestic economy. The eating, or dining-room, is almost invariably one of the best in the house.

Although fitting Cooper's description as spacious and heavy, this sideboard has graceful carving, skillfully worked veneers, and subtle metallic accents that make it anything but "ill-looking."

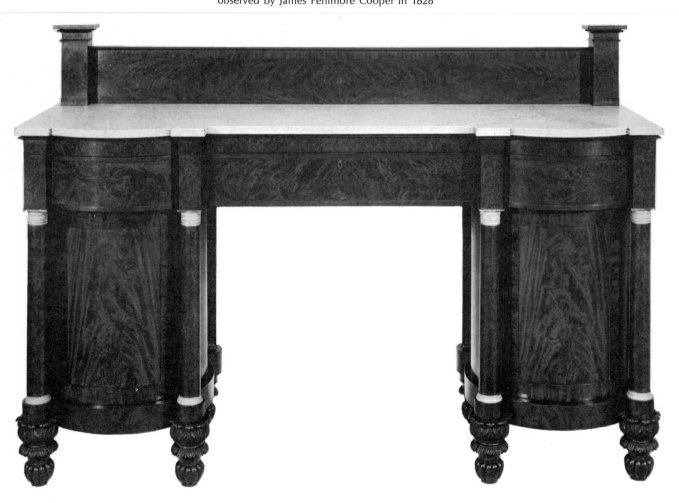

L. 78³/₄ inches
Museum of the City of New York, Gift of Mrs. Frederick Suydam Polhemus

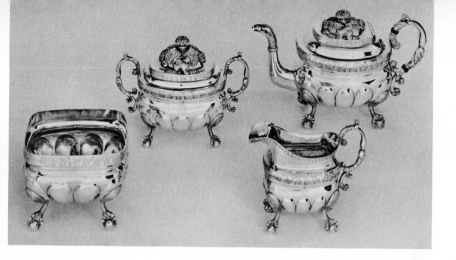

74 This Empire silver tea set of the 1820s by William Thomson features bulbous bodies with melon reeding and a wide border of ornament on the shoulder, in this case sheaves of wheat, a symbol of American prosperity and Jeffersonian agrarianism. Smaller bands of wheat sheaves embellish the lips of three pieces, and a standing sheaf surrounded by fallen ones forms the finial on the two covers. All of the pieces are supported by carefully articulated feathered legs with bird's claws curving around ball feet. The spout of the teapot is a bird's head, a feature of this style. The handles, however, with their scrolling foliate forms, are manifestations of the beginning of the rococo revival. Each piece is marked "W. Thomson" in script, in a shaped reserve; the teapot twice. On the side of each is an unidentified monogram, "E M F," under a stag's-head crest.

H. teapot 7³/₄ inches

Mr. and Mrs. Samuel B. Feld, New York

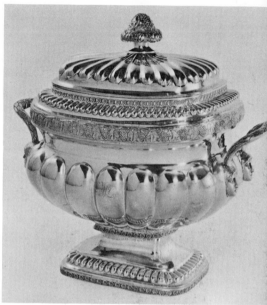

76

Marked "W. Thomson" in script within a rectangle on the underside, this silver tureen in the Empire style was made in New York by William Thomson, who worked from 1809 to 1845. The bulbous body has melon reeding, which is repeated on the base, shoulder, and cover. Three bands of cast palmettes, a wide border of chased grapes and leaves on the shoulder, berries and leaves on the large finial and curved handles, and cast masks at the junctures of handle and body make up the remainder of the ornament. Although masks are not unusual on English silver of the period, they are rarely seen on American Empire silver.

H. 12¹/₄ inches

Mrs. Frances Whitney, Mrs. John V. Taggart, John David Lannon, Jr., on loan to The Metropolitan Museum of Art since 1967, L.67.13

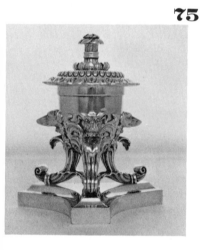

75 Marked around the base "O. RICH.," "BOSTON," and "fine," this inkstand is one of two made by Obadiah Rich about 1830 to 1835, believed to have been designed by sculptor Horatio Greenough. (The other is in the Garvan collection at Yale University.) Both follow the same classical pattern at the base: a plinth bearing a tripod of leafy scrolls that terminate in three Etruscan dogs' heads around an urn-shaped well. Here the hinged cover with its lip of double gadrooning has a classical finial of bound stalks and leaves.

H. 5⁵/₈ inches

Fogg Art Museum, Harvard University, Bequest of Mrs. William Norton Bullard

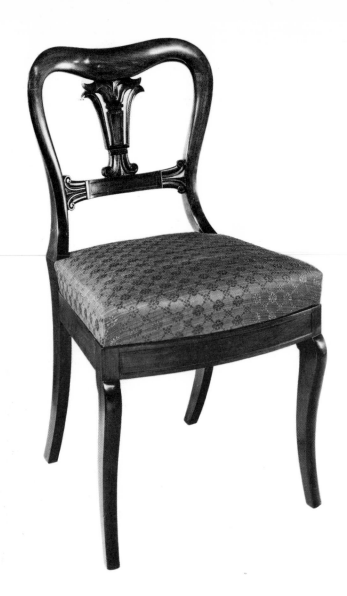

77

Decoration of Egyptian derivation is shown on the splat and stay rail of this rosewood side chair made about 1830 in New York in the style of the French Restauration. While light woods were favored in France for furniture in this style, the dark woods like mahogany and rosewood were used in America as the style took hold in the late twenties and the early thirties. The chair descended in the Bloomfield family of New Jersey and is a more elaborate version of chairs in a set made by Duncan Phyfe for his daughter Eliza Vail. The use of the wood's handsome grain, the play of flat against curving surfaces in the splat of inverted lotus shape, and the grace and restraint of the design suggest that this chair is also from the Phyfe workshop.

H. 32³/₄ inches
The Metropolitan Museum of Art, Edgar J. Kaufmann Charitable Foundation Fund, 68.202.1

78

New York merchant and art patron Luman Reed was credited by his contemporaries with a "natural pictorial perception and good taste." These qualities showed not only in the gallery of paintings occupying one floor of his home on Greenwich Street, but also in the furnishings of the private apartments. Shaped like the *fauteuil gondole* of the French Restauration, this armchair was made for Reed about 1832, probably in the workshop of Duncan Phyfe. The chair is distinguished in its subtle curving lines and mahogany of excellent quality. It is further enhanced by touches of carving: scrolls on front legs and arms and at the juncture of arm and back stile. Perhaps the finest detail, a common one on the best Phyfe furniture in the Restauration style, is the beautifully carved Egyptian motif of Ionic lotus leaves.

H. 39 inches
Ronald S. Kane, New York

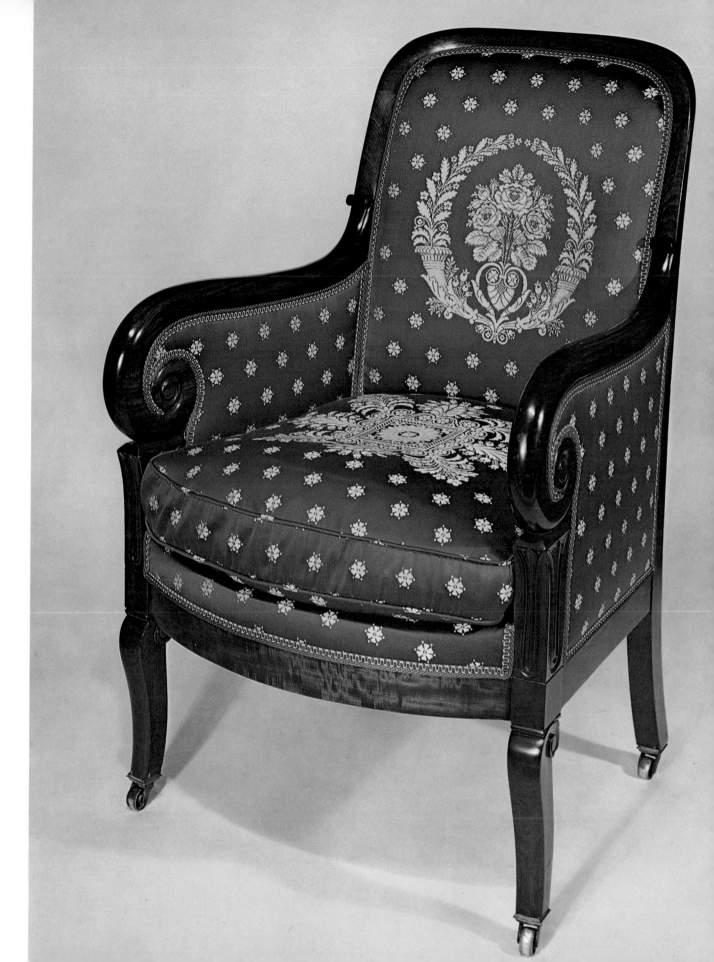

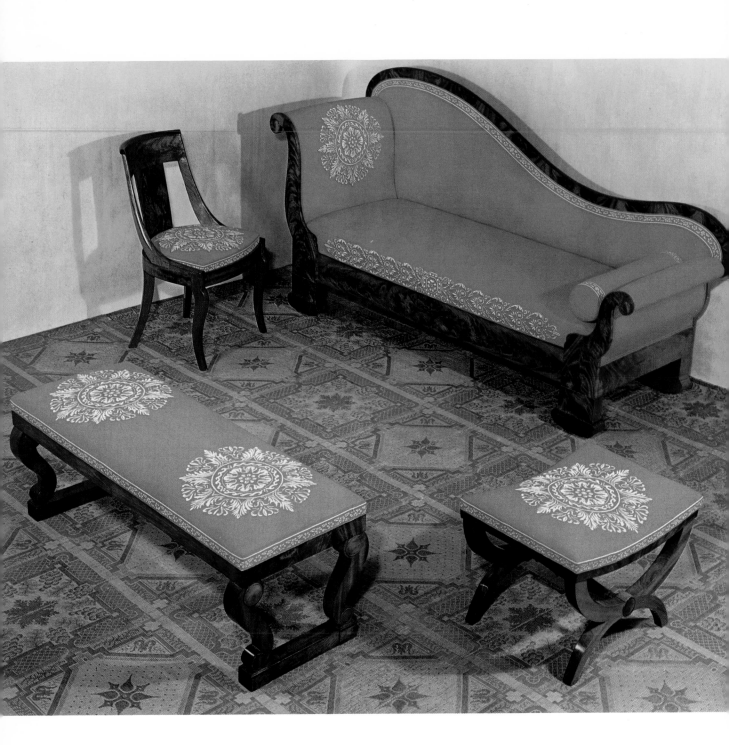

79

In 1837, according to family tradition, Samuel A. Foot, a New York lawyer, ordered from Duncan Phyfe a parlor set for his new house at 678 Broadway. In this grouping are four pieces from the set: a *méridienne*, or daybed, a curule stool, a window bench, and a *chaise gondole*, or gondola chair, all reflecting the influence of the French Restauration style. Ernest Hagen, a late nineteenth-century cabinetmaker and the first person to study Phyfe's work, characterized Phyfe's late Empire furniture (after 1830) as "the abominable heavy and Nondescrip [sic] veneered style." Such a description is scarcely applicable here, for, despite their heaviness, the *méridienne* with its curving back and sharply scrolled asymmetrical arms has a kind of monumental grace, and the *chaise gondole* and scroll-supported window bench an understated elegance. The rich color and grain of the mahogany are enhanced by the crimson linen and wool rep upholstery with woven gold medallions, a copy of the original fabric.

L. méridienne 72 inches
The Metropolitan Museum of Art, Purchase, L. E. Katzenbach Fund Gift 66.221.1, 3, 7, 9

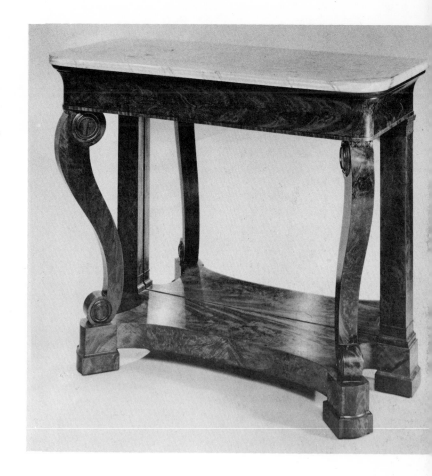

80

Of the same style and period as the Foot furniture (no. 79), this mahogany pier table is attributed to the workshop of Duncan Phyfe. Two other similar pier tables are known: one, for which there is an 1834 bill of sale, is in the collection of the White House; the other, bearing Phyfe's label for the years 1837 to 1840, was made for his daughter Eliza Vail. Both have frontal scroll supports, but they are not canted as here. Other differences that set this table apart from the documented pieces include the carved detailing of the capital and base of the pilasters flanking the mirror, the shelf, the reeded edge on the white marble top, and the carved Egyptian design, perhaps a lotus, on top of the scrolled supports. The design source for this table may have been a plate in La Mésangère in the period 1825 to 1827. Except for its carved detailing and block feet in place of casters, the Phyfe example is virtually identical to the French prototype.

L. 42¹/₄ inches
The Metropolitan Museum of Art, Edgar J. Kaufmann Charitable Foundation Fund, 68.201

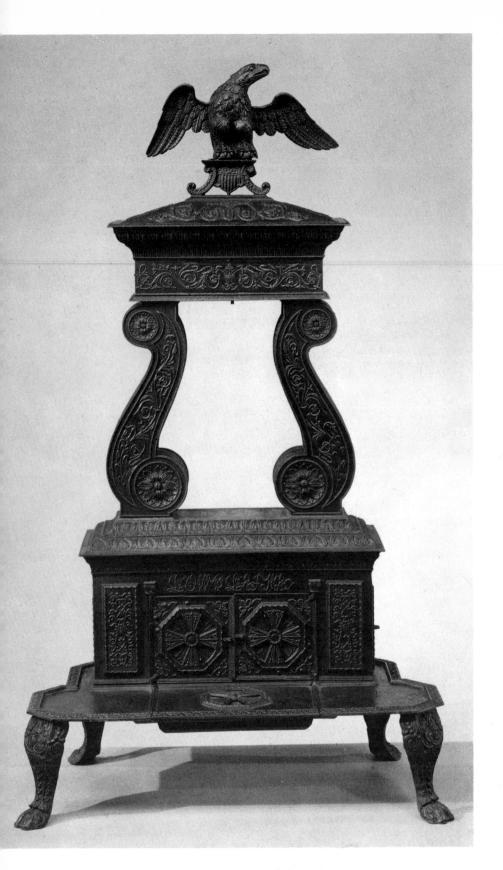

81

For all its utility and unglamorous material, the cast-iron stove was nonetheless stylish. Its function required it to be given a prominent place in even the most elegant rooms. This parlor stove, made by Low and Leake of Albany in the 1840s, would have been a worthy addition to a room furnished in the Empire style. Two scroll-shaped pipes, suggesting the sides of a lyre, support its gabled top, and a shield and flanking scrolls form a stand for a spread eagle. Virtually every surface is ornamented in the classical taste; a strict symmetry is adhered to; and the upper corners of the front doors are topped with stylized Ionic capitals. The makers' names, on a panel above these doors, and the word "Albany," on both sides of the firebox, are in a feathery script meant to contribute to the decoration. Albany and Troy were principal centers for the manufacture of cast-iron products, which industry provided the prosperity that demanded such elaborate utilitarian pieces. This stove is marked on the back "PATENTED AUGUST 10TH 1844," a date when the classical style was beginning to take second place to the other revivals. An almost identical stove, made by Groma and Low, is in Henry Sleeper's house, Beauport, in Gloucester.

H. 57½ inches
The Metropolitan Museum of Art,
Gift of Dick Button

82

An oval label on this bronze lamp reads: "CORNELIUS & CO./PHILAD./PATENT/APRIL 1ST. 1843." Christian Cornelius had begun as a silversmith in 1812, but soon turned to bronze casting, and his company became one of the foremost manufacturers of lighting devices during the nineteenth century. This is an astral lamp; that is, its oil reservoir is in the shape of a ring, at the level of the burner. The idea of using a circular font at burner level had been patented first in 1808 in a chandelier, and in 1810 was modified to serve in a table lamp. The principle of the Argand lamp was applied (see no. 83), with the thin round font less of an obstruction to the spreading light than the urn-shaped reservoir used on Argand lamps. Astral lamps became *de rigueur* in well-

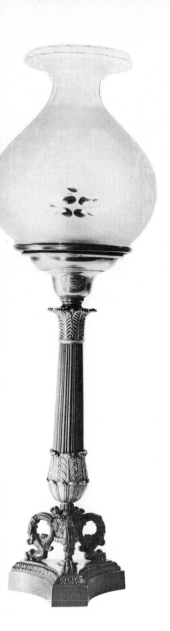

appointed houses, and detailing matched that of other late neoclassical furnishings: the shaft is a fluted pillar, supported on leaflike scrolls ending in paw feet, which rest on a tripod base with flat leaf cavetto molding. The leaf casting at the base and top of the shaft are gilded; the shade, also in late classical shape, is frosted and cut glass.

H. 29 inches
The Newark Museum

83

In 1783 Aimé Argand, a Swiss chemist, introduced a new principle in oil-burning lighting devices. He fitted a hollow cylindrical wick between two metal tubes, of which the inner extended down through and below the oil reservoir. In this way oxygen reached the flame from the interior as well as the exterior,

making it brighter and more smoke-free. Argand's name became attached to lamps using this principle, such as this example in bronze, made about 1835 or 1840 and labeled "B. GARDINER/N. YORK," for Baldwin Gardiner, a well-known retailer. Combining classical and rococo elements, the lamp has a center oil font in the shape of a Greek amphora; the ormolu scroll handles, the egg-and-dart decoration applied to the amphora and the two small oil reservoirs, the ormolu acanthus along the oil pipes, and the ormolu paw feet emerging from corner sockets shaped like acroteria are all from the classical repertory. But the overall tendency to heaviness and the loose feathery quality of the ormolu show that the classical was in its late stage and the rococo revival was becoming evident.

H. 17⅞ inches
The Metropolitan Museum of Art, Gift of John C. Cattus, 67.262.6

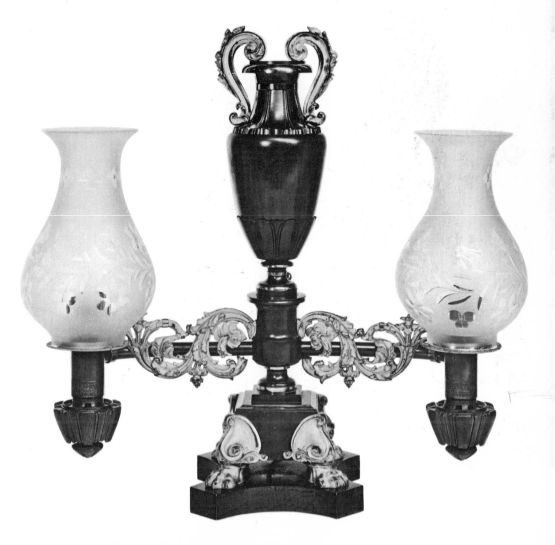

84

While numerous Philadelphia-made hanging light fixtures or chandeliers of the 1840s have been identified, almost none from New York is documented. The present example is an exception. The cylindrical wick-holders of this brass and gilt-bronze chandelier bear rectangular, stamped brass labels reading: "CLARK COIT & CARGILL/N. YORK." The lighting system is identical in principle with that of the standing Argand lamp sold by Baldwin Gardiner (no. 83); the small brass urn serves as the oil reservoir. Thomas Webster illustrates a nearly identical piece in his *Encyclopaedia of Domestic Economy* (1845), describing it as a suspended Argand lamp, "with the chains very ornamental, and the branches concealed by very rich brass work." The naturalistic leaves in the rococo style here certainly fit this description. Webster also explains the introduction of the triangular prisms, or lusters, hanging beneath the fixtures: "Instead of the forms, with many facets, into which these drops were formerly cut, glass, cut into the shape of triangular prisms, are now generally used, being more easily made, and refracting the light as much or more than any other shape."

H. 51 inches

The Metropolitan Museum of Art, Rogers Fund, 67.199

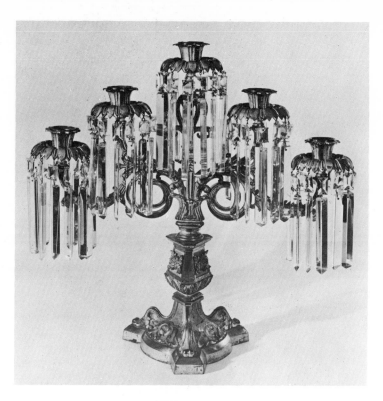

85

During the 1830s the rococo revival was increasingly evident in decorative accessories, such as this gilt-bronze and glass girandole. One of a pair used by the Poe family of Baltimore, it may have been locally made. The center support combines the free leaf and scroll motifs with a more classical tripod pedestal. The arms are typical rococo branches with petal-shaped bobêches and holders to carry out the floral conceit. The glass drops add a touch of elegance and a contrast in material, especially effective when they pick up the reflections of candlelight.

H. 20 inches

The Metropolitan Museum of Art, Anonymous Gift Fund, 68.151.1

86

"Candles," wrote Thomas Webster in his *Encyclopaedia of Domestic Economy*, "from their portability and other qualities, supply . . . the most convenient and the most general mode of obtaining artificial light for domestic purposes." Webster did not mention specifically the beauty and mystery of the live, uncovered flame, but it was doubtless for these qualities, too, that Philip Verplanck purchased this elaborate seven-branch ormolu candelabrum, even though the bright, relatively smokeless oil lamp was already in full fashion. Verplanck began Plum Point, his Greek revival country house overlooking the river near Cornwall-on-Hudson, in 1834. The furnishings, including this candelabrum, must have been ordered about 1836. Unlike the house, this piece is not wholly one style: the intertwined female figures are neoclassical in their lightness, elongated proportions, and stylized poses; the individual branches have all the sinewy asymmetry of the rococo. By spacing the branches equally about the stem, however, the designer organized them into a symmetry acceptable for this classically inspired design.

H. 32½ inches

The Metropolitan Museum of Art, Gift of John C. Cattus, 67.262.8

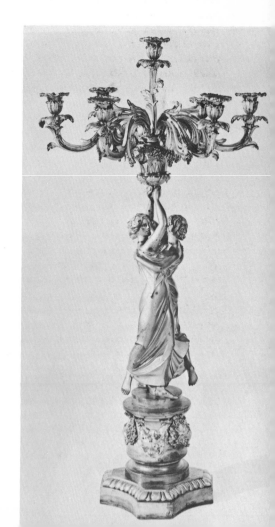

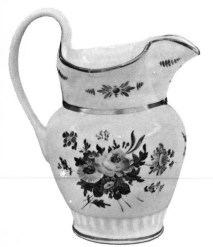

87 In the 1820s and 30s, when pitchers like this were made in quantity at the Tucker factory (see also no. 67), fashionable porcelain design was determined as much by the desire to show off the fine, thin white ceramic as by the interest in classical forms. The colorful floral ornament adds sparkle to the effect of translucent white surfaces. The shape and the reeding around the bottom are adaptations from ancient Greco-Roman models.

H. 9³/₈ inches
The Metropolitan Museum of Art, Rogers Fund, 13.145.7

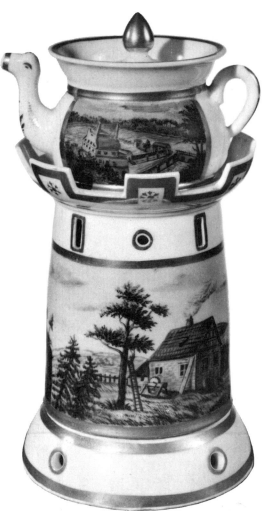

88 The night light and tea warmer was one of many gadgets popular in the nineteenth century to make life more comfortable and more elegant as well. The dual function is fulfilled only when the piece is made of fine porcelain, because only a translucent chimney permits the flame of the candle or oil font to radiate light while keeping the pot warm. This Tucker porcelain example, made about 1836, has the restraint characteristic of Empire design. The scenes, a view of the Philadelphia waterworks on the teapot and an imaginary landscape below, are in the sepia and black familiar from the publications of classical views popular in the 1830s.

H. 11¹/₄ inches
Philadelphia Museum of Art

89 Presumably made as a wedding present, this fine coffee service bears the initials of Mary Earp Tucker, who married Thomas Tucker, the manager of the porcelain works, in 1838, the year the factory closed. In its simplicity—with the wide gold line and letters with laurel spray as the only ornament—the service epitomizes the porcelain used on American dining tables between 1820 and 1860. The pieces, although not precise copies of ancient models, have the crisp outline characteristic of classical design. Tucker porcelain is very rarely marked although letters are occasionally found incised under pieces, some of which have been identified as the initials of molders. The set is more delicate than the work from French, German, and English potteries that was available in American shops.

H. coffeepot 8⅞ inches
The Metropolitan Museum of Art, Rogers Fund, 63.88.1,7-10,18

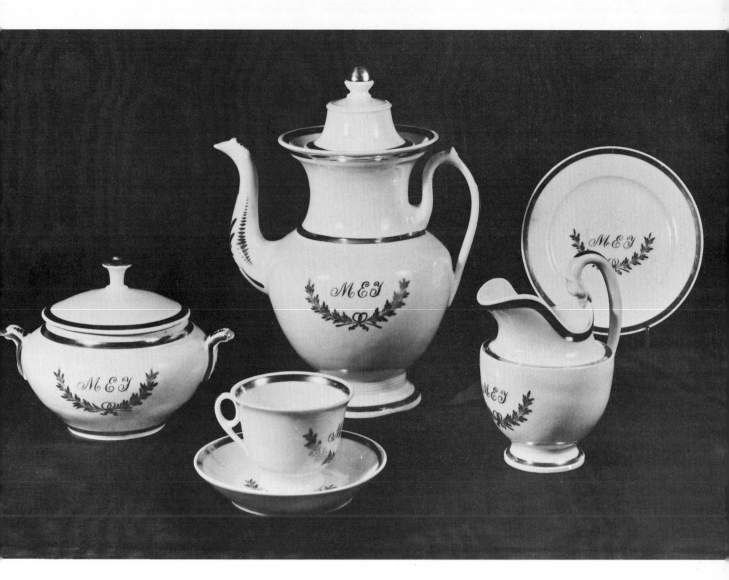

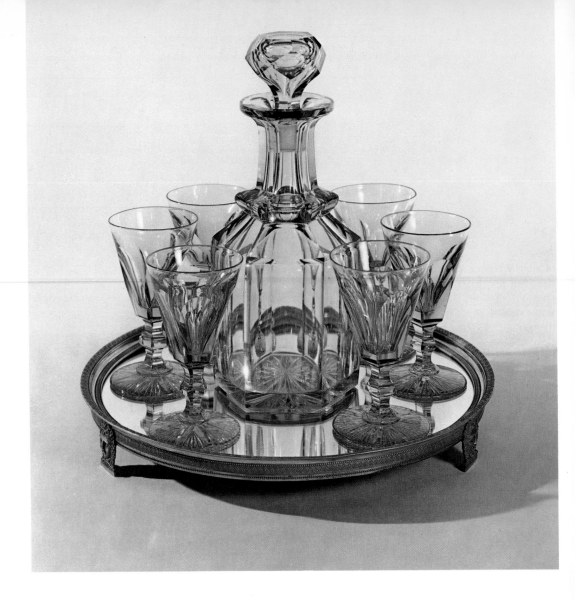

90 Originally owned by the New York collector Luman Reed, this decanter and six matching wine glasses were most probably American made. The most likely maker is Phineas C. Dummer of Jersey City, who produced handsome cut glass in the 1830s and sold it in New York. His reputation for high quality was well known, and he won prizes at trade exhibitions for both cut and pressed pieces. The unusual light-green color suggests experimentation with the addition of chemicals to the mixture of metal, perhaps to keep up with the new colored glass being introduced into America from Bohemia. The squat proportions and broad cut panels are characteristic of fashionable work of the 1830s.

H. decanter 10⅝ inches
Lent anonymously

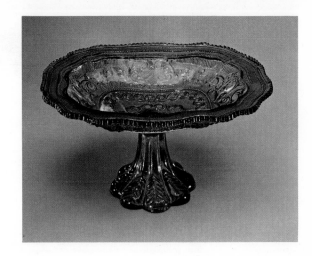

91

These three objects, a white lamp and pair of amethyst vases, are pressed in simple designs that may be contrasted to the intricate ones of lacy glass (see nos. 59, 92). An example of early pressed glass, the lamp is in the opaque white used to conceal imperfections obvious in clear glass. The lions and baskets of flowers on its pedestal are motifs that appear on pressed salts of the 1820s and 30s. It is very likely a product of the New England Glass Company. The vases are later and represent a reaction against lacy glass. The diamond pattern, an imitation of cut glass, is found on many pieces of the 1840s. Their shape, graceful and easily pressed, is characteristic of the late Empire style.

H. lamp 12 inches

Vases: The Metropolitan Museum of Art, Gift of Mrs. Emily Winthrop Miles, 46.140. 291, 292; lamp: lent anonymously

92

Although lacy glass was conceived as a substitute for the sparkling clear cut glass, occasionally examples were made in color. This amethyst compote molded in the princess-feather and medallion pattern, probably at Sandwich, is also found in blue, yellow, and clear glass. The pattern was favored in the decade 1830 to 1840, when whimsical, leafy arabesques and exotic motifs were used in reaction to classicism. The squat, curving form is related to contemporary designs in porcelain.

H. 6 1/16 inches

The Metropolitan Museum of Art, Bequest of Anna G. W. Green (Mrs. Charles W.), in memory of Dr. Charles W. Green, 57.131.14

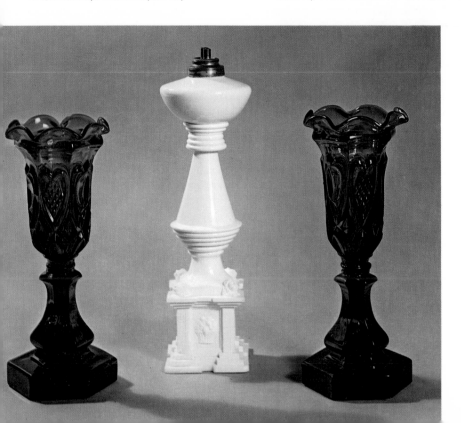

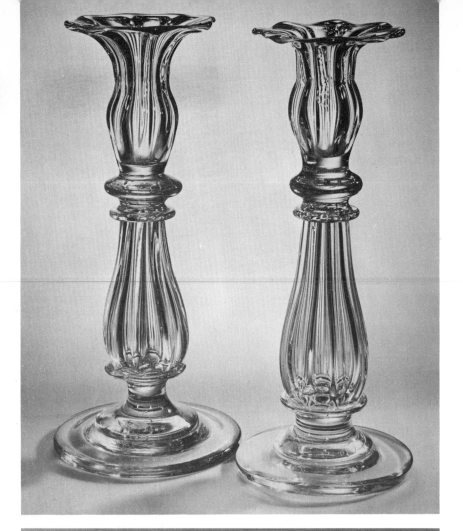

93

Pillar-molded glass with wide ribbing was made in the Pittsburgh area from about 1825 to 1850. This glass, a medium-priced ware used on riverboats and in taverns and hotels, was found most often in the form of decanters, cruets, and bowls. Candlesticks like these are rare. Pillar-molded glass was made by a special technique: the metal was blown into the mold twice and the outer surface fire-polished to remove the sharp edges left by the mold. The wide ribbing is also found on silver and pottery in the late Empire style.

H. 12³/₈ inches
The Corning Museum of Glass

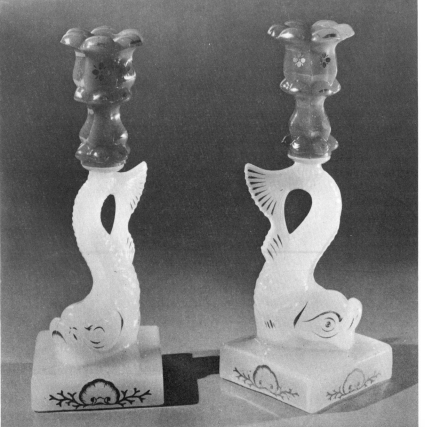

94

The dolphin-shaped glass candlestick was very popular from about 1840 to the 1870s. The motif was one of many familiar classical designs (see no. 45), and it persisted in glass long after it had been forgotten in other media. Probably made at Sandwich, these examples date between 1840 and 1850. They were pressed in opaque blue and white, the favorite colors for simple late classical glass and decorative ceramics, and have painted gilt details.

H. taller candlestick 10³/₈ inches
The Metropolitan Museum of Art, Bequest of Anna G. W. Green (Mrs. Charles W.), in memory of Dr. Charles W. Green, 57.131.3,4

95

Encasing loopings of colored glass in clear metal is a technique that gained popularity among American glassmakers in the mid-nineteenth century. A method of adding color that shows off the abilities of the blower, it produces a thicker, simpler version of intricate sixteenth-century Venetian *latticinio* glass. This pair of red-, white-, and blue-striped vases, with globular covers popularly known as "witch balls," are in classical shapes characteristic of the best work by the New England Glass Company of about 1840. Their airy grace would have added a festive note to an Empire parlor.

H. pair 13³/₈ inches
The Metropolitan Museum of Art, Edgar J. Kaufmann Charitable Foundation Fund, 69.84.1, 2

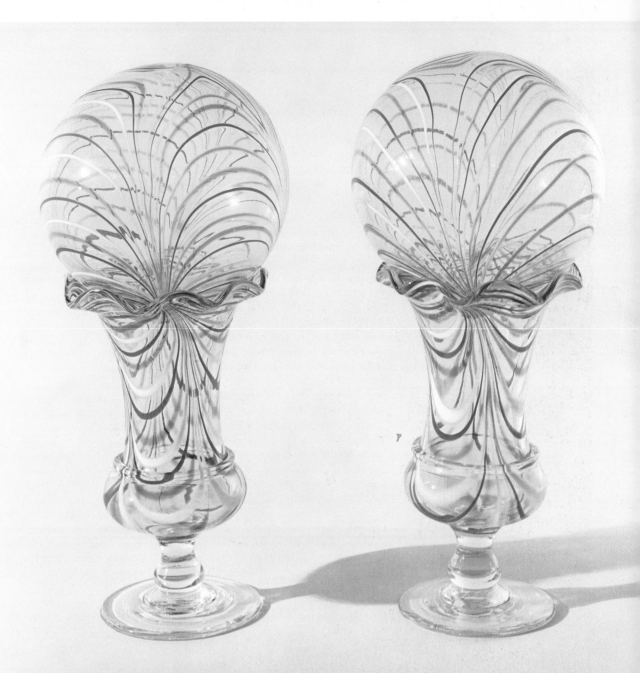

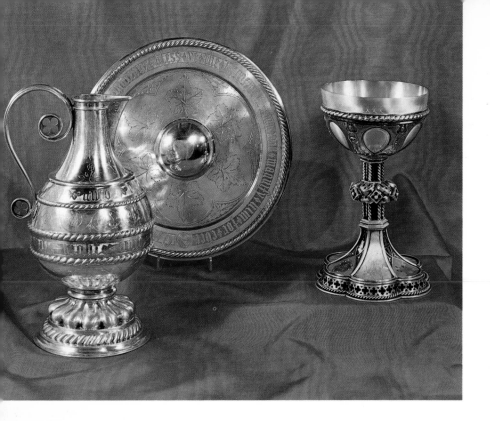

96

In England the Gothic revival style, popular in eighteenth- and early nineteenth-century architecture and decorative arts, had a resurgence in the 1820s and 30s. As used by designers like A.W.N. Pugin, it became more solid structurally and more accurate historically. In America this revival, beginning in the 1830s, became a major theme of the forties and fifties. At first it was used almost exclusively for either private mansions—"castles" for the new mercantile elite—or church buildings, where its soaring pinnacles could symbolize religious fervor. Often interiors and furnishings were also Gothic. Here the style is seen in sacred vessels made in the fifties for two New York churches, the Church of the Annunciation on Fourteenth Street and Richard Upjohn's Trinity Church on lower Broadway. The gold ewer, in a classical shape, has only minor details of Gothic or Renaissance inspiration. Most obvious are the Gothic quatrefoils pierced on its scrolling handle. The base has the bold repoussé often found on late fifteenth- and sixteenth-century mid-European, particularly German,

silver and gold vessels. On the underside appear the mark "F.W. COOPER" in a rectangle and the engraved inscription "Church of the Annunciation. N.Y. Whitsunday. A.D. Mdcccliii." Engraved pseudo-Gothic letters spell out Verse 2 of Psalm 19: "Day unto day uttereth speech And night unto night showeth knowledge." Around its rim the matching tray bears the message, from the Apocryphal Song of the Three Holy Children: "O ye Spirits and Souls of the Righteous bless ye the Lord praise him and magnify him for ever."

Closer to the Gothic in both shape and ornament is the silver and enamel chalice of about 1855, bearing the mark "COOPER & FISHER" underneath the base, as well as Cooper's address for the years 1853 to 1863, "131 AMITY St., N.Y." Cable moldings, which in a finer scale are found on fifteenth- to seventeenth-century silver and gold, appear here on the knopped stem, which is more attenuated than its historical precedents. On the hexagonal base enameled panels simulating medieval work contain religious symbols and scenes, nineteenth-century in their elaboration.

Francis W. Cooper is first in the New York directories of 1840/41 as a silversmith at 9 Sullivan Street. The last listing for him, as a "silverware manufacturer," is in the 1863 directory. There is no listing for his partnership with Fisher; Richard Fisher, silversmith, however, is entered in directories of 1855/56 to 1861/62 at the Amity Street address. According to Trinity Church records, a man named Segal did the chasing on the chalice and H. P. Horlor the enameling and engraving. Segal remains unidentified, but during several of these years the city directory records a Henry P. Horlor, engraver, on Nassau Street.

H. ewer 12 15/16 inches
Ewer and tray: Cathedral Church of St. John the Divine, New York; chalice: Trinity Church, New York

97

Seen here at Lyndhurst, William Paulding's Gothic revival Hudson River mansion for which they were made, probably in 1841, this oak table and pair of wheelback chairs designed by Alexander Jackson Davis illustrate two facts: first, that at its best the Gothic revival in America could equal the best of the Gothic revival in England, the source of many of its ideas and designs; second, that the Gothic revival in this country, even in furniture, was primarily the work of architects. Perhaps the most significant was Davis, whose diary, now in the Metropolitan Museum, records in July 1838 his studies for a "Country Mansion in Pointed Style, near Tarrytown for Wm. Paulding. . . ." In September 1841, Davis noted "Fifty designs for furniture, & various services [$] 50.00." Here Gothic motifs are used decoratively, so that the rose-window pattern is adapted for a chair back. In other instances the Davis designs were closer to actual Gothic furniture. Although this furniture can not be definitely attributed to a specific cabinetmaker, Burns and Trainque of New York are known to have made some of the Gothic furniture for the house, then called Knoll, Paulding Manor, or Paulding Place. Andrew Jackson Downing, horticulturist, writer, and arbiter of taste during the 1830s and 40s, who collaborated with Davis for a number of years, favored the firm of Burns and Trainque, and called their pieces "the most correct Gothic furniture . . . executed in this country."

H. chair 37¹/₄ inches
National Trust for Historic Preservation, Lyndhurst in Tarrytown, New York

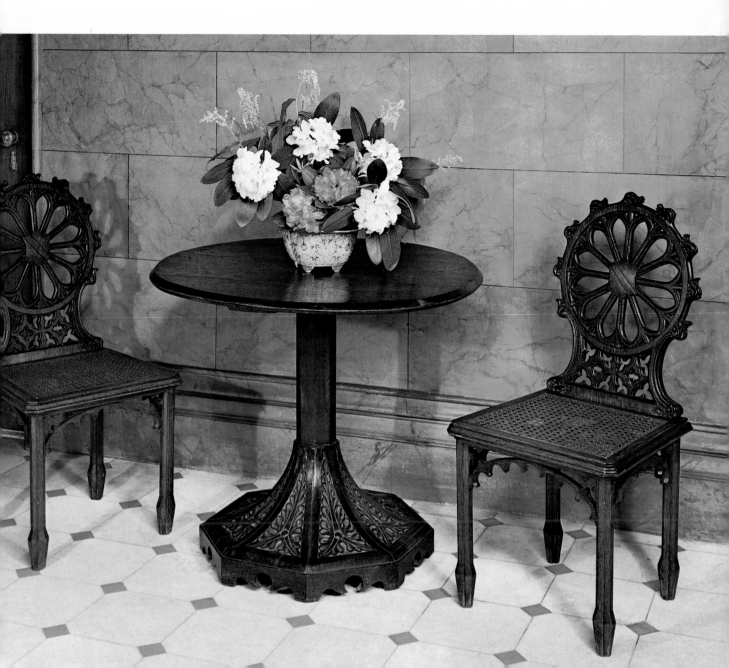

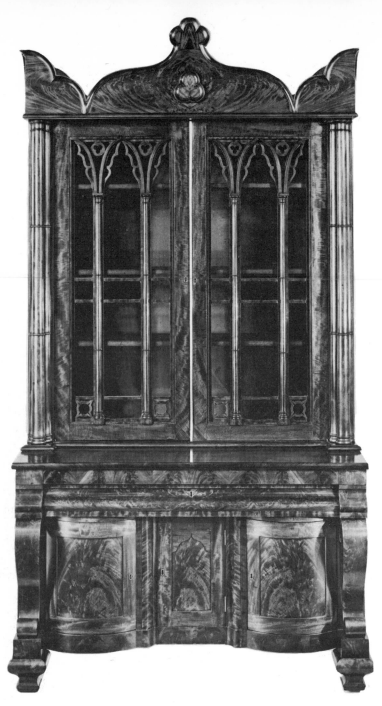

68). The upper, bookcase, section is Gothicized by clustered columns on either side of the doors; segmented columns, ogival arches, and trefoil mullions on the doors; and the trefoiled treatment of the pediment. The quality of the cabinetwork is excellent; the success of the whole design is typically reliant upon the masterful selection and laying on of richly figured veneers.

H. 91¹/₄ inches
The Metropolitan Museum of Art, Gift of John C. Cattus, 67.262.1

99

Inside the seat rail of this Gothic side chair is the stencil: "From/A. & F. ROUX/479 Broadway/N.Y." Alexander Roux, a Parisian cabinetmaker working in New York from 1837 to 1881, was joined in partnership by his brother Frederick for only two years, in 1847 at 478 Broadway and in 1848 across the street at 479. This oak chair can therefore be dated 1848. Based somewhat on French Restauration prototypes, chairs of this type owe their Gothic feeling to the pointed arches between the balusters and the trefoils pierced through the cresting rail. This kind of chair is best known through its association with the White House. A number

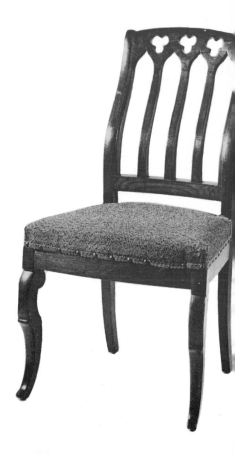

98

Designed and made in New York about 1835 to 1840 in the early days of the Gothic revival, this mahogany cabinet and bookcase is a curious combination of "pillar and scroll" Restauration and Gothic styles. The lower section, with its curved side doors and flat center one below a torus-front drawer, follows the general plan of a sideboard illustrated in Meeks's 1833 broadside (see no.

of them, made of walnut, have been shown in paintings and prints of Lincoln's cabinet room, and have been attributed to Joseph Meeks and Son on the basis of the Meeks bill to the White House for "12 BW [black walnut?]" Gothic chairs purchased in 1846 and 1847. Mahogany versions are also known, and it seems probable that several firms made chairs of this type. The Roux chairs are distinctive not only in being of oak but in the shape of the upper front leg, which has a scroll and French detailing, while the others have less successful thin, plain front legs.

H. 34³/₈ inches
Patricia E. Smith, New Canaan,
Connecticut

100

The slanted writing surface of this Gothic revival desk and bookcase lifts up to reveal the stenciled mark of the firm that made it, in the years between 1836 and 1850: "J & J.W. MEEKS/MAKERS/No 14 Vesey St/NEW YORK." Best known for their furniture in the late classical Restauration style (see no. 68) or the "pillar and scroll" style appearing in their widely circulated 1833 broadside, the Meekses also produced furniture in other styles with simple lines and elegant though restrained detailing, as here. On the lower section of this desk and bookcase rosewood panels are set off by moldings with Gothic cusps; behind the pointed-arch and quatrefoil tracery of the glass doors is a superb satinwood interior. When the molded desk drawer is pulled out and the curved rosewood slide pushed up, satinwood appears again in drawers, pigeonholes, and compartments of the desk interior. Few pieces of furniture of the period can surpass this one for quality of craftsmanship. The same high standards are apparent in the only other known Gothic revival Meeks desk and bookcase, privately owned, which is virtually identical to this one except that it is made of walnut and has slight variations in the mullions.

H. 91³/₄ inches
The Metropolitan Museum of Art, Rogers Fund, 69.19

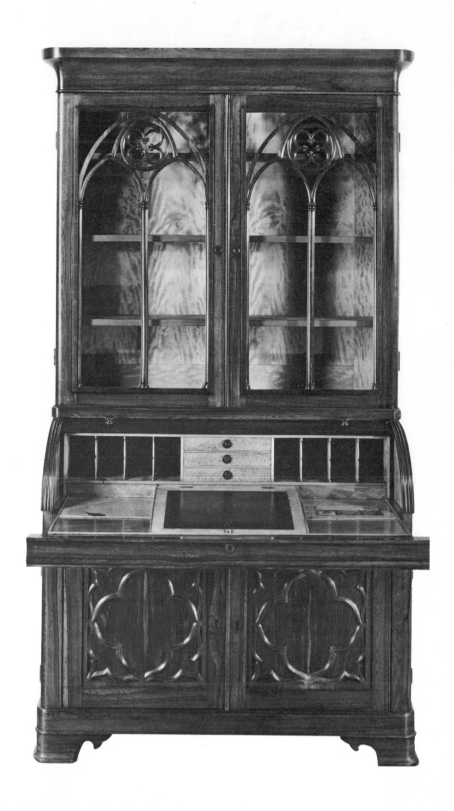

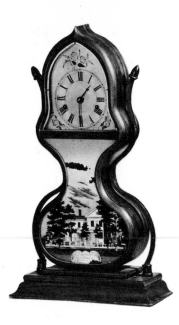

101

The name "acorn clock" has been given to examples like this with an acorn-shaped top on the case and acorn finials on the side bracings. Those that are marked bear the paper label of Jonathan Clark Brown, which sometimes includes his company name and location, Forrestville Manufacturing Company, Bristol, Connecticut. Made between 1847 and 1850, this type of clock is an unusual form. When inexpensive coiled springs were developed for clock movements, small shelf clocks could be manufactured and marketed at a low price. For the small movement Brown worked out this distinctive casing, which is particularly fitting for the period. The shape of the case, here pine veneered with laminated rosewood, can be interpreted as neoclassical, Gothic, or rococo, depending upon whether one sees the form as the acorn motif of the Empire style, the arch as pointed and Gothic, or the whole case as whimsical and rococo. Painted on the glass is the Greek revival house Brown purchased in 1847.

H. 24 inches
Henry Ford Museum, Dearborn, Michigan

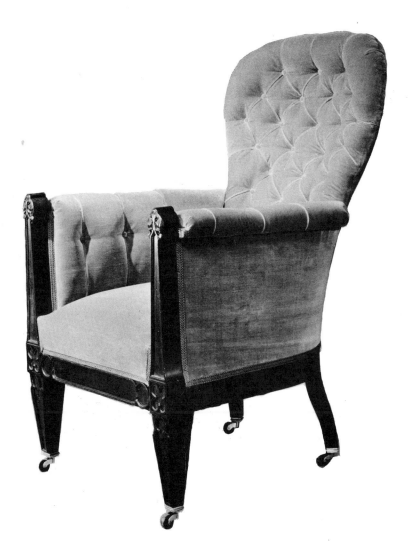

102

Paneled and carved front stiles, seat rails, and legs were not new when this walnut Gothic easy chair was made, probably in New York about 1850. Such treatment had occurred in the 1820s on late classical furniture illustrated in the pattern books of Smith, Nicholson, and Ackermann, but here Gothic arches, quatrefoils, and leaf carving were added to the front of the chair to make it fashionable. Fashionable also was the unusually deep seat, the high rounded back, and the tufting, which here follows the pattern of the original upholstery. The chair descended in the Delano family of Barrytown, New York, and was probably among the furnishings of the original part of their house *Steen Valetje* ("Stone Valley"), built in 1852, which included a library with Gothic architectural ornament. By the middle years of the century the concept had developed that certain styles were appropriate for the different rooms in a house; thus, Louis XV was thought correct for bedrooms and parlors, while Gothic, perhaps because of its connotations of remoteness and scholarly asceticism, was thought suitable for libraries.

H. 43⁵/₈ inches
The Metropolitan Museum of Art, Rogers Fund, 67.148

103

This bronze and brass Gothic chandelier once
lit the parlor of a Gothic revival cottage at
86 Spring Street, Portland, Maine. Designer of
the cottage was Scottish-born architect Henry
Rowe, who worked in London, Boston, and
New York before coming to Portland early
in 1845. In that year he advertised that "H.
Rowe would refer to J. J. Brown's Gothic Cottage in Spring street, as a specimen of his
workmanship and *design.*" For the cottage,
rich in Gothic ornament, the owner chose,
perhaps with Rowe's advice, this chandelier.
On its four scrolling branches are Gothicized
classical anthemia with pendants; the paneled urn from which they radiate has a band
of Gothic pendants below freestanding
leaves; the brass baluster is decorated with
applied cast-bronze Gothic ornament. The
Gothic revival seems particularly suitable in
a chandelier, for it was a style that depended
to a great extent upon the romantic contrasts
of light and shadow.

H. 40 inches
The Metropolitan Museum of Art, Rogers
Fund, 67.193

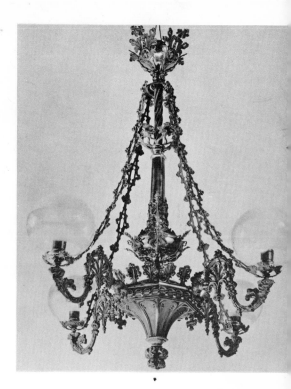

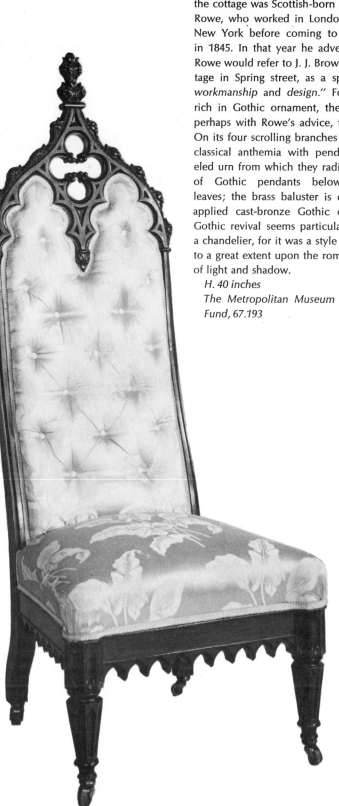

104

New York City cabinetmakers were not the
only ones to produce stylish furniture in the
mid-nineteenth century; there were also
talented and up-to-date craftsmen in the
smaller cities in the environs of the growing
metropolis. John Jelliff, who worked in Newark from 1835 to 1890, executed this handsome rosewood Gothic revival side chair
about 1855; it is said by family tradition to be
based on a design by his daughter Mary. Like
much of his furniture it has finely carved detailing, in the pierced quatrefoil and the elaborate finial. Jelliff worked principally in walnut and rosewood and made pieces in the
rococo and Louis XVI styles as well as the
Gothic. There are pencil sketches in Jelliff's
hand for Gothic furniture ornament, including chair tops with quatrefoils and crockets
similar to those here.

H. 58³/₄ inches
The Newark Museum, Gift of the Estate of
Florence P. Eagleton

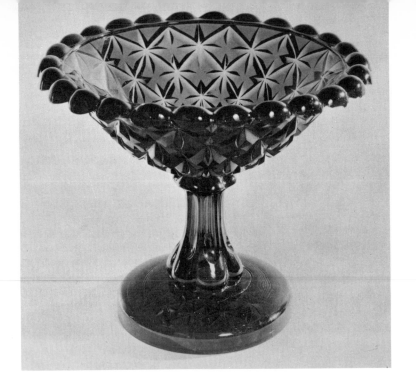

105

In this amethyst pressed glass compote, made at Sandwich in the 1840s, the star motif, which had appeared first on neoclassical English cut glass of the end of the eighteenth century, is employed in a symmetrical pattern. The star is deeper and larger than in the earlier examples, suiting the taste for monumental forms evident in furniture of the late Empire style. The paneled stem and the boldly gadrooned lip of the bowl emphasize the massiveness of the piece. Mixtures and processes for creating a certain color, difficult to achieve, were carefully guarded secrets of each of the glasshouses. This amethyst color, particularly popular in the period, was proof of the skill of the Boston and Sandwich Glass Company as well as a reaction against the clear glass important earlier.

H. 9¹/₂ inches
Mr. and Mrs. Samuel B. Feld, New York

106

Inspired by the colored and cut glass produced in Bohemia, American glasshouses in the 1840s began to produce glass both in different colors and in combinations of colors by overlay and cutting. This lamp, made at the Boston and Sandwich Glass Company in the 1850s, is of opaque white laid over ruby glass, a warm and vibrant combination. The dome-shaped foot and baluster create a form whose squat proportions—a reaction against the earlier classicism—are exaggerated by the character of the cutting. William E. Kern, later a superintendent of the factory at Sandwich, was given this lamp as a reward for his achievement of the combination of white and ruby glass.

H. 19 inches
The Metropolitan Museum of Art, Funds from Various Donors, 67.7.23

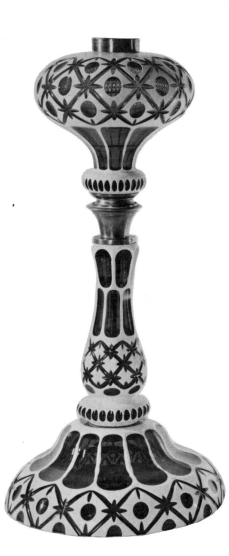

107

References to two-color Bohemian glass were plentiful during the 1830s and 40s in advertisements and on billheads of glass dealers. At manufacturers' exhibitions, like those held at the American Institute in New York, dealers tended to emphasize imported works as having more cachet, but American-made Bohemian glass was also shown. Typical of the American products is this tall covered vase in ruby and clear overlay glass cut in a rosette and diamond pattern, made at the New England Glass Company about 1845. It has a bolder, simpler design than would European work, which often combined engraving and cutting for a much richer effect. As in the lamp no. 106, the details of this vase, taken one by one, are classical, but the relationship between the parts and the intricate surface treatment are anticlassical and give the whole an almost Gothic feeling.

H. 29³/₄ inches
The Toledo Museum of Art, Gift of Dr. Frank W. Gunsaulus

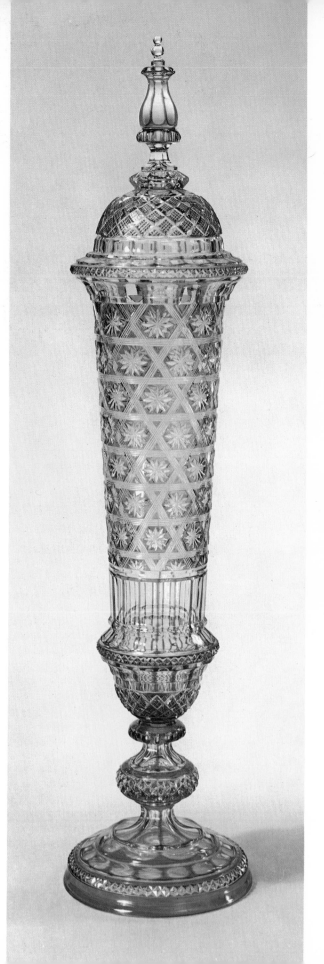

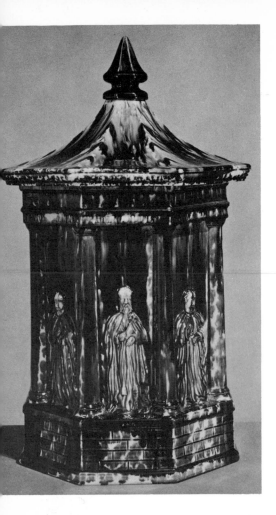

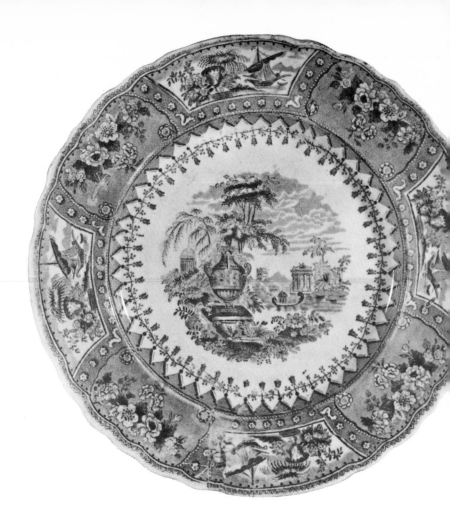

108 Eight apostles stand in niches around the outside of this octagonal water cooler, made by the United States Pottery Company of Bennington, Vermont, for exhibition at the New York Crystal Palace of 1853. Apostles had been introduced in Gothic revival designs for such diverse objects as pitchers and spittoons, so that the least of details in a room might carry out the Gothic spirit. Here, however, the architectural setting for the figures is more like an eighteenth-century garden pavilion than a medieval chapel. The United States Pottery Company, a result of the reorganization in 1852 of Lyman, Fenton and Company, was run by Christopher Webber Fenton, whose innovations and experiments made Bennington famous as a center for pottery. The cooler was one of the first pieces produced after Fenton hired an able modeler, Daniel Greatbach, to make molds. The glaze on this piece, flint enamel, is a variation of the ordinary mottled brown glaze called Rockingham, which had been popular since it was first made in England in the eighteenth century. The flint enamel had additional colors, particularly blue. On the underside of the cover is a circular mark reading: "Lyman Fenton Co./BENNINGTON, Vt./Fenton's / ENAMEL / PATENTED / 1849." The frieze is marked over six of the eight figures: "FENTON'S ENAMEL/PATENTED 1849/LYMAN FENTON & CO/MANUFACTURERS/BENNINGTON/VERMONT."

H. 23½ inches
The Brooklyn Museum

109

Blue and white ceramics were the most popular wares for the American table in the nineteenth century. Most of them were imported in quantity from England. Made by the American Pottery Company, active in Jersey City in the 1840s, this plate is a rare example of a domestic blue and white product based on English Staffordshire designs.

The engraved transfer-print decoration of a landscape framed by a paneled border of flowers and landscapes is derived from the English models, but is less detailed. English manufacturers often decorated their American exports with views of American landmarks; this American manufacturer has used a more general, romantic theme. The mark on the underside is an oval with, in the outer border, "AMERICAN POTTERY/JERSEY CITY," and in the center, "MANUFACTURERS," an urn, and "CANOVA," the name of the pattern.

Diam. 9¹/₈ inches
The Brooklyn Museum

110

Hound-handled pitchers, a standard mid-nineteenth-century form first produced in England in the Staffordshire region and then at many American potteries, are evidence of the technological improvements and esthetic changes of the period. The pitchers are made of yellow ware, a pottery developed for mass production and usually covered with Rockingham glaze. They are cast in molds to simplify the manufacturing process and also to enable the enterprising potter to utilize a sculptor's talents for the relief designs. This example of about 1847 was marked in a relief circle on the underside by its maker, Harker, Taylor and Company, East Liverpool, Ohio. This company was one of several potteries founded in East Liverpool by English potters, who introduced new methods of production to the United States. The theme of the pitcher is a deer hunt, which is rendered with some sophistication. The same scenes were often repeated on pitchers made by different manufacturers, suggesting that to be a moldmaker required technical proficiency rather than originality.

H. 11 7/16 inches
The Metropolitan Museum of Art, Edgar J. Kaufmann Charitable Foundation Fund, 69.70

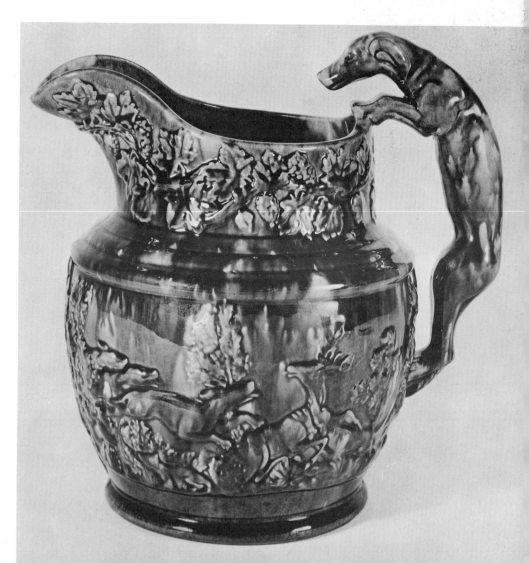

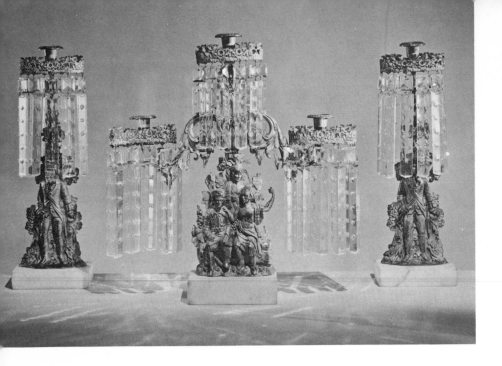

112

The first American attempts at gas lighting were made at the very beginning of the nineteenth century. In Baltimore, where this ornate gas lamp, one of a pair, was used, there were gas street lights as early as 1817, but not until about 1855, when the lamp was made, were many homes lit by gas. The gilt-bronze stand and arms are typical of rococo revival designs, but the pair is distinguished by the small heads and busts on the arms and the putto at the juncture of arms and stand—elaboration found only on the best bronze work of the time. The glass pendants add their elegance to the richness of floral, leaf, and scroll motifs that conceal the functional piping, and floral leaf motifs on the glass shades are in keeping with the rococo spirit.

H. 34¹/₂ inches

The Metropolitan Museum of Art, Rogers Fund, 67.27.1

111

Cornelius and Company of Philadelphia, one of the largest manufacturers of light fixtures in the United States during much of the nineteenth century, represented a variety of themes in mantel sets such as this candelabrum with flanking candlesticks made about 1840 to 1850. Early in the century technological innovation had made molded bronze inexpensive and easily worked, and thus sculptured stands became a popular medium for a growing American interest in historicism. Pocahontas and Ivanhoe were among the subjects offered by Cornelius and Company; the man in the center here is very likely Daniel Boone, who became a world-wide celebrity after Byron devoted seven stanzas in "Don Juan" to him in 1823. Boone sits beside an Indian with another behind him. The scene is completed by eighteenth-century soldiers on the candleholders. The pieces are marked on the back with the company name and stamped "PATENT/AP [. . .] 18 [41?]." The patent of 1841 was for a gas lamp; reference to it would have shown progressiveness, so important to prospective customers in the nineteenth century. The rings that hold the cut-glass prisms are in a floral pattern with birds, in the rococo revival style.

H. 17³/₄ inches

The Metropolitan Museum of Art, Gift of Mary E. Steers, 61.231.1-3

113

Bohemian-style glass, blue over clear, is used for the baluster-shaped column and the bowl of this gilt-bronze gas chandelier made about 1850. The chandelier was used in Massachusetts and very likely originated there, either at the Boston and Sandwich Glass Company or the New England Glass Company, both of which were making fine Bohemian-style glass at the time (see nos. 106, 107). Decoration of glass with color instead of deep-cut patterns was common at mid-century, achieving a richness and softness consistent with the rococo revival. The gilt-bronze framework—in the curve of the arms, motifs of rose and leaf on the rings, and scrolled links making up the connecting chains—is also typical of the rococo revival. These parts could well have been made by Henry N. Hooper and Company, the foundry that probably supplied lighting devices to the Boston area in as great quantity as did Cornelius and Company for Philadelphia (see no. 111).

H. 54 inches

The Metropolitan Museum of Art, Rogers Fund, 69.170

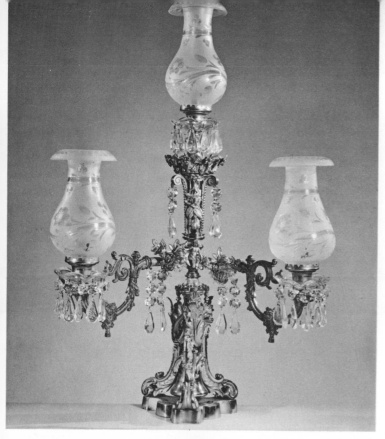

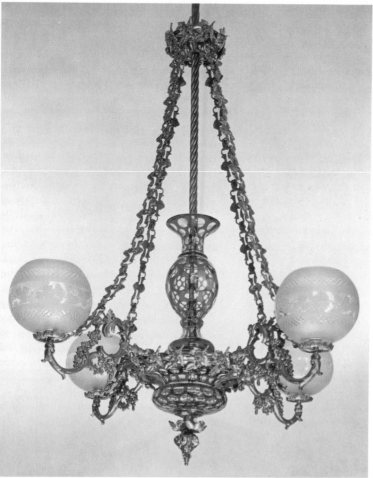

114

Thomas Webster in his *Domestic Economy* (1845) described the solar lamp, of which this is an example, as a "late improvement of considerable importance," in which a specially constructed cap on the wick feeds more oxygen to the flame. "But a still greater advantage . . . of this principle," Webster went on to say, "is that . . . Argand's lamp can be made to burn the coarse oils without either smoke or smell, equally with the best spermaceti oil." Here the font is a vase with a flat rococo revival leaf decoration, and just below, supporting the ring of air holes, is another vase of leaflike forms. Subtlety is shown in the use of the rococo scroll and leaf on the foot and in the matte finish of most of the gilt-bronze surface. The frosted glass on the shade, which diffused the light, is cut with Gothic arches and a classical basket of flowers, insuring the lamp's suitability for any room, no matter what its style. "E. F. JONES./BOSTON./PATENT./JANUARY. 11. 1859." is marked on the head of the screw that adjusts the wick. The patent was probably for an improved wick casing, since the lamp form had been introduced in the 1840s.

H. with globe 26¹/₄ inches
The Metropolitan Museum of Art, Anonymous Gift Fund, 68.111.2

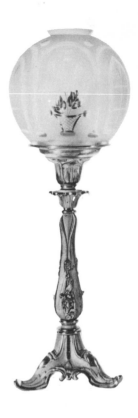

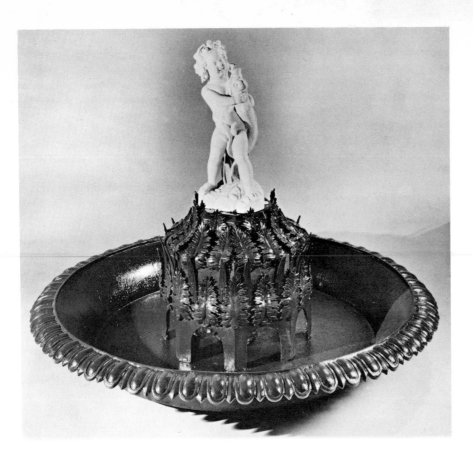

ary, urns, arbors, trellises, and summer houses; tables, chairs, beds, and piano stools; stands for umbrellas, hats, coats, flowers, or music—even foot scrapers and spittoons. Fountains such as this were made in separate component parts, which clients could order in different combinations. A fountain of this small size would probably have been for a private garden; a more elaborate combination might have embellished one of the many public parks established in American cities in the 1850s.

Diam. 58³/4 inches

The Metropolitan Museum of Art, Rogers Fund, 69.8

115 Among the techniques that came into widespread use through the industrialism of the nineteenth century was the molding, or casting, of iron. As early as 1823 Rudolph Ackermann in London could write, in *A Series, Containing Forty-four Engravings in Colours, of Fashionable Furniture:* "The rapid improvement that has taken place in the manufacture of cast iron, has elevated it from its late uses in ponderous and gross articles merely, to those of ornamental embellishment; not only where strength is required, but where lightness and elegance are purposed to be united, and to which may be superadded, a considerable economy." By 1851 the cast-iron and glass Crystal Palace that housed the great London exhibition was indisputable recognition of the usefulness of the material—although many were still to be persuaded of its beauty—and the New York Crystal Palace two years later copied both materials and name. By the mid-1850s, American foundries were advertising a great diversity of objects available in cast iron: railings and grilles; stoves, grates, and mantels; fountains, statu-

116

Patterns for cast-iron furniture were copied by rival manufacturers almost as soon as an item came on the market, and the advertisements of the different companies thus include many virtually identical pieces, which if they proved popular continued to be made through the century. This settee and matching chair were called "rustic" by all the firms that advertised them, including, among others, the Boston Ornamental Iron Works, which advertised the settee in 1857 in a three- or four-foot-long model, the J. W. Fiske Company of New York, which advertised it during the 1860s, and Samuel S. Bent of New York, who was still selling it in the early 90s. The desire for rusticity is part of the same nineteenth-century romanticism that sought to revive the Gothic spirit, and apparently the incongruity either in the multiplication of the model or in the cold heaviness of the cast-iron branches did not disturb the customer. Characteristic of mid-nineteenth century is the naturalism that showed the branches and leaves to be unmistakably of oak, and, in two places on the back of the settee, even a cord binding the branches.

L. settee 48 inches

The Metropolitan Museum of Art; settee: Edgar J. Kaufmann Charitable Foundation Fund, 69.158.2; chair: Rogers Fund, 69.159.2

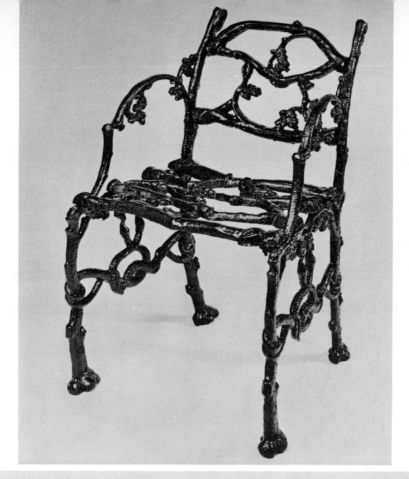

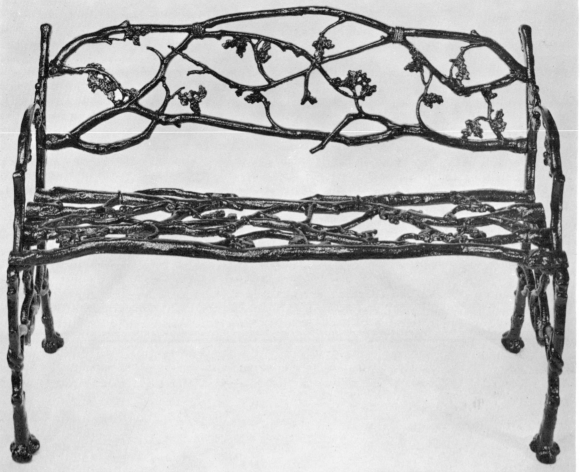

117

Urns were widely available in cast iron in different shapes, most, like this one, with a Renaissance and ultimately a classical prototype. The gadrooning, the heads at the juncture of handles and body, and the decorative rinceaux are all from the classical repertory. Similar vases were advertised in Boston and New York during the 1850s and 60s; this one is illustrated in a catalogue of the Van Dorn Iron Works of Cleveland, Ohio, published in 1884. Since this catalogue shows pieces that existed in the fifties, the pattern for the vase may have been made at that time; in any case, like other cast-iron pieces, it certainly remained available long after it first appeared on the market.

H. 36³/₄ inches

The Metropolitan Museum of Art, Edgar J. Kaufmann Charitable Foundation Fund, 69.158.3

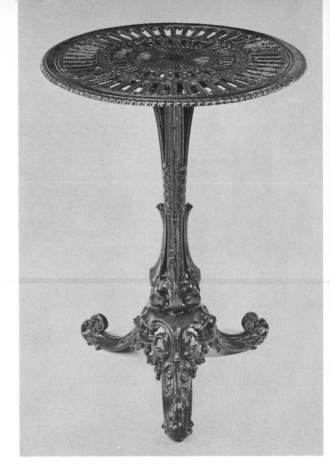

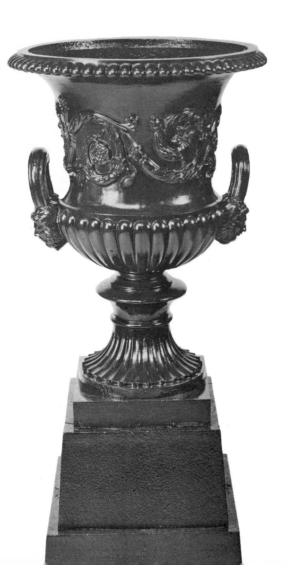

118 The pattern of the table shown here is one of a large number pictured in catalogues of cast iron, and further variation was provided by the fact that pedestals and tops were made separately and combined to suit the buyer's need and taste. Pieces in cast iron thus, quite naturally, were the earliest kind of furniture to be made on principles of standardization and interchangeable parts, the marks of industrial production that by the end of the century were to become the norm for manufacture of most household items.

H. 28¹/₂ inches

The Metropolitan Museum of Art, Anonymous Gift Fund, 68.168

119 Patented in England in 1846, the design for this cast-iron bench was copied and patented in the United States by 1848. The existence of a patent, however, was no deterrent to the enterprising businessman, and in the 1850s the piece was cast by numerous American foundries, from Chase Brothers and Company of Boston to the Vulcan Iron Works of New Boston, Illinois. This example, probably from the Vulcan Works, was purchased by pioneer nurseryman Suel Foster for his garden at the Fountain Hill Nursery, Muscatine, Iowa. Basic-

ally rococo revival in style, with decorative scrolls and leafage, the bench also has elements of the Gothic revival in the arch pattern of the back. In the 1854 catalogue of a New York City firm and in later catalogues it is designated a "Gothic settee." The pattern remained popular until the end of the nineteenth century.

L. 44¹/₂ inches
The Metropolitan Museum of Art, Gift of
Mr. and Mrs. James B. Tracy, Inst. 66.4

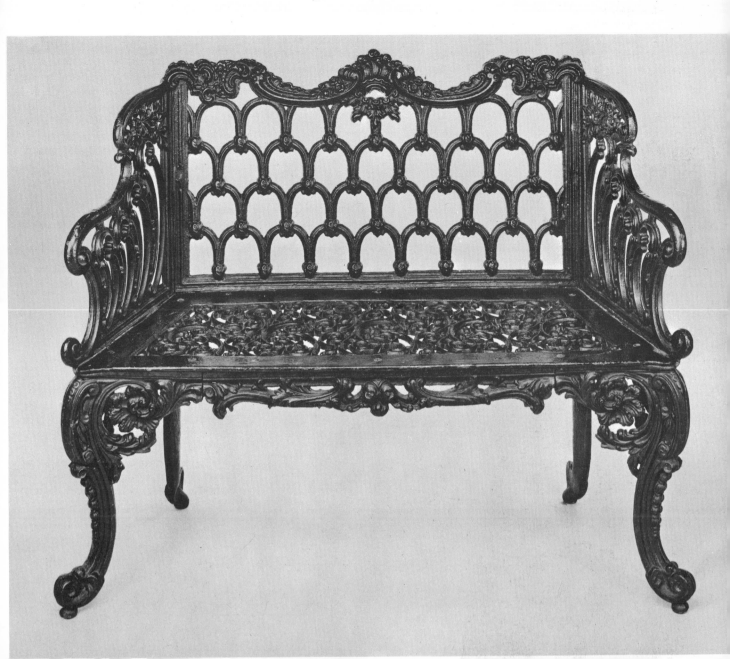

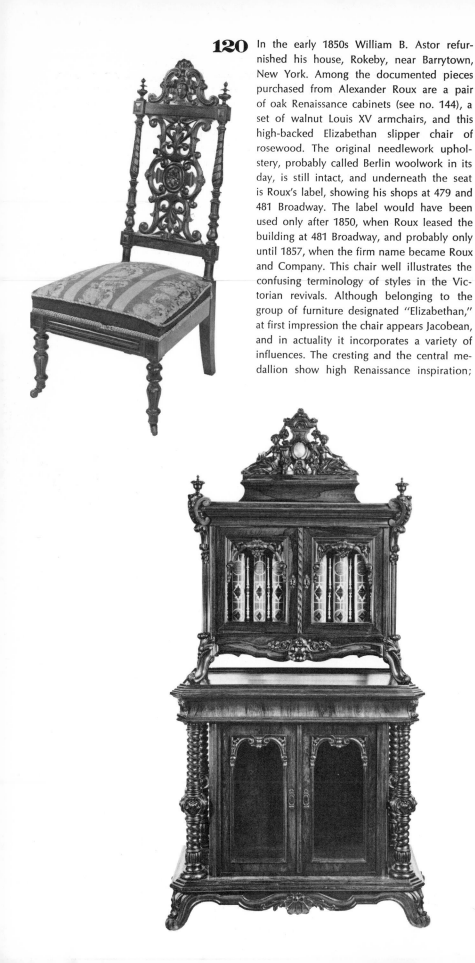

120 In the early 1850s William B. Astor refurnished his house, Rokeby, near Barrytown, New York. Among the documented pieces purchased from Alexander Roux are a pair of oak Renaissance cabinets (see no. 144), a set of walnut Louis XV armchairs, and this high-backed Elizabethan slipper chair of rosewood. The original needlework upholstery, probably called Berlin woolwork in its day, is still intact, and underneath the seat is Roux's label, showing his shops at 479 and 481 Broadway. The label would have been used only after 1850, when Roux leased the building at 481 Broadway, and probably only until 1857, when the firm name became Roux and Company. This chair well illustrates the confusing terminology of styles in the Victorian revivals. Although belonging to the group of furniture designated "Elizabethan," at first impression the chair appears Jacobean, and in actuality it incorporates a variety of influences. The cresting and the central medallion show high Renaissance inspiration; the turned stiles are close to seventeenth-century prototypes; and the C-scrolls of the back and cresting are similar to the scrolls of the baroque and rococo. The lightness of the chair, the delicacy of the turnings, and the shortness of the legs, however, mark it as of the nineteenth century.

H. 43 inches

The Family of Richard C. Aldrich, Barrytown, New York

121

In 1850, in a gesture that sounds like a presentation pun, New York firemen gave Jenny Lind, the "Swedish Nightingale," a specially bound set of Audubon's *Birds of America;* it was, she felt, her "most beautiful souvenir of America." It was given to her in a rosewood bookcase with a presentation plaque and the label of the Brooks Cabinet Warehouse, 127 Fulton Street, Brooklyn. In effect two bookcases, one on top of the other, the piece is an excellent example of the confusion of styles during the 1840s and 50s. The molded and carved aprons, curved legs, and French scroll feet are taken from the rococo. The twisted columns were considered by Victorians to be Elizabethan, although they actually derived from earlier sources, including Roman and baroque, and are also found on furniture some seventy years after Elizabeth during the reign of Charles II. The pediment, with its arched cresting and seated goddesses holding the symbols of music and plenty, flanking the dedicatory cartouche, has its source in sixteenth-century Renaissance furniture. Brooks Cabinet Warehouse was the firm of Thomas Brooks, first listed in the Brooklyn directories as a cabinetmaker in partnership with Lorenzo Blackstone in 1841 and 1842. In the 1853 New York Crystal Palace exhibition he displayed a fantastic sideboard also combining various styles. To the writer in *The World of Science, Art, and Industry Illustrated from Examples in the New-York Exhibition,* however, it was "Renaissance," a "style which began a few years ago [and] keeps pace with the increase of wealth and the prevalence of ornamental architecture."

H. 72 inches

Museum of the City of New York, Gift of Arthur S. Vernay

122

Delicacy without frailty, strength without stiffness, ornamentation without over-elaboration—the best qualities of two revival styles, rococo and Gothic, are combined in this rosewood side chair made in New York in the 1850s. Still bearing its original red and buff needlepoint covering in a modified fleur-de-lys pattern, the chair is basically rococo in its curving planes. Molded front apron and legs ending in volutes, scrolling stiles and stay rail, and leaf-carved cresting all follow the precepts of the Victorian rococo. Gothicism is apparent only in small details: leaf carving at the base of the balusters, a suggestion of arches formed by the scrolls above, and the turned pendants at either side of the cresting rail. Pendants of the same kind decorate the top of the rosewood stand, which has a scrolled apron like the scrolled rail of the chair back. The leaf carving at the center of the stretcher and at the base of the channeled side columns is similar in design to that on the balusters of the chair.

H. chair 34 inches
The Metropolitan Museum of Art; chair: Edgar J. Kaufmann Charitable Foundation Fund, 68.202.2; stand: Gift of Ronald S. Kane, 67.269.1

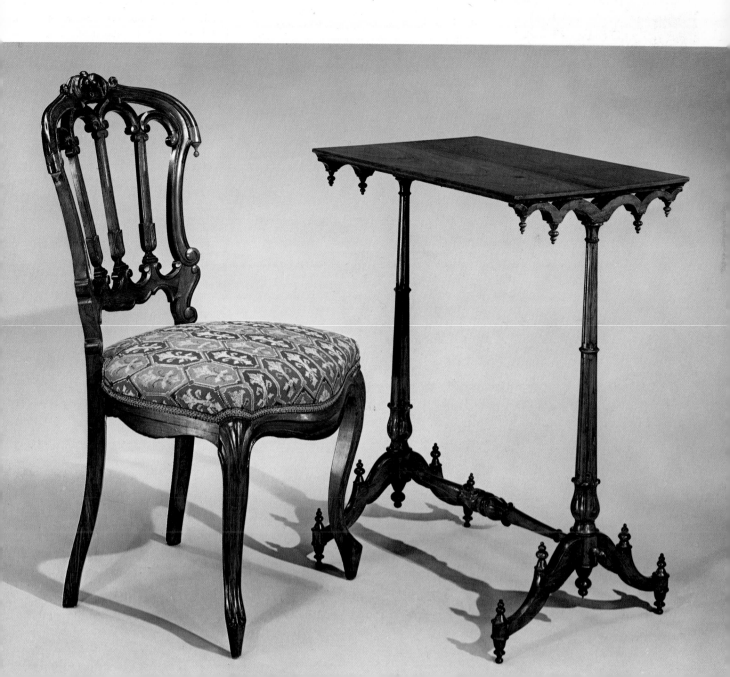

123

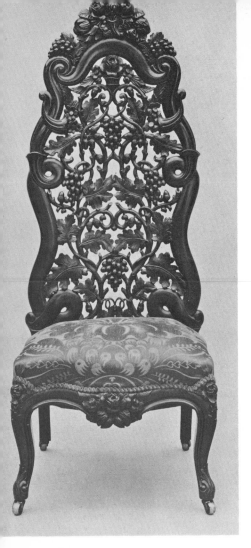

The rococo revival in furniture, which had begun in Europe in the 1820s and 30s, became a significant trend in America by 1845 and dominated the mid-century medley of styles into the 1860s. In this rosewood side chair made in New York about 1855 are almost all of the characteristics of the style variously called by Victorians "the antique French style," "the modern French style" (since it was in vogue), "Louis Quatorze," and "Louis Quinze" (both of which are inaccurate, although the latter is less so). Based upon the eighteenth-century rococo, with its strong C- and S-curves and scrolls, furniture of the Victorian rococo often had, as here, cabriole legs, French scroll feet—sometimes with a leaf scroll like these—and extravagant use of carved naturalistic curving ornament. On this chair, branches bearing oak leaves and acorns intertwined with a vine heavy with grapes form the laminated back. Crowning the whole is a small basket of roses, and above the cresting rail a correspondingly small cornucopia overflowing with roses and leaves. Although furniture of this type—either carved or laminated and carved—was produced by many craftsmen, it has been par- ticularly associated with one master, John Henry Belter (see nos. 124, 125).

H. 44¹/₄ inches

The Metropolitan Museum of Art, Gift of Mr. and Mrs. Lowell Ross Burch and Miss Jean McLean Morron, 51.79.9

124

At the top of a leg of this rococo revival rosewood center table is the label used by John Henry Belter between 1856 and 1861: "J.H. BELTER & CO./FACTORY WAREHOUSE /3rd Avenue 76th St 552 Broadway / MAN- UFACTURERS OF/ALL KINDS OF FINE FUR- NITURE/NEW YORK." Born in Germany in 1804, Belter was in New York by 1844, with a home and his first shop at 40¹/₂ Chatham Square. He had learned his trade, carving and cabinetmaking, in Württemberg, where he served his apprenticeship. In this country his German brothers-in-law, the Springmeyers, became his partners. Belter had up to forty apprentices, and many of the artisans working in his Broadway shops, first at 372, then at 547, at 552, and at 722, and also in his Third

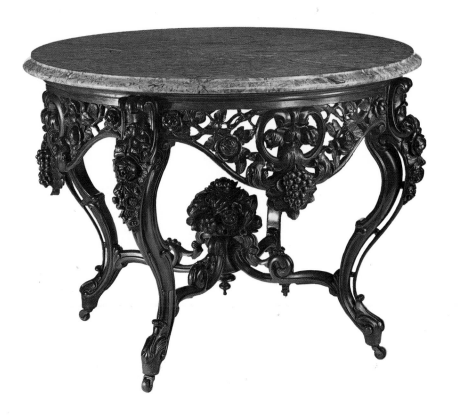

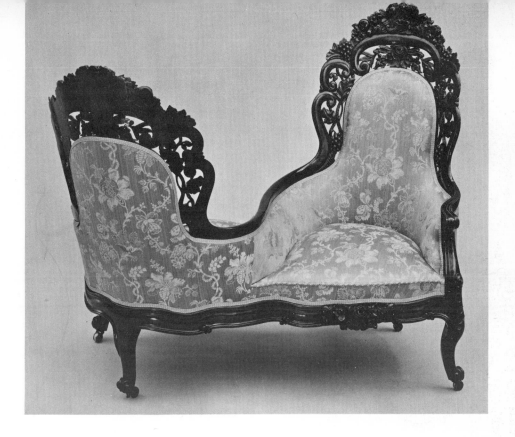

Avenue factory, were German immigrants who came to America after the European revolutions of 1848. The sure touch of a master carver can be seen here in the flowered brackets on the graceful curving legs, a scrolled saltire stretcher with a central bouquet of flowers, and lacy laminated, pierced apron of flowers, leaves, and grapes. The top is an oval of veined green marble.

H. 28¹/₄ inches

Museum of the City of New York, Gift of Mr. and Mrs. Ernest Gunther Vietor

125 Victorian love of innovation showed in a number of new furniture forms, among them the tête-à-tête, or love seat, sometimes made as two chairs facing in opposite directions and joined at the sides. This rococo revival example in laminated rosewood was made in New York in the 1850s, possibly in the Belter factory. As in the chair no. 123 bold S- and C-scrolls outline the backs and form the seat rail and cabriole legs; the decoration is carved flowers, leaves, vines, acorns, and grapes. The sinuous shape illustrates the im-

portance of lamination and bending, techniques not original to Belter, but which he perfected for the sake of strength, pliability, and lightness and for which he received a series of patents between 1847 and 1858. Belter used any number from four to sixteen layers; this piece has but eight, with total thickness approximately one-half inch. The wood was pressed in steam molds to achieve its curves. Writing, in 1908, memoirs called *Personal Experiences of an Old New York Cabinet Maker*, Ernest Hagen gave an invaluable record of mid-century New York cabinetmakers, their shops, and their working methods. Of lamination, he wrote that the whole procedure "made a very strong and not heavy chair back . . . all the ornamental carved work glued on after the perforated . . . back was sawed out and prepaired [*sic*]." Actually extra wood usually was glued on only for the high reliefs, as here.

H. 44¹/₂ inches

The Metropolitan Museum of Art, Gift of Mrs. Charles Reginald Leonard, in memory of Edgar Welch Leonard, Robert Jarvis Leonard, and Charles Reginald Leonard, 57.130.7

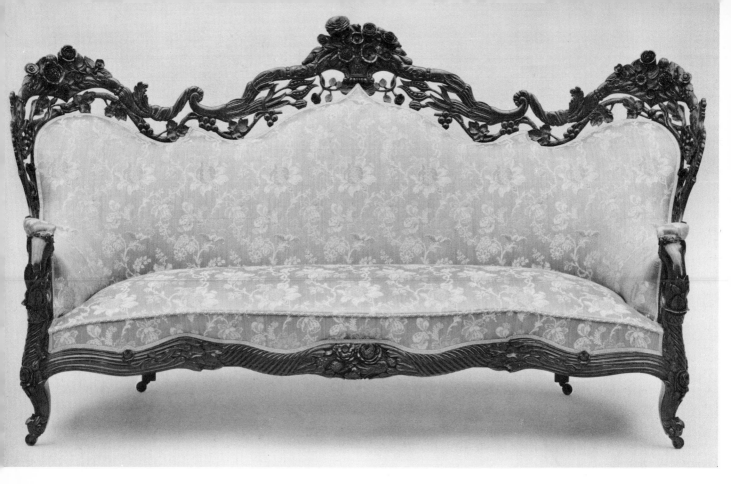

126

"Arabasket" was Belter's term for ornate carved and pierced rosewood furniture in the rococo revival style of the 1850s. The word is obviously a combination of "arabesque" and "basket." With its connotation of curving lines, sometimes in the shape of cornucopias, naturalistic flowers, leaves, fruit, vines, and acorns, arabasket seems appropriate, especially when, as on this sofa made in New York or the table no. 130, the central bouquet is in fact in a basket. That this type of furniture was never inexpensive is shown by a Belter invoice of September 1855 for similar pieces:

2 Arabasket Rosewood Sofas			175	$350.00
2	"	" Arm Chair	80	160.00
4	"	" Parlour "	45	180.00
1	"	" Centre table		175.00
1 Fine		" Etagere		300.00

All of this was designated "parlor furniture." Assembled in one room, it was a suitable material reflection of the flourishing, optimistic, expansive qualities of mid-century America.

L. 89³/₄ inches

The Metropolitan Museum of Art, Gift of Mrs. Charles Reginald Leonard, in memory of Edgar Welch Leonard, Robert Jarvis Leonard, and Charles Reginald Leonard, 57.130.1

127

With a back laminated in seven layers, bent, and carved, this New York rococo revival rosewood armchair of the 1850s, by an unknown maker, is similar to Belter's documented work. Belter, however, was not the only cabinetmaker producing such furniture. Competing with him were Charles A. Baudouine, Joseph Meeks and Son, and Charles Klein, all of New York, and Ignatius Lutz of Philadelphia. Of these the most serious competition came from Baudouine, whose work in the Belter style has been described in Hagen's memoirs. According to Hagen, Baudouine's

most conspicious [sic] productions were those rosewood heavy over decorated parlour suits with round perforated backs generally known as "Belter furniture" from the original inventor *John H. Belter, 372 B'dway, who had a shop near by. . . . Baudouine infringed on Belter's patent by making the backs out of 2 pieces with a center joint, and this way got the best of Belter, who died a very poor man.*

Baudouine, on the other hand, when he died, "left a fortune between 4 and 5 Millions."

H. 50 inches
The Metropolitan Museum of Art, Gift of Mrs. Charles Reginald Leonard, in memory of Edgar Welch Leonard, Robert Jarvis Leonard, and Charles Reginald Leonard, 57.130.2

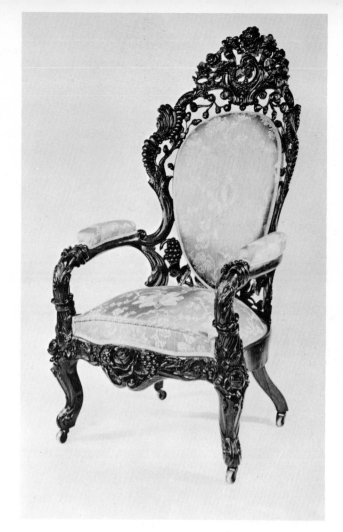

128

Extravagant carved solid rosewood C-scrolls and cornucopias form the stretcher of this rococo revival center table made in New York in the Belter style of 1850 to 1860. Each leg is composed of two contiguous S-scrolls with fruit and flowers at the juncture. Around the circular top is a wavy machine-made molding found also on late Empire furniture. The pierced and carved apron of scrolls, leaves, flowers, and acorns is made of laminated wood to achieve the strength needed for such an open and delicate design. The plain white marble top with its simple molded edge contrasts with the intricately worked rosewood.

H. 28¹/₂ inches
The Metropolitan Museum of Art, Gift of Mary E. Steers, 61.230

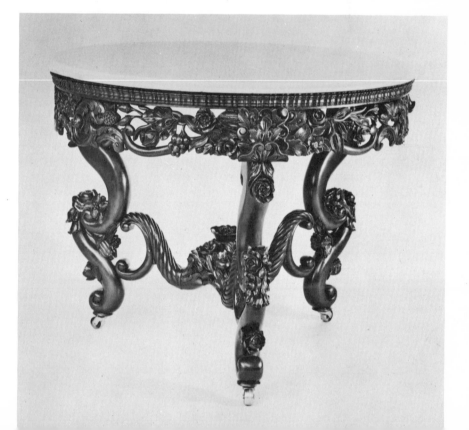

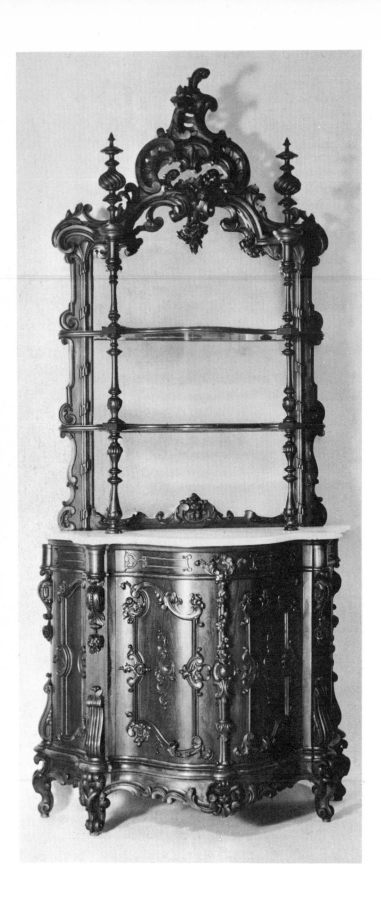

129 Not all ornate furniture of the rococo revival was laminated; this étagère made in New York about 1850 to 1860, perhaps by Roux, is of solid rosewood. Although walnut was often used for carved furniture, rosewood was favored for both solid and laminated pieces, because of the rich color, fine-patterned grain, and the high polish that could be attained. The wood derives its name from the faint roselike odor it gives off when cut or sawed. Here it has been shaped into a curving cabinet base and a mirror and shelf frame above, the whole surmounted by a bold and typically rococo cartouche flanked by turned finials. "Etagère" was simply the French name for a whatnot, a piece to display the varied knickknacks so dear to the Victorian heart. The mirrored backing makes a particularly effective place for objects in glass or porcelain.

H. 107¹/₄ inches

The Newark Museum, Gift of the Museum of the City of New York, 1934

130 The "line of beauty," as Hogarth called the serpentine curve of the eighteenth century, is the basis for the design of this rosewood rococo revival New York pier table of the 1850s. In a symmetrical and balanced plan, an S-curve forms each leg and each half of apron and stretcher. The center of the stretcher is a lifelike basket of flowers (see also nos. 123, 124, 126), and a female head in high relief is in the center of the apron, a touch more often found on furniture of the eighteenth-century European rococo or of the Renaissance revival. The incised diapered pattern on the apron is common to the 1850s, and is seen also on wallpapers and upholstery fabrics and in floral Brussels carpets. The unusual depth and fullness of the carving might have pleased Hogarth, whose doctrine in his 1753 *Analysis of Beauty* made it clear that the line of beauty is three dimensional and that beauty is based on seeing things in the round. A century later Victorians echoed his sentiments in both creations and words. The unknown author of an article on rococo furniture published in August 1850 in *Godey's Magazine and Lady's Book* might have been writing of this table when he said:

If we stop a moment to examine details, we will be especially struck . . . with the varied, in fact ever changing, curves of artistic carving of some beautiful wreath, with the boldness, depth, and sharpness of a *bouquet* or cluster; in another, with the hanging foliage, budding flowers, and waving scrolls, many of which are triumphs of the chisel.

In quality this superb table has much in common with documented work of Alexander Roux. There is a virtually identical table in the Madison, New Jersey, house (now part of Drew University) of Thomas Gibbons, for whom Roux is known to have made furniture. The gilt-bronze garniture on the table, a pair of candelabra and a double candelabrum supporting a fluted glass fruit bowl, came from the Van Rensselaer house in Albany. Its scrolling grapevine bearing leaves and grape clusters and the putti on lily pads at the bases complement the rococo quality of the table.

L. table 80 inches
Table: Museum of the City of New York, Gift of the Estate of Harold Wilmerding Bell; garniture: The Metropolitan Museum of Art, Gift of Mrs. F. Carrington Weems, 55.75.1-3.

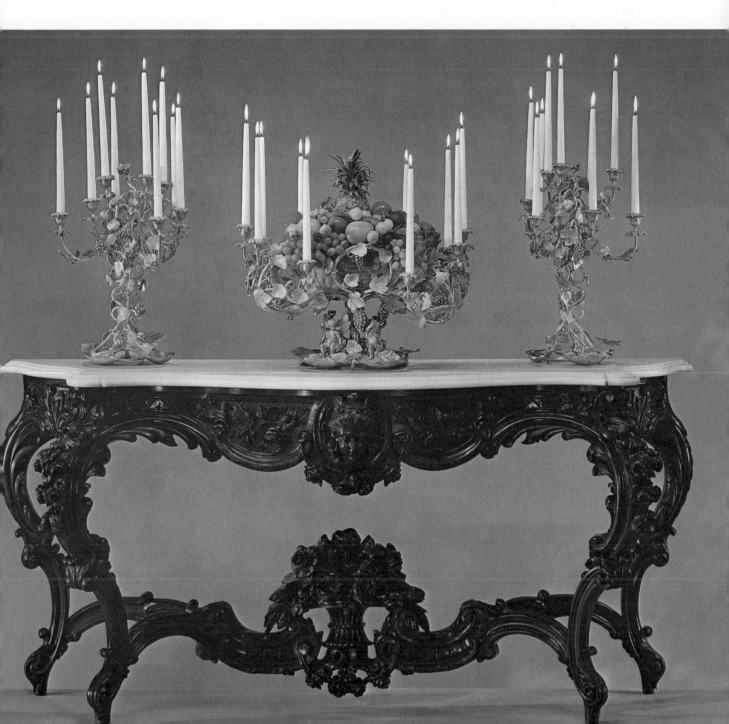

131

This gilt pier mirror, as well as the pair of sconces and bronze and gilt chandelier (nos. 134, 135), was part of the original furnishings of the parlor of a house that stood at 115 Elm Street, North Attleboro, Massachusetts, built for Edmund Ira Richards in 1853. The mirror reflected a room rich in the embellishments of its day: floral Wilton carpet, classical woodwork, diaper-patterned wallpaper in panels with elaborately molded borders centered by large rococo-Renaissance medallions. Primarily rococo in style, with its leafy scrolls and cartouche, the mirror also has a variation of the spiral twist molding often used in the period.

H. 112 inches
The Metropolitan Museum of Art, Gift of Mrs. Frederick Wildman, 64.36.2

132

Of carved, solid walnut, this rococo revival center table made in New York in the 1850s is an interesting contrast to flamboyant laminated furniture of the style and period (see nos. 123, 124). In its restraint, integration of decoration and structure, and emphasis upon the central motif of a shell framed by C-scrolls, it is close to eighteenth-century French rococo. Rococo probably de-

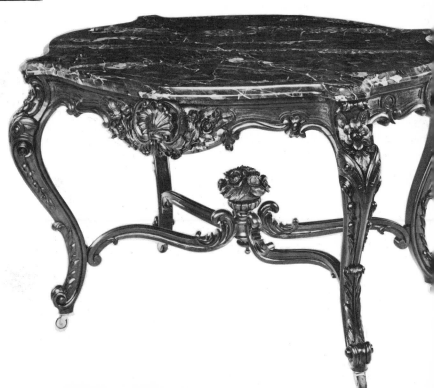

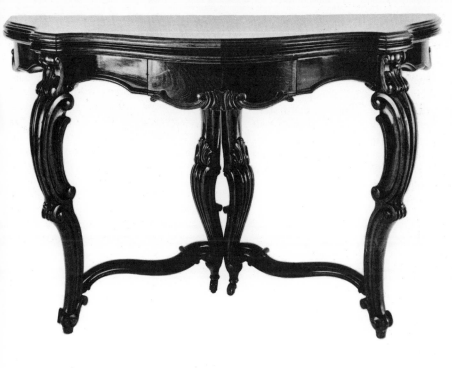

133

In March 1849 New York attorney George Templeton Strong, then building a house at 74 East Twenty-first Street, wrote of the efforts of his wife, Ellen, to furnish their new home: "If I hadn't spent money like an extravagant fool in my bachelor days I should have enough now to be able to tell her to march down to Baudoine's [sic] and order . . . whatever pleased her fancy. . . ." There was probably much to please her, for Charles Baudouine was at this time, according to Hagen, "the leading cabinetmaker of New York." The quality of his work can be seen in this rosewood rococo revival card table, bearing his stenciled mark for 1849 to 1854: "FROM/ C.A.BAUDOUINE / 335 / BROADWAY / NEW-YORK." Purchased by J. Watson Williams of Utica in 1852, the table is one of a pair that with tops closed could be put together to form what the original bill called a "multiform table." Its bold shape is emphasized by skillful touches of carving; its rear legs on casters pivot to support the baize-lined folding top. Baudouine, of French descent, was born in New York in 1808; he was first listed in the directories of 1829/30 at 508 Pearl Street. By 1839/40 he had moved to Broadway, where he remained at various locations until he apparently retired about 1855 or 1856. Hagen, who worked for him for two years after 1853, says that at the time Baudouine "employed about 70 cabinet makers, and including carvers, varnishers and upholsterers nearly 200 hands all told."

L. 46 inches
Munson-Williams-Proctor Institute, Utica

rived its name from the words *rocaille,* or "rockwork," and *coquille,* "shell," and was characterized by the use of these motifs as well as flower garlands. The frame of this table, which also bears flower and leaf motifs, shows how well black walnut lends itself to sharply defined carving. In the 1850s walnut came back into fashion. It was admired for its rich, dark, purplish-brown color, fine grain, and high luster. In addition it had strength and impermeability and contrasted strikingly with the brilliant stained-glass colors popular for upholstery, rugs, and draperies. John Fanning Watson in *Annals of Philadelphia* (1857) chronicled the return of the wood: " . . . in former days Walnut was the *common* furniture wood—as being second to Mahogany—As men got more wealthy it was discarded . . . and was sold as common fuel in my time—But now, it is again a wood of luxury. . . .".

L. 47¹/₂ inches
The Metropolitan Museum of Art, Gift of Mrs. Charles Reginald Leonard, in memory of Edgar Welch Leonard, Robert Jarvis Leonard, and Charles Reginald Leonard, 57.130.8

134 Bright gilding contrasts with the black flying Cupid in this gaslight sconce, one of a pair, from the North Attleboro parlor (see nos. 131, 135). It is clearly in the rococo spirit, with exuberant scrolls, cartouches, and spiraling floral and leafy forms hiding the gas pipes. Bearded and helmeted masks stand out at the midpoint on the curving descent of the arms, and small dog's heads in cartouches face front and back above the pendants. The nineteenth-century hand is evident in the fact that each rococo element is a focal point, rather than being submerged in the work as it would have been in the eighteenth century. The round glass globes are frosted and etched.

W. 24 inches

The Metropolitan Museum of Art, Gift of Mrs. Frederick Wildman, 64.36.4

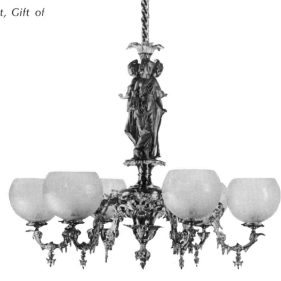

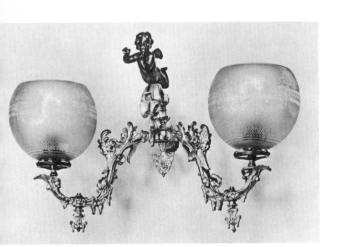

135 The parlor from which this bronze and gilt chandelier came, along with mirror and sconces (nos. 131, 134), was typical of its period in its mixture of several styles: rococo, Gothic, and Elizabethan in furniture, and classical in woodwork. In the chandelier is a similar combination. The twisted cable is a good example of the Victorian's disdain for too nice a distinction between styles. The spiral turning was applied liberally in the nineteenth century to furniture of the Renaissance, baroque, and rococo revivals, and even of the late Empire style. The scrolled arms are the same as those of the sconces. In the middle of the cable is a baroque element incorporating female busts; above the urn stand three full-length female figures representing

—in an expression of the Victorian love of symbolism—Art, Science, and Industry.

H. 66½ inches

The Metropolitan Museum of Art, Gift of Mrs. Frederick Wildman, 64.36.3

136

The cable seen on the mirror and chandelier (nos. 131, 135) and other decorative art forms of the mid-century appears on the crestings of this laminated rosewood sofa and armchair, where it resembles also classical gadrooning. The pieces are part of a set of rococo revival furniture made in New York about 1850 to 1860. Although furniture of this type has usually been associated with

Belter, this set differs from his documented pieces, which are lacier and more intricate. The bold curving shapes of this set and the Renaissance revival type of ornament on the center of the cresting and seat rails make it resemble a documented parlor suite produced by the Meeks firm in 1859 as a gift to Joseph W. Meeks's daughter, Sophia Teresa, on the occasion of her marriage to Dexter Hawkins. The suite, which descended in the family, has recently entered the American Wing collection. The backs of the pieces shown here are less attenuated and elaborate, but the bold simplicity of the shaping, particularly in the lower back of the chair, the arms, seat rails, and legs, strengthens the attribution of this sofa and chair to the firm. The Meekses, better known for their late classical furniture (see no. 68), were still among the most important furniture makers in New York in the fifties and sixties, and were known to have advertised rococo revival furniture during this period.

L. sofa 65 inches

The Metropolitan Museum of Art, Gift of Mr. and Mrs. Lowell Ross Burch and Miss Jean McLean Morron, 51.79.1,3

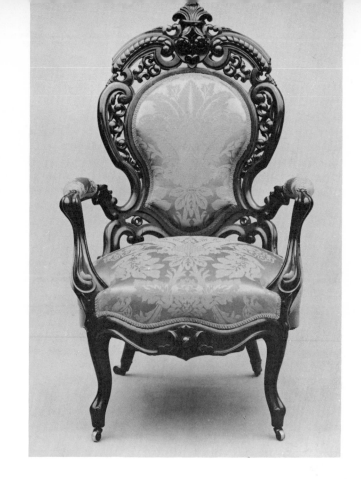

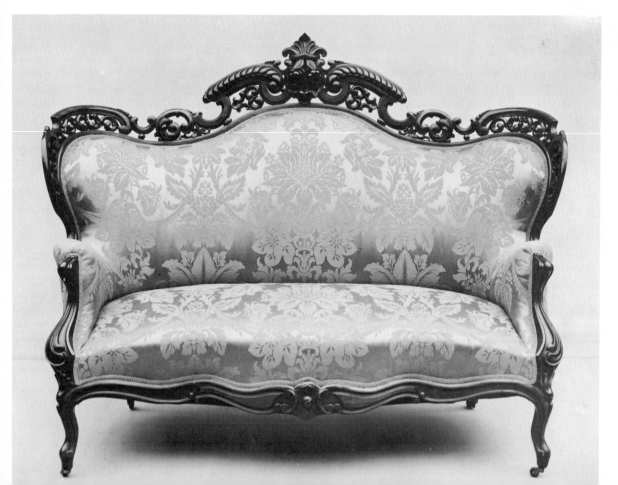

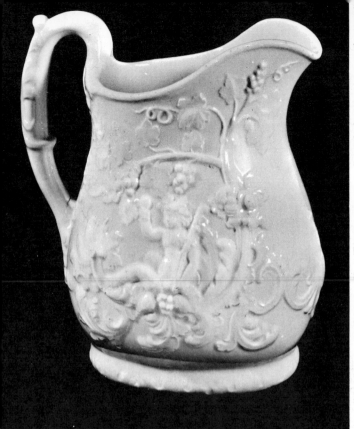

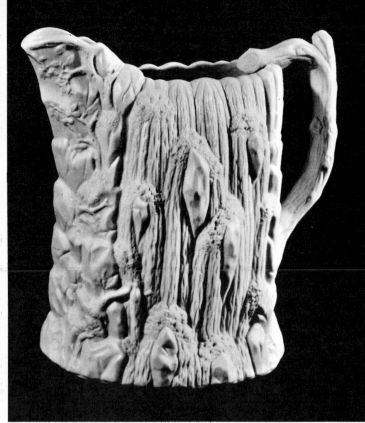

137

William Boch and Brother, later known as the Union Porcelain Works, began making porcelain in Greenpoint, New York, about 1853. The firm was ultimately taken over by Thomas C. Smith and did not close until about 1910. Early examples by Boch are scarce, but several pitchers like this one, made soon after the company's founding, have turned up. The squat, curving shape is an adaptation of a rococo design, and the young Bacchus in the grape arbor and foliate and scroll motifs framing the scene were inspired by eighteenth-century pattern books. This pitcher bears the mark "WB & BR'S./GREEN POINT L.I." on its underside; one from the same mold, decorated with gold and blue, now at the Henry Ford Museum, has the mark of the Union Porcelain Company rather than of William Boch.

H. 9³/₄ inches

The Metropolitan Museum of Art, Anonymous Gift Fund, 68.112

138

"Niagara Falls" is the name given to this pitcher made about 1853 and marked as the work of the United States Pottery Company, Bennington, Vermont. The material is Parian ware, a porcelain first introduced in England during the 1840s. Made from a special formula developed for producing unglazed pieces, Parian ware was less expensive and sturdier than ordinary unglazed porcelain, called biscuit. To have the body of a pitcher simulate a waterfall is a purely nineteenth-century phenomenon. Here the naturalism of rococo decoration has been carried to an extreme, but the crags, rocks, and trees have been subtly arranged in an orderly pattern. The pitcher was celebrating American natural wonders in the same way as did many paintings of the time (see paintings and sculpture volume, nos. 15,105).

H. 8¹/₄ inches

The Metropolitan Museum of Art, Gift of Dr. Charles W. Green, 47.90.15

139

The gilt and polychrome decoration on this porcelain cup and saucer made about 1850 by Charles Cartlidge and Company of Greenpoint, New York, adds light, rococo revival elements to a large, heavy form. The decorator used realistic flowers framed by a gilt arcade to echo eighteenth-century designs, but both the shapes of the pieces and the relationship of decoration to form are distinctly of the nineteenth century. The eighteenth-century rococo artist would have used more intricate interlacing to create a fantasy with his motifs, whereas the nineteenth-century designer clearly outlined the panels and centered the floral motifs within. The cup and saucer are also much larger than eighteenth-century ones; the size answered the demands of the period, for coffee and tea had become cheaper and were drunk in greater quantities than before. The decoration on Cartlidge's cup and saucer, although similar to ordinary imported wares, is simpler than that on European work.

Diam. saucer 7 inches

The Brooklyn Museum, Gift of Mrs. Henry W. Patten

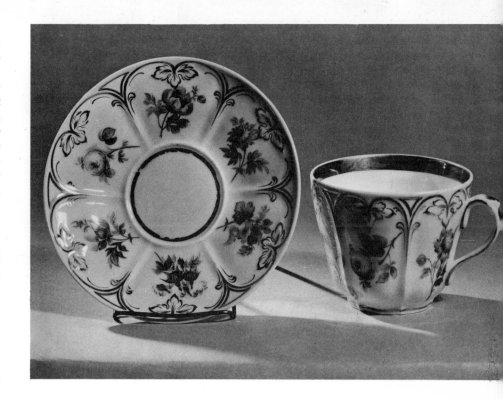

140

Changes in style between 1838, when the Tucker factory closed, and a decade later, when new ventures in American porcelain were being undertaken, are evident when a Tucker pitcher (see no. 87) is compared with this one made about 1850 by Charles Cartlidge and Company. The simple classical lines of the earlier piece have given way to more intricate shapes and decoration inspired by the rococo. The naturalistic relief elements and the squat shape are typical of rococo revival design. This porcelain pitcher was made as a presentation piece and is inscribed: "To the Assembly of the State of New York Presented by the M and M Union." Unfortunately the M and M Union, which ordered the pitcher, did not take it. It was preserved in the family of a potter who worked with Charles Cartlidge.

H. 13 inches

The Brooklyn Museum, Gift of Miss Alice Corey Robertson

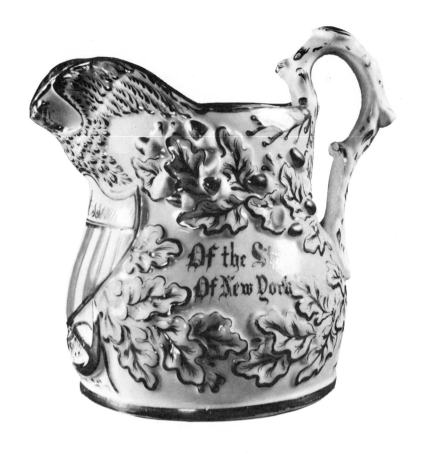

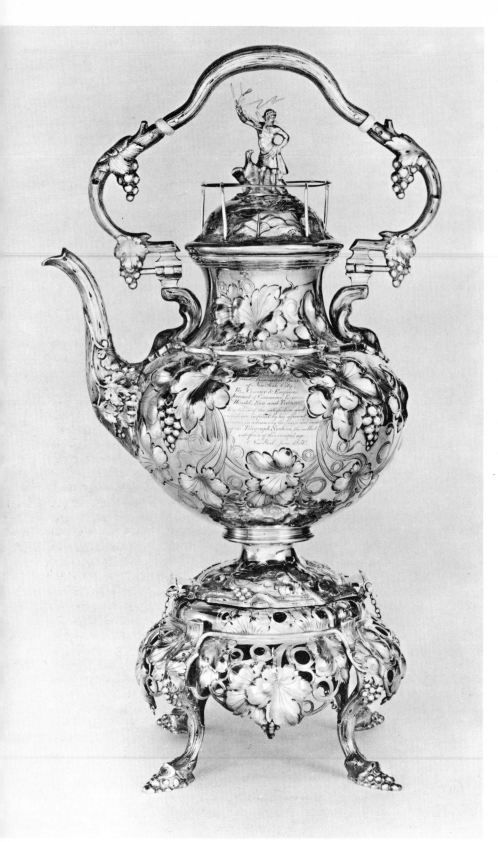

141

This hot-water kettle and stand, part of a silver tea service made by John Chandler Moore for Ball, Tompkins, and Black, New York, rewarded the head of the companies that ran the first telegraph lines from New York to Boston and Buffalo. Marked "BALL TOMPKINS & BLACK/NEW YORK/J.C.M/22" on the underside, it is inscribed on one side "To MARSHALL LEFFERTS, ESQ. President of the New York and New England and New York State Telegraph Companies," and on the other: "From the Stockholders and Associated Press of New York City . . . As a token of . . . his . . . advancing the cause and credit of the Telegraph System, the noblest enterprise of this eventful age. New York, June 1850." The kettle is rococo in its pear shape with repoussé decoration of grape vines and leaves, and its rustic handle and spout. More ornate than the rest of the set, this piece has a domed lid with a scene including a train, sailboat, and telegraph lines, encircled by a gallery of poles and wires; the finial is an eagle beside a figure of Zeus. This repoussé pattern was used elsewhere by Moore. It appears on two ewers at the Museum of the City of New York (one is from this set) and on a gold tea set presented in 1851 to Edward K. Collins. Moore worked from 1832 to 1851: one year, 1835/36, with Garret Eoff, and from 1839 as head of his own firm, making silver for Marquand and Company, and their successors, Ball, Tompkins, and Black. After his retirement, John C. Moore and Son Silversmiths continued under the direction of his son, Edward, working solely for Tiffany and Company and becoming incorporated with that firm in 1868.

H. 17 5/16 inches

The Metropolitan Museum of Art, Gift of Mrs. F. R. Lefferts, 69.141.1

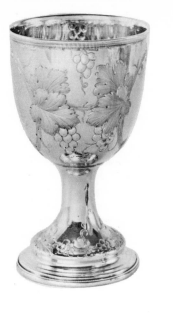
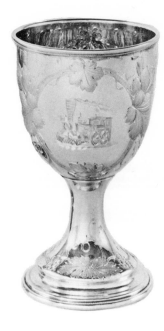

142 A pair of gold goblets made by the New York silversmiths Wood and Hughes about 1848 bears the same type of rococo naturalistic ornament as the Lefferts tea set (no. 141). Repoussé decoration of grapes and grape leaves outlines both the circular base of the stem and the two circular cartouches, one on either side of the cup. In one of these is an unusually fine engraving of a steam engine; the other, probably intended for a presentation inscription, remains blank. Jacob Wood and Jasper W. Hughes worked in partnership from the 1840s through to the end of the century. Their mark of this period, "W & H" in a rectangle, appears on the goblets, on the underside of the cup.

> H. pair 5¹/₂ inches
> Philip Hammerslough, West Hartford, Connecticut

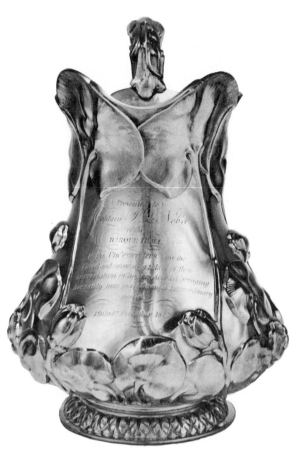

143 J. E. Caldwell and Company of Philadelphia manufactured this silver pitcher, which was, according to the inscription under the spout, "Presented to Captain P. L. Nobre of the BARQUE IRMA, by the Underwriters on the Vessel and cargo as a token of their appreciation of his services in bringing her safely into port through extraordinary perils. Philad.. a December, 1857." It is marked "J.E. CALDWELL & CO./PHILA./STERLING," and with an eagle and shield and pseudo-hallmarks. The decorator of the pitcher chose, rather than ship or captain, a motif of water lilies, especially popular after 1849 when Sir Joseph Paxton introduced the spectacular *Victoria regia* variety. The large flat petals at the rim and spout rise—as if floating on water within the vessel—from the smaller leaves and flower buds at the base, in a handsome rococo revival synthesis of shape and ornament. The "extraordinary perils" were chronicled in the New York *Shipping and Commercial List* of November 14, 1857: "Barque IRMA, Nobre, was driven ashore on a reef off Cat Island, San Salvador, during a violent gale from N.W. on the night of the 22d ult., but succeeded in getting off two days after by discharging half of her cargo, which was taken on board again. She afterwards (Nov. 2) put into Nassau, N.P. . . ." In the November 25 issue of the same paper *Irma* is listed as having arrived in Philadelphia.

> H. 10 1/16 inches
> Philadelphia Museum of Art

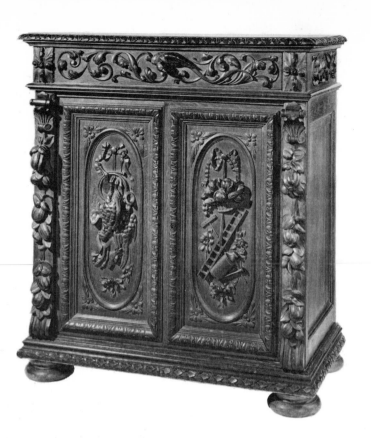

144. The Renaissance revival in furniture appeared in America about 1850. It was first characterized by architectural forms, chiefly of late sixteenth- or seventeenth-century inspiration, and decoration, often trophies, carved with the exuberance of the French baroque. This oak cabinet, one of a pair made for Rokeby, the William B. Astor house at Barrytown, New York, bears the label used by Alexander Roux from 1850 to 1857. From 1837 until 1881 Roux worked the gamut of historical revival styles. In the early fifties, like his contemporaries, he favored the rococo and Renaissance revivals: at the New York Crystal Palace he exhibited a rosewood rococo sofa and a massive black walnut Renaissance revival sideboard, its base decorated with four arched panels framing pendent bunches of flowers, fruit, or birds, some carved in high relief, like the ones on this cabinet. This carved "French" style was apparently considered most appropriate for dining rooms, as a number of sideboards and buffets were shown—all of them displaying heavy architectural-looking forms and high relief carving of leaves and fruit, naturalistic birds, game, or fish, and sometimes grotesque heads and figures combined with strapwork and cabochons or medallions. That in the 1850s this style was considered distinctive, and an acceptable alternative to

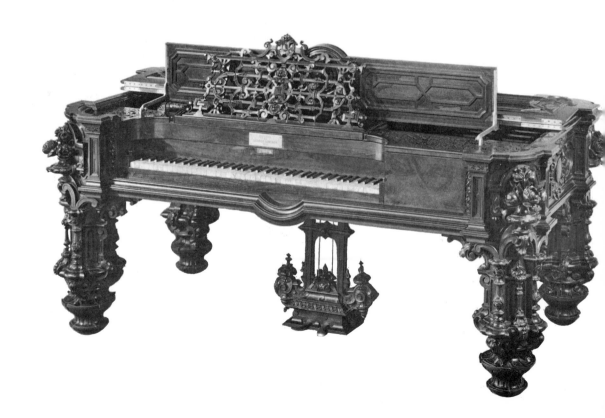

the rococo, is borne out by Ernest Hagen's remark on the shop of Roux's rival, Baudouine: "The work produced in his establishment consisted mostly of the gaudy, over ornate, carved rosewood furniture [i.e., rococo], although some oak dining room furniture was made, all in French carved style with bunches of fruit and game hanging on the pannels [sic]."

H. 43 inches
The Family of Richard Aldrich, Barrytown, New York

145

Among the most publicized and influential mid-century designs were the decorative objects exhibited at the London Crystal Palace in 1851, where this rosewood piano by Nunns and Clark of New York won a first prize. Its massive scale and baroque vigor are typical of the first phase of the Renaissance revival in America. Typical also is the eclectic quality of the design, with motifs drawn from styles of the fifteenth to the eighteenth centuries, and employed with considerable imagination and abandon. The panels, volutes, balusters, and arches on the legs and corners are architectural elements, but used decoratively rather than structurally. The legs, perhaps based upon clustered columns of the late Renaissance and baroque, terminate in volutes that do not logically support the pseudo-pilasters above. Between the pilasters a bouquet in an urn, set before a niche, rests precariously upon other volutes. All these elements, including the Renaissance cartouche at the center of each end panel, are carved in high relief. In contrast is the flat pattern of the music rack, derived from northern Renaissance strapwork, particularly that of the Elizabethan age. Its tight, almost geometric pattern is relieved by molded edges, carved classical palmettes, and small bosses. The opulence characteristic of the period is seen in the mother-of-pearl and tortoise-shell keys and the silver pedals. The makers, Robert Nunns and John Clark, became partners in 1833 and continued in business until 1858.

L. 87¹/₂ inches
The Metropolitan Museum of Art, Gift of George Lowther, 06.1312

146

By mid-century increased mechanization and the nation's expanding population had created new furniture centers in the Midwest. Cities like Grand Rapids and Cincinnati, located on rivers providing power and avenues of transportation, produced furniture that was often both economical and stylish. This rosewood dressing bureau, in a mixture of Renaissance revival and rococo styles, was made in Cincinnati about 1860 by the firm of Mitchell and Rammelsberg; a matching bedstead bears their stencil. According to J. Leander Bishop's *A History of American Manufactures from 1608 to 1860* (1868), this company started in 1844 and by the 60s was the largest furniture firm in the Midwest, and one of the largest in the country, manufacturing furniture in every style, finish, and price. Although probably not the most costly, this bureau is of excellent quality. The base, solid to the floor, with its corner columns, panels created by moldings, and applied carved cartouches and escutcheons, is typical of factory-made Renaissance revival furniture of the 1860s and 70s; so is the extremely heavy pediment, here arched above a cartouche. The rococo lingers on in the leafy scrolls sweeping out from the pediment, the naturalistic carved flowers and leaves flanking the mirror, and the scrolls of the candlestand supports. The finest details of the piece, these scrolled stands are probably derived from one of a group of rococo designs by Thomas Johnson originally published in 1758 as the *New Book of Ornaments*, and republished in 1834 by J. Weale, who mistakenly credited them to Chippendale.

H. 99 inches
The Newark Museum, Gift of Miss Grace Trusdell, 1926.

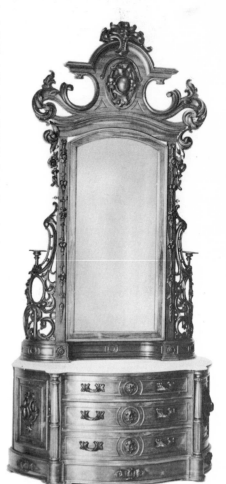

147

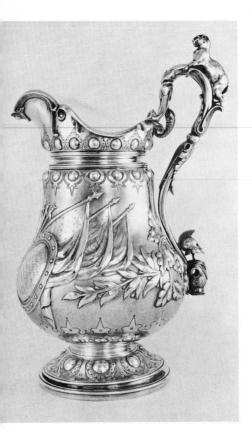

Rococo and Renaissance revival merge in this pitcher of 1859. The shape of the pitcher, pyriform body, molded and scrolled lip, and scrolled handle are rococo, while texture and ornament are characteristic of the Renaissance revival. In 1856 Owen Jones published in England his *Grammar of Ornament*. The first comprehensive study of historic styles of decoration, it had a profound effect on mid-century design in America as well as in England. Although the motifs seen here are not identical to any found in Jones, plate 82 (no. 9 in the Renaissance section) has similar examples of leaves, lambrequins, and bosses. In contrast to the usual ornament of the 1850s—whether flowing naturalistic rococo or sculptural baroque—that used here is tight, stylized, repetitive, and in low relief, presaging the flat, restrained decoration typical of the sixties. Within the circular cartouche is the inscription: "To Col.l A. Duryee this TESTIMONIAL IS PRESENTED on his retireing [*sic*] from the Colonelcy of the SEVENTH REGIMENT NATIONAL GUARD as a mark of high appreciation From his Fellow Citizens for his soldierlike qualities and for the valuable services rendered by the REGIMENT during the eleven Years that he commanded it. New York. 1859." The pitcher is marked on the base: "TIFFANY & CO./1004/ ENGLISH STERLING/925-1000/6248/550 BROADWAY," and with a Gothic "M" at each side, standing for the Moore silversmiths (see no. 141).

H. 14³/₄ inches
Museum of the City of New York, Bequest of Emily Frances Whitney Briggs

148

French names—Baudouine, Ringuet LePrince, Marcotte, and Roux—were dominant in the New York furniture industry at mid-century. To these can be added the name of Julius Dessoir, whose stenciled mark appears inside the drawer of this rosewood étagère made about 1855 to 1860: "J. DESSOIR/MAKER/ No. 543 BROADWAY. N.Y." Of the French New York cabinetmakers, Dessoir is the least known, although his career spanned two decades. The first listing of him as a cabinetmaker appeared in the 1842/43 city directory; the last, in that for 1865/66. In the New York

Crystal Palace of 1853 he exhibited an arcaded rosewood bookcase, "excellently and beautifully finished," as well as a table with caryatid supports and a black walnut armchair, "executed with taste and spirit." This étagère, like the pitcher no. 147 a mixture of rococo and Renaissance revival styles, has not only carving of fine quality but also a restraint that contrasts with the floridity of much furniture of the period. Highly architectural in overall appearance, it is rococo in the curving shape of its turreted table top, more Renaissance in the tight symmetrical cresting and scrolling brackets. These volutes terminate in framed bosses similar to those on the pitcher. Renaissance too is the extensive use of turned balusters; these balusters are not only structural but also, in their contrast with the plain surfaces behind them, an important part of the decorative scheme.

H. 68⁷/₈ inches
The Metropolitan Museum of Art, Anonymous Gift Fund, 69.89

149

In its simple lines and flat surfaces this child's bed by Alexander Roux represents the more restrained aspects of the Renaissance revival style. On the headboard and footboard appear Roux's stencil of the period 1850 to 1857: "FROM /A. ROUX/FRENCH/CABINET MAKER / Nos. 479 & 481 BROADWAY / NEW YORK"; and the bed can be dated even more specifically since it was ordered by Nason B. Collins, who married Sarah Louise Schofield on February 22, 1855. Roux's skillful design contrasts the curves of the pierced rosewood veneer sides with the straight solidity of the rails and corner posts. Their heaviness is relieved by moldings and a carved leaf and scroll motif near the top. The only other details of carving are the scrolls at the juncture of post and top rails, and the applied Renaissance medallion on each side. Although at first glance the pierced pattern of the sides resembles some of the scrolled decoration of rococo furniture, it is closer to strapwork patterns of the late Renaissance, particularly as interpreted by Boulle or his contemporaries in the period of Louis XIV.

L. 55¹/₂ inches
Museum of the City of New York, Gift of Miss Louise Coskery

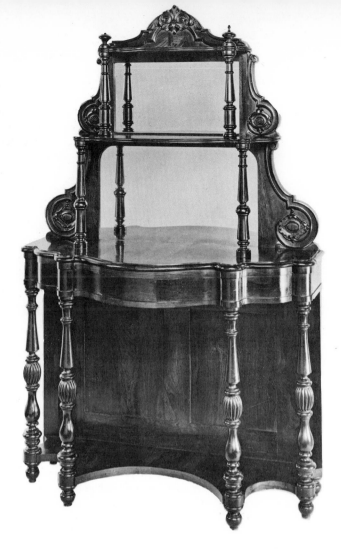

150

The design for this sword appears on a page headed "Straight Swords, for Generals" in a catalogue, *Presentation Swords, Made by Tiffany & Co.*, undated but published after 1862. It is described there as follows: "Washington pattern. Octagonal Grip of silver, surmounted by head of Washington in gilt. Knuckle-guard heavy gilt, with medallion relief of Hercules in silver. Wrist-guard, a crosspiece, with ram's head finials, and draped with flags. Scabbard chased and gilt. Blade etched and gilt." The Renaissance revival style is seen in the classical motifs of Hercules, rams' heads, drapery swag, stylized palmettes, and fasces, and in the symmetry and formality of treatment of each decorative element. The scabbard bears the mark "TIFFANY & CO./M" and the inscription: "TO Major Genl. Schofield. From the Citizens of St. Louis, Mo. Jany. 30th 1864."

L. 31½ inches
West Point Museum

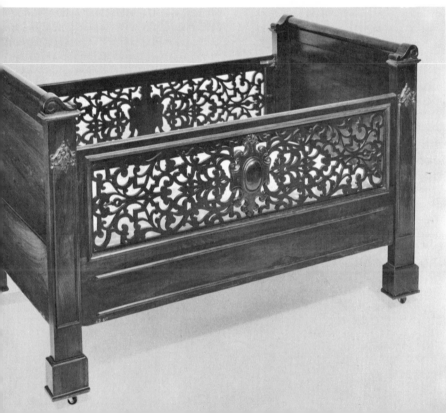

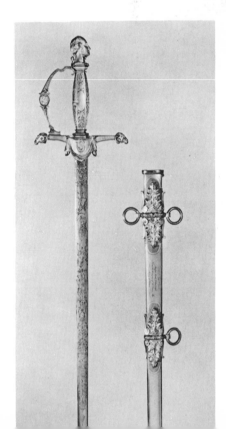

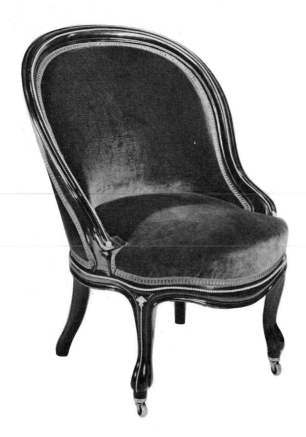

151

This slipper chair in a modified rococo shape with Louis XVI ornament originally bore the label of Alexander Roux of New York. Probably made about 1860, it is an interesting contrast to Roux's earlier Gothic and rectilinear Elizabethan chairs (nos. 99, 120). "Finger rolled" carving is the term sometimes given to the distinctive molding; it is often found on rococo revival sofas and chairs manufactured by western factories. Midwestern finger-rolled pieces, however, usually bear a modicum of carved ornament, particularly at the cresting, while decoration here is dependent upon the restrained use of brass trim against the ebonized maple frame. Beading emphasizes the curving lines; a delicate brass leaf tops the front legs; and brass banding and casters finish the front legs.

H. 30⅝ inches

The Metropolitan Museum of Art, Gift of Mrs. Zelina C. Brunschwig, 68.158

152

> When the proprietors of our great steamers and hotels can afford . . . to lavish far more in the furniture, gilding, and decoration of their saloons, than our best private fortunes will allow . . . the only resort for a gentleman who wishes his house to be distinguished by good taste, is to choose the opposite course, viz. to make its interior remarkable for chaste beauty, and elegant simplicity. . . .

The writer was Andrew Jackson Downing, and the philosophy expressed might well have been that of the John Taylor Johnstons in the 1850s, when, according to family tradition, they chose from the New York-Paris firm of Ringuet LePrince the group of furniture to which this rococo revival chair and table belonged. Rich but restrained, these pieces illustrate the best of the French taste in America at mid-century. Even the curving lines are subdued, and decoration, though ornate, is never flamboyant. Dark frames—ebonized apple or pearwood of the chair and table top and apron; ebonized walnut of the table legs—are an effective foil for gilt-bronze ornament, used to emphasize form rather than merely to embellish it. Leafy scrolls at the center of the table apron and the seat and cresting rails of the chair give a focal point to each piece; scrolls on the cabriole legs draw attention to their graceful swell, and ormolu shows off form equally effectively on table top, apron, and chair frame.

John Taylor Johnston and Frances Colles were married in 1850 and in 1855 began building a house on Fifth Avenue at Eighth Street. This set, and the classical pieces ordered from Marcotte about 1860 (no. 153), may have been intended for this house, or the set may have come to them from Frances Colles's parents, who had been customers of Ringuet's Paris firm in the 1840s. Numerous letters between the Colleses and Ringuet attest to their patronage and that of their friends, perhaps a determining factor in his decision to set up a New York shop in 1849. First listings for the firm of Ringuet Le-Prince and his son-in-law, Leon Marcotte, occur in the 1849/50 New York directories. For the next eleven years the Ringuet-Marcotte listing continued; beginning in 1855 Emmanuel Ringuet LePrince also listed himself separately at the same address as that of the firm, Ringuet LePrince and Marcotte.

Ringuet LePrince's furniture had appeared in exhibitions in Paris and London; in the 1853 New York Crystal Palace, under the name "Ringuet, LePrince & Co.," he showed a cabinet of ebony with inlaid panels and an elaborately carved black walnut buffet. Of the buffet the reviewer said: ". . . we are informed, [it] was manufactured in this city, although it is placed among the other contributions of the house which come from Paris." That Ringuet brought or so quickly found artisans capable of producing an important exhibition piece suggests that his New York shop, even in its early years, was considerably more than a warehouse for French imports; if that is the case, the Johnstons' highly sophisticated suite could well have been made in New York.

L. table 53³/₄ inches

The Metropolitan Museum of Art; table: Gift of Mrs. D. Chester Noyes, 68.69.3; chair: Gift of Mrs. Douglas Williams

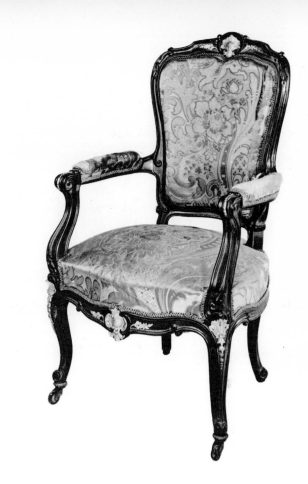

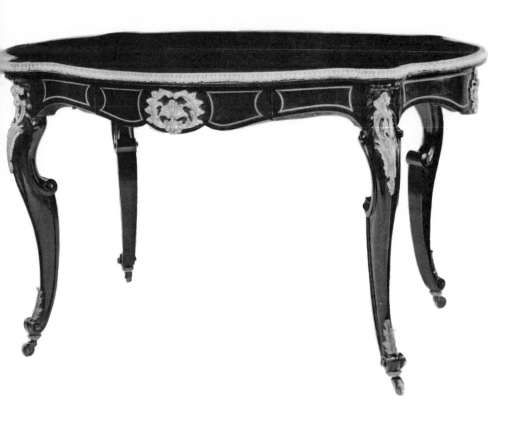

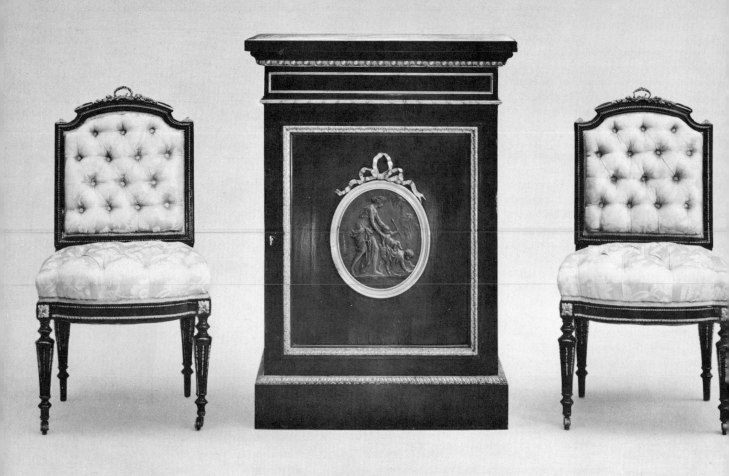

153

"Very rich suites of Black Wood and Gilt, covered in Moire Antique," proclaimed an advertisement in the New York *Evening Post* of 1860, and also "elegant Rosewood Parlor-Suites, covered in rich Satin; Black and Gilt Centre Tables with very rich Gilt Bronzes; elegant Cabinets to match; superb Black and Gilt Carved Centre Tables, marble tops." The advertisement, that of the firm of Ringuet LePrince and Marcotte, describes the kind of furniture seen here, part of an ebonized maple and fruitwood suite purchased, according to family tradition, by the John Taylor Johnstons about 1860 from Leon Marcotte. The suite consists of two sofas, a pair of small cabinets, a large cabinet, six side chairs, two lyre-back chairs, two armchairs, and a firescreen, all of which in shape and decorative details follow superficially the neoclassical style of Louis XVI. The sofas and the chairs in late eighteenth-century classical forms have decoration in classical patterns: beading, egg and dart, bound stalks and leaves; their turned and tapered legs are fluted.

When this set was made, Marcotte's fame had already almost surpassed that of his father-in-law, Ringuet LePrince (see no. 152). Marcotte, who had trained in France as an architect, first gave this profession in the 1849/50 and 1850/51 New York directories. Beginning in 1852 he was listed under furniture at the same address as LePrince. Also in 1852 he listed himself as an architect in partnership with, in one directory, "D. Sienna," in another, "D. Lieman." Unquestionably these were both misspellings for Marcotte's lifelong friend, Detlef Lienau. The partnership apparently lasted only one year, but collaboration between the two continued, culminating in Marcotte's work for the interior of the mansion Lienau designed in the 1860s for LeGrand Lockwood of Norwalk, Connecticut. With the retirement of LePrince in 1861, the name of the firm became Marcotte and Company, and by the middle of the decade Marcotte was New York's most noted decorator.

L. sofa 72 inches
The Metropolitan Museum of Art, Gift of Mrs. D. Chester Noyes, 68.69.1, 6, 7, 16

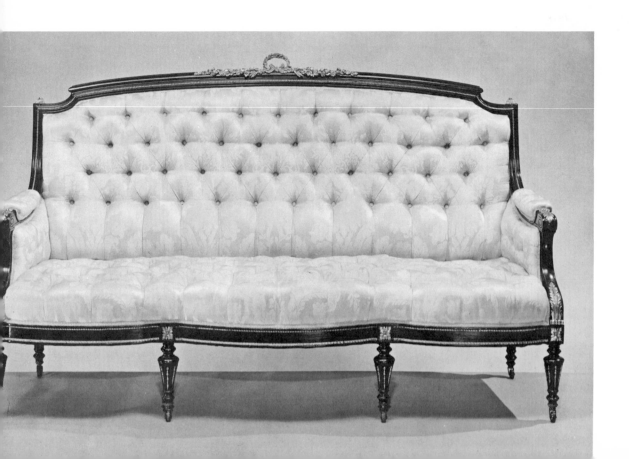

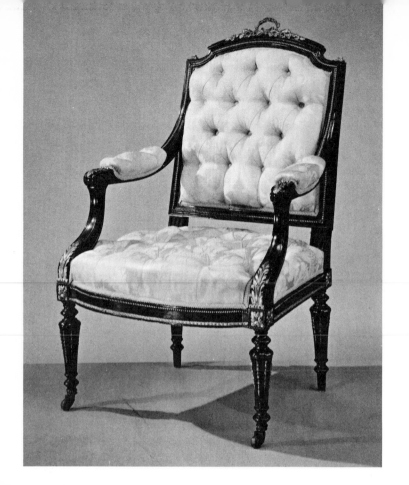

154 Part of the suite no. 153, this armchair is based on a late eighteenth-century straight-backed armchair called a *fauteuil à la reine;* it differs only in minor ways. The square back with arched cresting, the padded, curving arms, and the shaped seat rail are found on eighteenth-century models; the channeled legs are heavier and have an extra ring turning at top and base. The ebonized frame, popular for mid-nineteenth-century chairs, would have been gilt, white and gold, or even a pastel in the eighteenth century; the classical ormolu motifs—wreath and garland cresting, small finials, acanthus leaves at armrest and rail, and foliate pattern on the apron blocks—would undoubtedly have been carved in those places on the frame. Although gilt-bronze mounts were popular on eighteenth-century case pieces, they were seldom used on chairs. The earlier upholstery would probably have been à *tableau,* the padding deep and with a sharp edge at the back, but here the fabric (a replica of the gold damask original) is deep buttoned, a practice that appeared early in the nineteenth century and was standard by the Victorian era. Mid-nineteenth-century also are the casters on the front legs. Despite the differences, this chair was doubtless to Victorian eyes an excellent simulation of the Louis XVI style. It was just such furniture that elicited Hagen's praise of Marcotte's shop and this style: "They worked principally in the pure Louis XVI style and done the very best work. This style is really the best of all and will never go out of fashion, and, if not overdone . . . is simply grand."

H. 39 inches

The Metropolitan Museum of Art, Gift of Mrs. D. Chester Noyes, 68.69.2

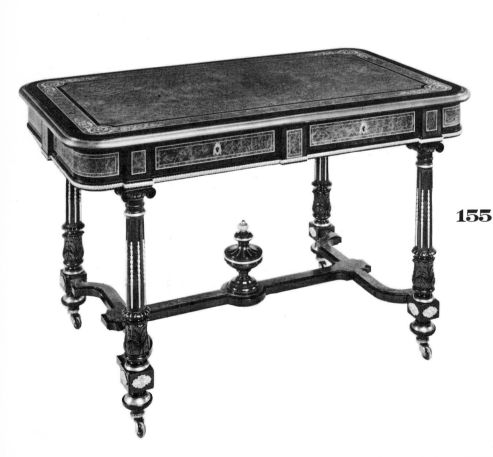

155 Acquired by Mr. and Mrs. Robert de Forest in 1872, the year of their marriage, this Louis XVI revival library table came, according to family tradition, from Marcotte's shop. Although in a style still fashionable at that time, the table may have been made earlier and given to the de Forests by Mrs. de Forest's parents, the John Taylor Johnstons. Certainly it is closely related to the Johnstons' Marcotte furniture (nos. 153, 154). Like that suite it shows a superb interpretation of the French classical style. Particularly noteworthy is the top, its amboina veneer bordered with alternating bands of stained hornbeam and amboina, and outlined in ivory stringing, with ivory leaves and scrolls in the corners. This type of elaborate marquetry was popular in France in the late eighteenth century and was revived before 1840; Marcotte could therefore have seen both Louis XVI and revival interpretations before he came to America about 1848. However derivative in general form and detailing, this table is nonetheless very much Marcotte's creation and bears the impress of his fine craftsmanship. Fifty years after the de Forests acquired the table, their interest in the best of American craftsmanship led them to present to the Metropolitan Museum a building to be devoted entirely to American decorative arts, the American Wing.

L. 49⁷/₈ inches
The Metropolitan Museum of Art, Gift of Mrs. Robert W. de Forest, 34.140.1

156

By using decoration of engraved brass and mother-of-pearl marquetry on a form derived from Louis XVI chairs, the New York maker of this ebonized maple side chair, perhaps Leon Marcotte, made it conform to the taste of 1865 to 1870. In shape and classical details, such as the column-like stiles and the ribbon cresting, it follows late eighteenth-century precedents. The brass beading, the carved fan, and the metal rings on the upper legs are nineteenth-century additions, as are the small turned spindles. Marquetry veneer is common to the period; here fashioned into a bird, foliage, and classical lyre, along with whimsical pierced designs resembling half-moons, it serves to lighten a back panel that might otherwise appear heavy on so delicate a form. Mother-of-pearl marquetry was often set into veneer panels on Marcotte furniture. The mother-of-pearl on the stay rail and seat rail of this side chair, however, is set into a composition ground in a technique used on papier-mâché furniture of the era.

H. 35³/₄ inches
The Metropolitan Museum of Art, Gift of Ronald S. Kane, 68.198.2

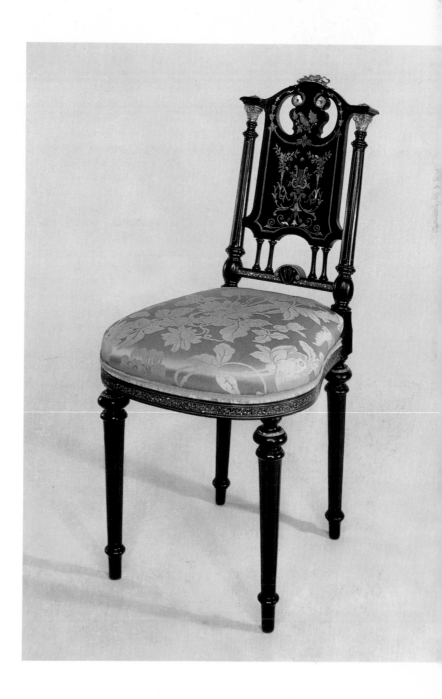

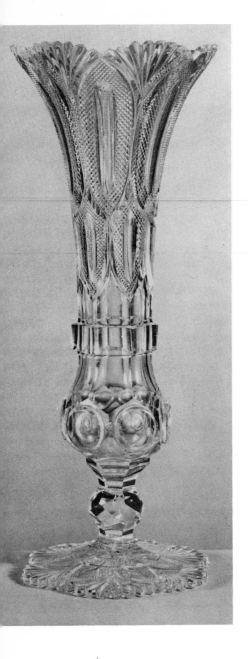

157

In one panel of this cut-glass vase is the inscription: "Presented by the officers & members of the Dorflinger Guards To Mrs. Dorflinger, January 14th 1859." The vase is cut in a small diamond and fan pattern that is more elaborate than was typical for the period, proving that the Dorflinger glass cutters retained this skill even though fashion demanded more engraving than cutting. Christian Dorflinger, born in Alsace and trained in Saint-Louis, Lorraine, had come to America in 1846 and founded the Long Island Flint Glass Works in Brooklyn in 1852. By 1860 he was operating three glasshouses there. The Dorflinger Guards were a colorfully uniformed, locally recruited group who served as a voluntary police force for the community. Dorflinger's local prominence soon became national, for in 1861 Mrs. Lincoln ordered the tableware for the White House from his firm —a commission that was a great boon to the American glass industry. Ill health forced Dorflinger's retirement in 1863, but by 1865, having moved to White Mills, Pennsylvania, he was back in business.

H. 17 inches
Miss Catherine Dorflinger, on loan to the Brooklyn Museum

158

The ancient Roman device of fusing bunches of colored glass rods and cutting them crosswise into patterns that suggest flowers was used by both Continental and American glassmakers to make designs called millefiori, "a thousand flowers." In this paperweight red and white overlays have been cut away to reveal the bright and intricate pattern; the heavy glass dome over the whole serves as a magnifying lens. The object has the stark, awkward quality characteristic of American work and is very likely the product of the New England Glass Company, dating from the 1860s. This company was capable of producing designs as elaborate as any made by then.

Diam. 2½ inches
The New-York Historical Society, Sinclair Collection

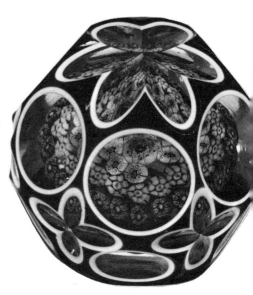

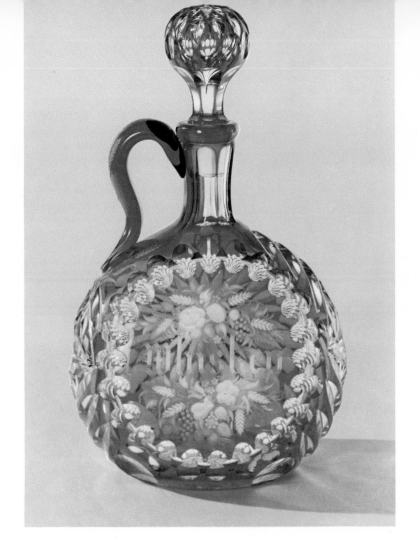

160

A classical shape, overlay glass of a rich blue, and an engraved scene with a matte surface made this goblet as fashionable at the time it was produced—about 1870—as it is skillful and handsome. Louis Vaupel, the most famous decorator of the New England Glass Company, created the ever popular hunting scene, with intricate detail showing his sure touch in the extremely difficult art of wheel engraving. Vaupel came to the New England company in 1856 from Germany, where he had acquired his expertise, and remained there until his retirement in 1885.

H. 8¹/₈ inches
Museum of Fine Arts, Boston, Bequest of Dr. Minette D. Newman

159 On the bottom of this decanter, a gift to William E. Kern when he left the employ of the Boston and Sandwich Glass Company (see also no. 106), is the inscription: "March 27ith/Sandwich Mass/1867/G.T. Lapham Eng." It is a superb example of American-made overlay glass, with brilliant ruby overlay cut away in engraving the still life and in cutting the simple geometric pattern on sides and back. The shape duplicates that of commercial whiskey bottles of the 1860s, a departure from the more ambitious and formal designs of the earlier nineteenth century. Nonetheless, the highly reflective faceting and the engraving—the equivalent in glass of handsome marquetry on furniture of the time —give the decanter great elegance.

H. 10¹/₈ inches
The Metropolitan Museum of Art, Funds from Various Donors, 67.7.22

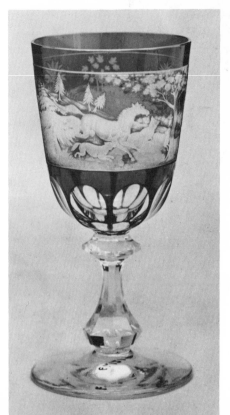

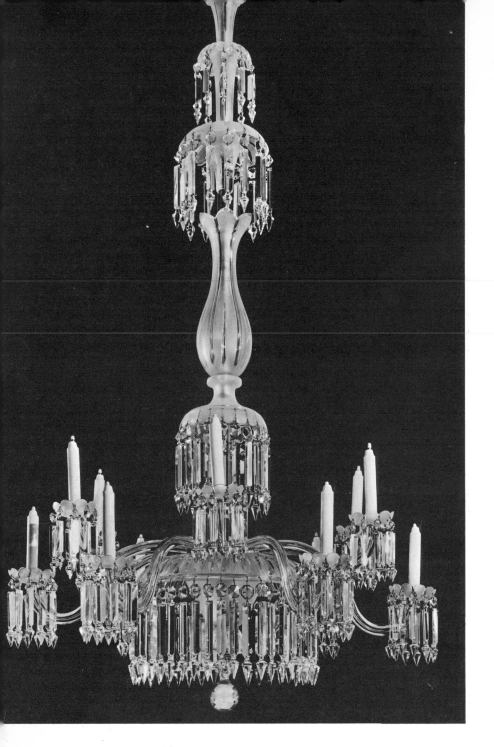

161

The simple grace of this gas chandelier shows the restraint typical of design in the 1860s. The frosted surface that conceals gas piping is as plain as the flat decoration favored on glass tableware of that decade. The shapes of the center support and the arms are repetitions of elements on eighteenth- and early nineteenth-century chandeliers in the neo-classical style but without the relief patterns cut into the earlier examples. The spirit is appropriately classical to harmonize with the Renaissance revival; the regularity of the prisms and their basis in Empire design fortify the classical feeling. Gillinder and Sons of Philadelphia were the foremost manufacturers of glass chandeliers at the time this one was made, and this is quite possibly their product.

H. 71³/₄ inches
The Metropolitan Museum of Art, Rogers Fund, 64.181

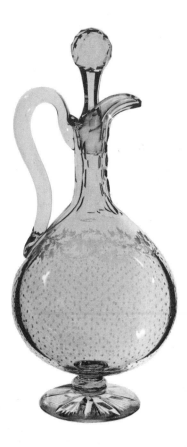

162

Similar in treatment to the decanter of no. 163, this elegant claret jug, made about 1860 by Dorflinger's Greenpoint Glass Works, shows cutting on neck, stopper, and base, but the body is engraved in a flat, small pattern typical of the period. The delicate foliate garland is also characteristic of the Renaissance revival.

H. 12¹/₂ inches
The New-York Historical Society

163

In cut glass of the 1860s and 70s there was less effort to create the deeply faceted, highly reflective surfaces than there had been in pieces made from 1810 to 1840. Following the trend in Renaissance revival furniture and silver, in which flat surface decoration was preferred to high relief, engraving was used more than cutting for decorating glass. The flat-cut and engraved wine glass and bowl, on the left, part of a service owned by John Taylor Johnston, are not positively identified but were probably made in Brooklyn by Dorflinger (see no. 157). The ribbon and shield enclosing the initial are classical elements in keeping with Renaissance revival design. The sugar bowl and decanter are from the service given to William E. Kern when he left the Boston and Sandwich Glass Company in 1867 (see also 106, 159). The engraved foliate decoration is light and graceful; the shallow cutting is in keeping with its delicacy.

H. decanter 12³/₄ inches
The Metropolitan Museum of Art; wine glass and bowl: Gift of Mrs. D. Chester Noyes, 69.144.3,4; sugar and decanter: Funds from Various Donors, 67.7.24, 13

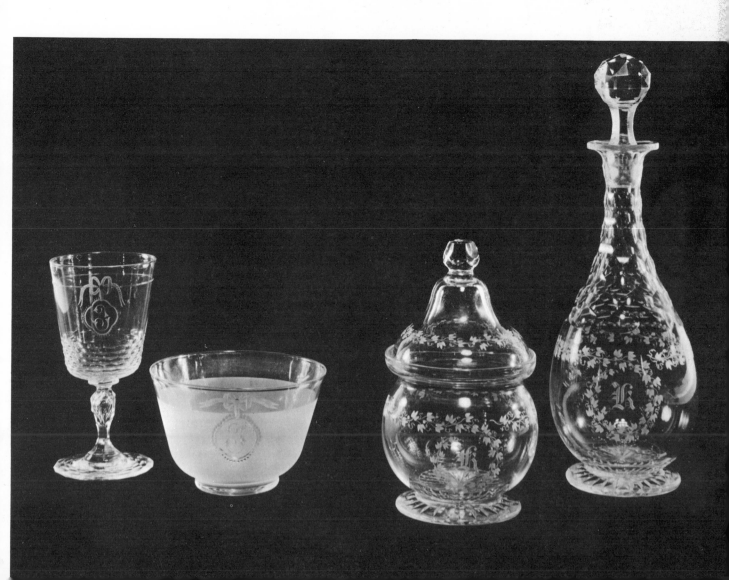

164 In the mid-1860s the Renaissance revival was often the eclectic combination of historic styles seen in this rosewood cabinet, which has Louis XVI ornament upon a Renaissance revival form. Made in New York, it can be precisely dated in the last four months of 1866 because of the fragments of a New York German-language newspaper of September 1866 found behind the porcelain plaques and the maker's label on its back: "FROM/ ALEXANDER ROUX,/479 BROADWAY,/43 & 46 MERCER ST./NEW-YORK,/FRENCH CABI-NET MAKER,/AND IMPORTER OF/FANCY BUHL / AND / MOSAIC FURNITUR[E] / Established 1836." Roux probably used this label

only for the decade 1856 to 1866; in the 1867 directories he is listed at 827 rather than 479 Broadway. The heavy form is typical of the Renaissance revival, as are the architectural qualities: three pseudo-Ionic pilasters across the front, excessive paneling through use of moldings and contrasting woods, and an unusual flat pediment. This curious addition with its scrolls seems more like an Ionic capital, an illogical crowning piece for the whole cabinet. Side projections outlined in "neo grec" incised lines also have the angular look found on many Renaissance revival forms. More in the Louis XVI manner are ormolu moldings and

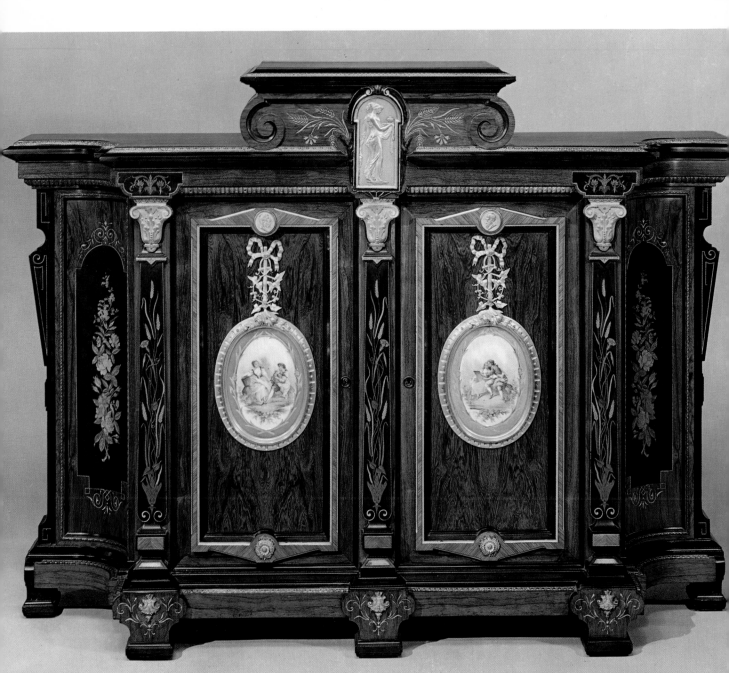

mounts, metal plaque with classical figure, and painted porcelain plaques on the doors, and marquetry, which perhaps owes its ultimate inspiration to Boulle as reinterpreted by late eighteenth-century craftsmen. The rich contrast of woods and the ornate decoration seen on this cabinet were featured by Roux in an 1859 advertisement in Carroll's *New York City Directory*: "We have now on hand a large and splendid assortment of Plain and Artistic Furniture, such as Rosewood, Buhl, Ebony, and Gilt, and Marqueterie of foreign and domestic woods. . . ."

Cabinets of this type were not unusual in the 1860s. The design may have been influenced by a much published cabinet exhibited by the London company Jackson and Graham at the International Exhibition of 1862. *Masterpieces of Industrial Art and Sculpture* (1862) described it as "made of ebony inlaid with ivory . . . with oval medallions of hymeneal subjects. . . . The style adopted is that of the best period of Louis Seize." "Louis Seize" might well have been used to designate Roux's cabinet, since stylistic nomenclature was as often based on ornament as on form. Or it might have been designated simply a "French cabinet." A trade catalogue of the period from a London firm lists under "Drawing Room" furniture: "French Cabinets (Black, inlaid with Ivory, or Brass, with Sevres Plaques or Medallions)."

H. 53⅝ inches

The Metropolitan Museum of Art, Edgar J. Kaufmann Charitable Foundation Fund, 68.100.1

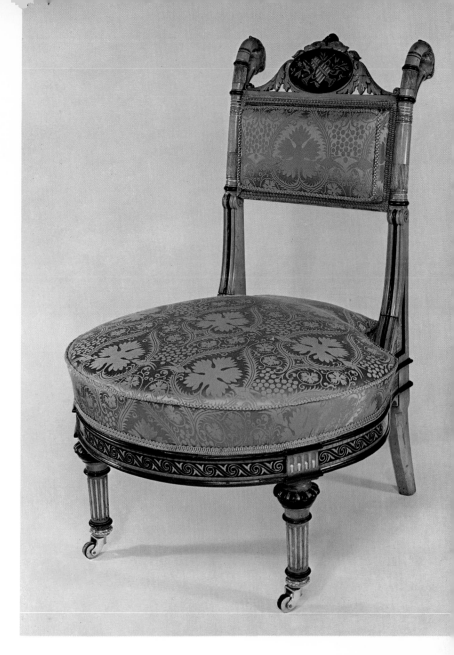

165 The style of France's Second Empire with its revival of light woods, Louis XVI delicacy, and motifs from antiquity obviously influenced the design of this slipper chair made about 1865, probably in New York, possibly by Herter Brothers. A pair of similarly carved light wood side chairs with swan's-head terminals and the Herter Brothers stamped mark has been found. The Herter stamp appears also on a light wood writing desk, part of a group of furniture made for Andrew H. Green. Tables from the group bear on their aprons the same breaking-wave pattern of inlay as appears here. Made of maple, this chair has ebonized and inlaid decoration and rosewood bead moldings on the rails. Channeled classical front legs with casters and cuff of brass beading are in contrast to plain rear legs. The marquetry wave pattern of the seat rail, found in ancient Greek and Pompeian art, and sometimes termed the Vitruvian scroll, emphasizes the roundness of the padded seat and the scroll of the stiles. The deep cushioning of the seat and backrest are typical of furniture in the style of the Second Empire, when Empress Eugénie introduced wholly upholstered pieces of furniture. Above the padded back the cresting rail bears an oval marquetry panel depicting a musical trophy. The stiles, broken up by volutes, bands of channeling, and ring turnings, are accented by ebonizing. They terminate in handsomely carved and scrolled swan's heads, a decorative motif reminiscent of the style of the First Empire.

H. 30¹/₄ inches

The Metropolitan Museum of Art, Gift of James Graham and Sons, Inc., 65.186

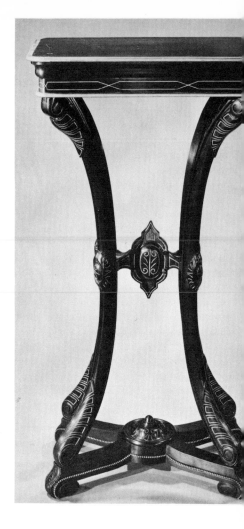

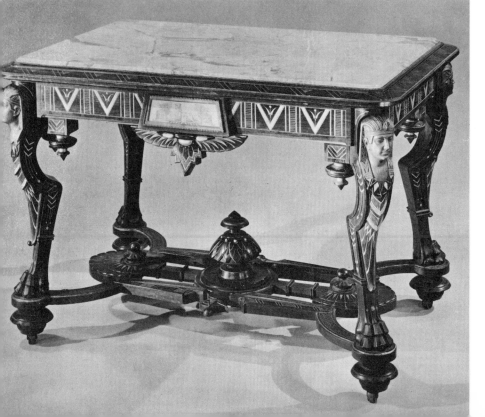

166

Egyptian, like Gothic, was throughout the nineteenth century more a survival than a revival. The influence of Egyptian motifs began with Baron Vivant Denon's publication in 1802 of sketches he made during Napoleon's expedition of 1798, and was renewed periodically by further archaeological discoveries. In 1852 the first major Egyptian collection to cross the Atlantic came to New York. During the same era the appointment of a Conservator of Egyptian Monuments to the Khedive ended the heyday of treasure-seeking enterprises and began a period of significant excavations, particularly at Giza. Thus in the sixties and seventies there was a resurgence of Egyptian decoration. Here in a rosewood center table with variegated marble top, made about 1865 to 1870 probably in New York, Egyptian ornament of sphinx head, animal feet, palmette, and lotus is superimposed upon a Renaissance revival form. Hagen had his own name for and opinion of this exotic phase of Renaissance revival furniture. Writing of the cabinetmakers Pottier and Stymus (see no. 207), he said:

> . . . their work was nearly all done in the "Neo Grec" most awfull gaudy style with brass gilt Spinx head on the sofas and arm chairs, gilt engraved lines all over with porcailaine painted medalions on the backs, and brass gilt bead moldings nailed on. Other wise, their work was good; but the style horrible.

L. 47 inches

The Metropolitan Museum of Art, Anonymous Gift Fund, 68.207

with classical Renaissance (no. 164), and, as here, in the exotic "style antique." The basis for this form was undoubtedly the same folding stool that influenced the Phyfe curule chair of the early nineteenth century (no. 17). Here, however, hocked animal legs embellished with water leaves terminate in gilded hooves. The shieldlike medallion at the juncture of the legs is a decoration common to Renaissance revival furniture. The sides of the stool, with their turned spindle ribs, are shaped like stylized open palmettes. A bold palette of umber, red, black, and gilt emphasizes the shape and decoration. The tufted brocade upholstery is original. On the underside appears the same Roux label as on the cabinet no. 164.

H. 23³/₄ inches

The Metropolitan Museum of Art, Edgar J. Kaufmann Charitable Foundation Fund, 69.108

167

Ebonizing on the cherry frame, incised gilded outlines around leaves and palmettes, and brass beading on the base decorate this stand made about 1870. It is therefore close in character both to the group of furniture that Hagen called "neo grec" and to the Renaissance revival. Particularly Renaissance in character is the shield linking the legs at midpoint and the applied embossed medallions on their outer surface. The stand descended in the Beckwith family and was originally part of the furnishings of the house near Garrison, New York, called Hurstpierpont.

H. 42¹/₂ inches

The Metropolitan Museum of Art, Anonymous Gift Fund, 68.97.2

168

The designation "neo grec" is perhaps even more applicable to this polychrome stool, made and labeled by Alexander Roux about 1865. Roux, ever the tasteful proponent of the latest style, worked in the forties in the Gothic (no. 99), in the fifties in the Elizabethan (no. 120), Renaissance (no. 144), and rococo (no. 151), and in the sixties in the Louis XVI, mixed

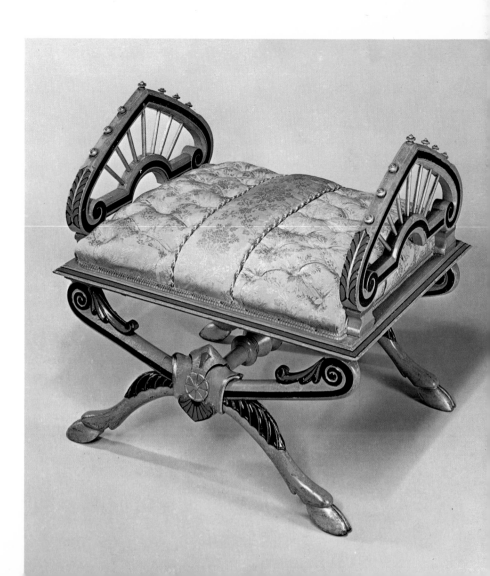

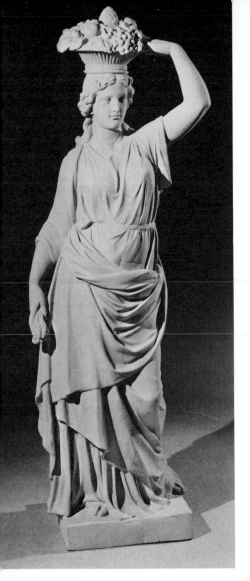

169

The best-decorated of America's parks and gardens after the Civil War had not only settees and chairs, urns and perhaps a fountain, but also statuary at selected spots along the walks or in an arbor. Catalogues of statuary showed animals—lions, dogs, stags—and allegorical figures. This example, made of zinc painted to simulate stone, represents Autumn, or Pomona, goddess of the orchard. The model was probably first cast in the 1860s or 70s; one is shown, as Autumn, among the Four Seasons, in an 1890 catalogue of the J.L. Mott Iron Works, New York. The back of this figure's base is marked: "M.J. SEELIG &c CO,/SCULPTORS &c/METALFOUNDERS/115-121 MAUJER ST./ WM, BURGH. N.Y." Seelig was at that address in Brooklyn from 1872 to the end of the century.

H. 55¹/₄ inches
The Metropolitan Museum of Art, Anonymous Gift Fund, 68.140.1

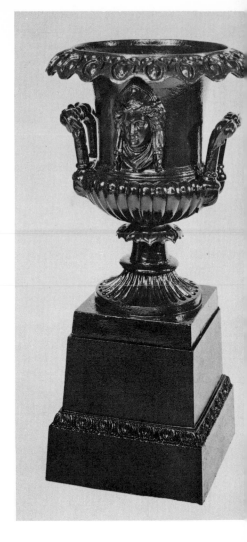

170

Writing in . . . *Landscape Gardening, Adapted to North America* . . . in 1841, Andrew Jackson Downing stated: "Vases of real stone . . . are decorations of too costly a kind ever to come into general use among us. Vases, however, of equally beautiful forms, are manufactured of artificial stone, of fine pottery, or of cast iron, which have the same effect, and are of nearly equal durability, as garden decorations." He went on: "As yet, we are unable to refer our readers to any manufactory here, where these articles are made in a manner fully equal to the English; but we are satisfied, it is only necessary that the taste for such articles should increase, and the consequent demand, to induce our artisans to produce them. . . ." Thirty years later, demand for cast-iron vases was high, and foundries offered them to buyers in half a dozen basic shapes, with or without handles or covers, plain or with decoration such as fluting or the classical heads on two sides of this one, and with a choice of pedestal. Here a formal elegance is achieved in the proportions of both vase and pedestal, heightened by the restrained use of decorative motifs of classical inspiration.

H. 36 inches
The Metropolitan Museum of Art, Edgar J. Kaufmann Charitable Foundation Fund, 69.158.4

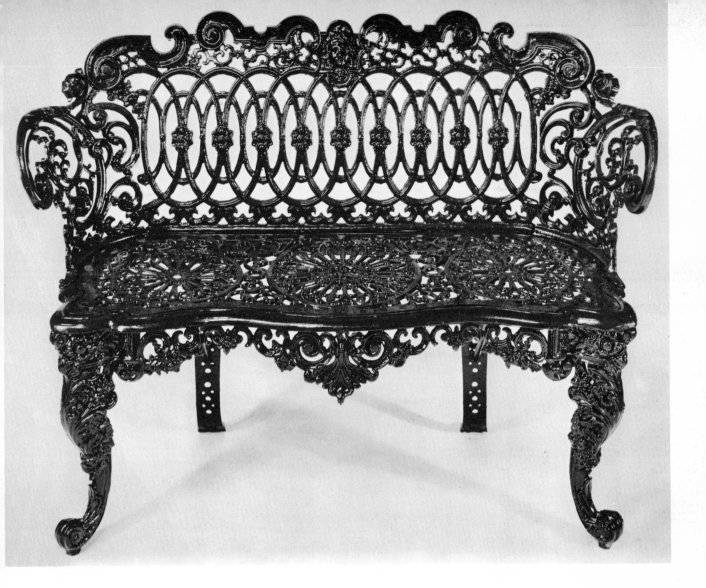

171 Not so common as the "Gothic" or the "rustic" cast-iron settee (nos. 116, 119) is this more elegant and elaborate piece, designed about 1870, which reflects both the rococo revival and the Renaissance revival styles. Although the cabriole legs with leafy knees, French feet, and scrolls—especially in their freer movement on the arms—are from the rococo repertory, symmetry and formality are the keynotes. The head used as a decorative motif, here in the center of the back, occurs on rococo furniture, but is seen also in this period on Renaissance revival silver and furniture (nos. 172-174) as well as on the cast-iron urn no. 170. The scrolls forming the back cresting are flattened and formalized by a raised outline, which creates an effect similar to that of the incised gilded outlines on a dark wood background of Renaissance revival furniture. While the rustic settee would have been at home in a rambling, overgrown English garden, this one would have been most appropriate to the planned formality of a French garden.

L. 44³/₄ inches
The Metropolitan Museum of Art, Anonymous Gift Fund, 69.90.1

172

Classical inspiration for the Renaissance revival is seen in this silver compote made by William Gale and Son in 1863. On the underside it bears the marks "W. GALE & SON/ NEW-YORK/ 925 STERLING," and "G&S" in a shaped reserve with four numbers. On the front is the inscription "James A. Patteson. from Maurice Faucon as a token of gratitude and esteem Dec. 25th 1863." To a variation of the classical cup shape, with large areas of plain surfaces, the silversmiths have added classical decoration. Perhaps the most prominent is the band of Greek key in polished pattern against striated ground on both base and bowl. The Greek key, or fret, pattern— sometimes called meander—is one of the most popular motifs from antiquity and was used on furniture of this period (no. 173) and on that of the earlier nineteenth-century classical revival (no. 45). The beaded trim of the base and lip also appears on furniture of the Renaissance revival and Louis XVI styles, usually in the form of applied brass edging (see nos. 151, 167). Animal-head and ring handles, here sheep's heads, were a favorite device of antiquity and were revived both in the Renaissance and in the eighteenth century, particularly in the work of Robert Adam. On the paneled base are cast medallions of heads in voluted surrounds; such medallions, typical of the Renaissance, are often found on decorative arts of the Renaissance revival.

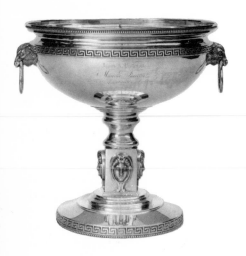

W. 10½ inches

The Metropolitan Museum of Art, Anonymous Gift Fund, 68.114

173

Pedestals became increasingly important after the Civil War, as more works of art came into fashionable American parlors. The small Parian figures of the 1850s were replaced by larger sculpture such as "Rogers groups" (see paintings and sculpture volume nos. 130, 131) or reproductions of famous statues. The stately, almost majestic character of this Renaissance revival pedestal of about 1870 suggests that it was made for a household of some importance, and evidence is provided by Clarence Cook in his popular book, *The House Beautiful* (1878), that such an item was out of the ordinary: "The pedestal in the corner is an ingenious provision for a much-felt need,—a pedestal for a statue, vase, or cast, being one of the pieces of furniture most difficult to find." The wood veneers—rosewood with tulipwood banding—and gilding are typical of Renaissance revival furniture. The Bacchic head in an oval medallion with beaded trim, the laurel swags, the Greek key, and the lambrequin design are Renaissance elements.

H. 45¼ inches

The Metropolitan Museum of Art, Rogers Fund, 64.122.3

174

In the 1860s John Jelliff, a cabinetmaker of Newark, made this Renaissance revival rosewood armchair for John Laimbeer, Sr., of New York. The trumpet-shaped legs, probably inspired by late seventeenth-century designs, support a broad, deeply padded seat. Comfortable padded and tufted armrests appear above caryatids, whose curving forms are echoed in the movement of the unusual arch-shaped rear armrest supports. Knobs pendent from these supports, an angular projection centering the front seat rail, as well as carved tassels hanging from the top corners, are all examples of the appendages often found on Renaissance revival furniture. The tassels seem a translation into wood of the current interest in fringes and upholstery trimmings. This interest in upholstery can be seen also in the way the tufted back is carried over the cresting rail, forecasting the look of the next decade, in which the totally padded and upholstered seat and back replace the visible frame.

H. 39 inches

The Newark Museum, Gift of Mrs. John Laimbeer, 1936

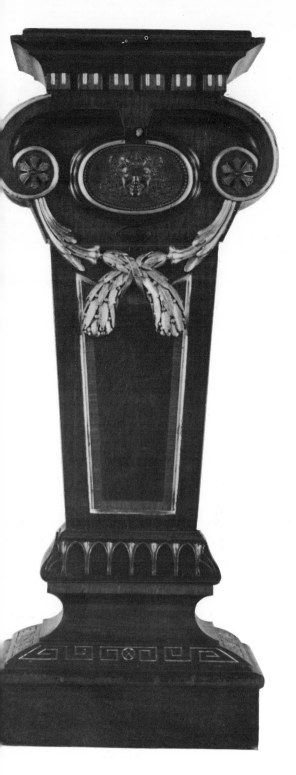

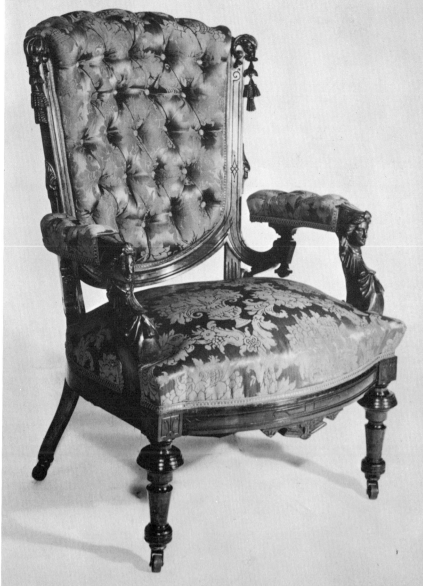

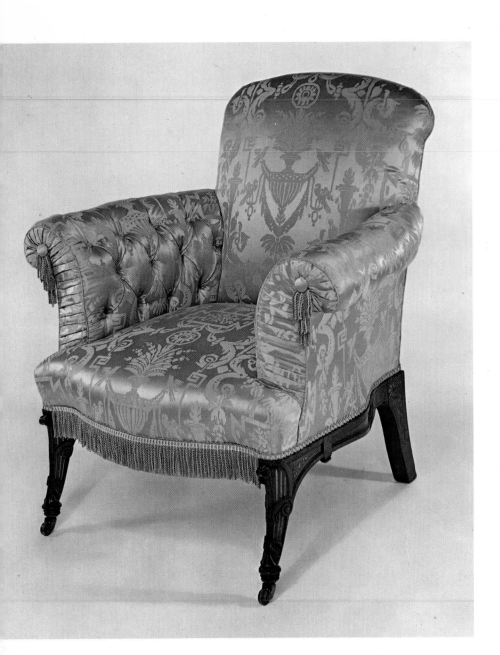

175

Upholstered furniture came into its own in the latter part of the nineteenth century. On this easy chair made about 1870 to 1875 are the ample padding, deep buttoning, and fringe that characterized upholstery in the last three decades. The rosewood rails and legs of the frame are an excellent interpretation of the Renaissance revival style, with carved palmettes, volutes, and incised and gilded lines and floral decoration. Tufted, or deep buttoned, easy chairs existed early in the nineteenth century, and one is shown in a plate from Ackermann's *Repository* of 1814; but deep luxurious upholstery became feasible only toward mid-century, when coil springs came into general use. The fashion for totally upholstered pieces gained great impetus from the styles favored by Empress Eugénie in the 1850s and culminated in the exotic "Turkish" chairs and cosy corners of the 1880s. Just such an easy chair as this one—more upholstery than frame—was described by Clarence Cook in *The House Beautiful* (1878):

> This chair is small, but amply large enough for a comfortable man, and nothing could be better managed than the flow of its lines. The original chair is covered with a material of a floriated pattern, and around the bottom is a silk fringe. . . . It is so pretty to look at, that one forgets to sit down in it. . . .

H. 36 inches
The Metropolitan Museum of Art, Rogers Fund, 64.237

176

This rosewood armchair is one of two included in a suite of Renaissance revival furnishings installed in the sitting room of a
house at 816 Broad Street, Meriden, Connecticut. Begun in 1868 and completed in 1870,
the forty-room house was built for wealthy
hoop-skirt and carpetbag manufacturer
Jedediah Wilcox at a cost of about $125,000.
The cost of the entire estate with grounds and
furniture was reported as $200,000; the house
was considered second only to that of Le-
Grand Lockwood in Norwalk, the greatest
mansion in the state. (Wilcox's square three-
story brick mansion in the "Franco-Italian
Villa style," doomed to demolition, will be
partially preserved through the removal by
the Metropolitan Museum of the richly ornamented entry, staircase hall, parlor, and
sitting room.) In a Meriden newspaper article
of November 1870, the elegant interior of
the house was described. "The furniture,"
states the article, "was all manufactured specially for the Wilcox mansion. . . . The parlor
. . . is upholstered in the Grand Duchesse
style. . . . The . . . sitting room . . . is fitted
up in the Marie Antoinette style of art, the
crimson curtains, sofas, lounges, chairs and
furniture generally, being covered with scar-
let satin."

H. 44¹/₂ inches

*The Metropolitan Museum of Art, Gift of
Josephine M. Fiala, 68.133.3*

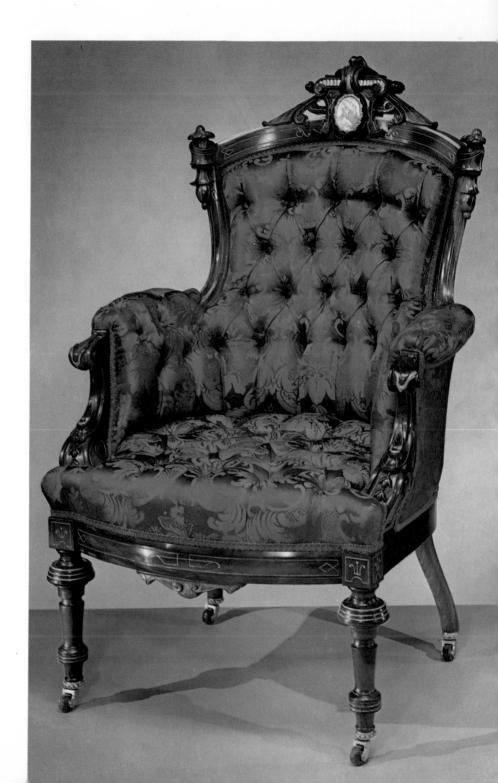

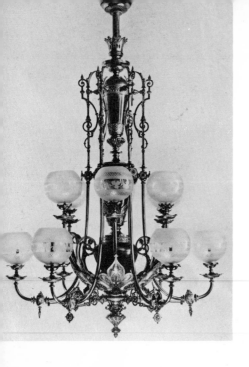

177

The twelve-branch brass gas-burning chandelier from the sitting room at Meriden, Connecticut (see no. 176), dates from about 1870. Pairs of two-branch gas wall-brackets on the end walls of the room completed the lighting scheme. The illumination provided by the twenty gas jets each refracted by an etched- and cut-glass globe must have been brilliant. The article describing the house stated: "The furniture was all manufactured . . . by Mitchell, Vance & Co., of New York." Doubtless "furniture" referred to the lighting fixtures, in which that company specialized; there is no evidence that it ever manufactured large pieces or provided interior decoration. The chandelier is exceptionally well preserved, never having been converted from gas to electricity. The burners are of different sorts: the jets on the lower rank have two rectangular openings over which a sliding brass sleeve with identical openings is fitted. By a twist of the sleeve, the amount of air to be mixed with gas is controlled, just prior to the point of combustion. The stopcocks controlling the flow of gas, at the low points of each curving arm, are camouflaged by oval medallions with male and female portrait heads, carrying out the motifs of the furniture. The chandelier is a typical nineteenth-century stylistic mélange, combining French motifs popular at the beginning of the eighteenth century with classical Greek and Gothic motifs fashionable in the 1830s and 40s.

H. 68 inches

The Metropolitan Museum of Art, American Wing Restricted Building Fund, 68.143.5

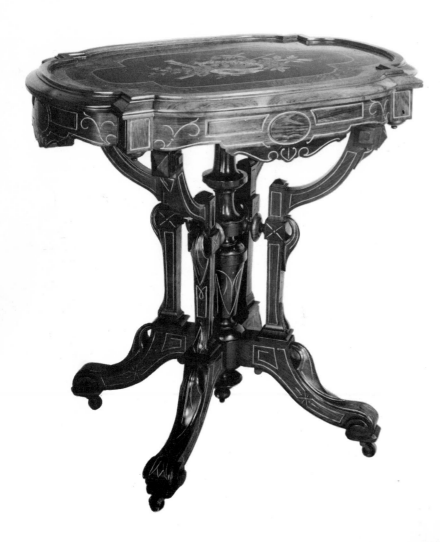

178

After the Civil War the common mid-century arrangement of parlor suites—sofa and chairs grouped around a center table—was no longer rigidly followed; groupings became more varied. Consequently, more small parlor tables were made, such as this rosewood one of about 1870 attributed to John Jelliff of Newark (see also nos. 104, 174). A handsome piece, it has the flat surface decoration of marquetry, paneling, and incised lines typical of the later phase of Renaissance revival design. The top bears an intricate inlaid floral panel; the base consists of four curving legs below angular supports linked by a center post in the shape of a Renaissance urn or baluster. The legs and supports have flat sides, and flat surface design rather than relief is emphasized throughout.

L. 31½ inches

The Newark Museum, Gift of Madison Alling

179

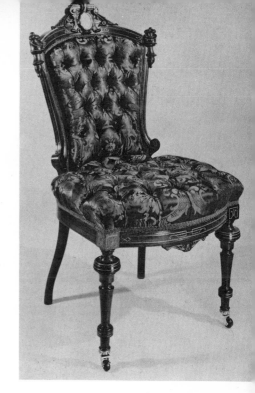

This sofa and side chair, part of the Renaissance revival set of furnishings for the sitting room of the Wilcox house (see no. 176), were made about 1870, probably in New York. The pieces are of rosewood and are ornamented with gilt incised lines. The tufted, three-dimensional upholstery creates a foil to the flat, linear ornament of the surrounding seat and back rails. The sofa was conceived both as three separate chair backs and as a single, coherent piece of furniture. The wide center section of the back repeats the cresting rail of the *en suite* side and armchairs, and the arms repeat those of the armchair; the end sections are upholstered over the cresting rail. Separate ornamental skirts depend from the seat rail,

emphasizing the tripartite design. Although these skirts, the incised lines, and the decorative medallions—here classical heads carved on mother-of-pearl—are all typical of the style now called Renaissance revival, many details of this set derive from late eighteenth-century neoclassical furniture. The use of urns flanking the sofa's center cresting rail and also the seat and leg designs are in that tradition. The confusion of stylistic terminology is therefore easy to understand. In its own age this furniture might well have been called "Louis XVI" or, as in the 1870 Meriden newspaper article, "Marie Antoinette."

L. sofa 76³/₄ inches

The Metropolitan Museum of Art, Gift of Josephine M. Fiala, 68.133.1,4

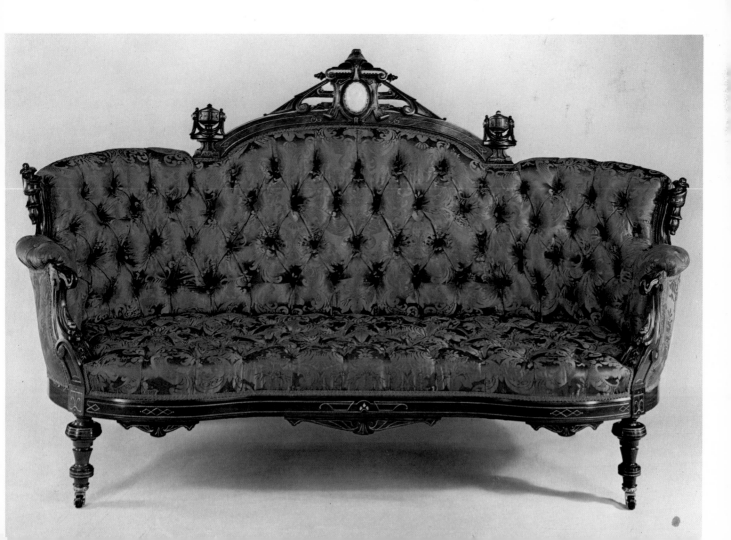

180

These two pieces of silver with Renaissance-inspired designs are part of sets that belonged to John Taylor Johnston, the first president of the Metropolitan Museum, who owned the Marcotte parlor furniture (nos. 153, 154). The smaller piece, a cheese scoop, is in the Medallion pattern patented by Gorham Manufacturing Company of Providence in 1864. The design is a circular medallion with a Grecian male or, as here, female head, surmounted by a stylized palmette; on the handle is a single reed with a patera. Pieces in this pattern are often found with the marks of other silver makers alone or together with the Gorham mark; the cheese scoop is marked with the Gorham lion, anchor, and "G" and "PAT. 1864," as well as with "TIF-FANY & CO./STERLING.," indicating that the piece, although made by Gorham, was marketed by Tiffany. The fish server is marked: "B TIFFANY & Co. STERLING PAT. 1870." The leaf, stem, and anthemion forms are to be found in cabinetwork of the same date. The engraving on the bowl is a stylized flower and leaf motif.

L. server 11¹/₈ inches

The Metropolitan Museum of Art, Gift of Mrs. D. Chester Noyes, 69.144.1,2

181

In 1866, when the laying of the Atlantic Cable was successfully completed, Cyrus W. Field, the principal sponsor, was presented with this silver tazza, the dish (no. 182), and a fruit bowl, by multimillionaire philanthropist George Peabody. As inscribed on each, they were a "Testimony and Commemoration of an act of very high Commercial integrity and honor." Made by the Gorham Company, the pieces exemplify the Renaissance revival style. The tazza has an elaborate pedestal, consisting of a conical base supporting a celestial globe on which stands the figure of Columbia, who in turn holds up the foot of the shallow bowl. A band of flat stylized leaves and flowers and human heads on a matte background decorate the base. Cast portrait medallions, here depicting Field and Peabody, are typical of the Renaissance revival, as are the bands of lambrequin and tassel and double guilloche, and the winged putti on the handles. The globe and the draped female figure are classical motifs; here they show the Victorian preoccupation with symbolism. The piece is marked with the Gorham lion, anchor, and "G," and "164."

H. 16³/₄ inches

Museum of the City of New York, Gift of Newcomb Carlton

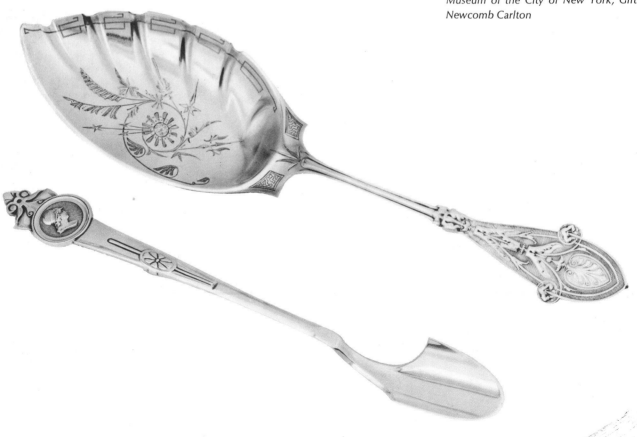

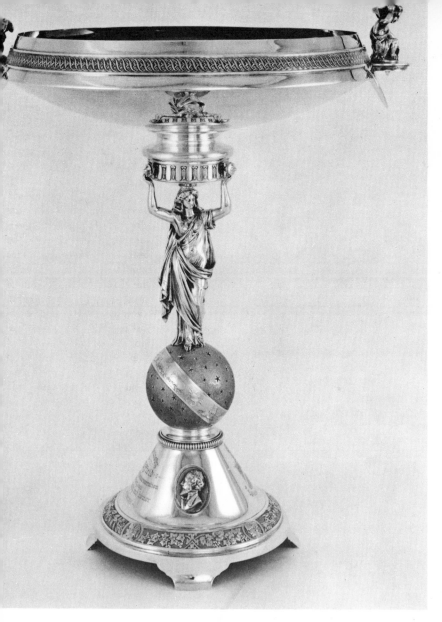

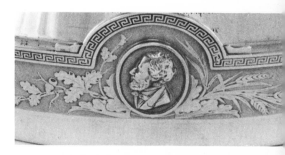

182 Also presented to Cyrus W. Field by George Peabody (see no. 181), this covered dish shares the formal, classical feeling of the tazza. The severe lines are emphasized by bands of the Greek key motif; the wider band has oak and wheat in repoussé against the matte finish characteristic of the Renaissance revival. Cast grotesque masks decorate the handles; a lion and shield form the finial of the cover. Portrait medallions of Field and Peabody are also shown, here round instead of oval. The dish is marked with the Gorham lion, anchor, and "G" and also "S & M," "30," and a star.

W. 15⅛ inches
Museum of the City of New York, Gift of Newcomb Carlton

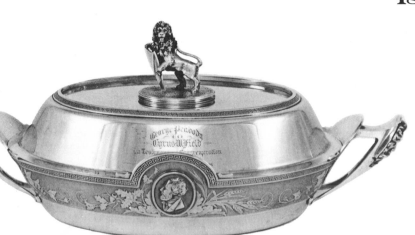

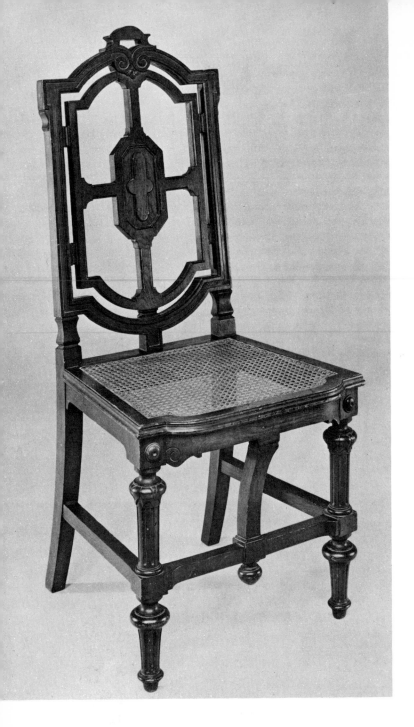

183

The architect James Renwick designed the country house of John Taylor Johnston in Plainfield, New Jersey, where this walnut hall chair, one of a pair, once stood. It was made about 1865 in New York, possibly from Renwick's design. With its simple, rectilinear shape and large areas of flat planes, the chair has an architectural look. It also has a number of the characteristics of the Renaissance revival style. The lines of the inner back, which resembles simple Renaissance strapwork, repeat those of the structural stiles, cresting, and stay rail. The hexagonal center panel is linked to the frame by supports, which form a cross. The molded edge of the outer back is typical of the Renaissance revival, as are the small arched cresting, here pierced, and the extension of the upper corners, where rail and stile meet to form a crossetted frame with corbel-like supports. The incised lines that are common on Renaissance revival furniture appear here only on each side of the front seat rail and echo the scrolls on the cresting. The front legs, channeled columns below bulbous turnings, are probably derived from late eighteenth-century neoclassical furniture, one of the influences in the Renaissance revival. Particularly characteristic of the Renaissance revival style is the vertical member between seat rail and stretcher, which, though shaped like supports of the period, serves no real structural purpose here and is decorative rather than functional.

H. 41¼ inches
The Metropolitan Museum of Art, Gift of Mrs. D. Chester Noyes, 68.69.12

184

This handsome example of Renaissance revival silver, a hot-water kettle made by Ball, Black and Company about 1870, shows the dignity and balance achieved by the best work in this style. Repetition gives a sense of symmetry: the body of the stand repeats the shape of the body of the kettle; the curves and angles of the legs repeat those of the handle. Variety and contrast give a sense of vigor: raised or incised surfaces are

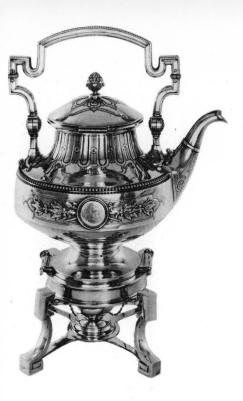

color marquetry representing a musical trophy. The base is constructed on a plan of cross-shaped angular supports around a central pillar, which rises to the top. Gilded incised lines outline the supports as well as decorate the turned feet, carved leaf scrolls, and tassel-like pendants. Pendent elements like these tassels and the scrolled partial apron often appear on Renaissance revival furniture.

H. 29¹/₂ inches
Grand Rapids Public Museum

shown against flat; matte against shiny; curved lines against straight. The legs are proportioned to create strength without heaviness and grace without mannerism—the effect sought, with less success, in the legs of the chair and table nos. 183 and 185. The kettle, a wedding present to Mary Phoenix Remsen, who married Robert Belknap on February 3, 1870, bears the crest of the Belknap family. It is marked on the underside "BALL, BLACK & CO./NEW YORK/210/ENGLISH STERLING."

H. with handle up 14³/₄ inches
Museum of the City of New York, from the collection of Waldron Phoenix Belknap, Jr.

185

Berkey and Gay, one of the major cabinet-making firms in Grand Rapids, Michigan, produced this Renaissance revival mahogany table in the 1870s. The company was founded as Berkey and Matter in 1862, although Julius Berkey had been making furniture as early as 1860. The table bears similarities to other Renaissance revival designs of the 1870s. The circular top of highly figured burl walnut is centered with a panel of elaborate multi-

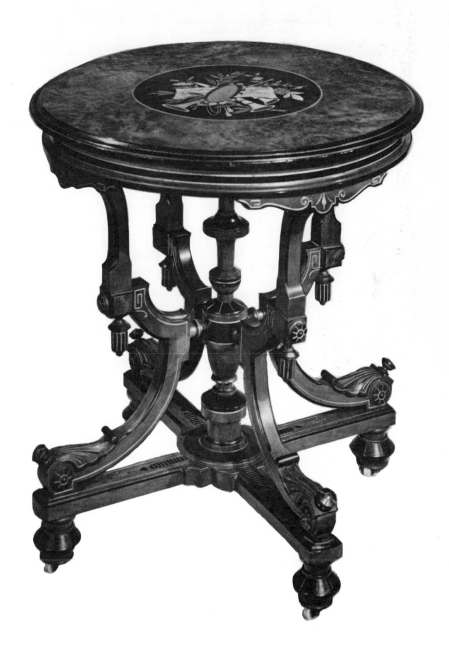

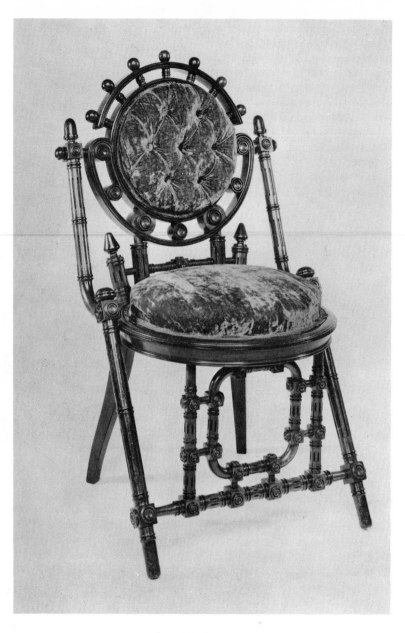

New York directories, listing his occupation as "chairs." He apparently found challenge enough in making the single piece of furniture, for the listing continued unchanged into the eighties. In 1876, in Kimball's *Book of Designs,* a retailers' catalogue, Hunzinger illustrated and described ten chairs. A side chair with the same underlying design as the one here is described as "Frame in Walnut, $18.67; upholstered in different colored Satin, with Star [that is, with the tufting creating a star pattern], $40.00." All of Hunzinger's chairs were inventive, so much so that their whimsey becomes the touch that makes them unmistakably his. Here, although there is a feeling of the Renaissance revival style in the decoration, the primary influence seems to have been an aesthetic of the machine. Interesting though the design is as a statement of the machine age that followed the Civil War, there is a certain incongruity in giving to an object intended for repose the characteristics of mechanical movement. Gazing at these chairs, one can only feel that turning a knob might set all the wheels and cogs into motion.

H. 32¹/₄ inches
The Metropolitan Museum of Art, Gift of Mrs. Florence Weyman, 67.210.1

186

Turned wooden parts that look like the components of an engine, or, in the base, cast-iron piping, characterize this walnut side chair, one of a pair, bearing the stamped inscription "HUNZINGER/N.Y./PAT. MARCH 30/1869." George Hunzinger was one of many furniture manufacturers of German origin who flourished in New York in the seventies and eighties. He was also an early specialist: he took out a patent for a reclining chair in 1861 and in 1866 first appeared in the

187

The Renaissance revival reached its peak in America at the time of the Philadelphia Centennial of 1876. By the 1870s the full range of Renaissance revival styles of the past two decades were used on major pieces like this rosewood cabinet made about 1870 to 1875. Monumental scale and architectural orders, part of the 1850s phase of the Renaissance revival, can be seen here. Evident too is an 1860s "neo grec" mixture of classic and exotic, in the combination of Ionic and lotus capitals on the pilasters and in the incised and gilded linear ornament. Marquetry, also part of the Renaissance revival of the 1860s, here resembles an eighteenth-century pattern more than the arabesques of the Renaissance. The wheel-shaped top of the free-standing central urn shows the current influence of the mechanical on decoration. As on many successful Renaissance revival pieces of the period, these separate trends of more than two decades are drawn together into one style in which the fascination of historicism is subservient to the overall design. Repetition of shapes and motifs unifies the whole. The large marquetry design with its straight sides and arched top above a vase shape repeats the form of the central arched recess and freestanding urn. Leaf carving on the urn appears again on carved scrolls and cresting. The wheel top of the urn is echoed in miniature in two circular spoked decorative knobs.

H. 81 inches
The Metropolitan Museum of Art, Rogers Fund, 64.236

188

Three of the qualities characterizing the best furniture of the Renaissance revival at its height, during the 1870s, are found in this center table made about 1875, probably in New York. First is the eclecticism of historical form and ornament; second, the extraordinary flat surface decoration of the late Renaissance revival; and third, and most important, the successful synthesis of the historical motifs and the 1870s approach to decoration into a complex but unified design. A floral marquetry panel on top is reminiscent of intricate work of the late seventeenth and early eighteenth centuries, particularly in France at the time of Louis XIV. The simple, cabriole-legged shape owes more to the period of Louis XV, while the broad flat channeling of the central urn and the painting of these channels is characteristic of Louis XVI furniture. Throughout the design the classical palmette is the unifying decorative motif. It appears in a marquetry band around the edge of the top. On the legs the palmette is incised and gilded in the "neo grec" manner, and in a looser-petaled form it is carved on the elaborate stretcher. Incised and gilded on a dark panel applied to the apron, the motif becomes the focal point. This table, once owned by Mr. and Mrs. James Lancaster Morgan, of Brooklyn, is thought to have been part of a set awarded a first prize at the Philadelphia Centennial.

L. 30¹/₈ inches
Museum of the City of New York, Gift of John Hill Morgan and Lancaster Morgan

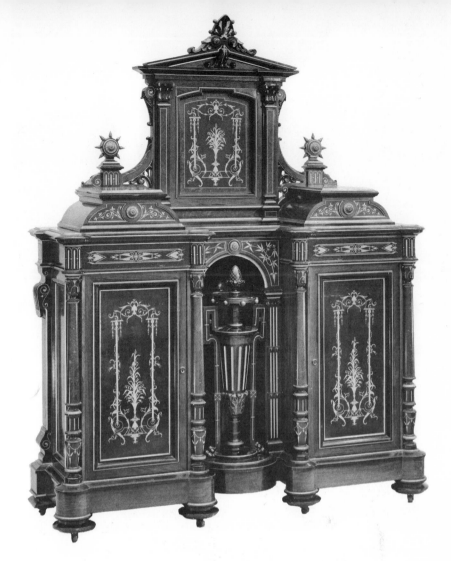

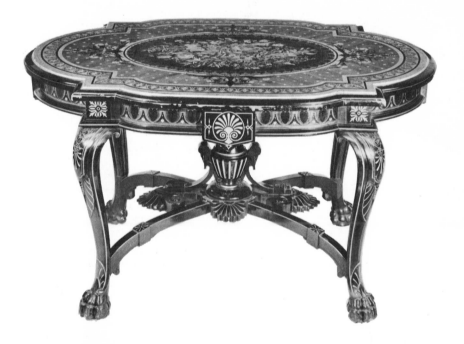

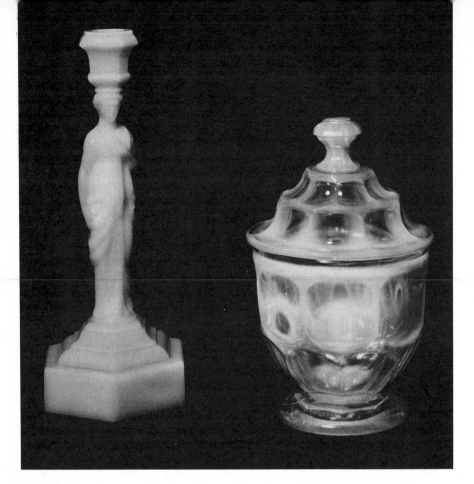

189

This opaque white candlestick and opalescent sugar bowl were pressed by the New England Glass Company. The candlestick, in a design patented in 1870, has as its shaft a caryatid, a motif of the Renaissance revival style. The caryatid was used by other glasshouses; it appeared, for example, on a variety of forms in the Boston and Sandwich Glass Company catalogue of 1874, but always cast as a separate piece—the New England Glass Company was unique in combining the caryatid with other elements in a single mold. The sugar bowl, illustrated in the New England Glass Company catalogue of 1869, is pressed in the Ashburton pattern. This is a free variation of a cut-glass pattern from the late eighteenth-century neoclassical style, which furnished many designs used on Renaissance revival objects.

H. candlestick 9⅝ inches
The Metropolitan Museum of Art, Gift of Mrs. Emily Winthrop Miles, 46.140.320, 336

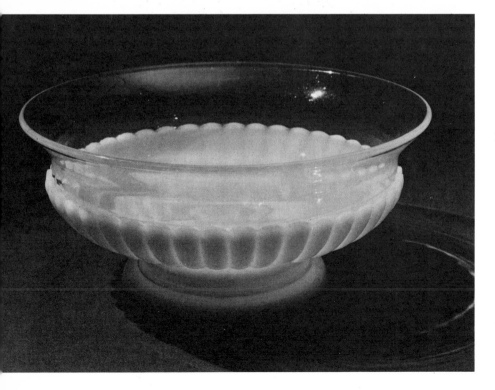

190

Bakewell, Pears and Company of Pittsburgh marked this pressed opal and clear glass bowl "B.P.&Co. Pat. Sept 29th 1874." What the patent protected was the technique of combining these two kinds of glass. The smooth clear inner layer and the ribbed opal glass outer layer make up a simple classical design. Small late nineteenth-century objects made up of classical elements often are closer to the ancient models than the more complex larger pieces, in which the motifs have been modified to the predominantly linear patterns most popular in the 1870s.

Diam. 9 inches
Lowell Innes, Saco, Maine

191

Dating from the late 1860s, these pressed-glass pitchers were inexpensive tablewares. The patterns, the Lincoln Drape and the Cable, are characteristic of the pressed glass made after the Civil War, in sometimes complex but comparatively low-relief designs. Because of their high quality, these pitchers can be attributed to the Boston and Sandwich Glass Company, which turned out many similarly pressed objects. Each pattern referred to a contemporary event: the Lincoln Drape in its evocation of the assassinated president, the Cable in its commemoration of the laying of the Atlantic Cable (see also nos. 181, 182). Both have a formal dignity that would have added to their appeal.

H. taller pitcher 9 3/16 inches

The Metropolitan Museum of Art, Gift of Mrs. Emily Winthrop Miles, 46.140.846, 831

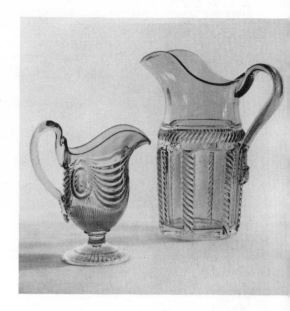

192

Because it was cheaper, glass made with lime, developed after 1860, replaced glass made with lead in the manufacture of pressed objects. The use of frosted glass, combined with clear glass in this covered compote by Gillinder and Sons of Philadelphia and Greensburg, Pennsylvania, was one way of camouflaging imperfections in the less than perfect lime glass. Pressing techniques had improved enough by then to allow representational relief patterns. The compote with its Indian finial is in the Pioneer pattern, introduced about 1880 and popularly called "Westward Ho."

H. 7½ inches

The Metropolitan Museum of Art, Gift of Mrs. Emily Winthrop Miles, 46.140.858

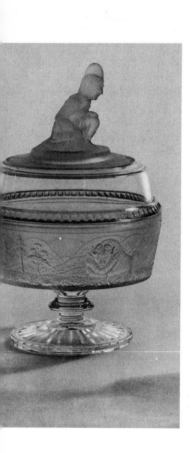

193

Made by Bakewell, Pears and Company, Pittsburgh, about 1865, this covered compote is pressed in a pattern called Argus, or Thumbprint, which was used at several factories in that city in the 1860s and 70s. The molded oval facets form a highly reflective surface that achieves the same effect as cut glass, but the metal is cruder; close inspection reveals imperfections that would not have been tolerated in fine cut glass.

H. 14⅛ inches

The Metropolitan Museum of Art, Gift of Mrs. Emily Winthrop Miles, 46.140.83

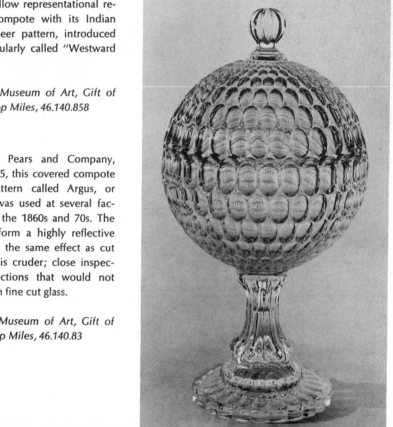

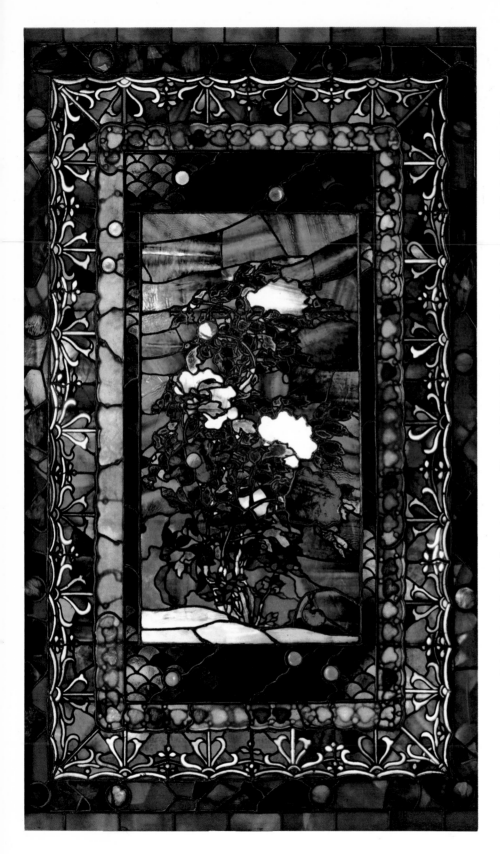

194

For the sale catalogue of the collection of Henry G. Marquand, second president of the Metropolitan Museum, John La Farge wrote of this window that it was among his earliest, "made in 1878-79. Part of the glass is the very first of what is called American glass . . . which I was the first to make. Sir Alma-Tadema and Hon. John Hay have similar subjects, with variations, of course." La Farge, who maintained a studio at 51 West Tenth Street, New York, was recognized internationally for his contribution to stained glass; he was also a painter (see paintings and sculpture volume no. 112). "American glass" is opaline, a translucent, iridescent metal. He made several thousand windows, many for prominent architects such as Ware and Van Brunt, H.H. Richardson, and McKim, Mead and White; Henry James called those he did for Richard Upjohn's Church of the Ascension, New York, "unsurpassably fine." Until the time of La Farge American stained glass had relied on late Gothic and Renaissance models, in which perspective was employed realistically. By the 1870s and 80s leading decorative artists had different precepts, stemming largely from William Morris—that a flat surface should be treated as such, and that the intrinsic qualities of materials should be brought out. The Near and Far Eastern sources—Turkish rugs or Japanese scrolls—from which artists were drawing fresh inspiration reinforced these ideas. The design of this window, one of several La Farge did of peonies blowing in the wind, is of Far Eastern, possibly Japanese, inspiration. The window was in Marquand's Newport house until 1930.

H. 75 inches

The Metropolitan Museum of Art, Gift of Miss Susan Dwight Bliss, 30.50

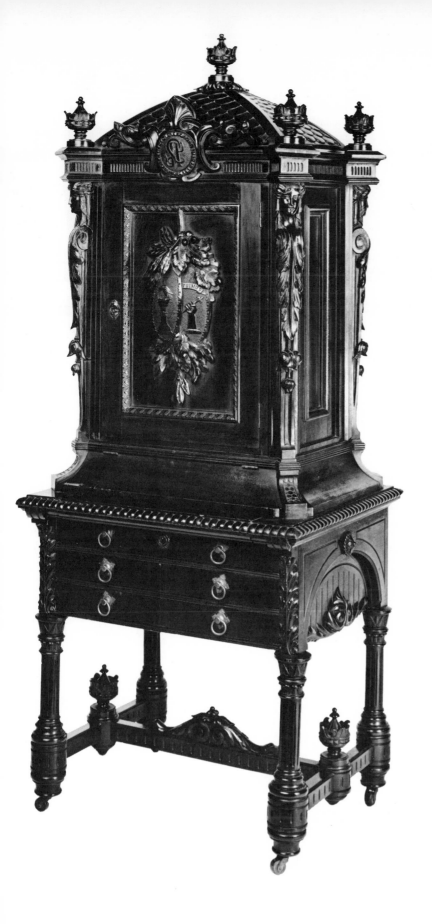

195

Bruce Price, who was to become a major architect of the 1880s, made the grand tour of Europe with his bride, Josephine Lee, in 1872, and during the next year designed this cabinet to hold the jewelry bought for her during the trip. Price later built, for America's newly wealthy families, houses in Tuxedo Park and "cottages" for those who summered in Newport and Maine; he worked in no single style of architecture, but often enough his designs had strong overtones of the French Renaissance at the time of Francis I. The Chateau Frontenac in Quebec is exemplary of that side of his work, and this ebonized cabinet seems a sort of preview of that imposing hotel. The cabinet is elaborate and formal, and highly architectural—not necessarily to be expected in furniture by architects, as a comparison of pieces by Richardson (no. 236) or Wright (no. 293) will show. Leafy scrolled brackets on the corners of the upper section become caryatids supporting projections, each topped by a crown-like finial, which is also found at the peak of the top and the center of each side stretcher. The top suggests a roof of scalloped French tile, which Price was later to use on homes in the Queen Anne, or shingle, style. An elaborate cartouche in the center of the front cornice bears his wife's monogram "JLP."

H. 69 inches

Museum of the City of New York, Gift of Mrs. Price Post

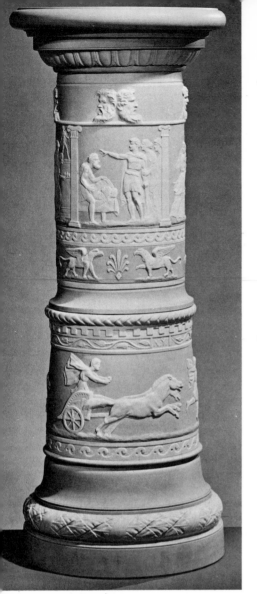

196

This pedestal was the creation of Karl Mueller, of the Union Porcelain Works, Greenpoint, New York, a sculptor of German origin who designed the company's exhibition pieces for the Centennial of 1876. Classical subjects were popular when the nation celebrated its one-hundredth birthday; prosperous Americans, anxious to prove their cultural level equal to their economic one, assumed that classical allusion would guarantee the good taste of their products. This truncated biscuit porcelain column, with figures in white against apricot, inspired by late eighteenth-century jasperware by Wedgwood, depicts the story of Electra. Three vignettes— Electra giving Orestes to a messenger, Electra mourning what she thinks are Orestes' ashes, and Clytemnestra's offering at Agamemnon's tomb—precede the scene shown here, in which Aegisthus uncovers what he expects to be the body of Orestes only to find it is Clytemnestra's; Orestes then proclaims himself to the usurper. Around the bottom is the chariot race in which Orestes was supposed to have lost his life. The column has two marks in the griffin frieze: one showing a figure of a horseman with the letters "K L H.M." around it, the other the letters "U.P.W." above an eagle's head with "S" in its beak, both inside two concentric circles. "N.Y." is marked in the vine band. Another column from the same mold, now in a private collection, is in green and gray stoneware with "ELEKTRA" in the middle band.

H. 42¹/₂ inches

The Metropolitan Museum of Art, Anonymous Gift Fund, 68.99.1

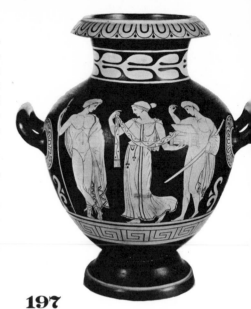

197

The Chelsea Keramic Art Works of Chelsea, Massachusetts, made this vase in 1876, the year it was acquired by the Museum of Fine Arts as part of its program to stimulate industrial art. This pottery was started by Alexander Robertson in 1866, but not until a reorganization of 1875, after Robertson had been joined by his father and brother, did art pottery become the specialty of the establishment. They followed the lead of the English potters who were working in small shops to retain traditions of craftsmanship. Art pottery was made with emphasis on the decorative rather than the useful; inspiration came from both classical and more exotic sources. This earthenware vase, based on the Greek hydria, was among the first decorative work produced at Chelsea. Its free adaptation of classical elements was in keeping with the still popular Renaissance revival style.

H. 13¹/₈ inches

Museum of Fine Arts, Boston, Gift of James Robertson and Sons

198

The taste for Egyptian subjects that continued through the century ran high in the 1870s. The 1872 memorial to the Union dead, in Mt. Auburn Cemetery, Cambridge, was a sphinx; Verdi's *Aïda*, commissioned to celebrate the opening of the Suez Canal in 1869, had its first American performance in New York in 1873; and Egyptian subjects were deemed suitable for the Philadelphia Centennial (see also no. 232). This bust of Cleopatra, in Parian ware, was made by Isaac Broome of Ott and Brewer, one of the largest ceramic producers of Trenton, New Jersey. Broome, a sculptor of some repute, was hired especially to make pieces for the Centennial (see also no. 201). The company, after reorganization in 1871, put special emphasis on work for exhibitions, with displays at both the Centennial and the Paris Exposition in 1878. The bust, colored olive-blue-black and decorated in gold and some silver, shows careful detailing of headdress, necklace, and garment. It is marked "BROOME, Sculp' 1876/OTT & BREWER/TRENTON, N.J."

H. 21 inches

New Jersey State Museum, Trenton, The Brewer Collection

Like the bust of Cleopatra (no. 198), The Finding of Moses is an Egyptian subject treated in a neoclassical manner, more in the spirit of Ingres's paintings such as Oedipus and the Sphinx than that of the later true search for exoticism. The group, in biscuit porcelain, was made about 1876 by the Union Porcelain Works of Greenpoint, New York, and designed by Karl Mueller (see also nos. 196, 203, 204). Both the crouching girl and the standing Pharaoh's daughter are in Roman rather than Egyptian dress. The inclusion of a sphinx was a standard way of setting the scene in Egypt.

H. 19¼ inches

The Metropolitan Museum of Art, Edgar J. Kaufmann Charitable Foundation Fund, 68.97.7

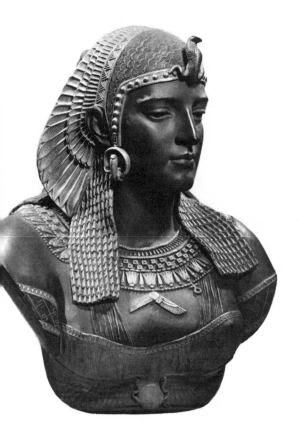

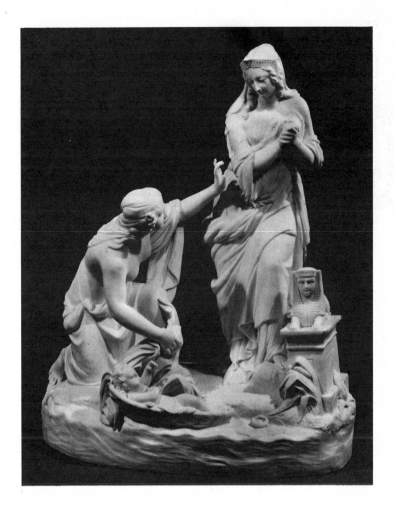

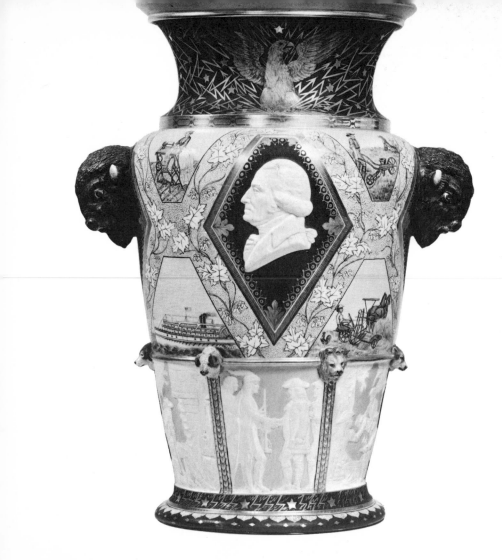

200

Also designed by Karl Mueller (see no. 196), this monumental Century Vase commemorates events of American history in six biscuit panels, while painted vignettes show the contemporary machines that were forging her progress in 1876. The relief profile of George Washington and the gilded American eagle above set the patriotic tone. The thunderbolt, customarily displayed only in the eagle's talons, has been combined with the star to become the gold border motif against a dark blue ground. Heads of North American animals such as the bison, walrus, and bighorn sheep adorn the porcelain vase, whose shape is basically classical. It is marked on the underside: "Century Vase/Exhibited at Centennial/Exhibition at Philadelphia/Manufactured 1876/By Union Porcelain Works/Greenpoint," and "UPW" with an eagle's head with "S" in its beak.

H. 22¹/₄ inches

The Brooklyn Museum, Gift of Carll and Franklin Chace, in memory of their mother, Pastora Forest Smith Chace, daughter of Thomas Carll Smith

201

Another piece made by the Union Porcelain Works for display at the Philadelphia Centennial, this Liberty cup demonstrates the approach to design of the 1870s. Each motif is selected from earlier styles and combined in a new shape. The handle is the personification of Liberty that Delacroix had used decades earlier. The white relief figures in the neoclassical style call to mind those introduced by Wedgwood in the late eighteenth century. The leaf borders are neoclassical motifs. The cylinder shape on a base and large size of the cup are typical of the time it was made. Both cup and saucer are marked on the underside, the cup in red, the saucer in black, "1876/UNION PORCELAIN WORKS /GREENPOINT/N.Y."

H. cup 4⁵/₈ inches

The Metropolitan Museum of Art, Gift of Mr. and Mrs. Franklin M. Chace

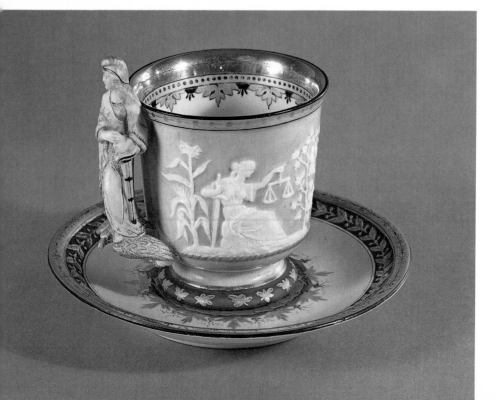

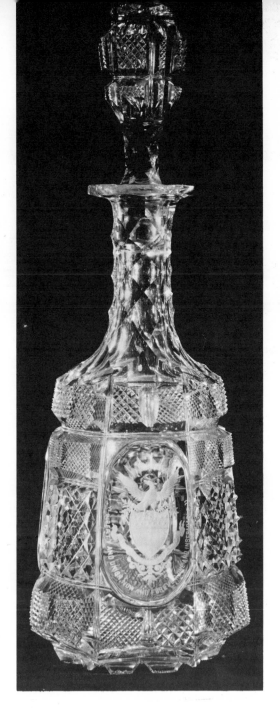

202

Elaborate cut glass became fashionable again in the 1870s, as this decanter and wine glasses by Christian Dorflinger's Wayne County Glass Works of White Mills, Pennsylvania, demonstrate. Made for the Centennial, where it received the highest award, the set shows off the makers' cutting skills. The several variations of diamond patterns were known earlier in the century, but they are more deeply cut here for a more emphatic effect. The decanter displays the United States shield and the motto "LIBERTY AND UNION, NOW AND FOREVER, ONE AND INSEPARABLE." Each of the thirty-eight glasses, one for every state in 1876, bears a medallion with the state's arms, its motto, and the name of its governor. The one on the left, representing Minnesota, shows a farmer plowing, the Falls of St. Anthony in the Mississippi at Minneapolis, and an Indian on horseback. Above is written *"L'ETOILE DU NORD"* (The star of the North) and below, "JOHN S. PILLSBURY." On the glass representing Massachusetts is an Indian with a bow and arrow. Around the crest is a wreath with an arm grasping a sword. The motto is *"ENSE PETIT SUB LIBERTATE QUIETAM"* (With the sword she seeks quiet peace under liberty); the governor's name is "A.H. RICE."

H. decanter 11⁷/₈ inches
Philadelphia Museum of Art

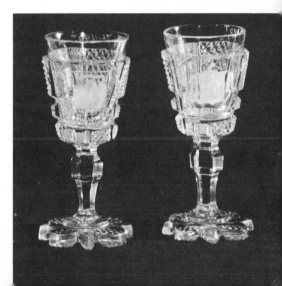

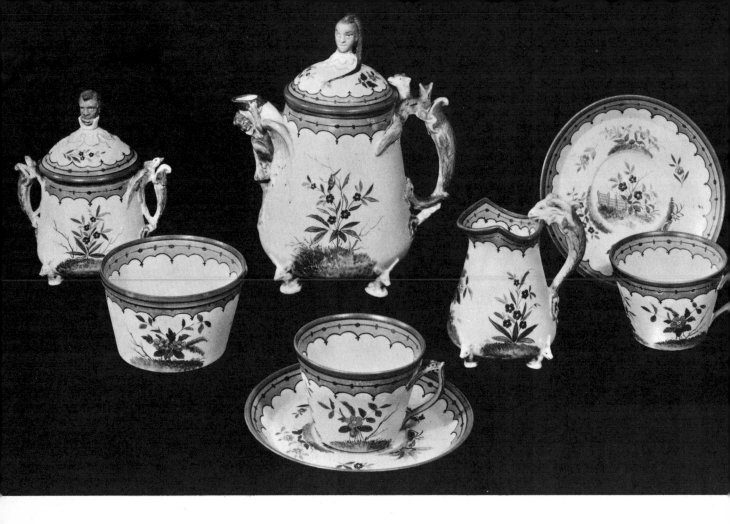

203 "Tête-à-tête set" was the name of a similar tea set when it was illustrated before 1900 in *The Pottery and Porcelain of the United States,* by Edwin Atlee Barber. Made by the Union Porcelain Works for the Centennial and designed by Karl Mueller, it combines rococo and neoclassical elements. The inspiration for the tapering forms is late eighteenth-century neoclassical porcelain, but the handles, feet, and finials are reinterpretations of eighteenth-century rococo whimseys. Mueller employed symbols as obvious as the Chinese head topping the teapot and the Negro head representing a West Indian sugar-cane picker on the sugar bowl. This, according to descendants of Thomas Smith, head of Union Porcelain, is the original biscuit porcelain model hand-decorated and unfired, for the set shown at the Centennial. It is marked on the underside of all but one saucer "U.P.W./S."

H. teapot 7 inches

The Metropolitan Museum of Art, Gift of Mr. and Mrs. Franklin M. Chace

204

Karl Mueller created the porcelain pitcher at the left for the Union Porcelain Works about 1880. The bear on the handle and the walrus on the spout, American animals that Mueller also employed, with other native species, on the Century Vase (no. 200), suggest the Pacific Northwest, possibly Alaska, as the setting for the Norse king or god offering beer to Uncle Sam on one side of the piece and the Chinese cardsharp being exposed and attacked on the other. The rest of the elaborate decoration includes a border derived from Near Eastern models. The shape of the pitcher is one first introduced about 1850 as a part of the rococo revival. Besides a "U.P.W." inscribed in the bisque barrel on one side of the pitcher, the underside has, in black: "UNION PORCELAIN WORKS/GREENPOINT/N.Y."

H. 9 1/2 inches

The Metropolitan Museum of Art, Anonymous Gift Fund, 68.103.2

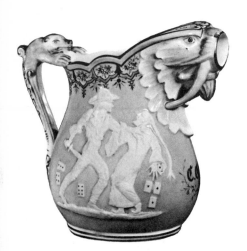

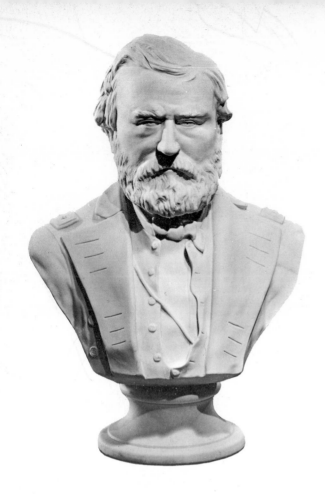

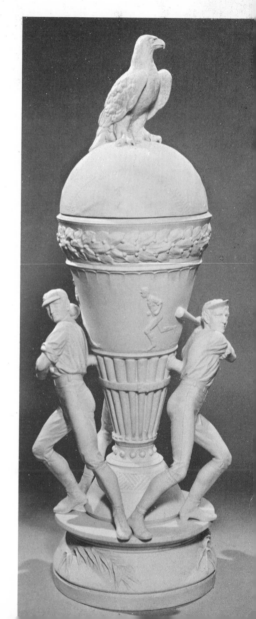

205

The Centennial inspired contemporary as well as older nationalistic themes, and the President of the United States, who also had commanded the victorious Union army, was the most natural of subjects for the celebration. This Parian ware bust of General Grant is stamped on the back: "MANUFACTURED/ BY/JAS. CARR, N.Y. CITY POTTERY,/1876./ W. H. EDGE,/SCULPTOR." James Carr had emigrated from England in 1844 to work in New Jersey potteries producing yellow ware. His company started making pottery in New York in 1853, acquiring renown for tableware and decorative Parian figures. The New York City Pottery was closed in 1888.

H. 18³/4 inches

The Metropolitan Museum of Art, Anonymous Gift Fund, 68.103.3

206

Also by Isaac Broome (see no. 198) of Ott and Brewer for the Centennial is this baseball vase of Parian ware. The conical shape is classical, based on the Roman fasces, although the rods are baseball bats tied with a nineteenth-century buckled belt; the laurel wreath and eagle are also Roman, borrowed in the service of nineteenth-century patriotism. The baseball topping the cone and those in a band around its base go with the large free-standing players and the ones in relief in celebrating the popular game. America's national sport probably first appeared in the 1830s, and by 1865 there were ninety-one municipal clubs. It remained essentially an amateur pastime until 1876, when the National League of Professional Baseball Clubs was organized, comprising eight clubs, including the Athletics from the Centennial city of Philadelphia.

H. 34 inches

The New Jersey State Museum, Trenton, The Brewer Collection

207 In 1888 Auguste Pottier of the firm of Pottier and Stymus, "Furniture & Decorations, 489 Fifth Avenue," offered these two black walnut chairs, made about 1875, to the Metropolitan Museum in a letter to the Museum's first director, General Luigi Palma di Cesnola. Pottier described them as "in the style of Henry II, made by our firm for the Centennial Exposition," when in fact they are of the style only in the use of Henry's cipher in the tapestry back of the side chair and the cipher of his mistress, Diane de Poitiers, on the back of the matching armchair. An imaginative composite in their decorative motifs, the chairs show both the traditional historicism that had pervaded furniture styles since the thirties and forties and, in details such as the decorative shallow carving and rows of small turned balusters, the new styles of the seventies and eighties. Renaissance inspiration can be seen in the skillfully carved lower back rail with its classical head flanked by scrolling leaves and flowers, in the stylized palmettes on the arm rails, and in the Ionic columns forming the center of the back stiles.

Auguste Pottier and William Pierre Stymus began their careers in the 1840s and ultimately became foremen of the New York French cabinetmaking firm of Rochefort and Skarren. According to Hagen, after Rochefort's death they continued his business on Broadway near Houston Street. The first individual listings for them occur in the New York directory of 1858/59 at 623 Broadway, with Pottier as a cabinetmaker and Stymus

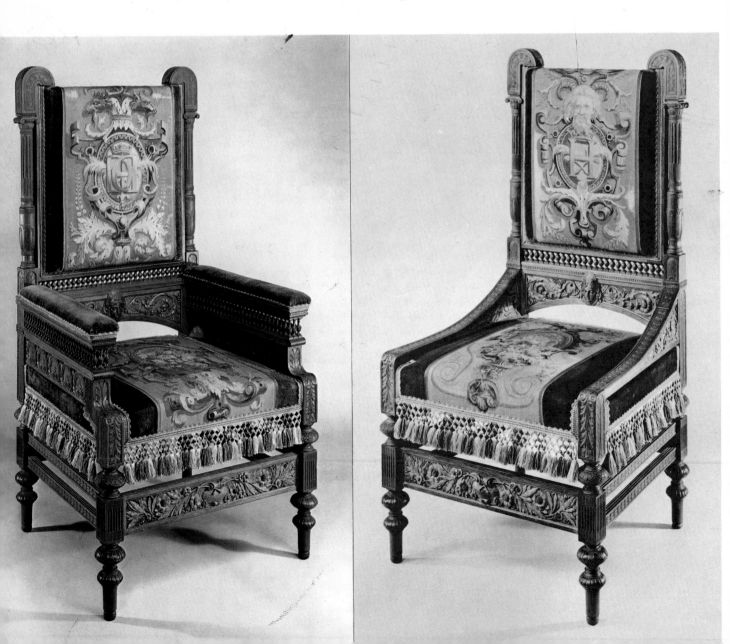

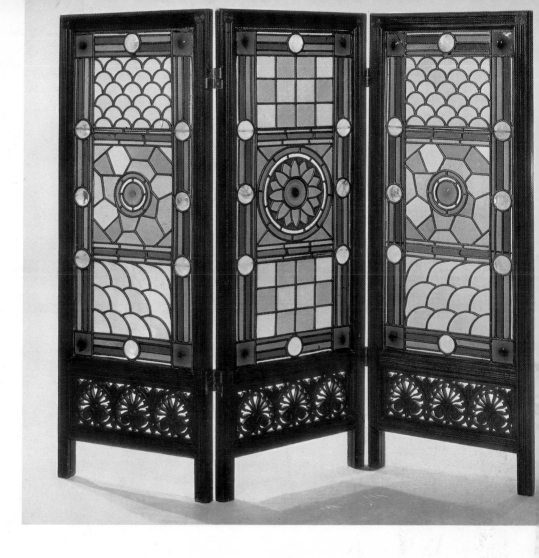

208

as an upholsterer. Their partnership listing at the same address began in 1859/60 as "Pottier & Stymus LATE B. E. Rochefort, upholsterers & cabinetmakers." By 1871 they also had a factory occupying a full block on Lexington Avenue between Forty-first and Forty-second Streets. In 1872 this location at 375 Lexington became their showroom as well, remaining their headquarters until 1883, when they began listing an office on Fifth Avenue. Like Herter Brothers and Leon Marcotte, Pottier and Stymus was one of the most important cabinetmaking and decorating establishments of the 1870s and 80s and, like these, a family business; by the 1880s a son of each of the founders was active in the firm.

H. 51³/₄ inches

The Metropolitan Museum of Art, Gift of Auguste Pottier, 88.10.2,3

Stained glass became extraordinarily popular in the 1880s. The Gothic revival had brought it back to the attention of designers, and the Pre-Raphaelites in England made it a fine art, exploiting its possibilities for rich color and flat pattern. In 1884 an Englishman, writing in *American Architect and Building News,* could say: " . . . it is a rare occurrence to find a new building or house of any pretension without some specimen of stained, painted or enamelled glass." In America, where John La Farge was doing his superb work (see no. 194), the case was virtually the same. This small firescreen is unsigned and is probably the work of a decorating firm like that of Christian Herter of New York (see no. 211). The breaking up of the surfaces in an entirely rectilinear way, into flat squares and rectangles—under the influence of Moorish tiles or Japanese architecture—was the rule in interior design of the day, for both entire walls and individual pieces of furniture. Here, within a strongly rectilinear cherry frame, the effect is of richness in simplicity, with enough variation in color, texture, and pattern to give great vitality to the piece.

L. 45¹/₈ inches

The Metropolitan Museum of Art, Edgar J. Kaufmann Charitable Foundation Fund, 69.127

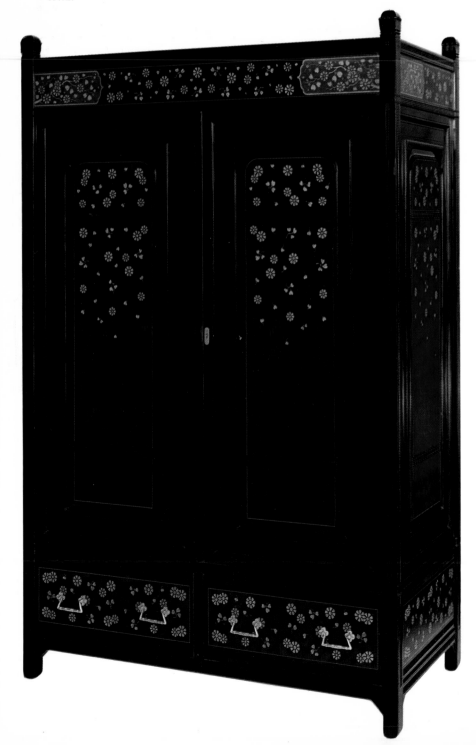

209

In the 1880s the stylish gowns and stage costumes of America's favorite prima donna hung in this elegant wardrobe. Lillian Russell—"airy, fairy, Lillian," as her admiring public called her—made her New York debut in 1880 and in the next few years, playing in such comic operas as Gilbert and Sullivan's *Patience* and *The Sorcerer*, she became the toast of Broadway. During this period, she is said to have acquired from one of New York's leading decorating firms this inlaid and ebonized cherry wardrobe; the back bears the mark, in incised letters, "HERTER BRO'S."

A comparison with earlier case pieces shows how much furniture design had changed. There is no architectural pediment here as there is on the Salem chest of drawers (no. 1), no rising of form through narrowing stages to a central terminating point, as on the rococo étagère (no. 129), nor even a suggestion of the cornice found on the Gothic secretary (no. 100). The incised top rail is the same thickness as the base rail; the corner finials, formed by the projection of the stiles, might just as easily be feet. Superficially the wardrobe has an "either-end-up" quality not present in earlier furniture and requiring exacting attention to decorative details more than to form. The shallow carving at the door corners points upward, as do the incised lines of the top stiles. Marquetry flowers and petals on the doors seem to be fluttering down from the branches in the lighter panels above. Through contrast of color and an inlaid frame, these panels become the focal points of the piece. Japanese influence, part of the exoticism of the 1880s (see also no. 212), is seen in the stylized character of the branches, the chrysanthemum-like flowers, the loose composition of the designs, and the large undecorated areas. For all the looseness of the pattern, there is a certain rigidity in the way the motifs are contained within the frame of the panels. This rigidity exists also in the severity of the rectilinear form, broken up only by the marquetry pattern, moldings, and incised lines.

H. 89 inches

The Metropolitan Museum of Art, Gift of Kenneth O. Smith, 69.140

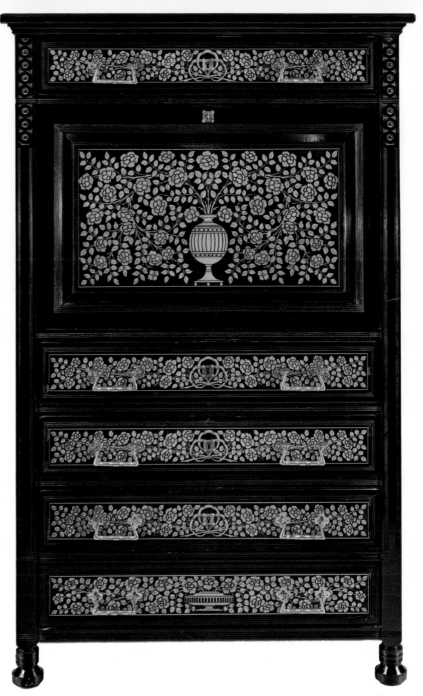

210 In *Hints on Household Taste* (1868) Charles Lock Eastlake stated:

> The best and most picturesque furniture of all ages has been simple in general form. It may have been enriched by complex details of carved work or inlay, but its main outline was always chaste and sober in design, never running into extravagant contour or unnecessary curves.

Explicit in Eastlake's words are not only a judgment of historic styles but also a criticism of the excesses of mid-nineteenth-century revivals. Implicit are the principles of the reform movement in furniture design. Although England shaped the philosophy, America produced some of the most sophisticated furniture following its tenets, as is shown by this ebonized cherry desk, part of a bedroom suite (see no. 211) made about 1877 to 1882 by Herter Brothers of New York. Whether called "art furniture," the most appropriate term here, "Eastlake," for its well-known popularizer, or "Queen Anne," the term applied to contemporary reform architecture, this kind of furniture stemmed from a reform movement that had begun in England as early as the 1830s. A. W. N. Pugin, John Ruskin, and the Pre-Raphaelites were all influential, but it remained for the leading proponents of the Arts and Crafts movement of the late 1850s and early 60s—architects like William Burges, Richard Norman Shaw, and Philip Webb, and designers like William Morris—to set the precepts of the style: rectilinear shapes, honesty of construction, and flat surface decoration —usually in panels—of painting, marquetry, or shallow carving.

The nomenclature "Arts and Crafts" is in itself significant. Leaders of the movement, particularly Morris, hoped to make decorative art objects once again worthy of the attention of the serious artist, while the master craftsman, as in the middle ages, would find joy in the integrity of his hand labor. However admirable the attempt to meld the art and the craft, there was a basic dualism in the Morris philosophy. "What business have we with art at all," queried Morris, "unless all can share it?" Yet his handicraft system precluded that sharing. Herter furniture, in design and method of production closely akin to works of the Morris school, was "reform" furniture in elements of style only. It was never meant to be mass-produced, nor aimed at a mass market. Part of the suite illustrated on the following two pages, made either for the town house or the country house of multimillionaire financier and railroad magnate Jay Gould (see also no. 215), this desk is listed on a March 1882 Herter Brothers invoice to Gould: "1 Inlaid Ebony writing desk to match Bedroom Suite $550."

H. 54 inches
The Metropolitan Museum of Art, Gift of Paul Martini, 69.146.3

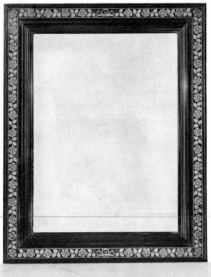

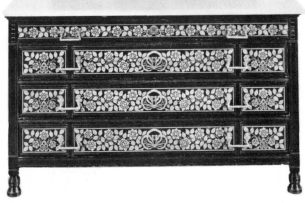

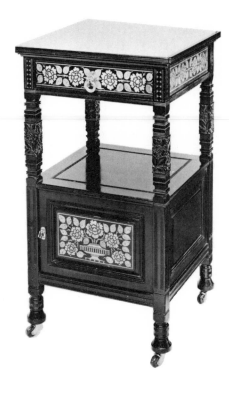

211 Most of the cost of this furniture, as well as the effect, lies in its extensive ornamentation of turning, shallow carving, and marquetry. The turnings are the bobbin and funnel feet of all the pieces of this set and the balusters relieving the almost completely straight lines of the bed. As on other furniture of the late sixties and the seventies, these balusters seem to have been influenced by mechanical devices, such as the cylinders, pistons, or valves of an engine (see also no. 186). It should not be forgotten that at this moment in history the machine was revolutionizing every aspect of life; it commanded both excitement for its power and reverence for its potential of spreading material well-being. Shallow floral carving, used sparingly on the night table and the bed to repeat the inlaid motifs, and incised lines are in the Eastlake-art furniture tradition.

A comparison of the marquetry on the pieces here with that on the wardrobe (no. 209) shows a quite different effect. With their closely knit patterns of natural forms, these panels resemble somewhat a wallpaper by William Morris. Here, however, the motifs within each panel are arranged in a single non-repetitive design, with a centering device, a vase or urn, a ribbon, or a central group of leaves or flowers. Even the hardware has been integrated into the pattern; the focal point of the drawer in the night table is a leaf pattern, of which the pull is a part; on the drawers of the bureau, as well as those of the desk no. 210, a keyhole escutcheon centers the design. Where there was no escutcheon, as on the bottom drawer of the desk, a different design was used.

Although a large firm with many designers and craftsmen, Herter Brothers in the

1870s and early 80s was dominated by the taste and influence of one man, its owner and director, Christian Herter. By both talent and training Herter was suited to pre-eminence in his field. Born in Stuttgart in 1840, he was named for his father, a well-known carver and cabinetmaker. Both Christian and his older halfbrother, Gustave Herter, were artistic. Christian was a student at the Ecole des Beaux-Arts at fifteen. Gustave studied in the atelier of a German architect before emigrating in 1848 to New York, where he became a silver designer for Tiffany's and three years later opened a cabinetmaking shop on Mercer Street. About 1860, when Gustave was a well-established furniture maker and decorator at 547 Broadway, Christian joined him in New York. The firm of Herter Brothers first appeared in the city directories for 1865/66. In 1868 Gustave sent Christian to France to study with Pierre Victor Galland, a successful decorative artist; when Christian returned in 1870, he bought out Gustave, who subsequently went back to Germany. During the next decade, under Christian's leadership, Herter Brothers became one of the greatest decorating firms in America.

H. bed 118 inches
The Metropolitan Museum of Art, Gift of Paul Martini, 69.146.1,2,4,5

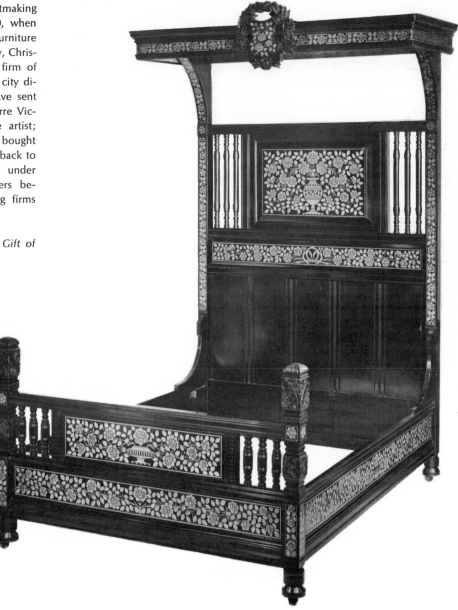

In the 1870s and 80s Herter Brothers kept pace with the latest international trends in furniture and accessories. Two of these trends can be seen in this blond maple bedroom suite, made by them about 1877 to 1880 for Lyndhurst, the Hudson River mansion owned by Jay Gould from 1880 to his death in 1892. The first is the use of decorative tiles; the second, the increasing importance of Japanese motifs. By the 1870s the practice of using tiles on furniture, as advocated by Bruce Talbert in *Gothic Forms Applied to Furniture* (1867) and Eastlake, had become widespread but was not always considered successful. The late nineteenth-century tastemaker Clarence Cook, writing in *The House Beautiful* (1878), inveighed against light wood furniture like this with "cold blue tiles let into its surface—tiles, things that, except for actual utility, have no right to be used in connection with wood." Here the tiles are used sparingly; at eye level,

each forms a decorative panel in the tradition of art furniture. Rather than "cold blue," each of these is painted with a different polychrome flower and bird scene in the Japanese fashion.

The rage for Japonica swept America from the 1870s through the early 80s, as it had swept England a decade earlier. In the 1850s Japan had been opened to trade with America and Europe. When Japanese wares were displayed at the London International Exhibition of 1862, English designers felt that Japanese art had the same simplicity and "honesty" they admired in medieval works. By the late sixties, architects like E. W. Godwin were designing Japanese art furniture, and in the seventies these designs were adapted commercially by English furniture manufacturers. In post-Centennial America Christian Herter is supposed to have been the first to import Chinese porcelain, Persian pottery and embroideries, and Japanese

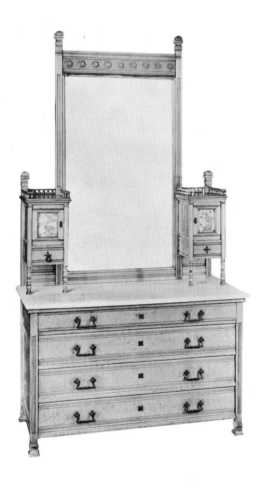

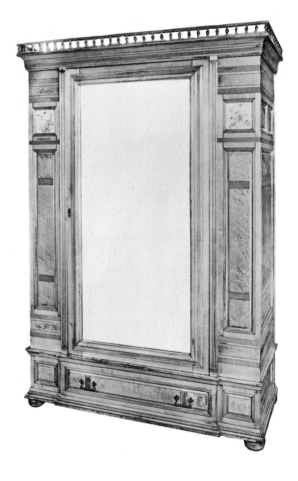

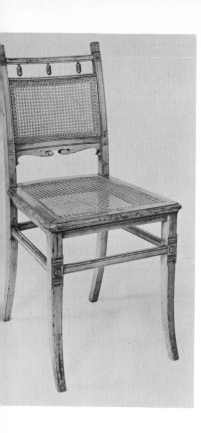

art objects, and the first decorator to employ Oriental motifs in his interiors. On this suite, as on the wardrobe no. 209, the Japanese influence is primarily a decorative one; it did not affect the basic shapes, which are simple and rectangular. There is, however, some influence of the forms of Anglo-Japanese furniture designed by Godwin. The modified saber legs of the side chair, though historically from the Greek and the English Regency classical revival, appear on many chairs and tables in Godwin's book *Art Furniture* (1877). The curious "stilt" cabinets flanking the dressing bureau mirror also seem to have derived from Godwin's designs, though much transmuted from similar forms on the advanced and rather severe Anglo-Japanese case pieces.

H. bureau and wardrobe 86½ inches
National Trust for Historic Preservation,
Lyndhurst in Tarrytown, New York

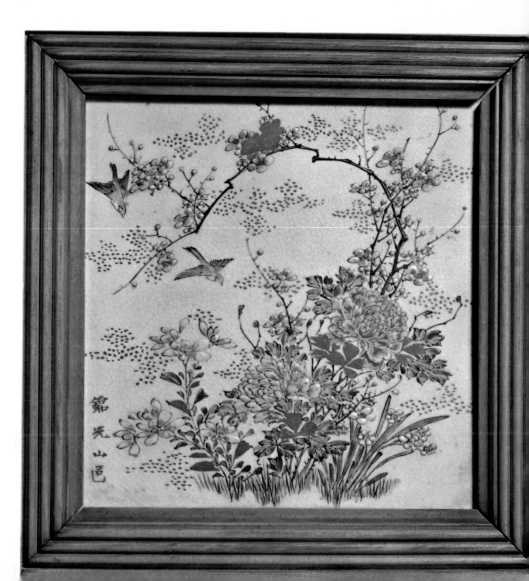

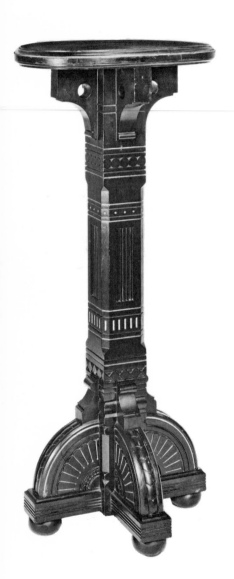

The reform furniture style usually designated "Eastlake" in America can be seen in this ebonized cherry pedestal made about 1880, probably in New York. The ebonized finish, chamfered corners of the shaft, and decoration of shallow geometric carving and incised lines are all characteristic of the style. The cross-shaped base joins the shaft with arc supports like the segments of a wheel. Flattened ball feet, a seventeenth-century form, appear on other furniture of the period (see no. 212).

Clarence Cook in *The House Beautiful* wrote of the Eastlake style in America, and the difficulty in assigning the term to sophisticated pieces of furniture such as this:

> The "Eastlake" furniture must not . . . be judged by what is made in this country, and sold under that name. I have seen very few pieces of this that were either well designed or well made. None of the cheaper sort is ever either. Mr. Herter has had some pieces made which were both well designed and thoroughly well made, as all his furniture is, however we may sometimes quarrel with his over-ornamentation; and Mr. Marcotte has also shown us some good examples in this style. But these are not . . . examples of cheapness, which was one of the recommendations of the "Eastlake" furniture. They are only referred to as doing the style (if it be a style) more justice than the lumps . . . though, in truth, these lumps are a good deal more like the things recommended in Mr. Eastlake's book than the stylish, elegant pieces designed by Messrs. Herter and Marcotte.

H. 40½ inches
The Metropolitan Museum of Art, Edgar J. Kaufmann Charitable Foundation Fund, 69.136.3

214

Classical saber legs tapering to slender brass ferrules support this rosewood table, made in the art furniture style about 1878 to 1884, probably in New York by one of the fashionable firms like Herter Brothers, Marcotte, or Cottier. In his *Art Furniture* E. W. Godwin illustrated a number of pieces with a leg of this shape; often on his Anglo-Japanese designs it was thin and spidery. The style was rapidly being adopted by American manufacturers, for Clarence Cook in *The House Beautiful* showed a large table by Cottier with saber legs and a Herter Brothers suite with similar, though heavier, legs on the settee. In addition to the form of the legs and the flat stretcher, the table shows art furniture characteristics in its decoration. The use of rich contrasting materials—here marble, brass, and wood—is often found on art furniture, as is marquetry, which appears on this table in a delicate leaf and flower pattern containing mother-of-pearl and brass.

H. 29¼ inches
Museum of the City of New York, Gift of Mrs. John S. Taber and Charles M. Clark, Jr.

215

"A chair made by Herter or Marcotte is put together in such a way that only violence can break it; and it can be re-stuffed and re-covered for fifty years, and be as good as new," wrote Clarence Cook in *The House Beautiful* (1878). This ebonized side chair made by Herter Brothers about 1880 incorporates the sturdy construction he admired in this furniture as well as qualities he praised elsewhere in his writings—a simple design and conservative decoration. Part of the furnishings for Jay Gould's Lyndhurst, it is only one of a number of pieces Gould purchased from the Herter firm (see no. 210). He was not alone in his taste. To the superb decorating abilities of Herter Brothers were entrusted the mansions of the wealthy and famous across the continent—those of men like Pierpont Morgan, Jacob Ruppert, and William H. Vanderbilt in New York, D. O. Mills in Menlo Park, New Jersey, and Mark Hopkins and Senator Milton Latham in San Francisco. In a photograph of a room furnished by Herter for Ruppert and published in *Artistic Houses* (1883/84) appears a side chair, which, though painted white, is very similar to this one. It has the same rectilinear back pierced by a shaped finger hole, the same incised lines, and front legs shaped in the characteristic Herter style: bulbous at the top, tapering to a ring-shaped ankle above a trumpet-like foot.

H. 33¾ inches
National Trust for Historic Preservation, Lyndhurst in Tarrytown, New York

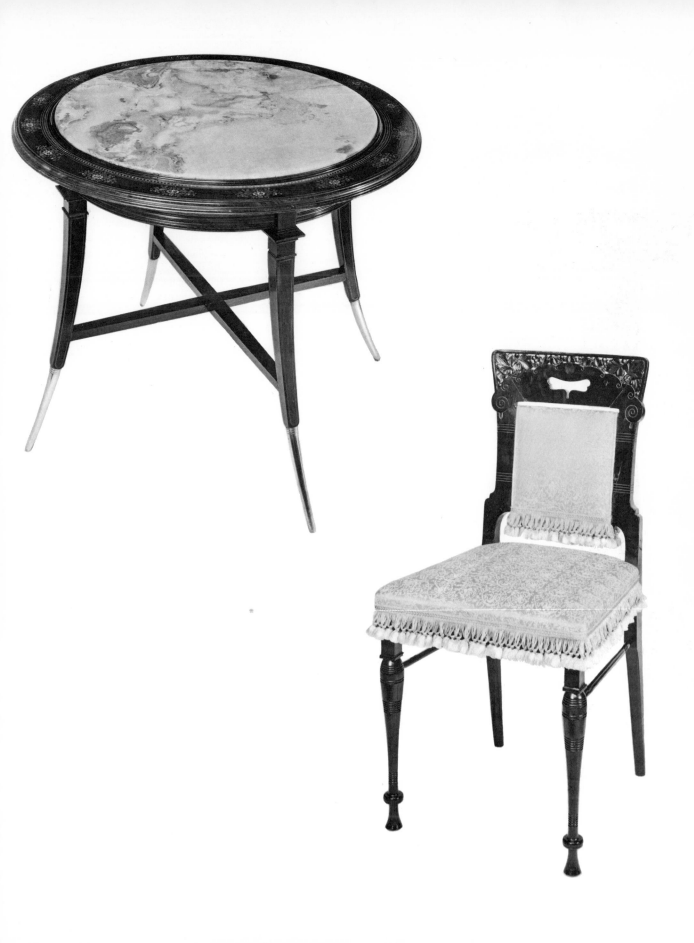

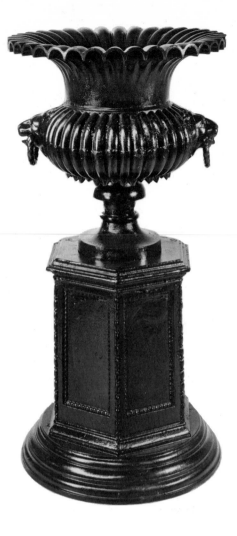

217

The graceful pattern of this small settee, probably designed in the 1870s, was less widely known than that of some other cast-iron pieces (see nos. 116, 119). Naturalism is subdued—in favor of a flat decorative quality in the leaves and a smooth line in the branches. The cabriole legs with paw feet, the floral brackets at the knees, and the symmetry of the back give the piece some of the formal quality of the Renaissance revival style, but the easy flow of line and the prettiness of the silhouetted leaves would have won approval for the piece from the reformers of design following the ideas of William Morris.

L. 39 inches

The Metropolitan Museum of Art, Anonymous Gift Fund, 68.140.2

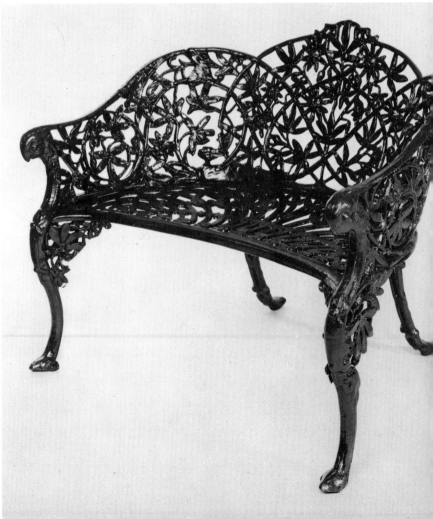

216

In the catalogues of ornamental works issued by iron foundries in the 1860s and 70s, this vase is one of the common models. Called in most of the catalogues the "Woodbury vase," although in at least one instance it was called "Venetian," it did not vary and seems always to have been placed on a hexagonal pedestal like this one. The lion's-head handles are a classical allusion, but the shape has no direct classical prototype.

H. 38³/₄ inches

The Metropolitan Museum of Art, Gift of Mrs. M. E. D. McConnell, 69.51.1

218

Another cast-iron design that remained popular through much of the second half of the century was the fern pattern, available in a settee and matching chair. The pattern is found in a catalogue published by A.B. and W.T. Westervelt of New York and again in that of Samuel S. Bent and Son, New York, published between 1890 and 1894. The chair shows the realism that often during this period produced unhappy effects, reproducing natural forms in a totally incongruous medium; but the inherent flatness of the fern and its simple pattern here seem appropriate and graceful even rendered in cast iron.

H. 35³/₄ inches
The Metropolitan Museum of Art, Edgar J. Kaufmann Charitable Foundation Fund, 69.158.5

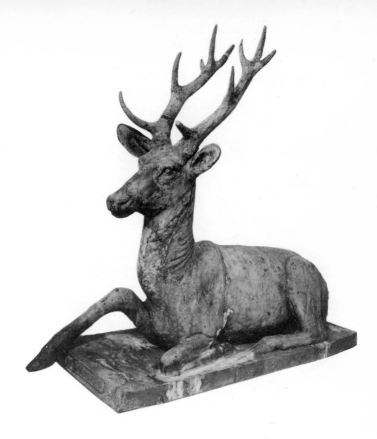

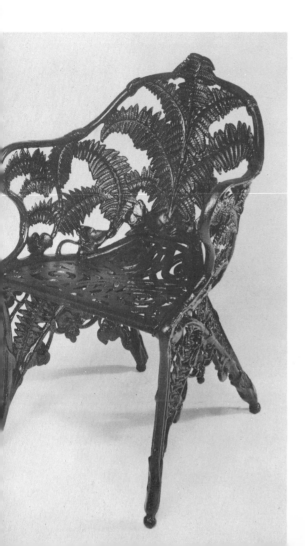

219

Among the animals cast in iron or zinc with which Americans decorated their lawns and gardens, the stag, either standing or reclining, was the most popular. This example is marked "J.W. FISKE. MANUFACTURER" in a ribbon, "PARK PLACE," "NEW YORK," and the numbers "25 8 23." Joseph W. Fiske was first listed in the New York directories in 1864/65, at 120 Nassau Street, occupation "iron." He clearly prospered, for by 1870 he listed his occupation as "manufacturer of ornamental iron work, fountains, vases, statuary, settees, chairs, &c. iron and wire railings, iron stable fixtures, copper weathervanes, &c., &c." A business address on Park Place was added in 1874/75, becoming the sole address in 1878/79, and the firm continued on that street into the twentieth century. A similar stag, but with the left front leg extended instead of the right, was sold by the J. L. Mott Iron Works of New York.

L. 47¹/₂ inches
Fenton L. B. Brown, New York

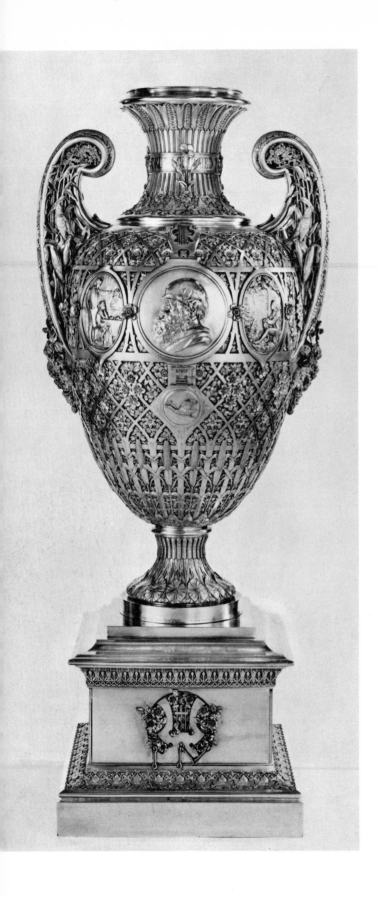

220 To honor the poet William Cullen Bryant on his eightieth birthday in November 1874, a silver vase was commissioned by a group of his friends, described by Samuel Osgood, one of them, as "the leading elements in our business, culture, government, and religion," in an article on the vase in *Harper's New Monthly Magazine* of July 1876. Winner among the designs, presented by major silver companies, was the one for this vase, by James H. Whitehouse of Tiffany and Company. Whitehouse is quoted in the article as saying: "When the Bryant testimonial was first mentioned to me, my thoughts at once flew to the country . . . and to a general contemplation of Nature; and these, together with a certain Homeric influence, produced in my mind the germ of the design—the form of a Greek vase, with the most beautiful American flowers growing round. . . ." Symbolism abounds—American flora, and Renaissance revival medallions representing Bryant's life and work, such as one of the waterfowl, the subject of his Victorian allegory of faith and piety. Osgood doubtless spoke for his contemporaries in his opinion of the vase: ". . . in its severity of form and in its careful and exquisite details there is a combination of simplicity and beauty. . . ." The eclectic decoration and the symbolism of the vase, along with the donors' estimation of it and of themselves, epitomize the spirit—earnest, optimistic, and self-satisfied—prevailing among America's gentry in the 1870s. The vase is marked "TIFFANY & CO UNION SQUARE NEW YORK," "DESIGN PATENT MAY 1875.," and "TIFFANY & Co MAKERS."

H. 33³/₈ inches
The Metropolitan Museum of Art, Gift of William Cullen Bryant, 77.9

221 Tiffany's silverwares were known throughout the world—at the Paris Exposition of 1867 they won the first award ever given to a foreigner, and they gained special recognition at the Centennial exhibition of 1876. The intricate work of which the manufactory was capable can be seen in this hot-water kettle, part of an elaborate tea and coffee set, made, according to the company's records, in 1875. Applied stylized Italianate tendrils are overlaid with berries and leaves, small birds and their nests, in a profusion of ornament that emphasizes rather than de-

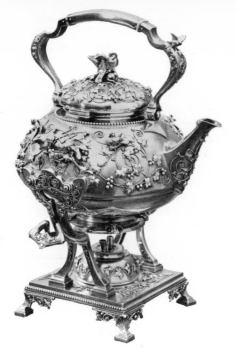

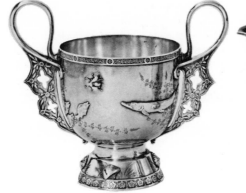

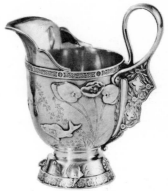

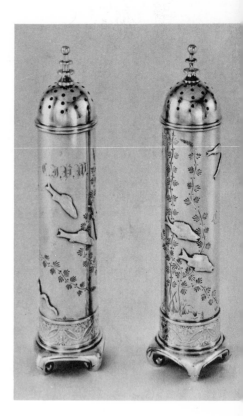

nies the basic simplicity of the form. Upon the incorporation of Tiffany and Company in 1868 the Moore silverworks at 53 Prince Street were united to Tiffany's commercial department and were much enlarged, Edward C. Moore becoming a director in the company and manager of its manufacturing interest. The set is marked: "TIFFANY & CO/ 2325 / QUALITY / STERLING / M / 628 UNION SQUARE," the M being used from 1868 to 1891, the years that Moore was supervisor and head designer of the silver plant.

H. 13¹/₂ inches
Mrs. John B. Greer, Shreveport, Louisiana

222

Tiffany and Company also made this sugar bowl and creamer, in 1874, and their decoration exemplifies several current stylistic trends. The applied flattened fish, lily pads, and shells on the body and foot of each piece and, even more, the engraved seaweed and grass have the flat quality and flowing line of Japanese art, a particularly strong influence at the time (see nos. 211, 212). The handles, with their openwork and flat floral ornament, are similar to "Eastlake" furniture (see no. 225). On the other hand, the basic shapes of the pieces as well as the tightly designed ornamental bands around

top and bottom could be well suited to pieces in the Renaissance revival style. Both pieces are marked "TIFFANY & Co/3737 MAKERS 8114/STERLING-SILVER/925 - 1000/ M," and inscribed "M.K.C April 15th 1880."

H. sugar bowl 5 inches
The Metropolitan Museum of Art, Edgar J. Kaufmann Charitable Foundation Fund, 69.128.1,2

223

Although not part of the same service as the sugar bowl and creamer no. 222, these pepper shakers, made in 1874, use the same fish and engraved seaweed motifs. The Oriental feeling is made stronger here by the finials, which recall Eastern pagodas, and by the wide band around the bottom, with its design in low relief. The tall cylindrical bodies, because of their simplicity, provide a more effective background for the motifs than the forms of sugar and creamer. Each pepper is marked "TIFFANY & Co/3551 M 6613/ STERLING-SILVER," and engraved on the outside "C.T.V.W." for a member of the Van Wyck family. One is inscribed "From Emily"; the other, "From Mamie."

H. 5¹/₂ inches
Museum of the City of New York, Bequest of Miss Katharine Van Wyck Haddock

224 By 1884 when Charles Tisch of New York made this elaborate rosewood cabinet, the Victorian love of knickknacks had become a rage for all exotica. Oriental porcelain, geological curiosities, archaeological souvenirs—all these and more found their way into the standing and hanging cabinets essential in any fashionable house. Wrote Eastlake in *Hints on Household Taste:* "The smallest example of rare old porcelain, of ivory carving, of ancient metal-work, of enamels, of Venetian glass, of anything which illustrates good design and skilful workmanship, should be acquired whenever possible, and treasured with the greatest care. . . . An Indian ginger-jar, a Flemish beer-jug, a Japanese fan, may each become in turn a valuable lesson in decorative form and color." Cook in *The House Beautiful* saw the use of a cabinet such as this for "the preservation of all the curiosities and pretty things gathered in the family walks and travels."

Tisch's cabinet is closely based upon the art, or Queen Anne, furniture then being produced in England by such firms as Gillow,

Cooper and Holt, and Collinson and Lock. A cabinet designed for the last-named firm by T. E. Collcutt in 1871 and exhibited at the Centennial in Philadelphia in 1876 helped to set the style, which was carried out in architectural details such as overmantels as well as in furniture. Many characteristics of this style can be seen in Tisch's work: coved top, straight lines and turned balusters, rows of small spindles, panels of surface decoration—here elaborate marquetry incorporating various woods and brass—shallow surface carving, mirror, and beveled glass. More boldly asymmetrical than its English prototypes, the Tisch cabinet has compartments of various sizes. Cook, describing a curio cabinet, explained the plan: "The object of the irregular arrangement is first, I think, to avoid monotony, but it finds a better excuse in the accommodation it gives to articles of different sizes and shapes. Here are places for little things and places for larger things, and each is at home in its own compartment. . . ." The asymmetrical cabinet he described showed Oriental influence, and in the present example there is something of the Anglo-Japanese style in the pierced fretwork of the apron. The influence of eighteenth-century revivals can be seen in the exaggerated bracket feet, which Tisch undoubtedly thought appropriate for the eclectic Queen Anne style.

Little is known about Charles Tisch. He was first listed in New York directories in 1870 as a carver. In 1871/72 the listing was for "chairs" at 166 Mott Street; in 1872/73 he was at 164 Mott as a cabinetmaker. He remained there for the next sixteen years, adding another shop at 14 East Fifteenth Street in 1886/87. The last directory to list his business is that of 1889/90, when he was at 174 Fifth Avenue, dealing in "art." At this time, 1889, with a letterhead giving this Fifth Avenue address and the name "Galerie Des Beaux-Arts," Tisch offered this cabinet as a gift to the Metropolitan Museum, stating: "This piece of Furniture received the first price [sic] at the New Orleans Exposition 84/85. It is a purely American production of my own Manufacture and consider it worthy of a place in the Museum."

H. 82³/₄ inches
The Metropolitan Museum of Art, Gift of Charles Tisch, 89.13

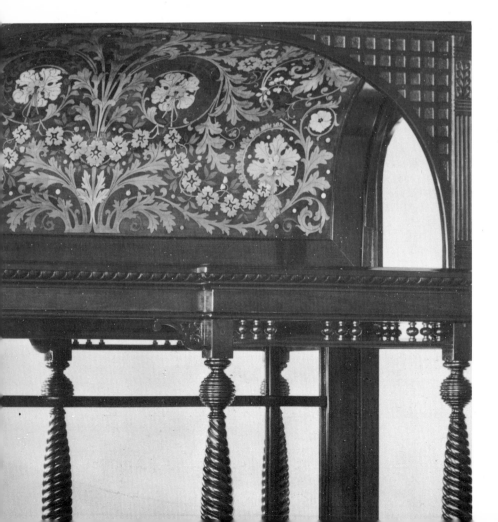

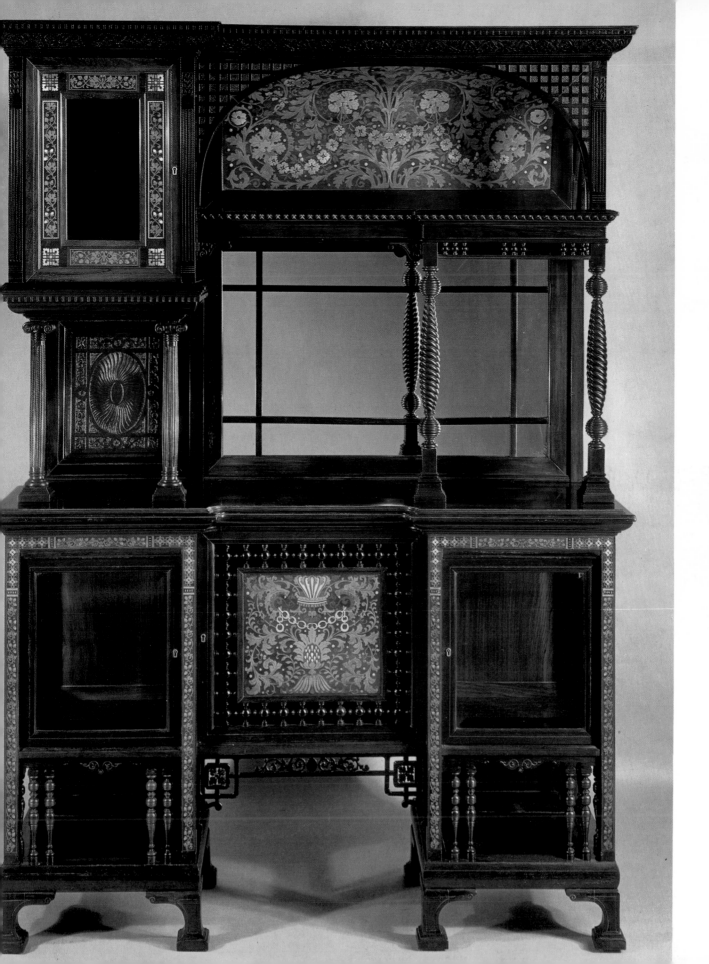

225

The rectilinear panels, ebonized frame, and shallow surface decoration, including incised lines, place this maple table in the American Eastlake-art furniture tradition of 1880 to 1885. Its high quality of craftsmanship and fine detailing suggest it is the work of a major firm, perhaps Herter Brothers. The shallow floral carving of the end panels is similar to that on documented Herter pieces (see no. 211). The motifs of the apron panel resemble the Japanese flowers and fans on the title page of the most influential book of Anglo-Japanese furniture, *Art Furniture Designed by Edward W. Godwin F.S.A. and Manufactured by William Watt* (London, 1877). The table has a top of marble, often used on furniture by Herter.

L. 34¹/₄ inches

Henry Ford Museum, Dearborn, Michigan

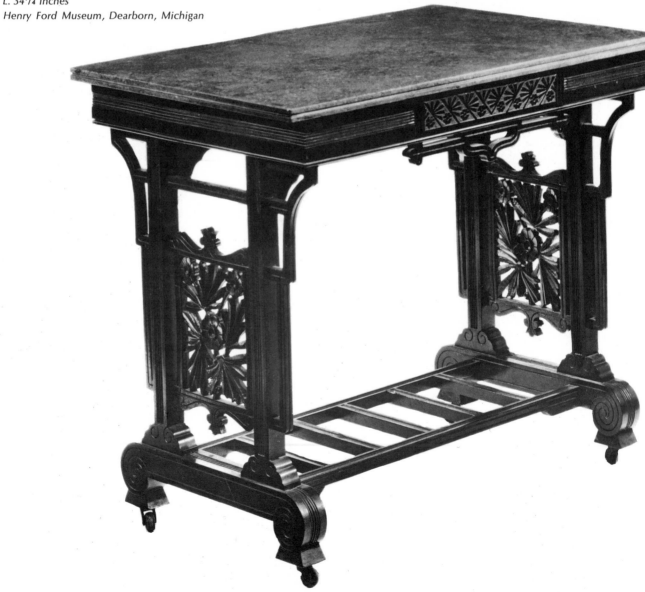

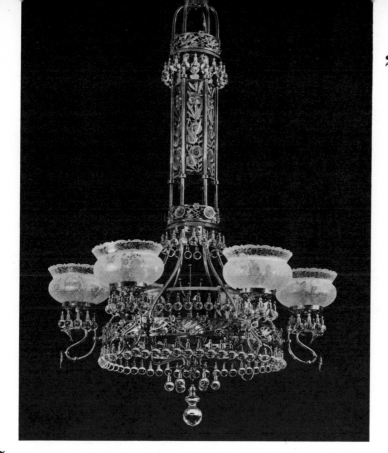

226 Chandeliers changed with changing styles as much as did tables and chairs, and this one of bronze, with its openwork design of chrysanthemums and other flowers, has the flat decoration within panels characteristic of art furniture of the 1880s. It also has a suggestion of exoticism in the glass balls recalling a Moorish fringe. Catalogues of I.P. Frink of 551 Pearl Street, New York, of the years 1882 and 1883 show a chandelier, one of several "special designs to order," the upper half of which is very similar to this, and it seems likely that the chandelier was ordered from that company. It was bought for a house in Dubuque, Iowa, built after the Civil War by William ("Hog") Ryan, a wealthy meat packer and friend of General Grant. In the 1880s Ryan's daughters redecorated the dining room, with a high cherry wainscoting, a built-in cherry serving table, which probably matched the dining set, now sold, a wallpaper designed by William Morris, and this chandelier. The contained quality of the chandelier, and the simplicity of its structure—essentially a series of rings linked by the pipes for gas—made it perfectly suited to a room designed in the new aesthetic.

H. 54³/4 inches

The Metropolitan Museum of Art, Edgar J. Kaufmann Charitable Foundation Fund, 69.92

227

The Robertsons attempted to combine serious aesthetics and popular appeal in these earthenware Chelsea Keramic Art Works vases of the 1880s. The blue-green, yellow-green, and green-brown glazes were inspired by the early Chinese pottery studied by potters of the eighties and nineties. The shapes are based on more familiar sources. The small square example is a variation of a contemporary Japanese brush pot, but with Westernized decoration. This is marked "CHELSEA KERAMIC/ART WORKS,/ROBERTSON & SONS." The piece behind it, marked "CKAW" in a diamond pattern, is a flattened version of a Near Eastern bottle, with classical lion's-head handles. The elephants' heads for the vase on the right were taken from a famous eighteenth-century Sèvres design, but the overall shape is typical of the 1880s. It is marked "HCR" in a monogram, for Hugh C. Robertson, and "CHELSEA KERAMIC ART WORK/ROBERTSON & SONS."

H. taller vase 12³/4 inches

The Metropolitan Museum of Art, Edgar J. Kaufmann Charitable Foundation Fund, 69.35; 69.38.2, 1

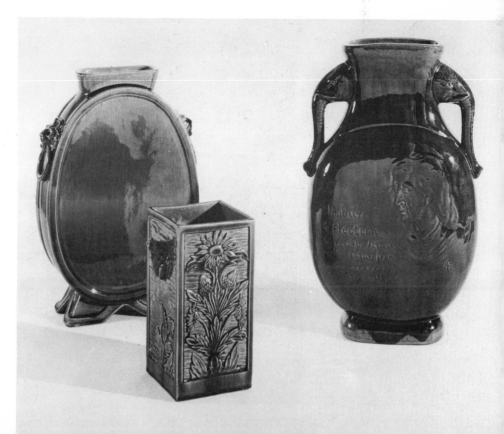

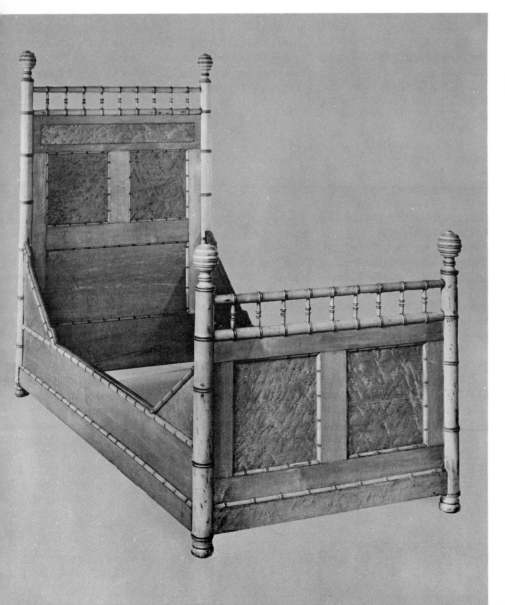

Like other exotic influences, the bamboo craze began in America about the time of the Centennial, and reached its peak in the 1880s, the period when this imitation bamboo suite of maple was manufactured, probably in New York. In the late 1870s Clarence Cook wrote of the charm of real bamboo furniture from the East; he cited Vantine's New York Emporium as a place to purchase such furniture, calling it "capital stuff" for furnishing a country house. In addition furniture of imported bamboo was manufactured in this country; two companies that specialized in it were Nimura and Sato of Brooklyn and J.E. Wall of Boston. Imitation bamboo pieces were made almost entirely of maple; in this set the maple is plain for the turnings and bird's-eye on most of the flat surfaces. In New York, during the 1860s, 70s, and 80s, George Hunzinger (see no. 186), Kilian Brothers, and C.A. Aimone were among those making imitation bamboo chairs and settees. In Kimball's *Book of Designs* (1876), Kilian Brothers featured, at a price of $8.67, a pseudo-bamboo chair similar to the one seen here. Although the inspiration for this furniture was Oriental, the form remained Western. Strong, rectilinear lines, extensive use of panels, and galleries of spindles are all in the tradition of reform furniture of the 1870s and 80s.

Although undoubtedly from the same showroom, the pieces of this bedroom suite have slight variations in decoration and turnings, suggesting that the customer could assemble his own set from harmonizing pieces according to his needs. In so doing he followed a fashion prevalent both here and in Europe, where similar furniture, usually made of fruit woods, was equally popular. In this country bamboo and pseudo-bamboo furniture seems to have been particularly favored for bedrooms. The June 1886 issue of *The Decorator and Furnisher* showed "an exceedingly tasteful bedroom" of real bamboo furniture, which was, according to the editor, "well suited to the general effect," a room "light and bright, summery and inviting."

H. chiffonier 61¹/₄ inches
The Metropolitan Museum of Art, Anonymous Gift Fund, 68.97.10,11,13-15

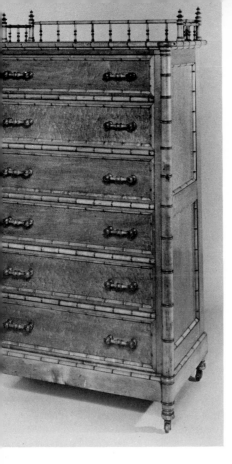

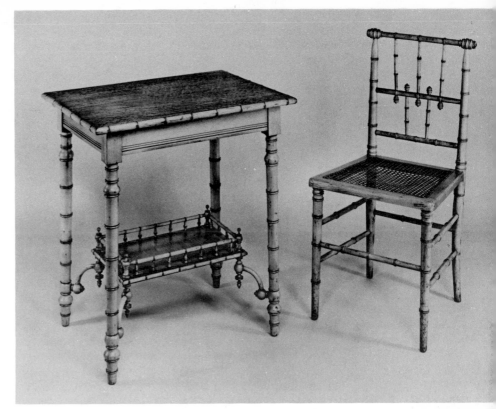

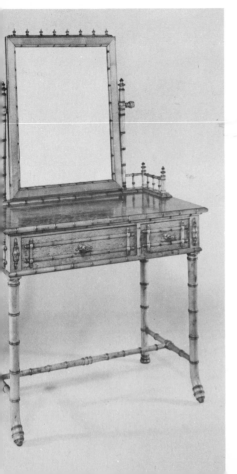

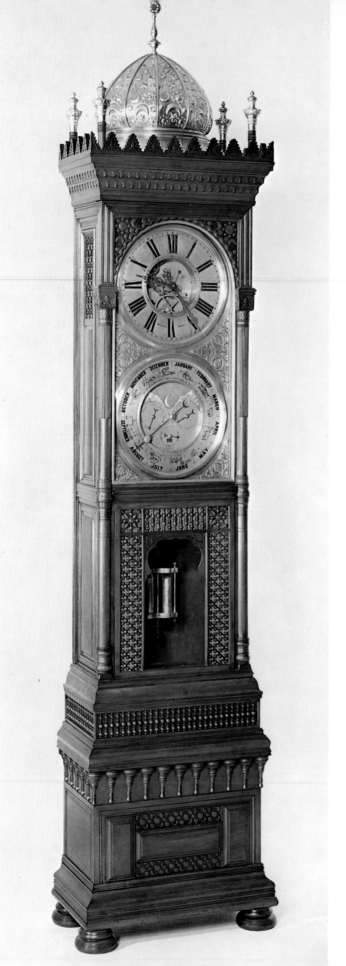

229 Near Eastern and Indian motifs have been used on this tall mahogany case clock made by Tiffany and Company in the 1880s. The repoussé brass dome with its star and crescent finial and the corner finials resembling minarets are Turkish elements. Indian are the floral motifs in brass around the dials and in wood on the square capitals and in the spandrels above the glazed "mihrab." The crenelated cornice is found in Near Eastern art from Babylonian times on, and deep-cut machicolations are an integral part of Islamic architecture. These exotic elements appear alongside panels and rows of decorative spindles on a basically rectilinear form—all characteristic of the art furniture of the time.

Edward C. Moore, by the 1880s both chief designer and a partner in Tiffany and Company, is one of several designers who disseminated a taste for Orientalia in the United States. He had a lifelong interest in the East, and possessed a superb collection of artifacts, mostly Eastern and Near Eastern, now in the Metropolitan Museum. Moore's position in the prestigious firm insured his taste an influential reception; furthermore, his encouragement of young Louis C. Tiffany's interest in his collection and in the decorative arts in general resulted in Tiffany's turning to decoration, eventually making his great contribution to the art of glassmaking (see nos. 263-272). In 1882 Louis Tiffany's decorating firm designed a room in the Moorish style for the Fifth Avenue mansion of Cornelius Vanderbilt II, using many of the motifs seen on this clock. The Indian motifs reflect the influence of Tiffany's partner Lockwood de Forest, who made and published studies of Indian architecture and design. According to a letter from the donor of the clock, Tiffany and Company made only two clocks with these works, which include dials showing the year, month, period of the zodiac, phases of the moon and sun, date, and day of the week, as well as the hour, minute, and second. The pendulum, a double vial containing mercury, suspended on a brass rod, regulates the swing despite fluctuations in temperature or pressure. The clock is marked "TIFFANY & CO. MAKERS." on each dial, and "TIFFANY & Co MAKERS/PATENTED NOV. 7th 1882/289" on the back of the works.

H. 105 inches
The Metropolitan Museum of Art, Gift of Mary J. Kingsland, 06.1206

230

Clearly Islamic in origin, too, are the design elements of this "tête-à-tête set," also made by Tiffany and Company, about 1888. A letter from the company when the set was presented to the Museum describes it: ". . . made . . . entirely by hand . . . without seams . . . each . . . from a single piece of silver. It is enameled, etched and gilded; and is also etched and gilded on the interior, which in itself is a very difficult and re-markable piece of work. . . ." The pieces are marked "TIFFANY & Co/8473 M 8147 [tea-pot, 8148]/ STERLING-SILVER." The decorative elements can be traced to Islamic and Indian metalwork. The colors of the enamels, primaries, purple, green, and white, are those of Turkish rugs and of Syrian Mamluk glass mosque lamps of the fourteenth century. Ivory finials are reminiscent of Indian chess pieces. Shortly after the time this set was produced Tiffany and Company received the Grand Prize for silverware at the Paris Exposition of 1889, and Edward Moore, who probably designed the set, was made a Chevalier of the Legion of Honor (see also no. 229).

L. teapot 11 inches
The Metropolitan Museum of Art, Gift of a Friend of the Museum, 97.1.1-4

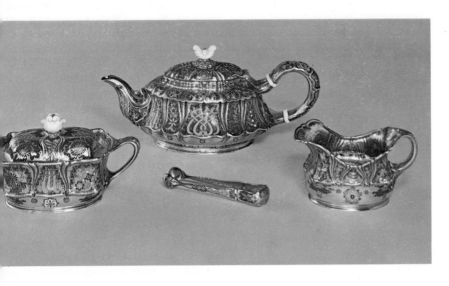

231

The design of these Tiffany and Company pieces, part of a tea service of 1874, was also drawn from the decorative arts of the Near East. Especially Islamic in feeling are the heavy niello work, the tripartite leaf on the lids, and the peacock feathers that join handles to bodies. The floral motifs, the leaf finial, and the running leaf motif around the neck of the sugar bowl are basically Indian. The coffeepot is a standard Near Eastern form, which was adopted in England and America in the 1870s and 80s. The set exemplifies what was described as the "new style, inspired by the Hindu, and baptised 'saracenic' by its creator, Mr. [Edward C.] Moore, one of the artistic directors of the Tiffany Company," in a review of the World's Columbian Exposition of 1893 in *Revue des Arts Décoratifs* (1893/94). Marked "TIFFANY & Co/3650 MAKERS 8920/STERLING-SILVER/ 925-1000 M," the set was presented at Christmas 1879 to Superintendent of Schools Henry Kiddle by the teachers of the public schools of New York City.

H. coffeepot 10¹/₈ inches
Mr. Alfred M. F. Kiddle, on loan to the Museum of the City of New York

232 Tiffany and Company made this ormolu and marble mantel set in about 1885. The company name and "New York" are on the face, with numbers that are meant to look Egyptian. The set represents a popular rather than an archaeological idea of Egyptian art —neither the hieroglyphs on the obelisks nor the sphinxes on the clock would bear the scrutiny of an Egyptologist. Of a clock decorated with Egyptian motifs made for the Centennial of 1876 by Mitchell, Vance, and Company, Walter Smith wrote in *Masterpieces of the Centennial . . .*: "There is something peculiarly suggestive and appropriate in choosing for the ornamentation of a clock—a mechanical apparatus that records the flight of time—emblems and figures taken from that country whose very existence to-day is a constant reminder of the centuries gone by, whose monuments stand as silent but sublime records of the glory of past ages." Interest in Egypt, renewed throughout the century by the publications of archaeological expeditions, received a special impetus in New York in February 1881 with the installation in Central Park, ac-

companied by speeches and a hymn composed for the occasion, of the obelisk known as Cleopatra's Needle.

H. obelisks 20³/₄ inches

The Metropolitan Museum of Art, Edgar J. Kaufmann Charitable Foundation Fund, 68.97.4-6

233

When Joseph Lycett decorated this white graniteware vase in 1889 it was considered one of the most noteworthy ceramic achievements of the day. Signed and dated in red paint on the underside "J. Lycett, 1889," the vase was made at the Greenpoint, New York, Faience Manufacturing Company, of which Joseph's father, Edward, was director. The exoticism of the eighties and nineties is evident in both the shape and decoration. Water lilies outlined in gold and bronze are painted on a pale ivory ground. The dolphin handles are covered with matte and dark gold. The elongated neck rises to a pierced and gilded dome of Near Eastern magnificence. Edwin

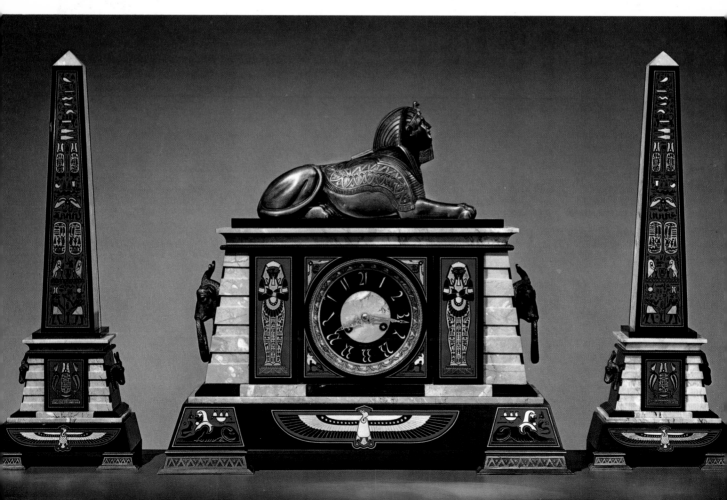

Atlee Barber, the first important historian of American ceramic art, owned the vase and published it in his book *The Pottery and Porcelain of the United States* (1893).

H. 28 inches
Henry Ford Museum, Dearborn, Michigan

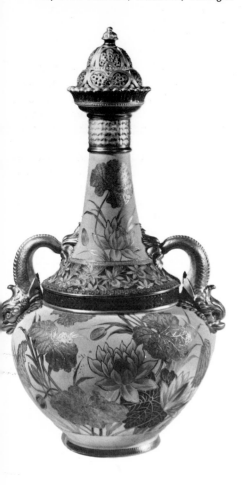

York Yacht Club Race Committee report for 1886, "by Capt. Ogden Goelet . . . for schooners and sloops, cutters and yawls of the New York Yacht Club. . . ." Paine's sloop *Mayflower* won the cup August 7, 1886. The writhing sea creature and twisting leaves and the unusual organic shape have a little of the art nouveau about them; the Egyptian or Indian maiden, suggesting a fig-urehead, gives an exotic flavor. The pitcher is marked "WHITING. MF'G. Co/NEW YORK," for Whiting Manufacturing Company, a major silver company that was established in New York in 1868 and stayed in business well into the twentieth century.

H. 19 inches
New York Yacht Club

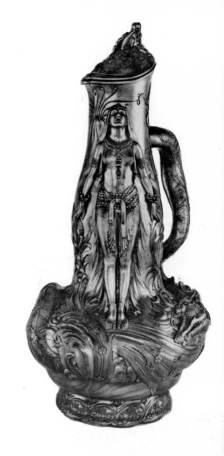

235

Another piece catering to the taste for things Egyptian is this small maple footstool, painted black with polychrome ornament, made about 1880. The legs are clustered columns with a lotus capital, representing in Egyptian art a grove of the plant. The flat incised and painted decoration, of lotus or papyrus on a zigzag line meant to represent water, and the winged orb are from the repertory of Egyptian motifs. The overstuffing and the fringe were popular at the time for seating furniture.

L. 16 inches
The Metropolitan Museum of Art, Rogers Fund, 67.230

234

Designers could lavish their most fanciful effects on the silver trophies to be awarded to the winners of America's sailing races in the 1880s; the trophy was sure to be proudly accepted, and the recipients were more than likely accustomed to extravagance and eclecticism in the furnishing of their houses. This pitcher was one of a number of trophies won by Charles J. Paine, railroad developer and yachtsman, defender of the America's Cup in 1885, 86, and 87. It is one of the Goelet Cups, offered, according to the New

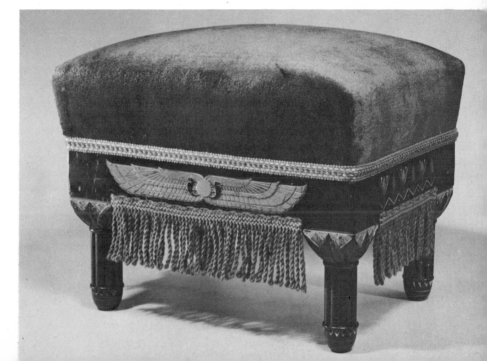

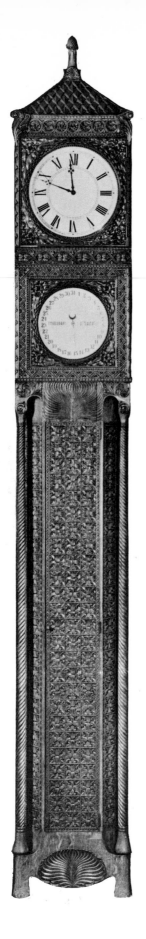

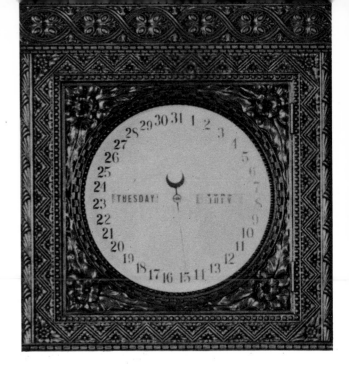

236

Henry Hobson Richardson, America's greatest architect since Benjamin Latrobe, was one of three architects appointed by the New York State legislature in 1875 to expedite the construction of the State Capitol, begun eight years earlier and still only up to the third story. The red oak clock and chairs shown here are part of the furnishing of the Court of Appeals chamber, designed by Richardson and installed in 1884. The carved motifs on the furniture echo those on the sumptuous mantel, also of red oak, which sets off a highly figured slab of marble over the fireplace. Richardson found his principal inspiration in the rugged Romanesque style, but in this room the overall flavor of the ornamentation is Byzantine. The swirling bosses, the ram's heads, the spiral turnings, and the seemingly inexhaustible variety of decoration of the clock are all very similar to decoration in that magnificent Byzantine monument, St. Mark's cathedral in Venice. The acanthus at the top corners of the clock and at the juncture of the chair arms and seats, also used in other parts of the room, is seen extensively on capitals in the Venetian basilica.

The room doubtless benefited directly from Richardson's vacation in 1882, during which he traveled in Europe photographing the monuments he admired. His own photographs and a lavish monograph on St. Mark's published in Venice under the auspices of the Queen of Italy, the first volumes of which appeared in 1881, very likely inspired him and his staff in their work on this chamber. The architectural motifs are adapted so skillfully that they are entirely appropriate to the furniture, which indeed seems to exemplify the functional yet dignified spirit sought for a courtroom. The exotic origin of the decoration of the chairs in no way diminishes their utility; they are graceful but strong, and the use of the simple oak is in keeping with current ideas of reform in furniture design (see no. 210).

H. clock 154 inches; chairs 36½ inches
Court of Appeals of the State of New York, Albany

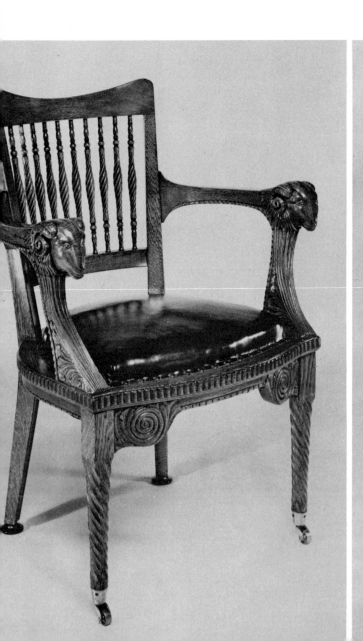
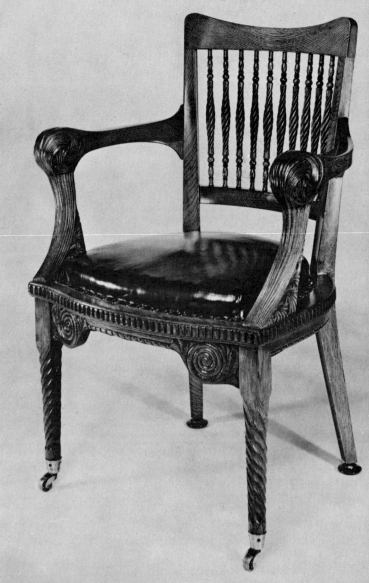

237

This cast-iron settee is of a general design called a "curtain" settee in the catalogues of the iron foundries, where it first appeared in the 1870s and 80s. This one is marked "PETER TIMMES SON BROOKLYN N.Y." The mark is doubtless for John Timmes, who had worked with his father, Peter, for a few years before beginning to list himself this way in the Brooklyn directory of 1878/79; he continued this listing to the end of the century, mostly as a maker of spikes but also as a galvanizer and a rivet manufacturer. The design combines elements of the revival styles used during the preceding decades: leafy S-curves and scrolls have the looseness of the rococo; the symmetry and formality of the back, especially the side panels with their central floral medallions, are typical of the Renaissance revival; while the overall rectilinearity of the back is in keeping with more current styles. The skirt, even though its motif is a heart or a stylized palmette, looks like the fringe used on furniture of Moorish inspiration.

L. 33 inches
The Metropolitan Museum of Art, Edgar J. Kaufmann Charitable Foundation Fund, 69.158.1

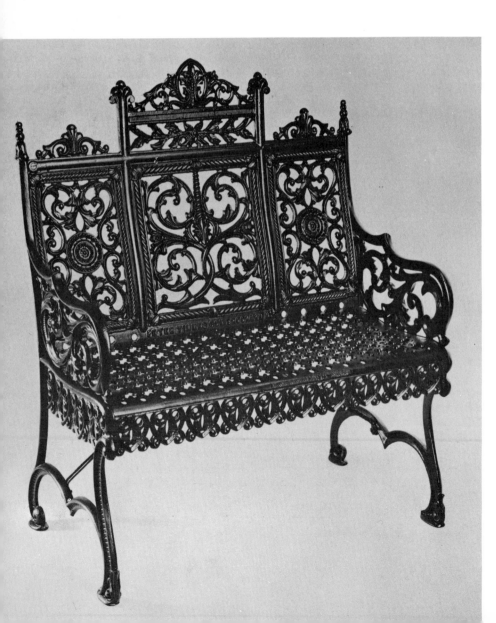

238

More directly in the Renaissance revival tradition is this cast-iron chair, although it too would have been called a "curtain" chair in the catalogues (see no. 237). The cresting, the oval medallion on the back, and the strapwork and the bosses of the seat valance are typically Renaissance revival elements, and the generous proportions of the chair are in keeping with this style. The chair is marked "THE NORTH AMERICAN IRON WORKS, N.Y." This foundry was listed in the New York directories from 1877/78 to 1896/97 at 88 Beekman Street.

H. 35¹/₄ inches
The Metropolitan Museum of Art, Rogers Fund, 69.159.1

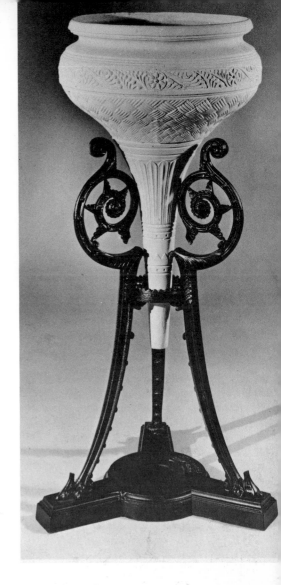

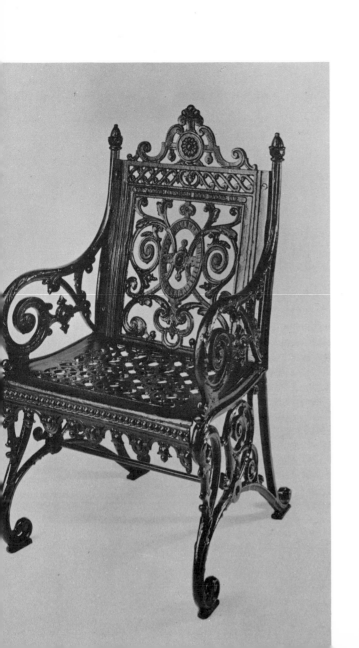

239

The urn in a tripod stand was known to the modern world through the excavations at Pompeii in the late eighteenth century, and interest in Pompeian art was revitalized toward the end of the nineteenth century with the renewed interest in flat surface decoration. The ornament on the urn, of lotus leaves, basketwork, and stylized flowers, is shallow and crisp, in keeping with this current taste. The mark on the base, "HECLA WORKS/NEW YORK," is that of a foundry in business in Brooklyn from 1885 until well into the twentieth century.

H. urn in stand 43³/₄ inches
The Metropolitan Museum of Art, Edgar J. Kaufmann Charitable Foundation Fund, 69.81.1

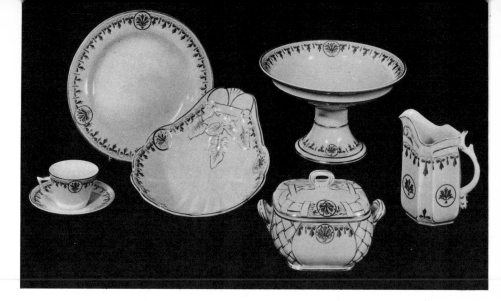

240

This group is part of a dinner set dating from 1885 that Thomas Smith, owner of the Union Porcelain Works, made as a gift for his daughter, Pastora Smith Chace, mother of the donor. Smith, according to the family, acquired the works after the Civil War as payment of a debt, after he had retired from his profession of architect and builder. The factory favored classical shapes such as these for the large dinner sets produced between 1880 and 1890. The bellflower and woven motifs used here were freely adapted from neoclassical models. Each piece bears the mark in dark green of an eagle's head with "S" in its beak and "U.P.W." above. The cup, saucer, plate, and compote are also marked "UNION / PORCELAIN / WORKS / GREEN-POINT / N.Y." in a reserve with the date "10'85" just below.

H. compote 5³/₄ inches
The Metropolitan Museum of Art, Gift of Mr. and Mrs. Franklin M. Chace

241

This oyster plate made by the Union Porcelain Works in the 1880s illustrates the type of luxury peculiar to life in the late nineteenth century, when many families lived in exaggerated comfort, and each culinary treat was served on its own special tableware. The overall shape of the plate is a clam shell in which oyster, scallop, and mussel shells, realistically molded to hold the table oysters, are surrounded by other evidence of shore life—a skate egg case, a snail, lobster claw, whelk, baby crab, and seaweed. The design

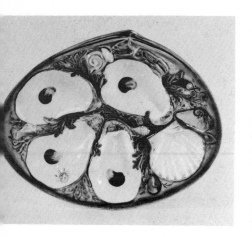

evokes the shore in the way a Harnett still life evokes the hunt (see paintings and sculpture volume no. 171). On the underside are the manufacturer's mark, "U.P.W.," an eagle's head with "S" in its beak, and "PAT. JAN. 4. 1881.," and the retailer's mark, "Tiffany & Co/ New York."

W. 8 9/16 inches
The Metropolitan Museum of Art, Anonymous Gift Fund, 68.99.2

242

In the East of the 1880s luxury and tradition often set the style. In the Midwest, however, reform concepts of utility and innovation were taking precedence. Nowhere was this more true than in Chicago, where the new school of architecture influenced all the decorative arts. There, about 1890, the Tobey Furniture Company, according to the donor's family, made this dining room set for the Jackson Boulevard home of prominent businessman Henry Lee Borden. The company, a partnership of the brothers Charles and Frank Tobey, received a corporate charter in 1875. It was apparently an outgrowth of two earlier companies, the Tobey Company retail shop, founded in 1856 by Charles Tobey, and the Thayer and Tobey Furniture Company started in 1870 by Frank Tobey and F. Porter Thayer. In 1888 with the formation of a subsidiary called the Tobey and Christianson Cabinet Company, the firm began specializing in expensive high-quality furniture. By about 1890, when this unusual dining room set was made, it was the most important furniture and dec-

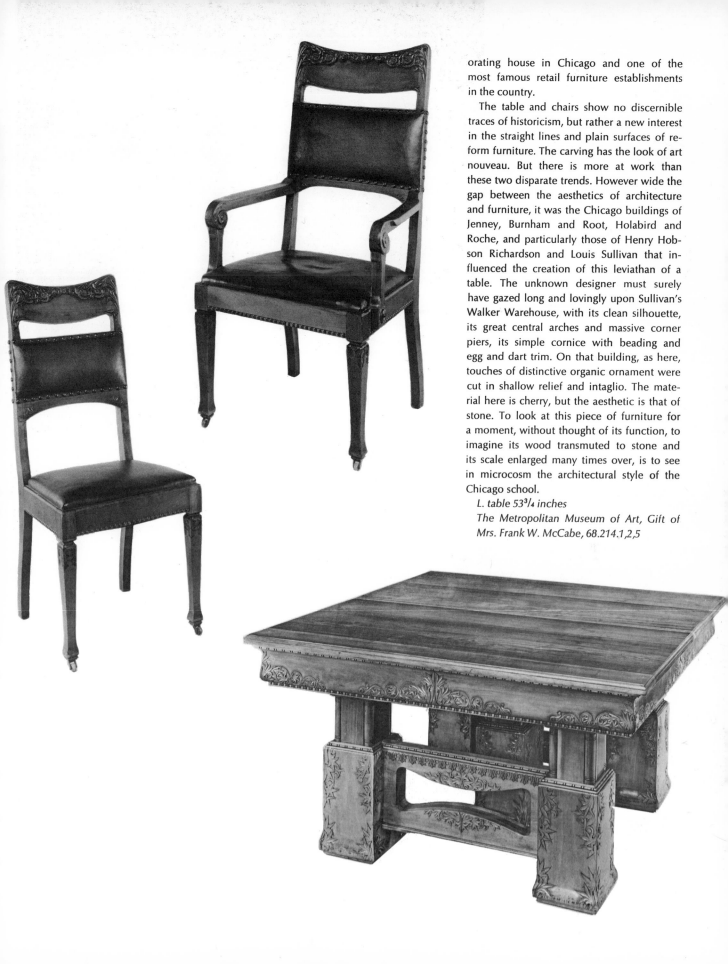

orating house in Chicago and one of the most famous retail furniture establishments in the country.

The table and chairs show no discernible traces of historicism, but rather a new interest in the straight lines and plain surfaces of reform furniture. The carving has the look of art nouveau. But there is more at work than these two disparate trends. However wide the gap between the aesthetics of architecture and furniture, it was the Chicago buildings of Jenney, Burnham and Root, Holabird and Roche, and particularly those of Henry Hobson Richardson and Louis Sullivan that influenced the creation of this leviathan of a table. The unknown designer must surely have gazed long and lovingly upon Sullivan's Walker Warehouse, with its clean silhouette, its great central arches and massive corner piers, its simple cornice with beading and egg and dart trim. On that building, as here, touches of distinctive organic ornament were cut in shallow relief and intaglio. The material here is cherry, but the aesthetic is that of stone. To look at this piece of furniture for a moment, without thought of its function, to imagine its wood transmuted to stone and its scale enlarged many times over, is to see in microcosm the architectural style of the Chicago school.

L. table 53³/₄ inches

The Metropolitan Museum of Art, Gift of Mrs. Frank W. McCabe, 68.214.1,2,5

243 Rookwood, the first and most famous of the American art potteries, was named for the home of its sponsor, Joseph Longworth, one of the Cincinnati family prominent in American art patronage in the nineteenth century. With the enthusiastic support of Longworth's daughter Maria Nichols, the pottery evolved from a small amateur center and opened as a commercial establishment in 1880. This earthenware vase, one of the earliest pieces of Rookwood pottery in existence, is marked "ROOKWOOD / POTTERY. / CIN O. / A.R.V./1881." The initials are those of the man in charge of the decorating department at Rookwood from 1881 to 1905, Albert R. Valentien, whose works rank among the finest American pottery. A considerable percentage of the large pieces produced in the early years survived imperfectly, if at all, because of difficulties with techniques of production. Success with glazes in light colors or white was also unusual, as the control of kiln temperature to achieve them was critical, and thus this fine piece takes on the value of rarity in addition to its intrinsic charm.

H. 17¹/₂ inches
Ronald R. Chitwood, Los Angeles

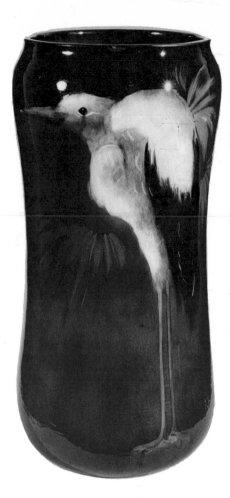

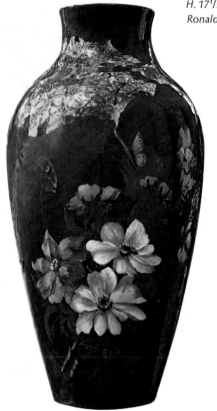

244 Brownish glazes as the background for light decoration—bird, animal, or floral—had been introduced at Rookwood but became a general type by the 1890s. This earthenware umbrella stand was made at the J.B. Owens Pottery Company, Zanesville, Ohio, and decorated by Albert Haubrich, whose signature is painted at the base. Haubrich was one of several Zanesville potters who worked in the decorated brown glaze, in shapes that varied from simple classical ones to the elongated forms of art nouveau. Here, the stork is derived from the Japanese models that also influenced Rookwood. Before joining Owens, Haubrich had worked for S.A. Weller, the largest pottery in Zanesville, where similar work was done.

H. 22 5/16 inches
The Metropolitan Museum of Art, Gift of Ronald S. Kane, 69.53

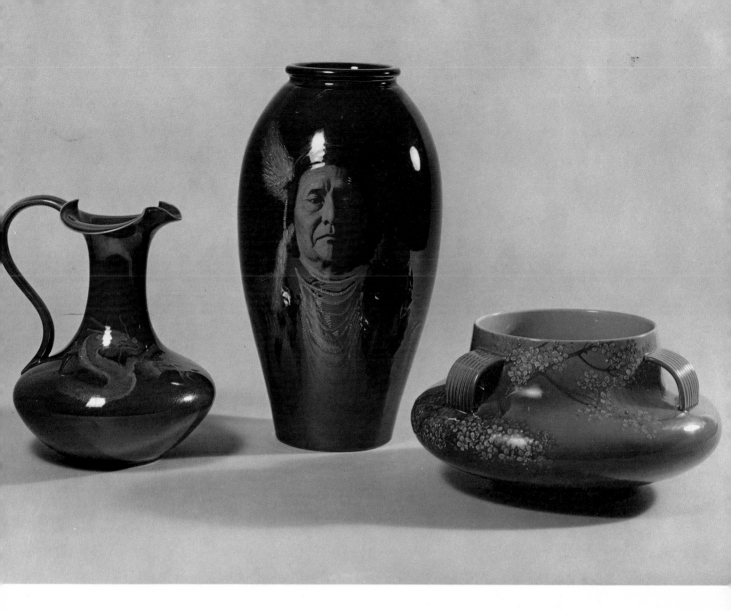

245 Craftsmen at Rookwood made these three earthenware pieces, which are marked and dated 1889, 1898, and 1890. Characteristic of late nineteenth-century design, the shapes and glazes reflect the Oriental and Near Eastern influences that reformers introduced in their desire to get away from the succeeding revivals of Western styles. The motifs of the dragon on the ewer and flowers on the bowl were inspired by Japanese models, while the vivid portrait of the beloved Chief Joseph of the Nez Percés is a sentimental reminder of the romance in the American West, to temper the prevailing exoticism. The ewer is marked with the initials of Albert R. Valentien; the Indian vase is signed "WP Mc-Donald"; and the bowl bears an indecipherable signature.

H. vase 14 inches
The Metropolitan Museum of Art; ewer and bowl: Edgar J. Kaufmann Charitable Foundation Fund, 69.37.1,3; vase: Gift of Wells M. Sawyer, 45.147

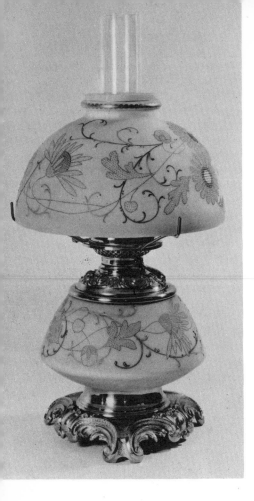

246

The Mt. Washington Glass Company produced this kerosene lamp of Burmese glass; the decoration of raised enamel details was probably inspired by a much coveted porcelain of the day known as "jeweled Sèvres." Mt. Washington obtained an English patent for Burmese in 1886 and presented an example of it, with a pattern similar to this, to Queen Victoria; thus patterns of this sort came to be called the "Queen's design." The rococo style of the brass mounts is a carryover from earlier in the century.

H. 19 13/16 inches
Lent anonymously

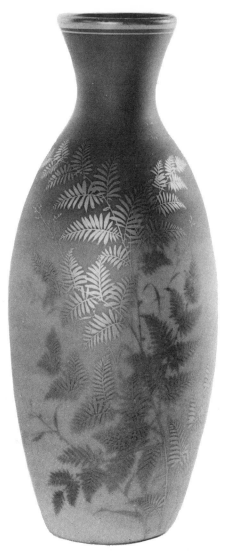

247

In the last two decades of the nineteenth century, many glasshouses produced art glass, works designed to fit the popular conception of what was difficult to produce, and therefore artistic. The glass with gradated colors called peachblow (see no. 248) was especially popular between 1886 and about 1900. The gradation of red to white in the peachblow of this vase is associated with the New England Glass Company. The colors go through the body, while in products by the rival Hobbs, Brockunier and Company the colors are only in the outer layer. The shape of the vase, a common form for pottery, and the gilt fern pattern were inspired by Japanese ceramics, then a major source of inspiration for Western artists.

H. 14³/₈ inches
Lent anonymously

248 In New York on March 8, 1886, a Chinese porcelain vase on a stand from the collection of Mrs. Mary Morgan was sold at auction for $18,000. Its appeal was due to its handsome shape and the delicate gradated colors of the glaze. Vases of this type were immediately in demand, and the manufacturers of art glass enabled customers to prove their good taste, and popularized their own product at the same time, by reproducing the vase and stand. Hobbs, Brockunier and Company of Wheeling, West Virginia, who made these three objects, were the first to capitalize on the idea; the vase on the left is a copy of the Morgan vase. The company produced a colored glass similar to the glaze of the Morgan vase, with either a matte or a glossy finish, calling it peachblow. The peachblow of this company was red to yellow. The colors were applied in a transparent layer on a ground of opaque white glass. The shape of the tall pitcher with matte finish is based on that of a Near Eastern ewer; that of the small pitcher on a combination of Near Eastern and classical forms. Hobbs, Brockunier made an extensive line of this ware for table as well as decorative use.

H. vase in stand 10 inches
Vase and ewer: lent anonymously; pitcher: The Metropolitan Museum of Art, Gift of Mrs. Emily Winthrop Miles, 46.140.762

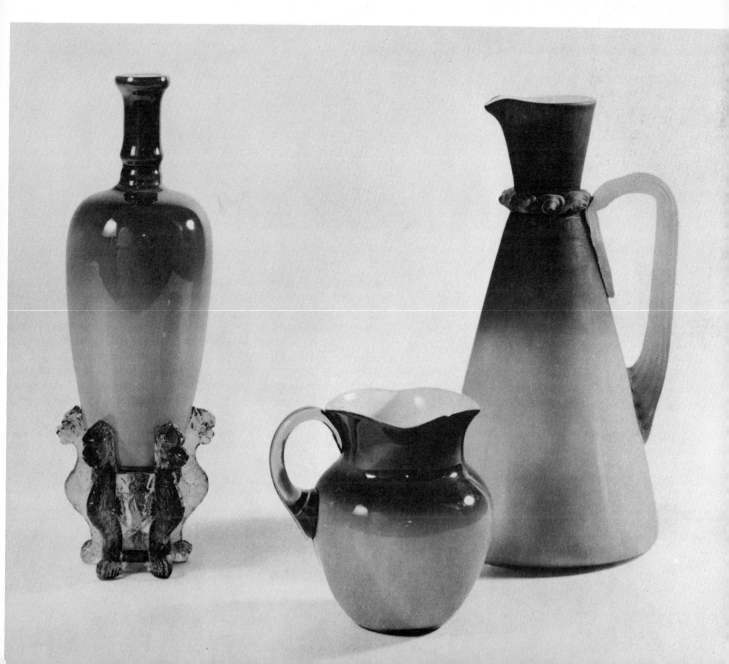

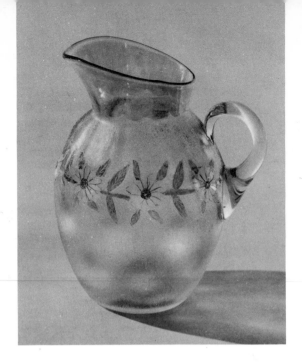

249

A matte finish was first used on glass for decorative effect by Joseph Locke of the New England Glass Company and was patented by him under the name "Pomona" in 1885. This delicate cream pitcher was decorated by the original process, called "first ground" by collectors, in which etching with acid was done by hand. Later the technique was simplified, and the hand work was eliminated; a patent for the newer technique was issued to Locke on June 15, 1886. The cost was much less, but the texture produced is more regularized and less appealing. The white, black, and gold floral band painted in enamels against the stippled surface is pale and delicate. Eighteenth-century Occidental works probably inspired the decoration; the shape has the simplicity characteristic of Islamic work.

H. 5¹/₂ inches
Lent anonymously

250

Works designated as "Royal Flemish" were advertised by the Mt. Washington Glass Company as early as 1889, although the patent for the process was not acquired by the foreman Albert Steffin until 1894. In this process, beige or brown enamel was applied to the acid-finished matte surface of the glass, and the design was outlined in gold. Islamic works of the fourteenth century influenced both the shape and the decoration of this vase.

H. 13 inches
The Corning Museum of Glass

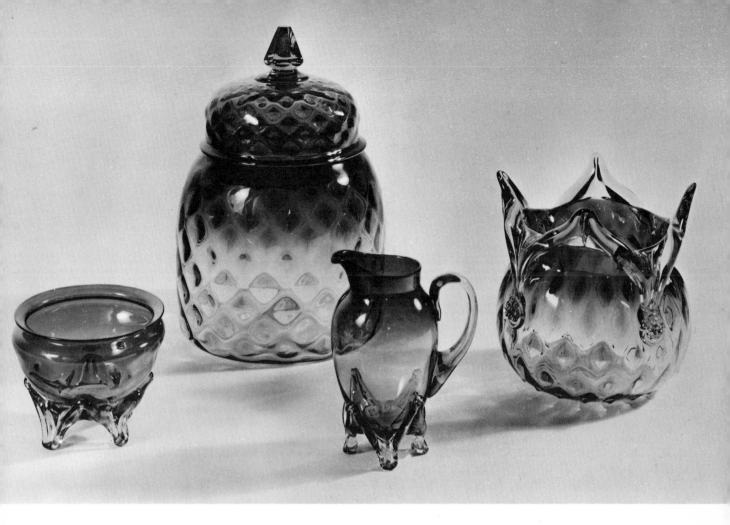

251

This sugar bowl, cracker jar, creamer, and decorated bowl were made in a type of art glass called amberina or rose amber, depending on where it was made. Amberina was described by Joseph Locke of the New England Glass Company, which made the cracker jar and large bowl, in the patent he received July 24, 1883: "Starting with amber glass as a base, I have been enabled by the action of heat alone to develop on a part of the article composed of homogeneous stock a more or less deep ruby color, and also develop in the said article a violet shade, and greenish, and a blueish, and other tinges." The Mt. Washington Glass Company, makers of the sugar bowl and creamer, called the same glass rose amber. All of these pieces, gradated from amber to ruby, were made to look novel and expensive by seeming to require virtuosity: the top of the decorated bowl and the tooled feet on the sugar bowl and pitcher suggest that the pieces are the work of individual craftsmen, although they are not. These details and the prunts on the bowl can be traced back to seventeenth-century German and English glass. The jar and the decorated bowl bear paper labels reading: "N E G W/AMBERINA/PAT'D/July 24, 1883."

H. cracker jar 8³/₈ inches
Sugar bowl, jar, creamer: The Metropolitan Museum of Art, Gift of Mrs. Emily Winthrop Miles, 46.140.483, 523, 524; bowl: Mr. and Mrs. Samuel B. Feld, New York

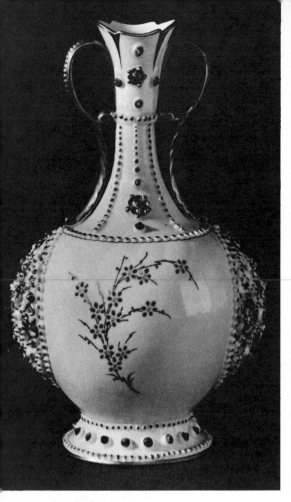

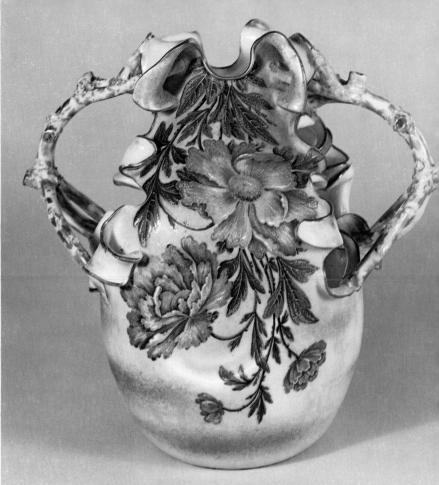

252 Made by Knowles, Taylor and Knowles of East Liverpool, Ohio, a large pottery that produced quantities of functional as well as decorative work, this vase shows the fashion in fine porcelain toward the end of the century. During the 1880s this factory had produced Belleek (see no. 253), but a fire in 1889 destroyed the kilns in which it was made. Subsequently Knowles developed this translucent bone china with a soft velvety glaze, marketing it as "Lotusware." Some of it was exhibited at the Columbian Exposition of 1893 in Chicago. The bottle shape was a popular one, inspired by pieces imported from China; the raised jeweled decoration, in a design from Near Eastern sources, was introduced several decades earlier at Sèvres. The piece shows a circular mark with a crown above; "LOTUSWARE" is outside the circle; "K T K Co." is inside, with a quarter moon and a star.

H. 9³/₄ inches
The Smithsonian Institution, Washington

253

Ott and Brewer, the major Trenton, New Jersey, pottery, produced this vase at the turn of the century. It is of Belleek, an especially thin porcelain developed at Belleek, Ireland. The mark on the underside is a crown with a sword through it, with "O & B" below and "BELLEEK" above. The odd shape, pinched at the sides, with an uneven, undulating mouth like folding leaves, is similar to contemporary Japanese work; its relationship to a natural growing form suggests that the designer was also influenced by the fashionable experimental style, art nouveau. The rustic handles were inspired by rococo models.

H. 9¹/₂ inches
The Metropolitan Museum of Art, Edgar J. Kaufmann Charitable Foundation Fund, 68.103.1

254

Walter Scott Lenox, most famous for founding the Trenton pottery that has borne his name since 1896, designed this Belleek pitcher in 1887 when he was art director of Ott and Brewer. "W.S.L./1887" is inscribed on the underside. The thin porcelain body lends itself very successfully to the shell form. The whimsical combination of the naturalistic shell with the classical elements of a putto and a ribbon serving as a handle is typical of the rococo-inspired designs of the last two decades of the nineteenth century. The shell is more detailed and the putto more schematic than they would have been in eighteenth-century rococo designs.

H. 9³/₈ inches
The Newark Museum

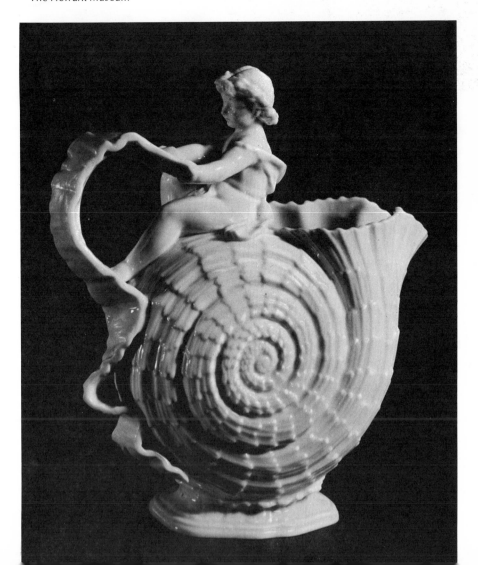

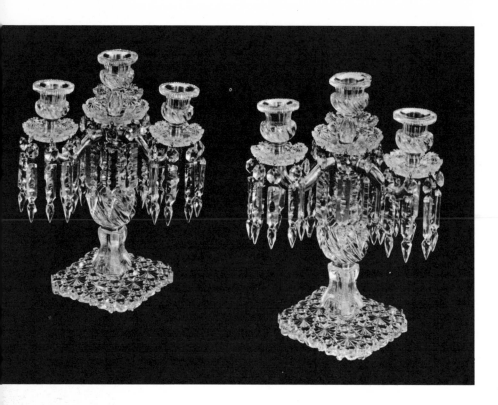

candelabrum is a form developed by English and Irish glasshouses in the late 1700s. The swirl-fluted knops on the columns and candleholders and the drops are updated versions of eighteenth-century details.

H. 11 11/16 inches

The Metropolitan Museum of Art, Edgar J. Kaufmann Charitable Foundation Fund, 69.121.1,2

256

The two emerald green overlay pieces at the left are of a hue perfected by William E. Kern. They were made by the Pairpoint Manufacturing Company, New Bedford, Massachusetts, where Kern worked at the turn of the century. The pitcher is in the prism and bullseye pattern, patented in 1898. The pattern, following turn-of-the-century practice, is much more intricate than the earlier style of cutting on the rose bowl. The same taste for intricacy is seen on the clear glass bowl, which, although characteristically American, has not been identified with a specific glasshouse. The deep-cut pattern includes the fan, star, hobnail, and diamond motifs, which were favored in the Brilliant period.

H. pitcher 9 inches

The Metropolitan Museum of Art; green bowl and pitcher: Funds from Various Donors, 67.7.19,20; clear bowl: Gift of John C. Cattus, 68.21

257

The Libbey Glass Company proudly proved the virtuosity of its craftsmen with this punch bowl made for the Chicago Columbian Exposition of 1893. The company, which changed its name from the New England Glass Company when it moved to Toledo, Ohio, in 1888, continued its tradition of workmanship of high quality. End-of-the-century historicism is suggested by the choice of subject—a hunting scene that recalls British sporting scenes of the beginning of the nineteenth century. The engraving technique, which mid-nineteenth-century designers adapted from Renaissance crystal carving, is carried to a high degree of excellence in this work.

H. 13 1/2 inches

The Toledo Museum of Art, Gift of the Libbey Glass Company

255

A counterpart of the historicism of the grander houses of the last quarter of the nineteenth century and of the furniture that filled them is the cut glass that came into fashion in about 1880. The glass designs echo the finest work of previous styles, but in more deeply cut patterns made possible by the introduction of first gas and then electric power. Popularly called Brilliant, this cut glass was made by a variety of manufacturers of fine lead glass. These candelabra, probably made as a special order by T. G. Hawkes and Company of Corning, New York, demonstrate the elegance of the glass. Here it is in the Russian pattern, one of the most important of the Brilliant designs, patented by Philip McDonald for the company in 1882. A refinement of the older star and hobnail pattern, its name derived from the fact that a complete banquet service was ordered for the Russian embassy in Washington shortly after it was introduced. In 1885 the Russian pattern was ordered for the White House by Grover Cleveland and was used there until the Franklin D. Roosevelt administration. The glass

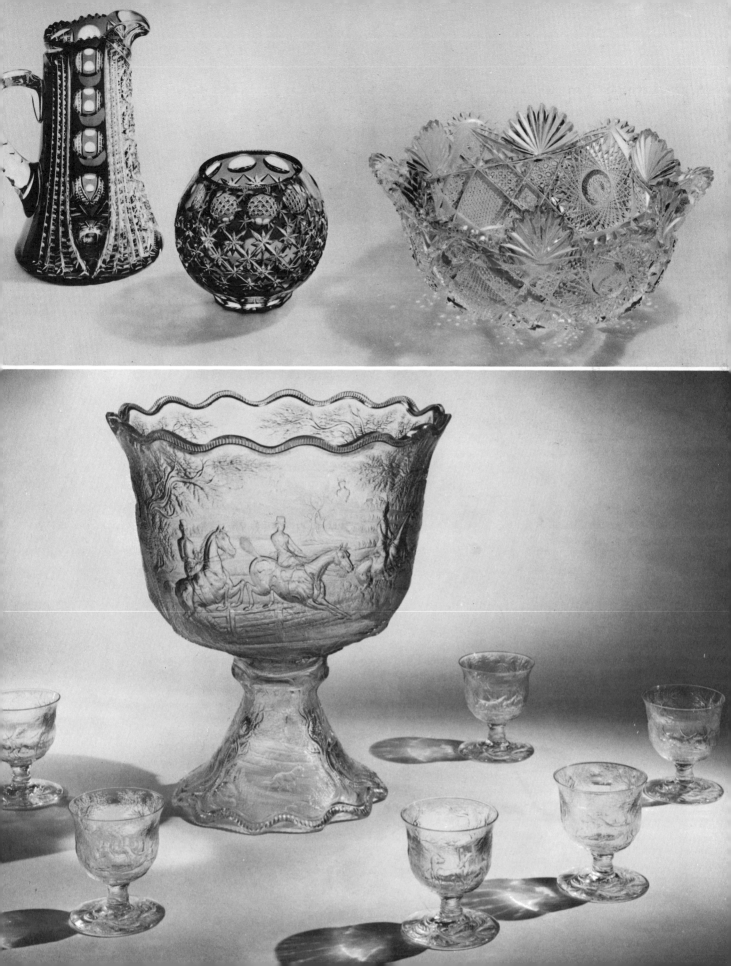

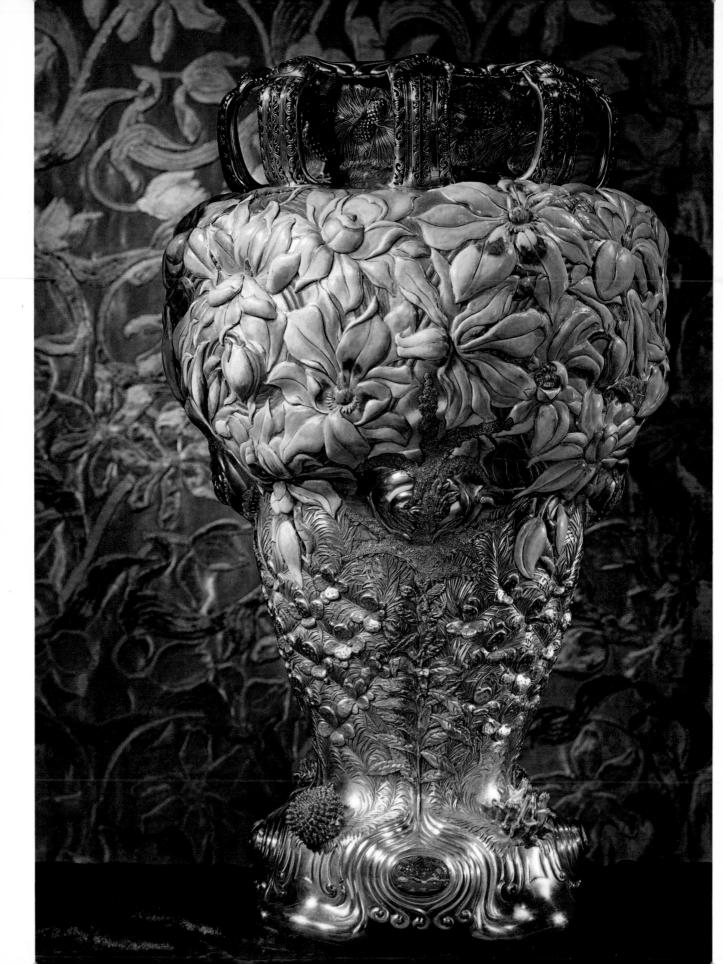

258 Perhaps only the closing decade of the nineteenth century could have produced an object so opulent and so eclectic as this enameled silver vase, almost three feet high, created by Tiffany and Company for the World's Columbian Exposition in 1893. The exposition itself was both opulent and eclectic; it brought together the products that were the pride of the industrialized countries and housed them in the "Great White City," consisting of buildings mostly in a style derived from classical Greece and Rome. Tiffany and Company had its own pavilion, a low building combining Spanish and Renaissance elements, supporting an immense classical column topped by an eagle on a globe.

An article on the Tiffany exhibit in *Godey's Magazine* for August 1893, by George Frederic Heydt, emphasized the American character of this vase: "The magnolia vase, the most prominent piece in . . . [the silver exhibit] is purely American; its form was suggested by the pieces of pottery found among the relics of the ancient cliff-dwellers of the Pueblos. The eight handles around the neck are Toltec, these together represent the early Americans. The decorations are composed of flowers and plants representative of the north, south, east, and west, making the vase in its entirety a characteristic American piece." Stylistically the vase combines several trends of the time: exoticism, as shown in the Toltec handles; the naturalism that characterized a great deal of nineteenth-century decorative art, in the plant forms; and, in the base, art nouveau. But the richness and beauty of workmanship and the overriding lushness manage, despite the great disparity in style among its parts, to give to the whole a feeling of unity.

On the underside of the vase is the manufacturer's mark "TIFFANY & Co./11168 MAKERS 3137/STERLING SILVER/T." "T" replaced "M" in this mark after the death in 1891 of Edward C. Moore (see nos. 222, 229); the letter from then on stood for the company president—Charles L. Tiffany, until his death in 1902. John T. Curran, then chief designer for the silver works, designed this piece. There is also the mark of all the pieces shown by Tiffany and Company at the World's Columbian Exposition, a globe with "[TI]FFANY & Co." superimposed on a "T."

The embroidery shown behind the vase was designed by and executed under the direction of Candace Wheeler, who with Louis C. Tiffany and others formed the decorating firm called Associated Artists (see no. 261) and then kept the name when she set up in business on her own in 1883. Mrs. Wheeler's company produced handsome tapestries, curtains, portieres, and wall hangings of all sorts of materials, for interiors to which fashion of the 1880s and 90s forbade any unadorned space. This portiere is of cloth of silver, with applied and embroidered velvet; the centers of the flowers are in silk.

H. vase 31 inches

The Metropolitan Museum of Art; vase: Gift of Mrs. Winthrop Atwell, 99.2; portiere: Gift of the Family of Mrs. Candace Wheeler (through Mrs. Boudinot Keith), 24.34.2

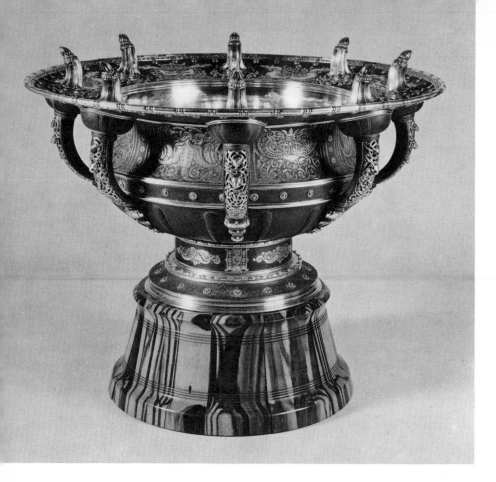

and with the globe superimposed on a "T" that was on all Tiffany pieces shown at the Exposition.

Diam. 20¹/₄ inches
The Metropolitan Museum of Art, Edgar J. Kaufmann Charitable Foundation Fund, 69.4

260

Exotic, too, is this horn chair, suitable for a room furnished in the masculine, somewhat heavy style of the eighties and nineties, with Near Eastern hangings, leather chairs and footstools, and copper, iron, or brass in abundance for balconies and lighting devices or simply used ornamentally. Chairs like this evoked the American West, but were also made in Europe for hunting lodges. Abraham Lincoln and Theodore Roosevelt both received horn chairs as gifts, and the Philadelphia architect Frank Furness had a smoking room described in *Artistic Houses* (1884) as filled with "trophies to make a Nimrod's mouth water, in the shape of bearskins, buffalo-skins, deer-skins . . . together with horns, antlers, and heads of many sorts. . . ." The provenance of this chair is unknown, but its feet—four-pronged brass claws enclosing glass ball casters—are like those used by Louis Comfort Tiffany's Associated Artists and successive decorating firms (see nos. 261, 262): this kind of foot seems to have been a Tiffany trademark. The Tiffany concerns decorated the Veterans' Room and Library in the Seventh Regiment Armory, New York, in 1880 as well as many of the palatial new houses being built by wealthy families, often with rooms that would have accommodated such a chair. The grace and proportions of this chair corroborate its possible attribution to the leading decorator of the day.

H. 37¹/₂ inches
Henry Ford Museum, Dearborn, Michigan

259

Next to the magnolia vase (no. 258), the most impressive metal object exhibited at the World's Columbian Exposition by Tiffany and Company was the Viking punch bowl. It shows the interest in the exotic, and also in the symbolic; structural and decorative elements are included as much for their connotative as their design value. Thus, like many works made throughout the century, the punch bowl does not copy but embodies a nineteenth-century concept of another age. It is bold and heavy, symbolizing the strength and will of the Vikings, at the same time demonstrating the admiration of the nineteenth century for those qualities. The picture caption in an article in *Godey's Magazine* for August 1893 describes the bowl as "Decarbonized iron, etched and demaskeen [*sic*] decorations inlaid with fine gold and silver, eight handles around body, terminating through flange on top of bowl in forms suggested by the prow of the Norseman's boat, plain silver lining." The bowl is marked "TIFFANY & Co 11171 MAKERS,"

261

This pair of andirons was made for the large library added in 1894 to the house at 7 Washington Square belonging to Robert W. de Forest, donor of the American Wing and president of the Metropolitan Museum from 1913 to 1931. The house had been built in 1832 for

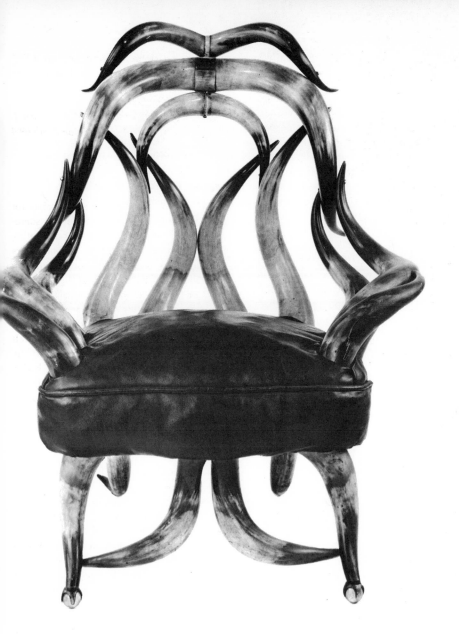

Mrs. de Forest's grandfather, John Johnston, in the current Greek revival style; the new room, no less up-to-date, was decorated by Louis Comfort Tiffany, scion of the well-known silver manufacturing and retailing family, who became one of the most important figures in the history of American decorative arts. Right after the Civil War young Tiffany began as a painter, studying briefly with George Inness in New York and Léon Bailly in Paris. But he became increasingly interested by the decorative arts, and in 1879 he founded, with the painters Samuel Colman and Lockwood de Forest (brother of Robert de Forest) and the textile designer Candace Wheeler, a decorating firm, calling it Louis C. Tiffany and Associated Artists. This soon disbanded, but in 1885 the Tiffany Glass Company was incorporated, becoming Tiffany Glass and Decorating Company in 1892 and Tiffany Studios about 1900. These small firms produced individualized and often experimental work by, or directly supervised by, Tiffany or one of his artist-associates —they were entirely distinct, both in law and in concept, from the larger, more traditional and solidly commercial Tiffany and Company run by Louis's father, Charles L. Tiffany. Louis Tiffany's personal interest, which developed into a profoundly original contribution, was in glassmaking. In the nineties work in metal was begun, most often combined with glass in the well-known Tiffany lamps. These black andirons, of iron with bronze heads with green and brown glass inserts, stood in a fireplace faced with slabs of highly figured marble. Around this was a mosaic mantel, about twelve feet wide, designed personally by Tiffany, depicting the marks of nine printers of the fifteenth and sixteenth centuries against an arabesque background.

H. 25¹/₈ inches

The Metropolitan Museum of Art, Gift of Mrs. D. Chester Noyes, 68.69.17, 18

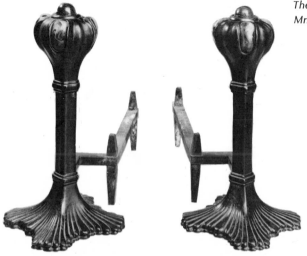

262 The romance of the East, fascination with antiquity, and flowing lines of plant forms, all important influences in late nineteenth-century design, meet and meld in this grouping of the arts of Tiffany Glass and Decorating Company and Tiffany Studios, made between 1890 and 1905. Perhaps the most familiar of the Tiffany forms here is that of the naturalistic lamp in the art nouveau style (see no. 269), with its green bronze base of lily pads and stems rising to support trumpet-shaped flower shades. The design won a Grand Prize in the Turin Exposition of 1902. The small bronze and oak table, marked, like the lamp, "TIFFANY STUDIOS/ NEW YORK." and a number, shows a debt to antiquity; its form, with slender legs, hoof feet, and X-shaped stretcher resembles that of collapsible Greek and Roman stands. The swelling plant form of the upper legs is an imaginative Tiffany touch that seems Near

Eastern in derivation. Plant and flower forms also appear carved in shallow relief on the cresting rail of the pair of ash chairs. More traditional in style than the lamp or stand, they are in the shape of a late eighteenth-century French bergère; their legs have reeding similar to that on the table. The naturalistic flower and leaf decoration has less connotation of the writhing forms of art nouveau, more of the quality of surface decoration found on art furniture.

Marquetry, the other decoration on these chairs, is also in the art furniture tradition; here it takes on the exotic look of the East. One is reminded that in the 1880s Tiffany's friend and associate Lockwood de Forest imported carved and inlaid Eastern furniture. Harriet Spofford wrote in *Art Decoration Applied to Furniture* (1878): "No marquetry exceeds for curiosity that which is occasionally brought now from India,

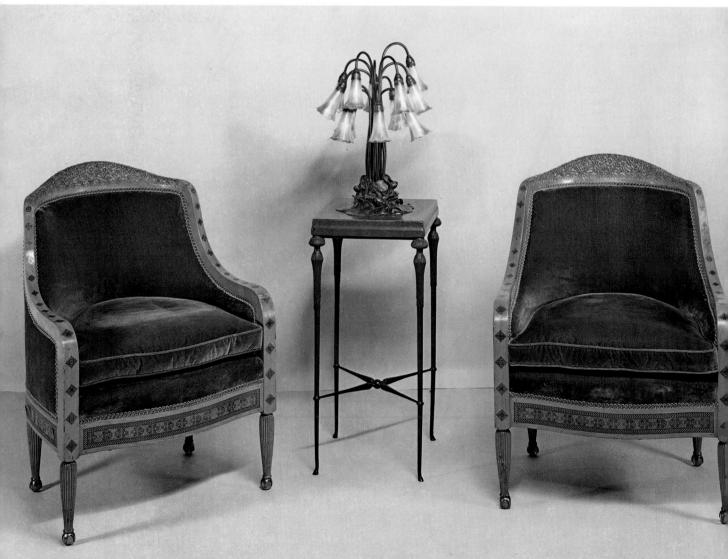

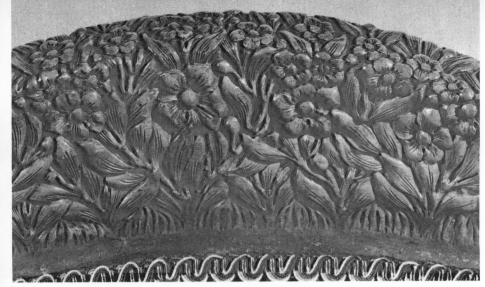

known as the mosaic of Bombay, and made of microscopic cubes of wood that produce a fine effect." In her chapter "Oriental Styles" she also spoke of "furniture in the East Indian style . . . in the satin-wood inlaid with the Bombay-work in its mosaic of minutest cubes. . . ." The inlay here is of a variety of woods, including mahogany, ebony, and boxwood; the minute cubes are outlined with brass.

Although these chairs are not marked, the attribution to Tiffany is strong. They are similar in shape and decoration to chairs made by Tiffany for the H.O. Havemeyer house; the glass ball held in a brass claw foot also appears on the Havemeyer chairs and other documented Tiffany furniture. In addition, the distinctive type of marquetry is discussed in the description of a "settle" in a catalogue of the Tiffany Glass and Decorating Company from the Chicago Columbian Exposition of 1893: " . . . our wood mosaic . . . is produced by an entire new method of work. The patterns upon this piece of furniture are made of thousands of squares of natural wood, sixteenth-of-an-inch in size, of different colors, and each individual square surrounded by a minute line of metal."

H. chairs 35⁵/₈ inches
Lamp: Mr. and Mrs. William G. Osofsky, Oyster Bay, New York; armchairs: The Metropolitan Museum of Art, Gift of Mr. and Mrs. Georges E. Seligmann, 64.202.1,2; table: The Metropolitan Museum of Art, Rogers Fund, 66.98

263

The leaded glass lampshades in floral patterns are probably the best-known product of Tiffany's decorating and glass companies. Tiffany was interested in all aspects of lighting; in 1885 he decorated the Lyceum Theater in New York, the first theater to be lighted completely by electricity. This dramatic new means of lighting focused public attention on lamps, and the handsome Tiffany products were quickly in demand. The peony, skillfully flattened and abstracted, provides the pattern of this shade, which is predominantly blue-green with purple, pink, green, and blue. The bronze shaft is decorated with attenuated stems having their roots in the rounded base and terminating at the top in fernlike volutes. Underneath the base is the mark "TIFFANY STUDIOS/NEW YORK./7985."

H. 63³/₄ inches
Mr. and Mrs: Walter P. Chrysler, Jr., Provincetown, Massachusetts

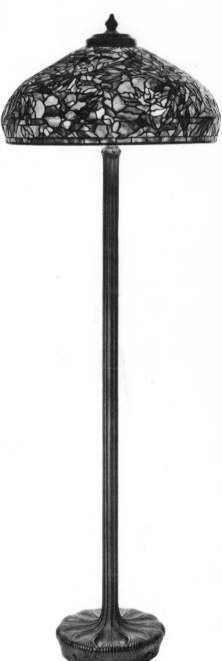

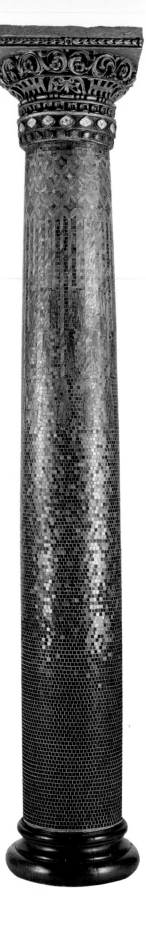

265 Among the best-known of the Tiffany designs for lamps is the wisteria pattern, with the base the conception of Tiffany himself and the shade usually thought to be the design of Mrs. Curtis Freshel, whose house in Chestnut Hill near Boston was surrounded by wisteria. According to tradition, when Mrs. Freshel moved into the house about 1900, she made designs for some of the furniture, including this lamp, which she then asked Tiffany to execute. Tiffany is said to have told her it would cost $10,000, but if she would agree to let him market the lamp, he would make it for $5,000; she agreed. As in all of Tiffany's floral lamps, the plant form is evoked rather than reproduced; the character of the materials—glass, lead, bronze—is emphasized, not belied. Thicker leading on top suggests branches nearer the stem, and the color becomes lighter, even pink, at the lowest edge of the cascading wisteria clusters. On the underside of the base is the mark "TIFFANY STUDIOS/NEW YORK./ 27770."

H. 27 inches

Mr. and Mrs. Walter P. Chrysler, Jr., Provincetown, Massachusetts

264

Byzantine mosaics, which Tiffany admired greatly, were the inspiration for this column from the studio building at his home, Laurelton Hall, in Oyster Bay, Long Island, completed about 1905. A booklet on glass mosaics published by Tiffany Glass and Decorating Company in 1896 states: "The most wonderful creation in glass-mosaic the world has ever seen was the interior of Sancta Sophia, at Constantinople." Tiffany's firm decorated a number of churches with mosaics, and this column gives a good idea of the subtlety he could achieve. Here as elsewhere Tiffany's inspiration in the past in no way limited his invention; the gilt diaper with rosettes and pendent cords with tassels are classical elements, but their treatment, in this flattened and sparkling iridescent design, transforms them from historicism into a superb personal expression.

H. 120 inches

The Metropolitan Museum of Art, Edgar J. Kaufmann Charitable Foundation Fund, 68.184

266

Like the lamp no. 265, this window by Tiffany Studios uses the graceful wisteria as its subject. Wisteria is well suited to such a decorative use, for one can have it cover a specific area and frame a scene without distorting its nature. The twisting vine seems to come entirely naturally from a point below and spread across the top. Purple mountains in the distance give the eye a resting point, while leaving a large area of sky and sea in light-colored glass to permit light to come through. The glass itself, in colors that are varied yet blend perfectly, shows the excellence that Tiffany demanded of all the works produced by his studios. Stained-glass windows were still very much in vogue around the turn of the century; this one was made about 1905 for the house of William Skinner at 36 East Thirty-ninth Street, New York.

H. 72³/₄ inches

Mr. and Mrs. Hugh F. McKean, Winter Park, Florida

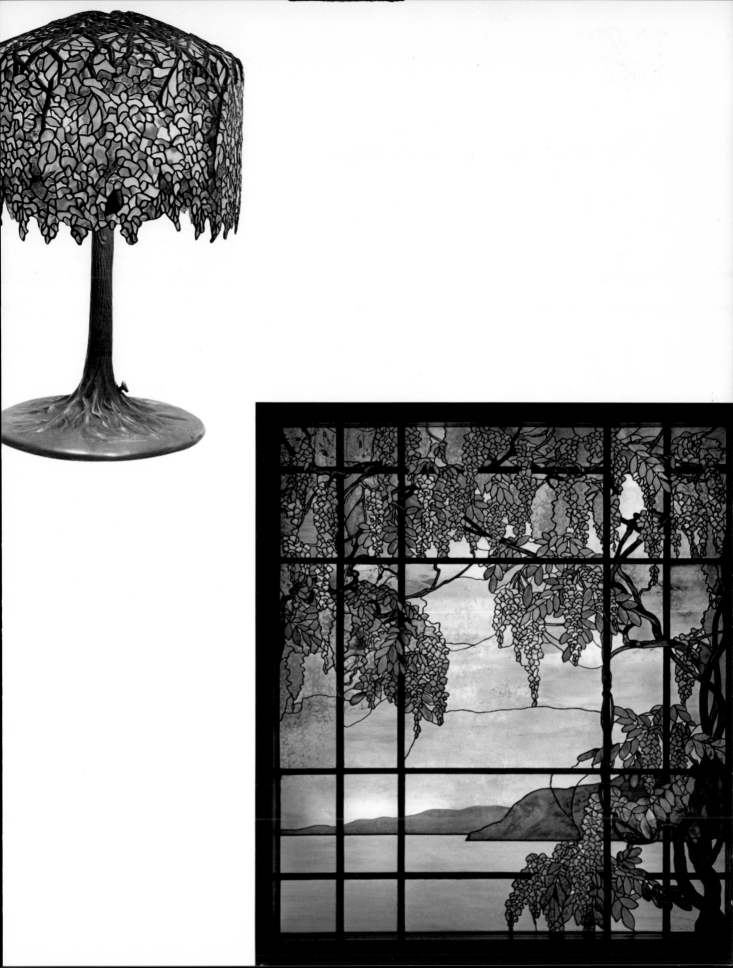

267

Late in the 1890s Tiffany and his associates began experimenting in the difficult medium of enamel, and first exhibited enameled pieces in Buffalo in 1901. These five examples—all enamel on repoussé copper—demonstrate the richness and variety of color that could be achieved, although not without extraordinary artistry. As Samuel Howe, once a Tiffany employee, wrote of enamel in *The Craftsman* in 1902: "In a word, as the price of its service, it demands from the artist the most unremitting care and the most exact calculation of effect." In all these pieces the motifs—apples and leaves on the iridescent glass and copper box, dragonflies, flowers, and lily pads on the other objects—are rendered with a sureness and seeming ease that are all the more testimony to Tiffany's skill. The smaller items are signed "L.C.T.," and the covered box "Louis C Tiffany"; each has an identifying number.

L. box 6 inches
The Metropolitan Museum of Art, Gift of the Louis Comfort Tiffany Foundation, 51.121.43,42,36,40,32

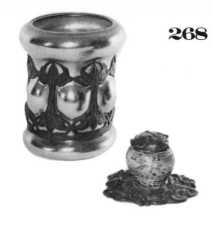

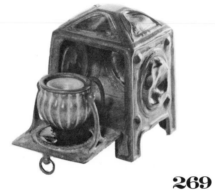

268

Unusual and striking combinations of metal and glass became an important part of Tiffany work—echoing the more rugged aspects of the history of design. Roman, Etruscan, Byzantine, and medieval works were all admired by Tiffany for the strength and sumptuousness of their colors and forms. In the enamels and in these three objects this admiration is evident, as is the originality with which Tiffany made the work unmistakably his. Iridescent gold glass is combined with bronze in a flat art nouveau leaf pattern in the vase on the left, marked "3586P L.C. Tiffany-Favrile." The bronze stand and cover of the small mosaic inkwell, marked "TIFFANY STUDIOS/29411," also show the fluidity of art nouveau. The larger piece has an inkwell, gimbaled on the door of a bronze and glass stand, that resembles a small jewel casket; it bears a glass insert marked "L.C.T."

H. vase 5³⁄₄ inches
Inkwells: Stuart P. Feld, New York; vase: lent anonymously

269

Tiffany, of course, produced objects solely of glass, like the four shown here. He created the word "Favrile" to describe his glass, stating at one time that the word came from old English "fabrile," meaning "pertaining to a craft or craftsman," and at another time that he derived it from the German *Farbe*, "color." In America it is with Tiffany's glass objects that the term "art nouveau" is popularly associated. This term denotes the international style that sprang up in northern Europe in the 1880s, and that was generally characterized by elongation, flowing lines, and the frequent use of certain natural forms—flowers, human hair, and waves. The name that stayed with the style came from the Paris shop of the dealer and critic Siegfried (known as Samuel) Bing, which opened as the Salon de l'Art Nouveau on December 26, 1895, with an exhibition including paintings by the Nabis group, sculpture, prints, drawings, and posters, as well as Tiffany glass objects and ten Tiffany windows. During the 1880s Bing's shop, where he sold Oriental *objets,* had attracted artists interested in the Orient; Tiffany knew the shop from his early trips to Paris, and in 1889 the two men began a close association, with Bing becoming Tiffany's sole European distributor.

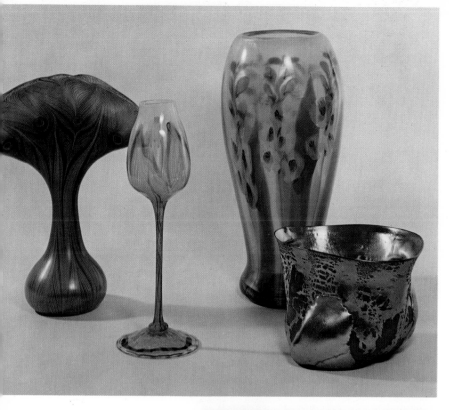

Peacock feathers, as on the vase at the left, made by 1896 and marked "01600," were a natural motif for Tiffany, who was fascinated by vibrant yet delicate combinations of color; the shape of this vase is of Near Eastern origin. The floral motifs of the stemmed vase, inscribed "01892" and made in 1895, and of the gladiolus vase, made in 1909, besides being popular among designers in art nouveau, provided a nearly infinite range of possibility for color. The large vase is marked "176A-coll. L.C. Tiffany [indicating that the piece was to be kept for Tiffany's own collection]—Favrile." Iridescence, almost a Tiffany signature, is seen on the lava bowl, made in 1908, which resembles an object excavated after centuries of burial—a more romantic simulation of antiquity than a mere copying of the shapes of the early pieces. It is marked "21A-coll. L. C. Tiffany-Favrile." The peacock vase and the stemmed vase were given to the Metropolitan in 1896 by Henry O. Havemeyer, whose house at 848 Fifth Avenue was decorated by Louis C. Tiffany and Samuel Colman in the early 1890s; the peacock vase bears the sticker of the Tiffany Glass and Decorating Company.

H. large vase 16 7/16 inches
The Metropolitan Museum of Art; peacock vase and stemmed vase: Gift of H.O. Havemeyer, 96.17.10, 36; large vase and bowl: Gift of the Louis Comfort Tiffany Foundation, 51.121.22,13

270

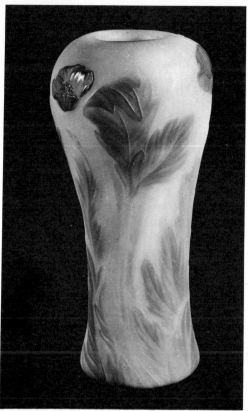

The technique used on this vase by Tiffany, that of engraving cameo reliefs on cased glass, was developed in Europe in the last quarter of the nineteenth century, at first in direct imitation of ancient Roman cameo glass. Toward the end of the century a group of French art-glass makers in Nancy, among whom the best-known is Emile Gallé, achieved a wide reputation by adapting the technique to free forms and floral patterns in the art nouveau style. Gallé's work was part of Siegfried Bing's first exhibition of art nouveau in December 1895 (see no. 269). With vases such as this one, in shades of white, cream, and brown, Tiffany proved himself the equal of the French glassmakers. The vase is marked "L.C. Tiffany Favrile 1761 C."

H. 8³/₈ inches
Lent anonymously

271

That Tiffany was considered one of the greatest designers of his time is apparent in the critical acclaim for his contributions to the Exposition Universelle at Paris in 1900. The piece that stood out in this collection was this astonishing punch bowl. The United States Commission to the Exposition, in its report on "Applied Arts" quoted in *American Art Annual* III (1900), declared:

Among the collection of Favrile glass sent by the Tiffany Company the most important piece was a punch bowl . . . about thirty inches in diameter. The glass is encased in a frame of chased and wrought golden metal [actually brass with gold plating], the design of the base suggesting the effect of breaking waves, while from their foaming crests spring six arms of peacock-hued Favrile glass, they in turn support the uprights of the frame, becoming a richly ornamental band at the top. Three of the supports end in quaintly twisted finials of lustre glass from which hang ladles of metal and iridescent glass.

The mount, in keeping with art nouveau principles, is based upon wavelike forms and is particularly well suited for a container filled with the froth of bubbling punch.

H. 14¹/₄ inches
Dr. and Mrs. Robert Koch, South Norwalk, Connecticut

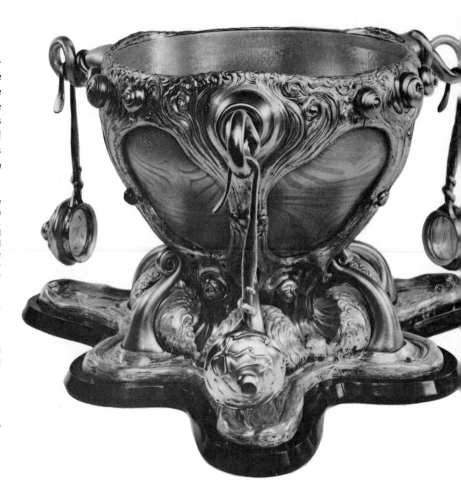

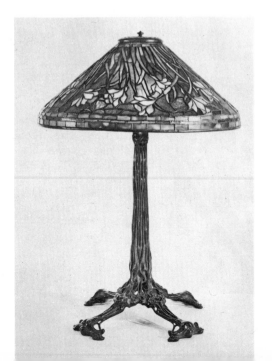

272

Shades of green are dominant, gradating into some yellow and light blue, in the glass of this leaded lampshade with daffodil motif. The pattern was probably made under the supervision of Clara Driscoll, a Tiffany designer. Its bronze base is organically shaped. Unlike some of the bases, it is in no recognizable plant form; the extremely contorted and fluid forms make it closest of all the Tiffany bases to the European art nouveau designs. The inside rim of the shade is marked "TIFFANY STUDIOS NEW YORK 1497-44."

H. 28¹/₄ inches
Lent anonymously

273

Although art nouveau had a profound—albeit short-lived—influence upon the other decorative arts in America, it had virtually no discernible effect upon high-style, fine quality furniture. So late was its influence on furniture here that by the time this mahogany curio cabinet was made in New York, about 1910, art nouveau was already waning in Europe. The cabinet bears on its back a metal plaque that reads: "TRADE/FFF MARK/ GEO. C. FLINT CO./WEST 23RD ST., N.Y." George C. Flint and Company, successors to the firm of Henry Bruner, was first listed in the 1868 New York directory. A Twenty-third Street address, with three additional addresses, first appeared in the directory for 1894/95; a listing only at Twenty-third Street ran from 1909 until 1913. The address on the label, as well as the style, indicates the cabinet was made in this period.

Most of the so-called art nouveau furniture made in this country in the early twentieth century was a much diluted commercial version lacking the grace and imagination of the better European pieces. This cabinet, however, is a rare example of American furniture in the sophisticated Continental art nouveau style, since it is an almost exact copy of a pair of cabinets made by the French designer Louis Majorelle of Nancy about 1900 to 1905. Majorelle made art nouveau furniture from 1897 until the decline of the style. He exhibited his pieces in a number of places, including the Paris Exhibition of 1900, the Turin Exposition of 1902, the Musée des Arts Décoratifs show of 1903, the 1904 Paris Exposition de la Société des Artistes Décorateurs, and the annual Paris Salons d'Automne of 1906 and 1907. Possibly his pair of cabinets was pictured in an exhibition catalogue, or perhaps a designer for the Flint firm saw and sketched them. This cabinet follows closely the Majorelle form and plan and pattern of carving; however, as in most copies, something of the original spirit is lost. Here the flowing lines, while well carved, seem tighter and more constrained than those on the European prototype.

H. 58³/₄ inches
The Metropolitan Museum of Art, Anonymous Gift Fund, 68.132

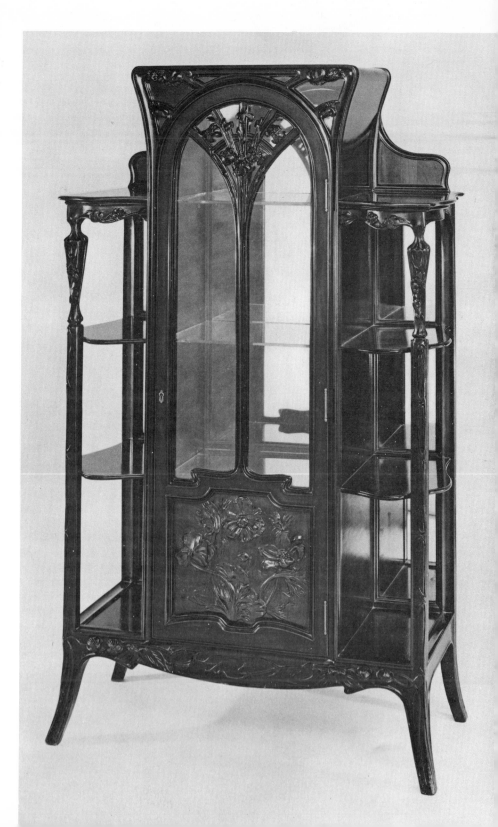

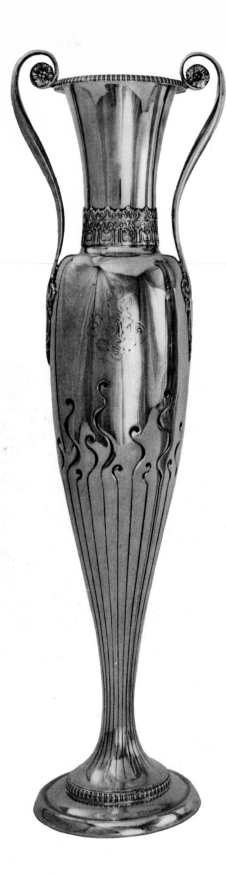

274

In this pair of vases by Tiffany and Company
are mingled two trends of the 1890s, the
Beaux-Arts tradition, and the quiet but insist-
ent influence of art nouveau. The vase shape,
the applied chased band on the neck, gadrooning on the lip, and rosetted scrolls at the
ends of the handles are all of classical derivation. Concurrent with the Arts and Crafts
movement and Tiffany's innovations was the
influence of the academic Ecole des Beaux-
Arts in Paris, where virtually all American artists and architects from the eastern states
went for their training, returning with a thorough knowledge of details of the classical
orders and the Renaissance architecture of
France and Italy. In all the decorative arts formal, even magnificent, objects were being
made in the Beaux-Arts spirit (see nos. 281,
282). The attenuation of the lower part of
the body, however, and the incised lines that
break free into undulating waves are from the
vocabulary of art nouveau. Marked "TIFFANY
& Co/1108[1?] MAKERS 5209[?]/STERLING
SILVER/925-1000/T," inscribed on the base
"April 25—1894.," and monogrammed "A L L"
on the body, the vases were a wedding present to Anne Louise Lamont, who married
Harry Harkness Flagler on April 25, 1894.

H. 17⁷/₈ inches

*Museum of the City of New York, Gift of
Harry Harkness Flagler*

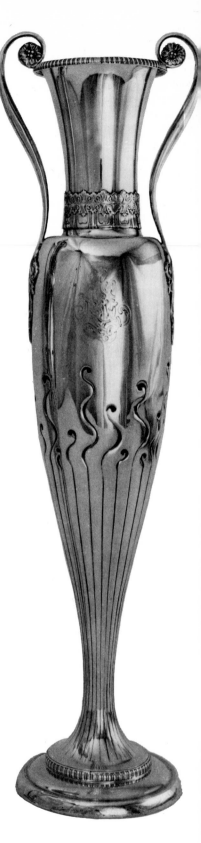

275

Art nouveau, in its brief and lovely life, is most
frequently associated in American art with the
very special products of Louis Tiffany (see
nos. 261-272). But although the style was too
short-lived ever to attain really widespread ap-

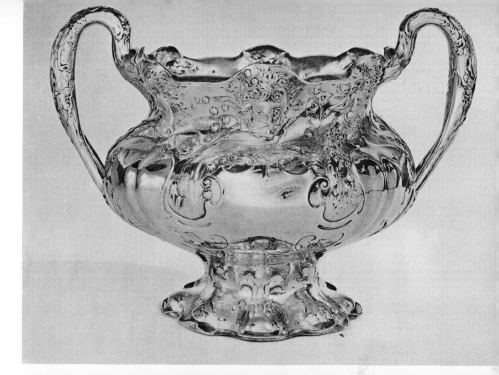

peal, certain of the smaller silver companies produced a lot of work in art nouveau, and the large Gorham Manufacturing Company of Providence had its own version of it, called Martelé. An example is this punch bowl, decorated with waves, mermaids, and various leaves and flowers, in flowing forms. William Codman, an English artist, came to Gorham in 1891, and under his direction the design department began to produce these works, each piece a unique design. Hammered by hand from silver of high quality, they were first marketed about 1900. The technique imparted a soft fluid look to the material, very apparent in this bowl. The symmetry and lack of elongation of this piece differentiate it from most work in art nouveau, but the motifs and the flowing quality are characteristic of the style. The bowl is marked with the Gorham lion, spread eagle above an anchor, and "G," "950-1000 FINE./2518," and with a monogram and the year "1900."

W. 20¹/₂ inches

Mr. and Mrs. Walter P. Chrysler, Jr., Provincetown, Massachusetts

276

Unger Brothers of Newark, in business from 1881 to 1910, was one of the small silver companies that by 1900 specialized in art nouveau designs, and this letter opener, brooch, and belt buckle are typical of their output, which included every conceivable article that could be made in silver for desk or dresser or for personal use. The motifs are the familiar ones that suited the flowing dreamy style: female heads with long loose hair, waves, and floral forms. The trident held in the mermaid's right hand extends the sweep of her figure upward, as the reins in her left hand carry it down. Each piece has the Unger Brothers mark: "U B" in monogram with "STERLING" above and "925 FINE" below, all in a circle. A more typical expression of art nouveau than the Martelé silver (no. 275), these pieces are fine examples of the style, showing it to be at its best as exquisite as it is unmistakable.

L. letter opener 9⁷/₈ inches

The Metropolitan Museum of Art, Gift of Ronald S. Kane, 67.35.1-3

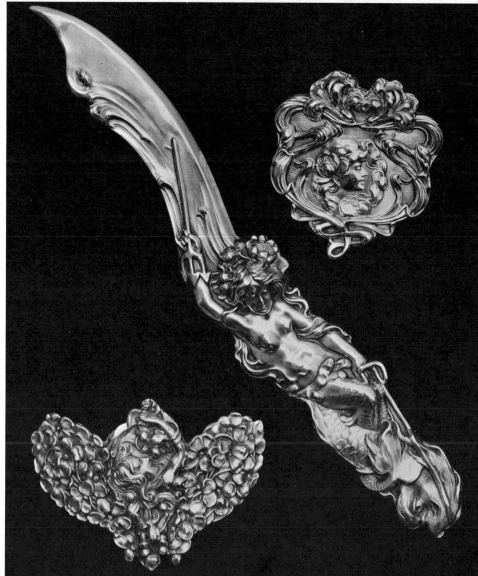

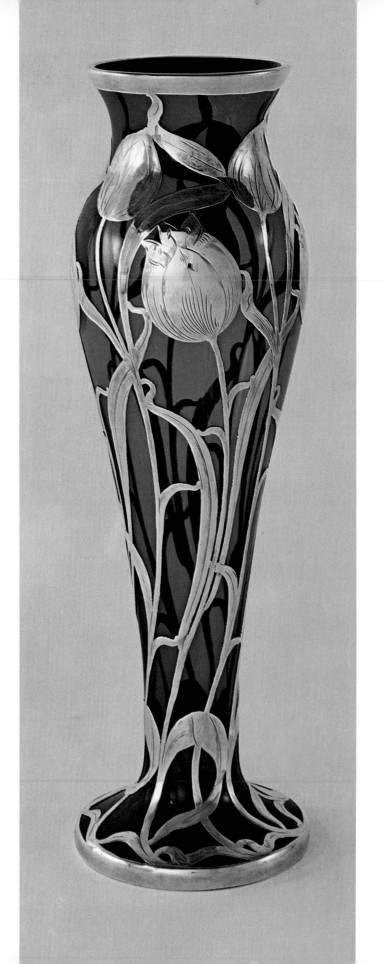

277

This graceful vase, probably dating from the first decade of the twentieth century, was made by the silver-deposit process, first developed in the 1880s and most popular between 1890 and 1910. In this process silver was deposited, through electroplating, upon a silver-flux design that had been previously applied to the glass. The Alvin Manufacturing Company of Providence specialized in silver-deposit work, and this vase, although unmarked, could well have been made by that company. The willowy tulips with interlaced leaves are a manifestation of the emphasis in art nouveau on motifs that, while naturalistic, seem to have their origins in eighteenth-century rococo design rather than in nature.

H. 12¹/₄ inches

The Metropolitan Museum of Art, Anonymous Gift Fund, 68.102

278

Islamic glass was the inspiration for the design on this vase, cased in brown and gold and etched in an interlacing pattern against a frosted ground. A fine demonstration of how traditional and advanced ideas in design were combined at the turn of the century, the flowing treatment echoes the art nouveau style, although applied with an unusually conservative hand. Gilt arabesques enliven the surface. Inscribed in gold on the underside is "Honesdale," for the glass-decorating company that Christian Dorflinger founded in 1901 in the Pennsylvania town of that name.

H. 14³/₈ inches

The Metropolitan Museum of Art, Anonymous Gift Fund, 69.91.1

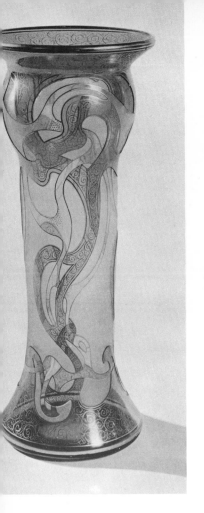

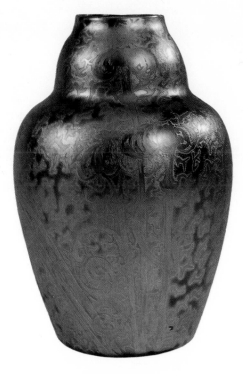

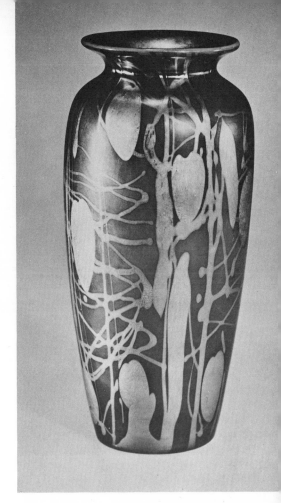

279

This earthenware vase made in 1903 by J. Sicard for S. A. Weller, one of the major potteries in Zanesville, Ohio, has the iridescence of Tiffany glass. Sicard learned the technique with Clément Massier, a potter in Golfe Juan, France, whose source of inspiration was Hispano-Moresque lusterware; the popularity of the iridescent Tiffany glass undoubtedly encouraged Sicard in its use. The form of the vase and the gold and silver pattern on the blue ground are a distinctive expression of art nouveau that Sicard evolved in Ohio. The names "Sicard" and "Weller" have been worked into the decoration, near the bottom of the vase.

H. 8³/₄ inches

The Metropolitan Museum of Art, Anonymous Gift Fund, 69.93

280

Made by the Steuben Glass Works, Corning, New York, of "Aurene," the company's iridescent glass registered under this trademark in 1904, this handsome vase uses rich colors and art nouveau patterns on a common shape. Frederick Carder, trained in England, was director of the glassworks from its inception in 1903; he ranks among the foremost designers of art glass. Although the shapes of Carder's glass remained for the most part traditional, he made technical experiments and innovations as bold as Tiffany's. "Aurene," so named because it shone like gold, was made in gold, blue, green, red, and brown, sometimes plain, sometimes decorated. Works in the deep red of this vase are rare today. The work is dated "1905" on the underside, presumably by Carder.

H. 6³/₄ inches

The Corning Museum of Glass

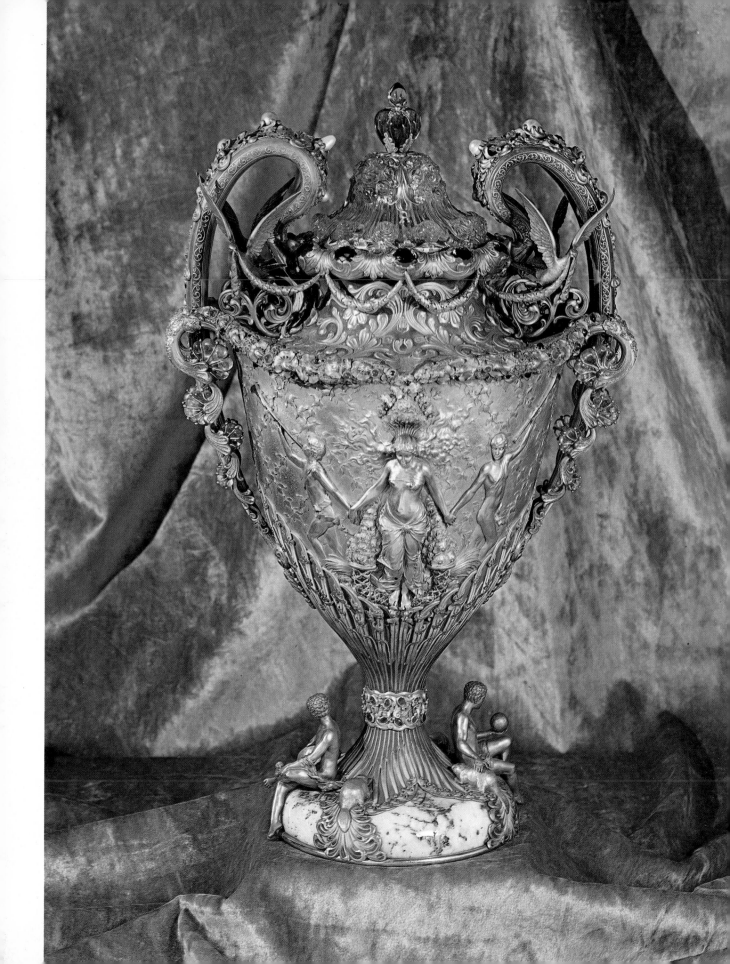

If one wanted to represent with a single object the segment of American society that earned for the end of the century the name of Gilded Age, that object might well be the Adams vase. The vase was made by Tiffany and Company during the years 1893 to 1895, from a design by Paulding Farnham, then chief designer and director of the jewelry division, for presentation to Edward Dean Adams, chairman of the board of the American Cotton Oil Company, by the stockholders and directors. Adams had worked tirelessly to save the company from financial ruin; he refused monetary compensation; so in 1891, the vase was conceived as a symbol of gratitude. Reform, exoticism, and art nouveau were all strong currents in American decorative arts during the 1890s, but along with these the classical tradition continued to run steadily. The World's Columbian Exposition in Chicago in 1893 was a triumph for Beaux-Arts architecture. As in architecture, so in the decorative arts did tradition and academicism seem to some the most suitable mode for artistic expression.

For the Cotton Oil Company directors, there could be no mistake about their gratitude if it were embodied in gold studded with pearls and semiprecious stones. Indeed, Tiffany and Company published a booklet about the vase, emphasizing the cost and time in its production: it required the services of three draughtsmen, fifteen modelers, eighteen goldsmiths, twenty-one chasers, twelve finishers, four molders, three turners, two enamelers, three stonecutters, and two lapidaries. The book also explained the symbolism. The cotton plant was the source for the colors of the vase. The gold quartz at the base signifies the "pure, rich principle at the root of all the construction." The two figures on the base are "young Atlas turning the financial world at his pleasure" and "Husbandry holding a cotton-branch in his hand." Circling the base is a platting of roots, signifying "power of conception." On one side of the vase the central figure is Modesty "encouraged by two heralds to announce the success of her great undertaking . . . supported by horns of abundance that signify the profusion of the cotton-flower." On the other side appears the figure of a youth, like Modesty, molded in full relief, his chin resting on his hand. Here Farnham's symbolism reaches its apogee: "The upper part of the body is clothed with a star-embroidered gar-

ment, which is an attribute of Genius. The meaning of the star is uncertainty resolved into definite form. The figure on the right is Agriculture giving his confidence to Genius, and that on the left represents Commerce warming his hands over the magic flames coming from the cotton-flower, which is supported on the pedestal of this growth. Genius holds in his right hand a vessel filled with the coins produced as the result of this industry." Perhaps the most telling point of the booklet is its emphasis on patriotism—even though all the stylistic elements came straight from the European tradition. Throughout, the word "American" appears again and again, and the last significant passage states that "every piece of material used, and the artist and his principal assistants, are American, which shows an independence that many countries in the old world might be proud of." The seal of the American Cotton Oil Company appears behind one handle, Adams's initials and the date 1891 are behind the other. The vase is marked on the underside "TIFFANY & Co./MAKERS/SOLID GOLD," and, on a tube inside, "TIFFANY & Co./STERLING SILVER/T."

H. 19½ inches
The Metropolitan Museum of Art, Gift of Edward D. Adams, 04.1

282

Designer of this gold cup was the sculptor Karl Bitter, who was born and trained in Vienna and came to America in 1889. Through work as an architectural modeler he became known to a leading architect of the Beaux-Arts school, Richard Morris Hunt, who made him his protégé. Bitter's sculpture eventually decorated many buildings in the Beaux-Arts style, including two of Hunt's most important structures, the Administration Building at the World's Columbian Exposition of 1893 and the Fifth Avenue facade of the Metropolitan Museum, designed in the early 1890s. Bitter's best-known work of sculpture is the figure of Abundance on the Pulitzer Fountain in front of the Plaza Hotel in New York. This carved and repoussé cup, made for the golden wedding anniversary in 1900 of Marcus and Bertha Goldman, grandparents of the donor, is in a traditional chalice form. Its sculptural, ornamental, and symbolic elements are also solidly classical. On the base the seated figure of Eros supports and protects two

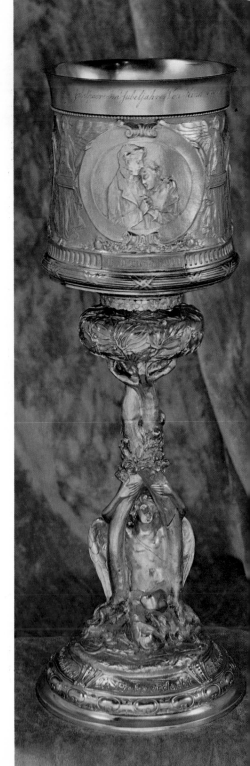

intertwined tree trunks that bear leafy branches. Three medallions on the cup show a young couple embracing, a couple with a baby, and an older couple with children and grandchildren. The cup is inscribed around the rim: *"Dem Yubelpaare Im Yubel-* *jahre Von Kind und Kindeskind geweiht, An Becher's Schwelle Aus edler Quelle Trinkt Glück und Kraft auf ferne Zeit* [Dedicated to the jubilee couple in the jubilee year by children and grandchildren, at the rim of the cup drink from the noble source good fortune and strength for a long time]." Below or between the medallions are the inscriptions: "1850 21ten Juli 1900." "ARBEITSLUST [love of industry]," "WOLTHAETIGKEIT [charity]," and "VATERLANDSLIEBE [patriotism]." Around the base are the words *"In Liebe erdacht In Liebe vollbracht Aus Goldener Tiefe Die Liebe Euch lacht* [Conceived in love, completed in love, from golden depths love smiles at you]." The cup shows the maker's mark on the underside: "WM. B. DURGIN CO./18 K D/CONCORD. N.H."

H. 14 7/16 inches
The Metropolitan Museum of Art, Gift of Marcus I. Goldman, 48.173

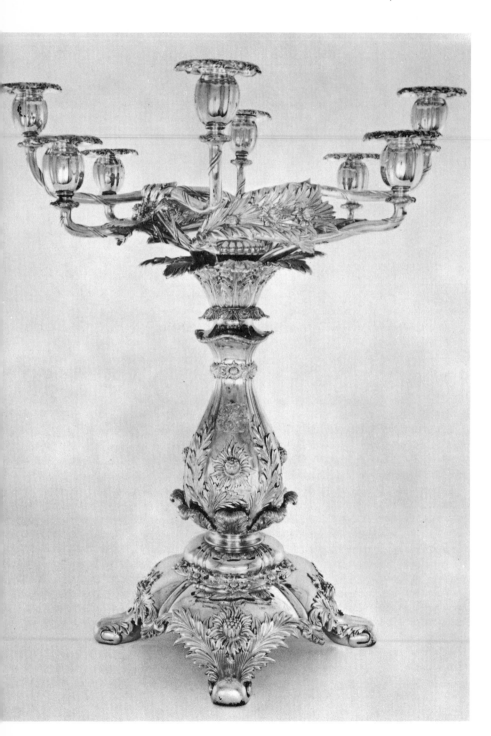

283

This elegant candelabrum is from a sterling silver-dinner set of about 165 pieces of hollow- and flatware, a wedding present to the mother of the donors in 1890. The chrysanthemum was a favorite motif in the last two decades of the nineteenth century, doubtless because of the influence of Japanese art, in which it stands for longevity. Those Victorians knowledgeable in the "language of flowers" would appreciate the touch of symbolism. The vine-clad branches sweep out gracefully like the long stems of wild chrysanthemums; they are overlaid with a wreath of leaves and flowers. There is an almost baroque sensibility in the contrast of these arms with the bulbousness and weightiness of the stem and the squat firm stance of the underturned feet. Tiffany and Company first brought out this pattern in 1880; some of the flatware in the set is marked "PAT. 1880." The mark on this piece is "TIFFANY & Co/ 5727 MAKERS 3128/ STERLING-SILVER/ 925-1000/M."

H. 21 1/2 inches
Museum of the City of New York, given in memory of Daisy Beard Brown by her daughters, Bertha Shults Dougherty and Isabel Shults

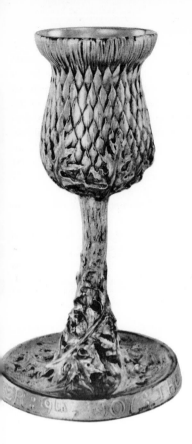

284

Shaped like a thistle to evoke the Scottish ancestry of Andrew Carnegie, this gilt-bronze goblet was one of several made for a dinner on December 9, 1907, celebrating the opening of the new clubhouse built by the Engineers' Club. Carnegie had donated the money for the twelve-story building at 32 West Fortieth Street in New York. Stylistically the goblet is outside of any single tradition; its naturalism recalls that of the middle of the century, while the roughness inherent in the thistle form and the interest of the surface treatment seem to relate it to the Arts and Crafts movement. Made by Tiffany and Company, it also shows the high degree of elegance this company maintained in all of its work, no matter what the style. The name of the club, the date of the dinner, and the mark "TIF-FANY & Co" are visible around the base of the goblet.

H. 7 9/16 inches
Museum of the City of New York, Gift of Alfred M. F. Kiddle

285

This massive silver tray presented to August Belmont upon completion of the New York City subway line about 1904 is, like the achievement it honors, a tour de force of design and execution. A loving cup most probably presented at the same time bears the inscription: "Presented to August Belmont, Esq. by the Board of Directors of the Interborough Rapid Transit Company in appreciation of his services as its President in the construction of the Rapid Transit Subway New York City, October 27th 1904." Within a formal neoclassical treatment the tray uses realistic vignettes and motifs to portray or symbolize the construction of the subway. The rectangular well shows an engraved map of the line. Around the wide rim, on a background of tracks, are cast and applied medallions, one of Belmont, the others showing sites of the construction. Each medallion is wreathed and linked to the next by the laurel, the classical symbol of victory. The handles, of an openwork laurel pattern, are in the shape of shovel handles, and are linked to the

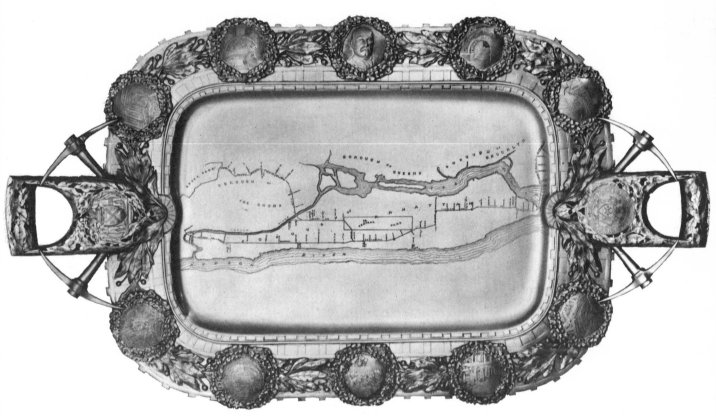

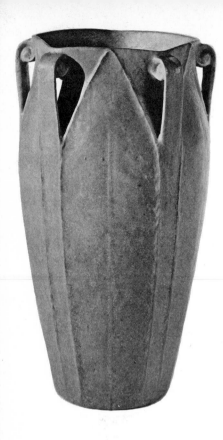

tray by pickaxes. The tray carries on the line of American silver presentation pieces made during the nineteenth century (see, for example, nos. 51, 143, 220): it is well-designed, although in a current established, rather than avant-garde, style, and it manifests the characteristically American love of symbolism and an earnest pride in achievement—especially technological—which continued into the twentieth century. The tray is marked "TIFFANY & Co/16015 MAKERS 6070/925-1000/ C."

L. 37⁷/₈ inches
Museum of the City of New York, Gift of August Belmont

286

In 1897 the Grueby Faience Company was established in Boston, growing out of Atwood and Grueby, a company that produced tiles and other pottery for architectural purposes. Much of the company's art work seems to have been influenced by Egyptian forms, and this yellow vase, with its small scrolls and flat leaves, is typical in that respect. Typical too is the matte finish. The company was a commercial enterprise but was associated with the advanced designers of the day; Grueby lamp bases were made for Tiffany shades, and the Grueby company and United Crafts of Eastwood, New York (see no. 295), exhibited together at the Pan-American Exposition in Buffalo in 1901.

H. 10⁷/₈ inches
The Metropolitan Museum of Art, Edgar J. Kaufmann Charitable Foundation Fund, 69.91.2

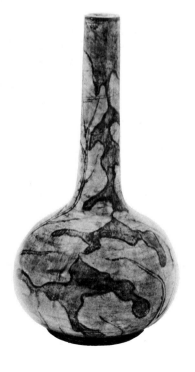

287

The pottery at Newcomb College, New Orleans, the women's division of Tulane University, was founded in 1895 to teach the craft to students of art. The products, made to be sold, were so fine that they were immediately in demand. Basic ceramic design rather than current fashion was studied, although some reflection of popular styles was to be seen in the work. An Islamic bottle was the source of the classic and graceful form of this piece, made about 1899. Motifs on Newcomb pot-

tery were to be only those familiar locally; the oak leaf used here is indigenous to Louisiana. The use of the motif may have been suggested by Italian fifteenth-century majolica, although the color scheme of the latter was usually dark blue on white, while here the motif is in light green on a mottled blue ground. The piece is marked with an "N" within a "C" for Newcomb College, another "N," and an "M" in a shaped lozenge.

H. 8 inches
Museum of Fine Arts, Boston, Anonymous Gift

288

Experiments with forms and glazes at Newcomb College produced work different in quality from the commercial wares of the day. Inspired by simple folk pottery, this vase, made about 1899, has a light green glaze on the upper section, while the lower section is an unglazed reddish-brown. The design looks surprisingly up-to-date seventy years later. The Newcomb potters found inspiration in the handsome products of the craft tradition and, with no need to appeal to a mass market, concentrated on the same honest functional designs that attract potters today. The vase is marked with an "N" within a "C," and an "F," probably for the decorator.

H. 5¹/₂ inches
Museum of Fine Arts, Boston, Anonymous Gift

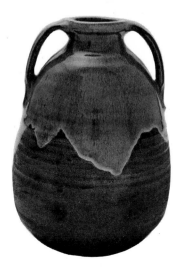

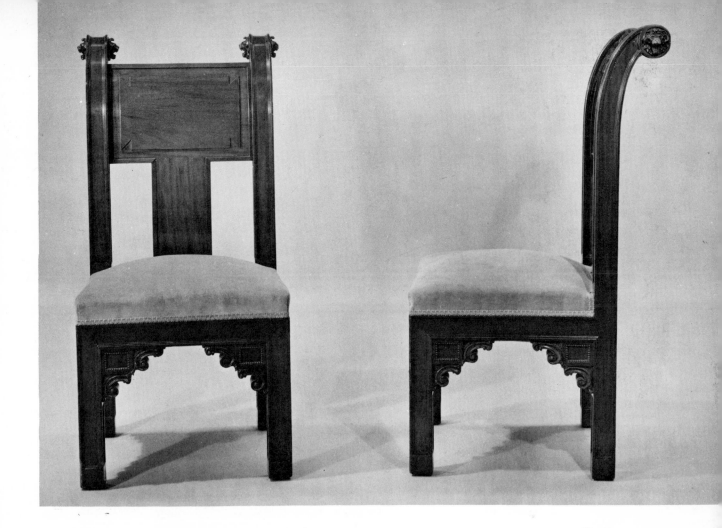

289 Prairie school architect George W. Maher designed this pair of mahogany chairs, two of a set of sixteen, for the dining room of the house he built in 1897 for John Farson in Oak Park, Illinois. A contemporary of Frank Lloyd Wright and Louis Sullivan, Maher became an apprentice in the firm of Bauer and Hill, moving soon to that of J. L. Silsbee, one of the largest architectural offices in Chicago. In 1887 he read to the Chicago Architectural Sketch Club a paper stating that "originality in American architecture rests . . . upon . . . studying the necessities of labor and life, and meeting them . . . there is as much chance of a national style forthcoming in this country as elsewhere in the world. . . . In most of our large cities a class of buildings can be seen which have no equal for interior arrangement . . . for nowhere are the wants of comfort and practicability so sought after as here. . . ." Strength and mass, straight lines and plain surfaces, all relieved by finely executed decor-

ative detail—the best qualities of prairie school architecture are visible in these chairs. At first glance somewhat Chinese in appearance, they also seem to draw heavily upon the medieval and Renaissance tradition, which with Oriental arts were the chief inspiration for the Arts and Crafts honesty of expression. Certain aspects of the chairs, such as the paneling, the deep back rest, and the scrolling stiles with carved animal heads, are reminiscent of furniture of the Low Countries in the sixteenth and early seventeenth centuries, and particularly the designs of Hans Vredeman de Vries. Probably Maher saw some of this furniture when he traveled to Europe in the early 1890s. In combining various influences, however, he managed to produce furniture with both the elegance of tradition and the simplicity of the coming modern design.

H. 43¹/₂ inches
Park District of Oak Park, Illinois

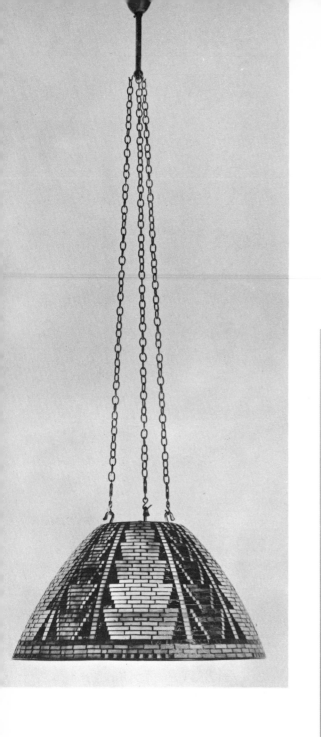

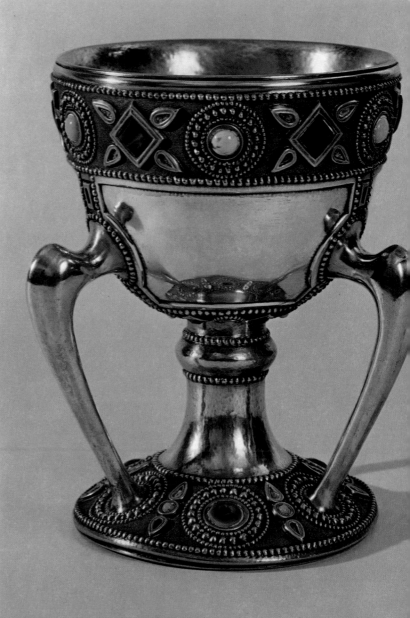

290

A geometric pattern is used on this handsome large hanging lamp, made in 1899 by Louis C. Tiffany as a special order for Robert W. de Forest for his house, Wawapek, in Cold Spring Harbor, Long Island, built the year before. Robert de Forest had asked Tiffany to design a lamp for the "hall" of the house, in the dark red of autumn foliage, but Tiffany said that the room should have an American Indian basket, and produced this lamp. It picked up the theme of the American Indian baskets and pottery in de Forest's collection, displayed on the high shelf around the room just under the ceiling. The leaded glass on the outside is in red, white, yellow, and black, while on the inside the glass pieces, in a similar bricklike pattern but larger, are in a milky blue and white.

Diam. 26 inches

The Metropolitan Museum of Art, Gift of Mr. and Mrs. Douglas Williams, in memory of Mr. and Mrs. Robert W. de Forest, 69.150

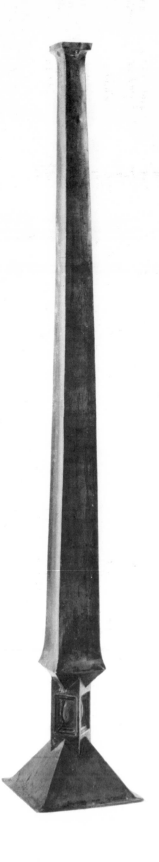

291

Another example of the inspiration found by Louis Tiffany in artistic sources ignored by less daring designers is this silver cup. The three-handled tyg is a traditional form, but this shape is completely new; it is a rather heavy classic goblet transformed by the handles, which somewhat resemble animal bones. The applied decoration, with inset emeralds and turquoises, recalls Mexican or American Indian work. The cup seems to have an affinity to the Arts and Crafts movement, but the simplicity and utilitarianism of that movement are not emphasized here; rather, the strong medieval quality of the vessel makes it look as though it might have belonged to a Frankish or Scandinavian king, and the cup clearly was at home in the boldly and extravagantly decorated halls of the nineteenth-century barons. It was made about 1905 and is marked "TIFFANY STUDIOS/NEW YORK./STERLING/925/1000/4787."

H. 8 inches

The Metropolitan Museum of Art, Edgar J. Kaufmann Charitable Foundation Fund, 69.36

292

Frank Lloyd Wright conceived his domestic architectural programs to encompass every interior detail, the furniture, and even decorative objects, such as this angular and attenuated copper vase, one of a pair. The vase originally graced the architect's own octagonal library in Oak Park, near Chicago, and presumably was made shortly after 1893, at the start of his independent practice. A photograph of the library with the pair of vases on the center table was displayed in the 1902 exhibition of the Chicago Architectural Club and published in that society's *Annual* for the same year. In the library were eight very similar built-in columnar electric lamp standards rising at each corner from dado-high bookshelves. The vase's verticality contrasts with the emphatic horizontality of all of Wright's domestic architecture, while the geometric design and autumnal color of the copper are in keeping with Wright's early concept of domestic design (see no. 293).

H. 28 inches

Edgar J. Kaufmann, Jr., New York

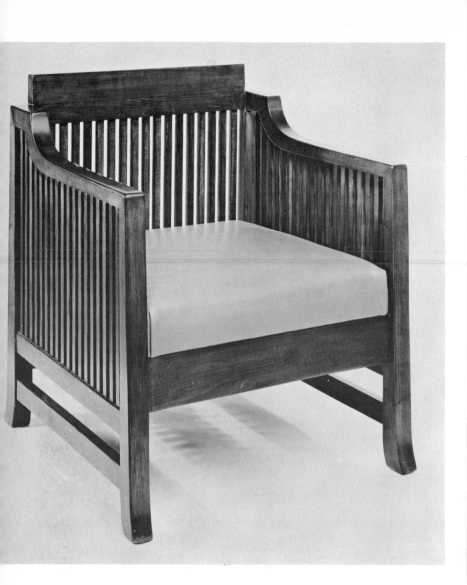

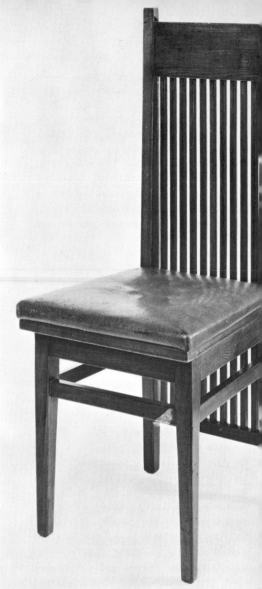

293 Among the first examples of Frank Lloyd Wright's furniture are the arm- and straight chairs shown here: the former was in Wright's studio near his house in Oak Park in 1895; the latter—a type of which he made many variations—may also have been in this building. Wright had arrived in Chicago in 1887, at the height of its greatest expansion, and two years later he was employed by the prestigious architectural firm of Adler and Sullivan. He established his own practice in 1893, and during the next year published some "Propositions," spelling out a philosophy that was to govern the work of his whole Oak Park period, ending in 1910. Buildings were to be organic—to appear to grow from their sites and harmonize with na-

ture in every detail. Interior furnishings were to follow the same principles. Wright's own words best state his ideas about furniture: "The most truly satisfactory apartments are those in which most or all of the furniture is built in as a part of the original scheme considering the whole as an integral unit." He advised: "Bring out the nature of the materials, let their nature intimately into your scheme. Strip the wood of varnish and let it alone—stain it. . . . go to the woods and fields for color schemes. Use the soft, warm, optimistic tones of earth and autumn leaves. . . ."

These chairs are of poplar, finished, as originally, with brown stain. George Niedecken, a Milwaukee cabinetmaker, is generally credited with executing Wright's progressive furniture designs—designs most mills at first refused to produce. Wright's earliest designs were a manifestation of the Arts and Crafts movement, in which hand work was extolled; but as time went by he became more and more pleased by the specific character of furniture made by machine. These chairs exemplify what he praised as "the clean cut, straight-line forms that the machine can render far better than would be possible by hand." The chairs descended to Wright's son John Lloyd Wright, from whom the present lender acquired them.

H. side chair 42¹/₈ inches
Edgar J. Kaufmann, Jr., New York

294

While architects like Richardson, Maher, Wright, and Greene and Greene were making furniture following the Arts and Crafts precepts specifically for buildings of their own design (see nos. 236, 289, 293, 296), two men spread the taste for honesty and simplicity in furniture to a wide public. They were Gustav Stickley, with his Craftsman furniture, and Elbert Hubbard, whose community of craftsmen, the Roycrofters, at East Aurora, New York, produced books and periodicals and portrait busts of such heroes as William Morris, Walt Whitman, and Hubbard himself, as well as simple oak benches, tables, chairs, and bookcases. This straightforward oak armchair, with leather seat and copper fastenings, was designed by Stickley between 1898 and 1901. Stickley's and Hubbard's furniture was called Mission furniture because it had a mission—to be used: a chair was to be sat in, a bookcase was to hold books; later, connotations of the Franciscan missions in California came to be associated with the style. Stickley's didactic intent is clear in the initial issue, in October 1901, of *The Craftsman*, the magazine he established to promulgate his ideas: he wrote that he sought "to substitute the luxury of taste for the luxury of costliness; to teach that beauty does not imply elaboration or ornament; to employ only those forms and materials which make for simplicity, individuality and dignity of effect."

H. 37 inches
Mr. and Mrs. Robert Mattison, Berkeley, California

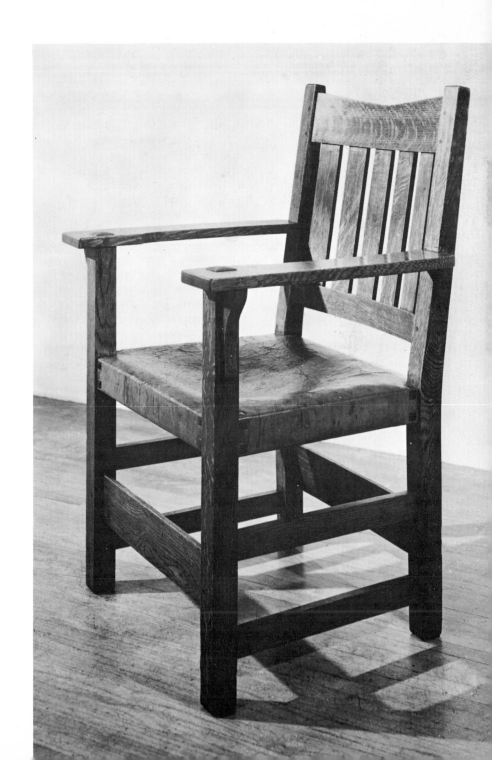

295 Gustav Stickley began designing his Craftsman furniture—of which all these pieces except the lamps, and also no. 294, are examples—in Eastwood, New York, in 1898, and first exhibited it to the public in 1900 at the furniture exposition in Grand Rapids, Michigan. Influenced by the Arts and Crafts movement, Stickley lost patience with manufacturing in the current ornate and—in his judgment—false taste. Each Craftsman trade catalogue contained an introduction by Stickley outlining the principles and history of the movement. Of his furniture he stated: "I had no idea of attempting to create a new style, but merely tried to make furniture which would be simple, durable, comfortable, and fitted for the place it was to occupy and the work it had to do."

Furniture was of native American woods, often oak like these pieces, with coverings of leather, canvas, or simple cloths, and fittings of copper or iron. Here the armchair covering is of canvas; the pulls on the desk are of copper. All the furniture shown here was designed by 1905; the reclining chair is one of the first three designs Stickley patented in 1901. The pieces were still advertised in a catalogue of 1913, in the introduction to which Stickley nicely combined modesty and smugness: "Most of my furniture was so carefully designed and well proportioned in the first place, that even with my advanced experience I cannot improve upon it." Craftsman furniture clearly filled certain requirements of the American public; it quickly flourished, but soon became all too popular, for by 1913 the catalogue emphasized that true Craftsman furniture could be distinguished by its bearing no less than three trademarks: the word "Craftsman"; the shop mark of joiner's compasses with the motto *Als ik Kan* ("As I can"), which Stickley took from Jan van Eyck; and the written signature "Stickley." Nonetheless, imitators drove Stickley into bankruptcy by 1916.

The lamps with isinglass shades are examples of the early work of Dirk van Erp, a coppersmith who worked in the San Francisco area until his death in 1933. The book on the desk is *Craftsman Homes,* published by Stickley in 1909.

H. desk 45¹/₂ inches
Chairs, table, lamps: Mr. and Mrs. Terence Leichti, Los Angeles; desk: Eric M. Schindler, Los Angeles

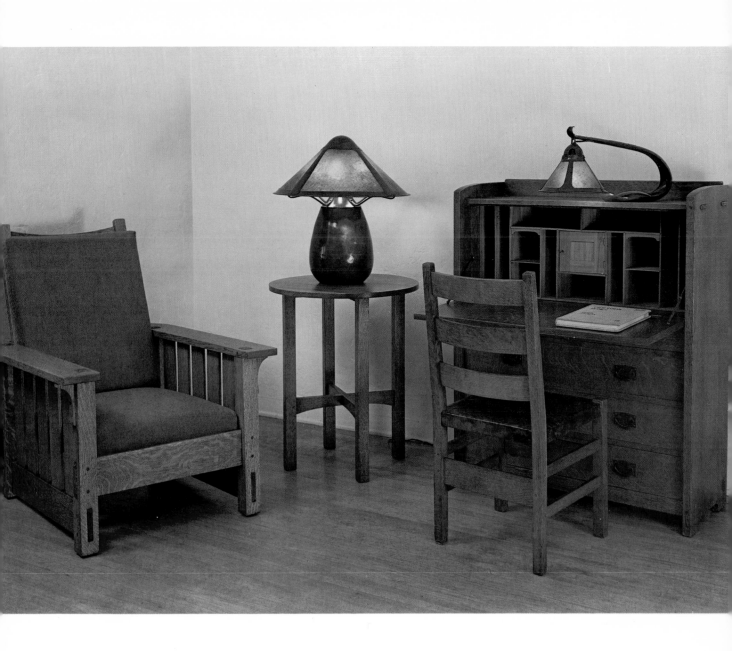

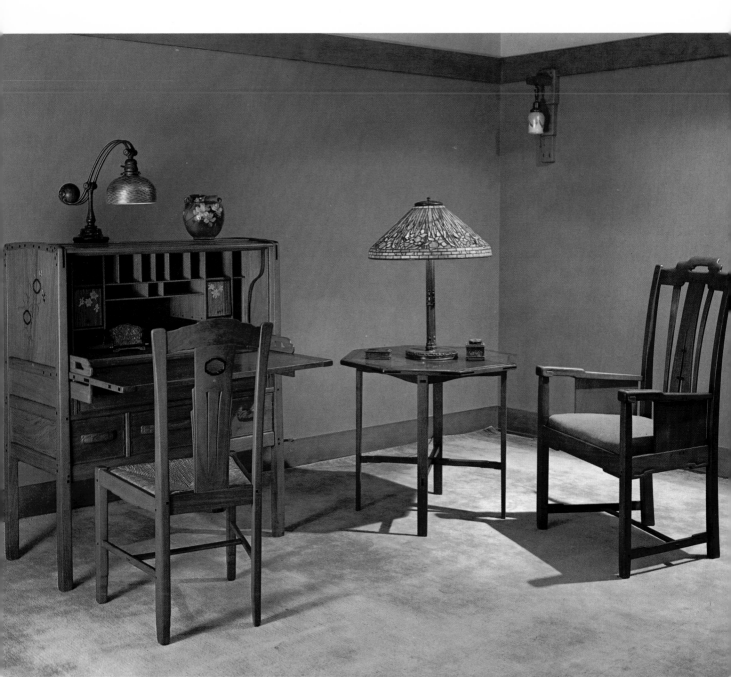

created a personal idiom for houses, which in smaller, less expensive versions evolved into the California bungalow style. Like those of their better-known contemporaries Louis Sullivan, Frank Lloyd Wright, and other architects of the shingle style, the Greene brothers' houses played up the qualities of natural materials and were integrated into the landscape.

In almost all cases the Greenes designed not only house and grounds, but interior fittings and furniture as well; the furniture shown here and the dining table no. 298 were designed and made for a house commissioned by David Gamble in 1907 and built in 1908. On the desk, the square ebony pegs that cover brass screw fastenings, contrasting with the walnut, and the splines are both typical of Greene and Greene furniture. The inlaid floral motif, of fruit woods and semiprecious stones, is taken from the Rookwood vase, owned by the Gambles, shown on top of the desk. The desk chair is also of walnut; the table and armchair are of mahogany, both with ebony trim. All the furniture for the Greenes was made by Peter Hall, a craftsman whose work so pleased them that they established him in business. Both lamps are from Tiffany Studios, as are the penholder, inkwell, and stamp box —the Greenes commonly incorporated Tiffany works into their houses.

A comparison of this group with the group including the same kinds of pieces by Stickley (no. 295) reveals immediately the great difference in effect possible despite similar precepts. The architects believed in the use of natural materials and in straightforward construction, and they eschewed historicism and sham ornament, but these pieces prove that furniture made with these premises need not lack beauty, grace, or elegance. That the ideals were the same, however, is shown by the fact that Greene and Greene selected Stickley furniture for some of the bedrooms of this house. Since 1966 the Gamble house has been owned by the city of Pasadena and operated by the University of Southern California as a museum for the work of Greene and Greene.

H. desk 45 inches

Table: Dr. and Mrs. Joseph D. Messler, Pasadena, California; other objects: The Gamble House, Greene and Greene Museum and Library, Pasadena, California

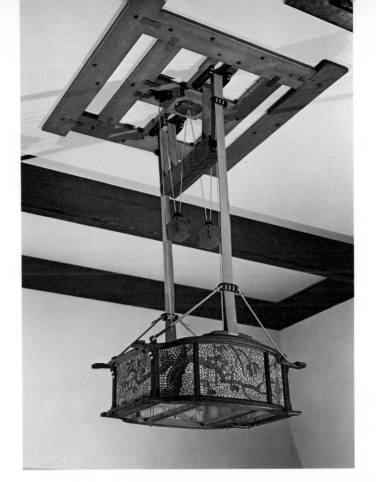

297

Iridescent Tiffany glass in a mosaic pattern of a stylized cherry tree—in both subject and style again showing the current Japanese influence—is used in this dining chandelier designed by Greene and Greene in 1906 for Mrs. L. A. Robinson of Pasadena. The glass itself was from the Tiffany Studios; the leading was fashioned in the Los Angeles studio of Emil Lange, who had formerly worked with Tiffany. The hand-shaped frame is of dark mahogany, as are the three boxes filled with buckshot that act as counter-balances; the straps and stabilizing thongs are of leather; the blocks on the straps and the rollers are of ebony; and the Craftsman-style ceiling plate is of cedar. Despite this disparity of materials, the design has complete integrity, and it is thus all the more eloquent as testimony to the artistry of the architect brothers.

Greatest h. 72 inches

Randell L. Makinson Collection, Los Angeles

298 Also by Charles and Henry Greene for the Gamble house (see no. 296), and shown there in the photograph, is this superbly finished dining table of mahogany with ebony pegs and splines. It can be extended to double its length by the insertion of five leaves, without separating the single pedestal support, which is stabilized by the extended base pieces. When the table is closed, the careful finishing of the ends of the cantilever supports is visible. The top is strengthened around the edge by a slightly heavier, doweled band; the elimination of the traditional apron support ensures visual continuity when leaves have been inserted. Tiffany Studios made the circular

flower bowl, the mosaic design of which is repeated around the fireplace visible to the left. The beautifully proportioned pedestal of the table, with its pieces of slightly different colors, gives a feeling of both lightness and strength, and the whole table achieves that combination of simplicity, utility, and beauty that the finest designers had been seeking during the last three decades of the nineteenth century. It sets a standard that may not be surpassed in the whole of the twentieth.

L. 65 inches
The Gamble House, Greene and Greene
Museum and Library, Pasadena, California

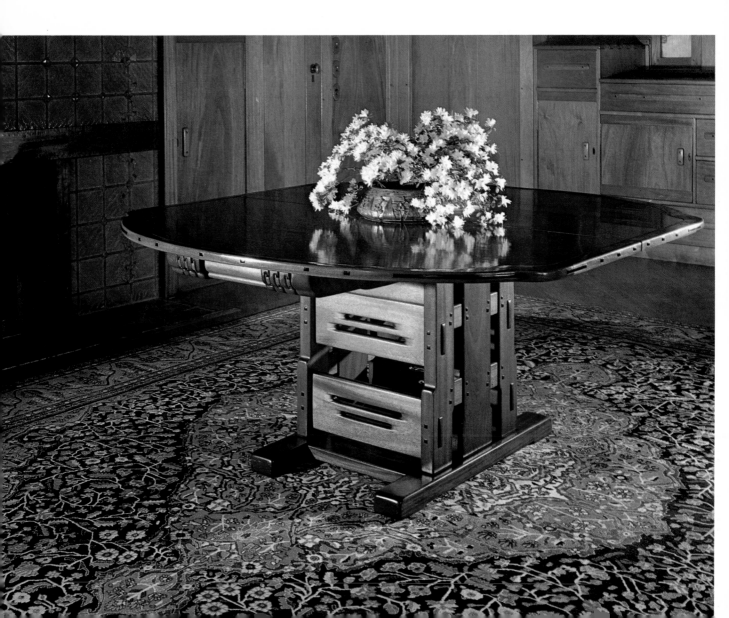

INDEX AND BIBLIOGRAPHY

INDEX

SELECTED BIBLIOGRAPHY

19th-Century Sources

Ackermann, Rudolph, ed. *The Repository of Arts, Literature, Commerce, Manufacture, Fashions, and Politics*, London, 1809-1828

Adam, Robert. *The Works in Architecture of Robert and James Adam*, vols. 1, 2, London, 1773-1779

Adam, Robert and James. *The Works in Architecture of Robert and James Adam*, vol. 3, London, 1822

Artistic Houses . . ., 2 vols. in 4 folios, New York, 1884

Bishop, J. Leander. *A History of American Manufactures, from 1608 to 1860; exhibiting . . .*, 3rd ed., rev. and enl., 3 vols., Philadelphia and London, 1868

Cook, Clarence. *The House Beautiful, Essays on Beds and Tables, Stools and Candlesticks*, New York, 1878

[Directories]. Many American cities and towns had annual directories listing the names, occupations, and addresses of residents.

Downing, Andrew Jackson. *The Architecture of Country Houses . . .*, New York and Philadelphia, 1850
Cottage Residences , . . . Adapted to North America, [5th ed.], New York, 1887
A Treatise on The Theory and Practice of Landscape Gardening, Adapted to North America . . ., London, 1841

Eastlake, Charles L[ock]. *Hints on Household Taste in Furniture, Upholstery, and Other Details*, London, 1868; ed., with notes, by Charles C. Perkins, 1st American, from rev. London, edition, Boston, 1872
A History of The Gothic Revival, London and New York, 1872

[La Mésangère, Pierre de]. *Meubles et Objets De Goût, 1796-1830, 678 Documents Tirés des Journaux de Modes et de la "Collection" de la Mésangère*, ed. by Paul Cornu, Paris, [n.d.]

Loudon, J. C. *An Encyclopedia of Cottage, Farm, and Villa Architecture.and Furniture: . . .*, 1st ed., 1833, new ed., London, 1835

Official Descriptive and Illustrated Catalogue of the Great Exhibition of the Works of Industry of all Nations, 1851, 3 vols. and supplement, London, 1851

Official Catalogue of the New-York Exhibition of the Industry of All Nations, New York, 1853

Percier, 'C[harles], and Fontaine, P[ierre] F. L. *Recueil de Décorations Intérieures . . .*, Paris, [1812]

Silliman, Benjamin, Jr., and Goodrich, C. R., eds. *The World of Science, Art and Industry Illustrated from Examples in The New-York Exhibition, 1853-54*, New York, 1854

Smith, Walter. *The Masterpieces of the Centennial International Exhibition, Vol. II: Industrial Art*, Philadelphia, 1875

Subject Matter Index of Patents for Inventions Issued by the United States Patent Office from 1790 to 1873 Inclusive, comp. by M. D. Leggett, 3 vols., Washington, 1874

Webster, Thomas. *An Encyclopaedia of Domestic Economy . . .*, New York, 1845

Wharton, Edith, and Codman, Ogden, Jr., *The Decoration of Houses*, New York, 1897

Wyatt, Matthew Digby. *The Industrial Arts of The Nineteenth Century . . . Illustrations of the Choicest Specimens . . . at the Great Exhibition of Works of Industry, 1851*, 2 vols., London, 1851

20th-Century Publications

Andrews, Wayne. *Architecture, Ambition and Americans*, New York, 1947

The Brooklyn Museum. *Victoriana, An Exhibition of the Arts of the Victorian Era in America* (Apr. 7-June 5, 1960), Brooklyn, 1960

Butler, Joseph T. *American Antiques 1800-1900, A Collector's History and Guide*, New York, 1965

Clark, Victor S. *History of Manufactures in the United States 1607-1860*, 2 vols., Washington, 1916

Davidson, Marshall B. *Life in America*, 2 vols., New York, 1951

Davidson, Marshall B., ed. *The American Heritage History of American Antiques, from the Revolution to the Civil War*, New York, 1968
The American Heritage History of Antiques, from the Civil War to World War I, New York, 1969

Dictionary of American Biography, ed. by Allen Johnson and Dumas Malone, New York, 1928-1964

Drepperd, Carl W. *First Reader for Antique Collectors*, New York, 1946
Victorian The Cinderella of Antiques, New York, 1950

Edwards, Ralph, and Ramsey, L. G. G., eds. *The Connoisseur's Complete Period Guide*, New York, 1968

Gibbs-Smith, C. H. *The Great Exhibition of 1851, A Commemorative Album*, London, 1950, reprinted, amended, 1964

Giedion, Siegfried. *Mechanization Takes Command*, New York, 1948

Hamlin, Talbot. *Greek Revival Architecture in America: Being an Account of Important Trends in American Architecture and American Life prior to the War Between the States , . . . ,* list of articles by Sarah Hull Jenkins Simpson Hamlin, introd. by Leopold Artaud, New York, 1944

Harbeson, Georgiana Brown. *American Needlework,* New York, 1938

Kaufmann, Edgar J., Jr., ed. *The Rise of An American Architecture: 1815-1915,* with essays by Henry-Russell Hitchcock, Vincent Scully, Winston Weisman, and Albert Fein, New York, 1970 [traveling exhib. cat.]

Kimball, Fiske. "Victorian Art and Victorian Taste," *Antiques,* vol. 23, no. 3 (Mar. 1933), pp. 103-105

Kouwenhoven, John A. *Made in America, The Arts in Modern Civilization,* Garden City, New York, 1948

Lichten, Frances. *Decorative Art of Victoria's Era,* New York, 1950

Little, Frances. *Early American Textiles,* New York, 1931

Lynes, Russell. *The Domesticated Americans,* New York, Evanston, and London, 1963
The Tastemakers, New York, 1954

McClinton, Katharine Morrison. *Collecting American Victorian Antiques,* New York, 1966

The Metropolitan Museum of Art. *The Greek Revival in the United States,* preface by Joseph Downs, (Nov. 9-Mar. 1, 1943), [New York, 1943]

Mumford, Lewis. *Sticks and Stones, A Study of American Architecture and Civilization,* New York, 1924
Technics and Civilization, New York, 1934
The Brown Decades, A Study of the Arts in America, 1865-1895, 2nd rev. ed., New York, 1955

Museum of Fine Arts, Boston. *Eighteenth-Century American Arts, The M. and M. Karolik Collection of Paintings, Drawings, Engravings, Furniture, Silver, Needlework & Incidental Objects . . . ,* by Edwin J. Hipkiss, notes . . . by Henry P. Rossiter, introd. by Maxim Karolik, Boston, 1941

The Newark Museum, Newark, New Jersey. *Classical America 1815-1845,* by Berry B. Tracy and William H. Gerdts, (Apr. 26-Sept. 2, 1963), Newark, 1963

Pevsner, Nikolaus. *High Victorian Design, a study of the exhibits of 1851,* London, 1951
Studies in Art, Architecture and Design, 2 vols., London, 1968
The Sources of Modern Architecture and Design, New York, 1968

Reade, Brian. *Regency Antiques,* Boston, 1953

Rogers, Meyric R. *American Interior Design . . . ,* New York, 1947

Singer, Charles, Holmyard, E. J., Hall, A. R., and Williams, Trevor D. *A History of Technology, Vol. IV: The Industrial Revolution ca. 1790 to 1850; Vol. V: The Late Nineteenth Century ca. 1850 to ca. 1900,* Oxford, 1958

Stokes, I. N. Phelps. *The Iconography of Manhattan Island 1498-1909,* 6 vols., New York, 1915-1928

The White House Historical Association. *The White House, An Historic Guide,* 4th ed., by Lorraine W. Pearce, rev. and enl., by William V. Elder, III, Washington, 1963

18th- and 19th-Century Sources—Furniture

Chippendale, Thomas. *The Gentleman and Cabinetmaker's Director . . . ,* London, 1754

Conner, Robert. *The Cabinet Makers' Assistant, Designed and Drawn by Robert Conner,* New York, 1842

[Godwin, E. W.]. *Art Furniture . . . Designed by Edward W. Godwin, F. S. A. and Manufactured by William Watt,* London, 1877

Hall, John. *The Cabinet Makers Assistant . . . ,* Baltimore, 1840

Hepplewhite, A., and Co. *The Cabinet-Maker and Upholsterer's Guide; or, Repository of Designs for Every Article of Household Furniture . . . ,* London, 1788

Hope, Thomas. *Household Furniture and Interior Decoration, Executed from Designs by Thomas Hope,* London, 1807

Jones, Owen. *The Grammar of Ornament,* London, 1856

King, T. *The Modern Style of Cabinet Work, exemplified . . . ,* London, 1829

Nicholson, Peter and Michael Angelo. *The Practical Cabinet Maker, Upholsterer and Complete Decorator,* London, 1826

[Price Books]. Cabinetmakers of the larger English and American cities issued price books in the late 18th to mid-19th centuries.

Pugin, Augustus Welby Northmore. *Gothic Furniture in The Style of The 15th Century . . . ,* London, 1835

Shaw, Henry. *Specimens of Ancient Furniture . . . ,* with descriptions by Sir Samuel Rush Meyrick, London, 1836

[Shearer, Thomas, et al.]. *The Cabinet-Makers' London Book of Prices, and Designs of Cabinet Work, calculated for the convenience of cabinet makers in general, . . . ,* London, 1788

Sheraton, Thomas. *The Cabinet-Maker and Upholsterer's Drawing-Book in Three Parts . . . ,* vol. 1 pts. 1,2, London, 1793; vol. II, pt. 3, London, 1794; 3rd ed., rev. and enl., in 4 pts., London, 1802
Appendix to the Cabinet-Maker and Upholsterer's Drawing-Book. containing . . . , London, 1802
The Cabinet Dictionary . . . , London, 1803
The Cabinet-Maker, Upholsterer and General Artist's Encyclopaedia, London, 1804-1806
Designs for Household Furniture, London, 1812

Smith, George. *The Cabinet-Maker and Upholsterer's Guide, . . . ,* London, 1826
A Collection of Designs for Household Furniture and Interior Decoration, . . . , London, 1808

Spofford, Harriet Prescott. *Art Decoration Applied to Furniture,* New York, 1878

Talbert, Bruce James. *Gothic Forms Applied to Furniture, metal work, and decoration for domestic purposes,* London, 1867, Boston, 1873

20th-Century Publications— Furniture

Albany Institute of History and Art, Albany, New York. *New York Furniture Before 1840 in the Collection of the Albany Institute of History and Art,* by Norman S. Rice, Albany, 1962

Aslin, Elizabeth. *Nineteenth Century English Furniture,* Faber Monographs on Furniture, New York, 1962

Bjerkoe, Ethel Hall. *The Cabinetmakers of America,* Garden City, New York, 1957

Butler, Joseph T. "American Mid-Victorian Outdoor Furniture," *Antiques,* vol. 75, no. 6 (June 1959), pp. 564-567

Comstock, Helen. *American Furniture: Seventeenth, Eighteenth, and Nineteenth Century Styles,* New York, 1962

Davis, Felice. "The Victorians and Their Furniture," *Antiques,* vol. 43, no. 6 (June 1943), pp. 256-259
"Victorian Cabinetmakers in America," *Antiques,* vol. 44, no. 3 (Sept. 1943), pp. 111-115

Downs, Joseph. "The Greek revival in the United States," *Antiques,* vol. 44, no. 5 (Nov. 1943), pp. 218-220

The Henry Francis du Pont Winterthur Museum. *American Furniture, The Federal Period, in the Henry Francis du Pont Winterthur Museum,* by Charles F. Montgomery, New York, 1966

Horner, William MacPherson, Jr. *Blue Book, Philadelphia Furniture William Penn to George Washington,* Philadelphia, 1935

Ingerman, Elizabeth A. "Personal experiences of an old New York cabinetmaker," *Antiques*, vol. 84, no. 5 (Nov. 1963), pp. 576-580

Jourdain, Margaret. *Regency Furniture 1795-1820*, London, 1949

Lea, Zilla Rider, ed. *The Ornamented Chair, Its Development in America*, Rutland, Vermont, 1960

McClelland, Nancy. *Duncan Phyfe and the English Regency 1795-1830*, New York, 1939

The Metropolitan Museum of Art. *A Loan Exhibition of New York State Furniture . . .*, (Feb. 5-Apr. 22, 1934), New York, 1934

Museum of Fine Arts, Boston. *American Furniture in the Museum of Fine Arts, Boston*, by Richard H. Randall, Jr., Boston, 1965

Museum of the City of New York. *Furniture by New York Cabinetmakers 1650 to 1850*, (Nov. 15, 1956-Mar. 3, 1957), New York, 1956

Musgrave, Clifford. *Regency Furniture 1800 to 1830*, London, 1961

Ormsbee, Thomas H. *Field Guide to American Victorian Furniture*, Boston, 1952

Otto, Celia Jackson. "Pillar and Scroll: Greek Revival Furniture of the 1830's," *Antiques*, vol. 81, no. 5 (May 1962), pp. 504-507
American Furniture of the Nineteenth Century, New York, 1965

Palmer, Brooks. *The Book of American Clocks*, New York, 1950

Ralston, Ruth. "The Style Antique in Furniture—I: Its Sources and its Creators," *Antiques*, vol. 47, no. 5 (May 1945), pp. 278-281, 288-289
"The Style Antique in Furniture—II: Its American Manifestations," *Antiques*, vol. 48, no. 4 (Oct. 1945), pp. 206-209, 220-223
"Nineteenth Century New York Interiors, Eclecticism Behind the Brick and Brownstone," *Antiques*, vol. 43, no. 6 (June 1943), pp. 266-270

Roe, F. Gordon. *Victorian Furniture*, London, 1952

Roth, Rodris. "American Art, The Colonial Revival and Centennial Furniture," *The Art Quarterly*, vol. 27, no. 1 (1964), pp. 57-77

Smith, Robert C. "The Classical Style in France and England 1800-1840," *Antiques*, vol. 74, no. 5 (Nov. 1958), pp. 429-433
"Late Classical Furniture in The United States, 1820-1850," *Antiques*, vol. 74, no. 6 (Dec. 1958), pp. 519-523
"Gothic and Elizabethan Revival Furniture 1800-1850," *Antiques*, vol. 75, no. 3 (Mar. 1959), pp. 272-276
"Rococo Revival Furniture, 1850-1870," *Antiques*, vol. 75, no. 5 (May 1959), pp. 470-475
"Furniture of the Eclectic Decades 1870-1900," *Antiques*, vol. 76, no. 1 (July 1959), pp. 50-53
"'Good Taste' in Nineteenth-Century Furniture," *Antiques*, vol. 76, no. 4 (Oct. 1959), pp. 342-345

Symonds, R. W., and Whineray, B. B. *Victorian Furniture*, London, 1962

Tracy, Berry Bryson. "19th Century American Furniture in the Collection of the Newark Museum," *The Museum* [published by The Newark Museum], n.s., vol. 13, no. 4 (Fall 1961), pp. 1-23

19th-Century Sources— Glass

Jarves, Deming. *Reminiscences of Glass-Making*, rev. ed., New York, 1865

Pellatt, Apsley. *Curiosities of Glass Making: with Details of the Processes and Productions of Ancient and Modern Ornamental Glass Manufacture*, London, 1849

20th-Century Publications— Glass

The Corning Museum of Glass, Corning, New York. *The Story of American Pressed Glass of the Lacy Period 1825-1850*, by James H. Rose, (June 21-Sept. 15, 1954), Corning, 1954, 1957

Daniel, Dorothy. *Cut and Engraved Glass 1771-1905*, New York, 1950

Grover, Ray and Lee. *Art Glass Nouveau*, Rutland, Vermont, 1967

Knittle, Rhea Mansfield. *Early American Glass*, New York and London, 1927

Lee, Ruth Webb. *Early American Pressed Glass*, 12th ed., Framingham Centre, Massachusetts, 1933
Victorian Glass, Specialties of the Nineteenth Century, 3rd ed., Northborough, Massachusetts, 1944
Sandwich Glass, A History of the Boston and Sandwich Glass Company, 8th ed., rev. and enl., Northborough, Massachusetts, 1947

McClinton, Katharine Morrison. *American Glass*, Cleveland, Ohio, 1950

McKearin, George S. and Helen. *American Glass*, New York, 1941
Two Hundred Years of American Blown Glass, Garden City, New York, 1950

Old Sturbridge Village, Sturbridge, Massachusetts. *Glass in New England*, by Kenneth M. Wilson, Old Sturbridge Village Booklet Series, Sturbridge, 1959, 1962

Pearson, J. Michael and Dorothy T. *American Cut Glass, for the Discriminating Collector*, New York, 1965

Revi, Albert Christian. *Nineteenth-Century Glass, its Genesis and Development*, New York, 1959
American Cut and Engraved Glass, New York, 1965
American Art Nouveau Glass, New York, 1968

The Toledo Museum of Art. *The New England Glass Company 1818-1888*, by Millard F. Rogers, Jr., [n.p.] 1963

Watkins, Lura Woodside. *Cambridge Glass 1818 to 1888, The Story of The New England Glass Company*, Boston, 1930
"Deming Jarves and the Pressing of Glass," *Antiques*, vol. 20, no. 4 (Oct. 1931), pp. 218-220
American Glass and Glassmaking, New York, 1950

Lighting Devices

Butler, Joseph T. *Candleholders in America 1650-1900 . . .*, New York, 1967

Thwing, Leroy. *Flickering Flames, A History of Domestic Lighting through the Ages*, Rutland, Vermont, 1958

Watkins, C. Malcolm. "Artificial Lighting in America 1830-1860," in *Annual Report Smithsonian Institution* (1951), pp. 385-407

Wyant, Major L. B. "The Etiquette of Nineteenth-Century Lamps," *Antiques*, vol. 30, no. 3 (Sept. 1936), pp. 113-117

Ceramics

Barber, Edwin Atlee. *Marks of American Potters*, Philadelphia, 1904
The Pottery and Porcelain of The United States, New York and London, 1893; 3rd ed., rev. and enl., New York, 1909

The Brooklyn Museum. *Preliminary Notes for a catalogue of Made-in-America Pottery and Porcelain assembled for exhibition at the Brooklyn Museum*, by Arthur W. Clement, New York, 1942
Notes on American Ceramics 1607-1943, by Arthur W. Clement, Brooklyn, 1944

Clement, Arthur Wilfred. *Our Pioneer Potters*, New York, 1947

Nelson, Marion John. "Indigenous Characteristics in American Art Pottery," *Antiques*, vol. 89, no. 6 (June 1966), pp. 846-850

New Jersey State Museum, Trenton. *Early Arts of New Jersey: The Potter's Art c. 1680-c. 1900*, (Jan. 24-Sept. 3, 1956), Trenton, New Jersey, 1956

The Newark Museum, Newark, New Jersey. *The China and Pottery of New Jersey from 1685 to 1876,* Newark, 1915
The Pottery and Porcelain of New Jersey 1688-1900, preface by Arthur W. Clement, (Apr. 8-May 11, 1947), Newark, 1947

The Philadelphia Museum of Art. *Pottery, catalogue of American pottery and porcelain,* by E. A. Barber, Philadelphia, 1893

Ramsay, John. *American Potters and Pottery,* Clinton, Massachusetts, 1939

Schwartz, Marvin D. "Fine American Ceramics of the Victorian Period," *Antiques,* vol. 77, no. 4 (Apr. 1960), pp. 386-389
Collectors' Guide to Antique American Ceramics, Garden City, New York, 1969

Spargo, John. *Early American Pottery and China,* New York and London, 1926

Stiles, Helen E. *Pottery in the United States,* New York, 1941

Watkins, Lura Woodside. *Early New England Potters and Their Wares,* Cambridge, Massachusetts, 1950

Young, Jennie J. *The Ceramic Art, a Compendium of the History and Manufacture of Pottery and Porcelain,* New York, 1879

Silver

Albany Institute of History and Art, Albany, New York. *Albany Silver 1652-1825,* by Norman S. Rice (Mar. 15-May 1, 1964), Albany, 1964

Avery, C. Louise. *American Silver of the XVII & XVIII Centuries, A Study Based on The Clearwater Collection,* New York, 1920
Early American Silver, New York and London, 1930

Brix, Maurice. *List of Philadelphia Silversmiths and Allied Artificers From 1682 to 1850,* Philadelphia, 1920

Currier, Ernest M. *Marks of Early American Silversmiths With Notes on Silver, Spoon Types & List of New York City Silversmiths 1815-1841,* Portland, Maine, and London, 1938

The Darling Foundation of New York State Early American Silversmiths and Silver. *New York State Silversmiths,* Eggertsville, New York, 1964

Ensko, Stephen G. C. *American Silversmiths and Their Marks III,* New York, 1948

Kovel, Ralph M. and Terry H. *A Directory of American Silver, Pewter and Silver Plate,* New York, 1961

McClinton, Katharine Morrison. *Collecting American 19th Century Silver,* New York, 1968

[The Metropolitan Museum of Art]. *Checklist of American Silversmiths' Work 1650-1850 in Museums in the New York Metropolitan Area,* comp. by Carl C. Dauterman, New York, 1968

Prime, Phoebe P. *Three Centuries of Historic Silver Loan Exhibitions under The Auspices of the Pennsylvania Society of the Colonial Dames of America,* Philadelphia, 1938

Rainwater, Dorothy T. *American Silver Manufacturers,* Hanover, Pennsylvania, 1966

The Virginia Museum of Fine Arts, Richmond. *Masterpieces of American Silver* (Jan. 15-Feb. 14, 1960), Richmond, 1960

REFERENCES

Sources for individual entries. Titles given in shortened form are cited in full in the selected bibliography.

1 McIntire double chest of drawers
Museum of Fine Arts, Boston. *Karolik Collection*, by Hipkiss, no. 41, supplement no. 41

2 Allison press cupboard
Winterthur. *American Furniture*, by Montgomery, pp. 440-441, pl. 452

3 Davey secretary
Gaines, Edith, ed. "Collectors' notes," *Antiques*, vol. 85, no. 4 (Apr. 1964), pp. 442-443, 472

4 Mills and Deming sideboard
Hepplewhite, A., and Co. *The Cabinet-Maker and Upholsterer's Guide; or, Repository of Designs for Every Article of Household Furniture . . .*, London, 1788, p. 6
Walcott, William Stuart, Jr. "Ten Important American Sideboards," *Antiques*, vol. 14, no. 6 (Dec. 1928), pp. 516-517

5 New York Sheraton-style armchair
Sheraton, Thomas. *The Cabinet-Maker and Upholsterer's Drawing-Book In Three Parts, Vol. II*, pt. 3, London, 1794, pl. 36, no. 1 (plate originally published Aug. 1792)
The New-York Book of Prices for Cabinet & Chair Work agreed upon by the Employers, New York, 1802, p. 56
Winterthur. *American Furniture*, by Montgomery, pp. 110-111, pls. 58-59

6 Baltimore pier table
Sheraton, Thomas. *Appendix To The Cabinet-Maker and Upholsterer's Drawing-Book . . .*, London, 1802, pl. 4 (plate originally published Mar. 27, 1793)
The Baltimore Museum of Art. *Baltimore Furniture, The Work of Baltimore and Annapolis Cabinetmakers from 1760 to 1810*, (Feb. 21-Apr. 6, 1947), [n.p.], 1947, no. 16, p. 43

7 Derby side chair
Hepplewhite, A., and Co. *The Cabinet-Maker and Upholsterer's Guide; or, Repository of Designs for Every Article of Household Furniture . . .*, London, 1788, Chairs nos. R and S (plate originally published Sept. 1, 1787)
Hipkiss, Edwin J. "Notes on Samuel McIntire and Elias Hasket Derby's Furniture," *Boston Museum Bulletin*, vol. 32, no. 189 (Feb. 1934), pp. 13-16
Museum of Fine Arts, Boston. *American Furniture*, by Randall, p. 201, pl. 160
Downs, Joseph. "Derby and McIntire," *The Metropolitan Museum of Art Bulletin*, n.s., vol. 6, no. 2 (Oct. 1947), pp. 73-80
Winterthur. *American Furniture*, by Montgomery, pp. 77-79, nos. 16, 17, 18

8 Salem easy chair
Hepplewhite, A., and Co. *The Cabinet-Maker and Upholsterer's Guide; or, Repository of Designs for Every Article of Household Furniture . . .*, London, 1788, pl. 15 (plate originally published Oct. 1, 1787)

9 Amelung-type decanter
McKearin. *American Glass*, pp. 100-114

10 Hutton candlesticks
Hatch, John Davis, Jr. "Isaac Hutton, Silversmith: Citizen of Albany," *Antiques*, vol. 47, no. 1 (Jan. 1945), pp. 32-35
Albany Institute of History and Art, Albany, New York. *Albany Silver 1652-1825*, by Norman S. Rice, (Mar. 15-May 1, 1964), p. 40, fig. 77, pls. 73-74.

11 Wiltberger tea service
The Henry Francis du Pont Winterthur Museum, Winterthur, Delaware. *American Silver in The Henry Francis du Pont Winterthur Museum*, by Martha Gandy Fales, Winterthur, 1958, no. 126
Davidson, Ruth. "Features: In the Museums," *Antiques*, vol. 84, no. 1 (July 1963), p. 84

12 Seymour sideboard
Adam, Robert and James. *The Works in Architecture of Robert and James Adam*, vol. 1, no. 1, London, 1773, p. 11
Biddle, James. "A Piece of Great Utility," *The Metropolitan Museum of Art Bulletin*, n.s., vol. 25, no. 8 (Apr. 1967), pp. 308-313

14 Seymour side chair
The London Chair-Makers' and Carvers' Book of Prices for Workmanship, London, 1802, pp. 38-41
Stoneman, Vernon C. *John and Thomas Seymour Cabinetmakers in Boston, 1794-1816*, Boston, 1959, p. 312, no. 209, p. 314, no. 211
Winterthur. *American Furniture*, by Montgomery, pp. 90-93, pls. 37, 38, 39

15 Seymour commode
Hepplewhite, A., and Co. *The Cabinet-Maker and Upholsterer's Guide; or, Repository of Designs for Every Article of Household Furniture . . .*, London, 1788, pl. 78 (plate originally published Oct. 1, 1787)
Stoneman, Vernon C. *John and Thomas Seymour Cabinetmakers in Boston, 1794-1816*, Boston, 1959, pp. 245-249, bill illustrated, pl. 159
Museum of Fine Arts, Boston. *Karolik Collection*, by Hipkiss, no. 42, supplement no. 42

**16 Sheraton-style Sister's cylinder book-
case-desk**
Sheraton, Thomas. *Thomas Sheraton's
Complete Furniture Works, The Cabi-
net Dictionary . . .*, 1st ed., London,
1803, reprinted New York, 1946, ed. by
Walter Rendell Storey, pl. 38 (plate
originally published Mar. 26, 1803)
First Presbyterian Church, Baltimore,
Maryland. Marriage Records of 1811,
p. 237
[Articles on Robert Oliver]. *The Baltimore
Sun,* (Mar. 9, 1924); (June 2, 1957)
Bordley, James, Jr. A Study of Baltimore
Furniture: Period 1785-1815, Baltimore,
1946, ms. at Maryland Historical So-
ciety, Baltimore
The Baltimore Museum of Art. *Baltimore
Furniture, The Work of Baltimore and
Annapolis Cabinetmakers from 1760 to
1810,* (Feb. 21-Apr. 6, 1947), [n.p.],
1947, no. 79, pp. 126-127

17 Phyfe armchair
McClelland. *Duncan Phyfe,* p. 289, pl. 276
Winterthur. *American Furniture,* by Mont-
gomery, pp. 124-127, pls. 72, 72a

18 New York sideboard
McClelland. *Duncan Phyfe,* p. 172, pl. 154

19 Phyfe-style dining table
Winterthur. *American Furniture,* by Montgomery, pp. 409-410

22 New York Hepplewhite side chair
Hepplewhite, A., and Co. *The Cabinet-
Maker and Upholsterer's Guide; or,
Repository of Designs for Every Article
of Household Furniture . . . ,* London,
1794, facsimile ed., New York, 1942,
pl. 2, Y of chairs (plate originally pub-
lished Sept. 1, 1787)
Sheraton, Thomas. *Thomas Sheraton's
Complete Furniture Works, Appendix
to the Cabinet-Maker and Upholsterer's
Drawing Book. containing . . .* London,
1802, reprinted New York, 1946, ed. by
Walter Rendell Storey, pl. 49, no. 4

23 New York cheval glass
*The New-York Book of Prices for Manu-
facturing Cabinet and Chair Work,* New
York, 1817, pp. 85-86

24 Phyfe-style dressing or work table
Fairfield Tercentenary Committee. *A Loan
Exhibition by the Citizens of the Town
of Fairfield,* (Summer 1935), Fairfield,
Connecticut, 1935, no. 40
[Keyes, Homer Eaton, ed.]. "The Editor's
Attic," *Antiques,* vol. 28, no. 6 (Dec.
1935), pp. 230-232, frontispiece
Victoria and Albert Museum. *Interna-
tional Art Treasures Exhibition,* London,
1962, no. 170, pl. 120

25 Phyfe eagle-back side chair
McClelland. *Duncan Phyfe,* pp. 267, 270,
pl. 254

26 Lannuier card table
Bonaparte, Joseph Napoleon. *Catalogue
of Rare, Original Paintings . . . Also of
Valuable Engravings, Elegant Sculpture,
Household Furniture, &c. &c, Belong-
ing to the Estate of the late Joseph
Napoleon Bonaparte, . . . to be sold
at his late residence, near Bordentown,
. . . Friday, June 25, 1847 . . .,* lists two
card tables with carved lyres, copy of
catalogue in the American Wing Ar-
chives, The Metropolitan Museum of
Art
Gottesman, Rita Susswein, comp. *The
Arts and Crafts in New York, 1800-
1804, Advertisements and News Items
from New York City Newspapers,* New
York, 1965, p. 148, no. 355
Swartzlander, Mary. Notarized statement,
re Bonaparte sale, (Doylestown, Pennsylvania, Jan. 9, 1967), in the American
Wing Archives, The Metropolitan Museum of Art
Tracy, Berry B. "For One of the Most
Genteel Residences in the City," *The
Metropolitan Museum of Art Bulletin,*
n.s., vol. 25, no. 8 (Apr. 1967), pp. 283-
291

27 Phyfe lyre-back side chair
Winterthur. *American Furniture,* by Montgomery, pp. 126-128, pl. 72a

28 Boston armchair
Sheraton, Thomas. *Thomas Sheraton's
Complete Furniture Works, The Cabinet Dictionary,* 1st ed., London, 1803,
reprinted, New York, 1946, ed. by
Walter Rendell Storey, pl. 8, no. 1
(plate originally published Feb. 1,
1803); quotation on first page [n.p.]

29 Boston writing and sewing table
Museum of Fine Arts, Boston. *American
Furniture,* by Randall, pp. 258-259, pls.
214, 214a
Winterthur. *American Furniture,* by Mont-
gomery, pp. 162-163

31 Churchill and Treadwell wine cooler
Wyman, Morrill. *Memoir of Daniel Treadwell,* American Academy of Arts and
Sciences Centennial vol. 11, Cambridge,
Massachusetts, 1888, pp. 325-524
Lovering, Joseph. "Boston and Science,"
in *The Memorial History of Boston, Including Suffolk County, Massachusetts.
1630-1880,* ed. by Justin Winsor, 4 vols.,
Boston, 1881, vol. 4, pp. 489-526, quotation p. 515

32 Lewis inkstand
Tracy, Berry B. "Late classical styles in
American Silver, 1810-1830," *Antiques,*
vol. 86, no. 6 (Dec. 1964), pp. 702-706,
fig. 10

34 Barry pier table
*Relf's Philadelphia Gazette and Daily Ad-
vertiser* (Jan. 19, 1810), Joseph B. Barry
and Son advertisement

**Sheraton, Thomas. *The Cabinet-Maker
and Upholsterer's Drawing-Book in
Three Parts, Vol. II,* London, 1794, no.
56 "Ornament for Frieze or Tablet"
(plate originally published Oct. 11, 1791)
Hornor, William MacPherson, Jr. *Blue
Book Philadelphia Furniture William
Penn to George Washington . . . ,* Philadelphia, 1935, pls. 432-434

37 Rasch silver sauceboat
Newark Museum. *Classical America,* by
Tracy and Gerdts, no. 93

39 Lannuier bed
Albany Institute of History and Art, Albany, New York. *New York Furniture
Before 1840 in the Collection of the
Albany Institute of History and Art,*
by Norman S. Rice, Albany, 1962, pp.
34-36

**40, 43 Lannuier window seat and lyre-
back armchair**
Pearce, Lorraine W. "The Work of Charles-
Honoré Lannuier, French Cabinetmaker
in New York," *Maryland Historical Society Magazine,* vol. 55 (Mar. 1960),
pp. 14-29

41 Lannuier pier table
The Metropolitan Museum of Art. *The
Greek Revival in the United States,*
preface by Joseph Downs, (Nov. 9-Mar.
1, 1943), [New York, 1943], no. 49
Pearce, Lorraine W. "The Work of Charles-
Honoré Lannuier, French Cabinetmaker
in New York," *Maryland Historical So-
ciety Magazine,* vol. 55 (Mar. 1960), pp.
14-29
Albany Institute of History and Art, Al-
bany, New York. *New York Furniture
Before 1840 in the Collection of the
Albany Institute of History and Art,* by
Norman S. Rice, Albany, 1962, p. 33
Pearce, Lorraine W. "The distinctive character of the work of Lannuier," *Antiques,* vol. 86, no. 6 (Dec. 1964), p.
714, fig. 6
Tracy, Berry B. "For One of the Most
Genteel Residences in the City," *The
Metropolitan Museum of Art Bulletin,*
n.s., vol. 25, no. 8 (Apr. 1967), pp.
283-291

42 New York or Boston easel
Museum of Fine Arts, Boston. *American
Furniture,* by Randall, pp. 262-263, pls.
216-216A

44 Lannuier card table
[La Mésangère, Pierre de]. *Meubles et
Objets de Goût, 1796-1830, 678 Documents Tirés des Journaux de Modes et
de la "Collection" de la Mésangère,*
ed. by Paul Cornu, Paris, [n.d.] Pl. 21
[Hone, Philip]. *The Diary of Philip Hone
[1828-1851],* ed. by Allan Nevins, 2
vols., New York, 1927, enl. ed., New
York, 1936

44 *continued*

Waxman, Lorraine. "The Lannuier Brothers, Cabinetmakers," *Antiques*, vol. 72, no. 2 (Aug. 1957), pp. 141-143

Pearce, Lorraine W. "The Work of Charles-Honoré Lannuier, French Cabinetmaker in New York," *Maryland Historical Society Magazine*, vol. 55 (Mar. 1960), pp. 14-29

"Lannuier in the President's house," *Antiques*, vol. 81, no. 1 (Jan. 1962), pp. 94-96

Tracy, Berry B. "For One of the Most Genteel Residences in the City," *The Metropolitan Museum of Art Bulletin*, n.s., vol. 25, no. 8 (Apr. 1967), cover, frontispiece, pp. 283-291

45 Empire dolphin sofa
Newark Museum. *Classical America*, by Tracy and Gerdts, no. 12

46 Baltimore side chairs
The White House Guide, pp. 95-96

47 New Jersey candlestick
McKearin. *Two Hundred Years of American Blown Glass*, pl. 93, no. 1

48 Haig and Co. coffeepot
Barber. *Pottery and Porcelain of The United States*, 1909 ed., pp. 116-118

Temple, Jacob Paxson. *The Jacob Paxson Temple Collection of Early American Furniture and Objects of Art Sold . . .*, sales cat., Anderson Galleries, New York, (Jan. 23-28, 1922), no. 115

49 Sugar bowl
The Toledo Museum of Art. *The New England Glass Company 1818-1888*, by Millard F. Rogers, Jr., [n.p.], 1963, p. 40, no. 13

50 Quervelle center table
Smith, Robert C. "Philadelphia Empire furniture by Antoine Gabriel Quervelle," *Antiques*, vol. 86, no. 3 (Sept. 1964), pp. 304-309

51 Fletcher vase
Report of the President and Managers of The Schuylkill Navigation Company, to the Stockholders, January 6, 1834, Philadelphia, 1834

Wood, Elizabeth Ingerman. "Thomas Fletcher, A Philadelphia Entrepreneur of Presentation Silver," *Winterthur Portfolio III* (1967), pp. 136-171

53 Astens center table
[Keyes, Homer Eaton, ed.]. "The Editor's Attic," *Antiques*, vol. 27, no. 3 (Mar. 1935), p. 88

54 Pittsburgh-type cut-glass tumbler
Pellatt, Apsley. *Curiosities of Glass Making, with Details of the Processes and Productions of Ancient and Modern Ornamental Glass Manufacture*, London, 1849

Daniel, Dorothy. *Cut and Engraved Glass 1771-1905 . . .*, New York, 1950, pl. 43

55 Philadelphia cut-glass tumbler
McKearin. *Two Hundred Years of American Blown Glass*, pl. 79, no. 5

Gilchrist, Agnes Addison. *William Strickland, Architect and Engineer 1788-1854*, Philadelphia, 1950, pl. 13

56 Pittsburgh-type punch bowl and cups
Daniel, Dorothy. *Cut and Engraved Glass 1771-1905. . . .*, New York, 1950, pp. 116-123

57 Boston & Sandwich Glass Co. oil lamps
Lee. *Sandwich Glass*, p. 191

58 Bakewell decanter
McKearin. *American Glass*, pp. 138-141

Innes, Lowell. "Glass Cut at Pittsburgh," *Carnegie Magazine*, vol. 20, no. 2 (June 1946), pp. 42-44

Carnegie Museum, Pittsburgh. *Early Glass of the Pittsburgh District 1797-1890*, by Lowell Innes, (Apr. 21-Sept. 6, 1949), Pittsburgh, 1949

59 Bowl and covered dish with tray
Lee. *Sandwich Glass*, pl. 60

60 Willard clock
Willard, John Ware. *A History of Simon Willard, Inventor and Clockmaker*, 1st ed., Boston, 1911; 2nd ed., Mamaroneck, New York, 1962

Palmer, Brooks. *The Book of American Clocks*, New York, 1950

O[wsley], D[avid] T., in "Some Recent Accessions," *Boston Museum Bulletin*, vol. 62, no. 330 (1964), pp. 134-136

61 Curtis girandole clock
Durfee, Walter H. "The Clocks of Lemuel Curtis," *Antiques*, vol. 4, no. 6 (Dec. 1923), pp. 281-285

Palmer, Brooks. *The Book of American Clocks*, New York, 1950

62 Willard lighthouse clock
Willard, John Ware. *A History of Simon Willard, Inventor and Clockmaker*, 1st ed., Boston, 1911; 2nd ed., Mamaroneck, New York, 1962

Palmer, Brooks. *The Book of American Clocks*, New York, 1950

63 Forbes plateau
Letter, Virginia Watkins Mitchell to the American Wing, including copies of older letters, (Boyce, Virginia, [May] 1965), in the American Wing Archives, The Metropolitan Museum of Art

65 Hancock sofa
Sheraton, Thomas. *Thomas Sheraton's Complete Furniture Works, The Cabinet Dictionary*, 1st ed., London, 1803, reprinted New York, 1946, ed. by Walter Rendell Storey, pl. 75

Thomas Sheraton's Complete Furniture Works, The Cabinet Encyclopaedia, [n.p.], [n.d.], reprinted New York, 1946, ed. by Walter Rendell Storey, pl. 2 of sofas (plate originally published Dec. 24, 1805)

Genealogy of the Family of Belcher and Ann Hancock, watercolor by William Hancock, 1808, in the possession of Mrs. Edward H. Smith

Billhead, with Grecian couch, pictured in *Antiques*, vol. 35, no. 4 (Apr. 1939), p. 171, copies in American Antiquarian Society and The Landauer Collection, The New-York Historical Society Collection

Boston Evening Gazette (Mar. 1827), William Hancock advertisements

66 Hancock library chair
Ackermann, Rudolph, ed. *The Repository of Arts, Literature, Commerce, Manufacture, Fashions and Politics*, London, 1809-1828, pl. 51 (plate originally published March 1813)

Hall, John. *The Cabinet Makers Assistant . . .*, Baltimore, 1840, pl. 28, figs. 147, 148

67 Tucker vases
The Philadelphia Museum of Art. *Tucker China 1825-1838 . . .*, (May 4-Sept. 9, 1957), [Philadelphia, 1957] nos. 489 and 490

68 Meeks pier table
Pearce, John and Lorraine W., and Smith, Robert C. "The Meeks Family of Cabinetmakers," *Antiques*, vol. 85, no. 4 (Apr. 1964), pp. 414-420, fig. 4

Pearce, John and Lorraine W. "More on the Meeks Cabinetmakers," *Antiques*, vol. 90, no. 1 (July 1966), pp. 69-73

70 New York stenciled secretary
The Metropolitan Museum of Art. *The Greek Revival in the United States*, preface by Joseph Downs, (Nov. 9-Mar. 1, 1943), [New York, 1943], no. 56

73 New York sideboard
Cooper, James Fenimore. *Notions of the Americans: Picked up by a Travelling Bachelor*, 2 vols., London, 1828, vol. 1, pp. 196-197

75 Rich inkstand
Newark Museum. *Classical America*, by Tracy and Gerdts, no. 116

Fales, Martha Gandy. "Obadiah Rich, Boston Silversmith," *Antiques*, vol. 94, no. 4 (Oct. 1968), pp. 565-569, fig. 2

77 New York side chair
McClelland. *Duncan Phyfe*, p. 126, pl. 109

79 Phyfe Foot parlor furniture
McClelland. *Duncan Phyfe*, pp. 272-274, pls. 260-261, pp. 315-317

80 Phyfe-style pier table
[La Mésangère, Pierre de]. *Meubles et Objets De Goût, 1796-1830, 678 Documents Tirés des Journaux de Modes et de la "Collection" de la Mésangère*, ed. by Paul Cornu, Paris, [n.d.], pl. 99
McClelland. *Duncan Phyfe*, p. 128
Pearce, Lorraine W. "American Empire Furniture in the White House," *Antiques*, vol. 81, no. 5 (May 1962), p. 517, fig. 6
Newark Museum. *Classical America*, by Tracy and Gerdts, no. 78

81 Low & Leake stove
Hollister, Paul. *Beauport at Gloucester*, photographs by Samuel Chamberlain, New York, 1951, p. 80

82, 83, 84 Cornelius astral lamp, Gardiner Argand lamp, Clark, Coit & Cargill chandelier
Webster, Thomas. *An Encyclopaedia of Domestic Economy . . .*, New York, 1845, pp. 140-206
Watkins, C. Malcolm. "Artificial Lighting in America 1830-1860," in *Annual Report Smithsonian Institution* (1951), pp. 385-407
Thwing, Leroy. *Flickering Flames*

85, 86 Baltimore (?) girandole, candelabrum
Webster, Thomas. *An Encyclopaedia of Domestic Economy . . .*, New York, 1845, p. 165
Butler, Joseph T. *Candleholders in America, 1650-1900 . . .*, New York, 1967

87, 89 Tucker pitcher, Tucker coffee service
Barber. *Pottery and Porcelain of The United States*, 1893 ed., pp. 126-153
The Philadelphia Museum of Art. *Tucker China 1825-1838 . . .*, (May 4-Sept. 9, 1957), Philadelphia, 1957

88 Tucker night light and tea warmer
The Philadelphia Museum of Art. *Tucker China 1825-1838 . . .*, (May 4-Sept. 9, 1957), [Philadelphia, 1957], no. 521, pl. 11

90 Decanter, glasses, tray
Daniel, Dorothy. *Cut and Engraved Glass 1771-1905 . . .*, New York, 1950, pl. 43

91 Lamp, amethyst vases
Lee. *Sandwich Glass*, pp. 481-486
The Toledo Museum of Art. *New England Glass Company 1818-1888*, by Millard F. Rogers, Jr., [n.p.], 1963, p. 53; no. 102

92 Pressed amethyst compote
McKearin. *American Glass*, pl. 161
Lee. *Sandwich Glass*, pl. 161

The Corning Museum of Glass, Corning, New York. *The Story of American Pressed Glass of the Lacy Period 1825-1850*, by James H. Rose (June 21-Sept. 15, 1954), Corning, 1954, 1957, no. 226, pl. 29

93 Pittsburgh candlesticks
McKearin. *Two Hundred Years of American Blown Glass*, pl. 92, no. 3

94 Sandwich dolphin candlesticks
Lee. *Sandwich Glass*, pl. 184

95 New England Glass Co. witch ball vases
Watkins, Lura Woodside. *Cambridge Glass 1818 to 1888, The Story of The New England Glass Company*, Boston, 1930
The Toledo Museum of Art. *The New England Glass Company 1818-1888*, by Millard F. Rogers, Jr., [n.p.], 1963

96 Cooper ewer and tray, chalice
Trinity Church in the City of New York. Insurance records, no. TR 69, in Appraisal of Fine Arts by William K Drewes, 1955

97 Davis table and chairs
Davis, Alexander J. Diary, ms. in The Metropolitan Museum of Art, entries for Sept. 1, 1841, May 26, 1848
Downing, Alexander Jackson. *The Architecture of Country Houses . . .*, New York and Philadelphia, 1850, p. 440
[Issue on Lyndhurst]. *Historic Preservation*, vol. 17, no. 2 (Mar.-Apr. 1965)
Pearce, John N. "A. J. Davis' greatest Gothic," *Antiques*, vol. 87, no. 6 (June 1965), pp. 684-689

98 New York cabinet and bookcase
Comstock. *American Furniture*, p. 310, no. 665

99 Roux Gothic side chair
The White House Guide, p. 120
Pearce, John N. and Lorraine W. "More on the Meeks Cabinetmakers," *Antiques*, vol. 90, no. 1 (July 1966), pp. 69-73, fig. 7
Hauserman, Dianne D. "Alexander Roux and his 'Plain and Artistic Furniture'," *Antiques*, vol. 93, no. 2 (Feb. 1968), pp. 210-217, fig. 1

100 Meeks Gothic desk and bookcase
Pearce, John N. and Lorraine W. "More on the Meeks Cabinetmakers," *Antiques*, vol. 90, no. 1 (July 1966), pp. 69-73, similar secretary, fig. 2

101 Brown acorn clock
Palmer, Brooks. *The Book of American Clocks*, New York, 1950

102 New York easy chair
Delano, Mrs. Lyman (Leila B.). Sales Catalogue of House Steen Valetje, Barrytown, New York (May 31-June 3, 1967), p. 90, no. 1616

103 Gothic chandelier
Shettleworth, Earl G., Jr. "Portland's Heritage . . . Henry Rowe's Structures were Outstanding," *Portland Evening Express*, vol. 84, no. 286 (Sept. 4, 1965), p. 16, cols. 1-5

104 Jelliff Gothic side chair
The Newark Museum, Newark, New Jersey. *Early Furniture Made in New Jersey, 1690 to 1870*, by Margaret E. White (Oct. 1958-Jan. 1959), Newark, 1958, p. 63
White, Margaret E. "Some Early Furniture Makers of New Jersey," *Antiques*, vol. 74, no. 4 (Oct. 1958), pp. 322-325

105 Sandwich compote
Lee. *Sandwich Glass*
The Corning Museum of Glass, Corning, New York. *The Story of American Pressed Glass of the Lacy Period 1825-1850*, by James H. Rose, (June 21-Sept. 15, 1954), Corning, 1954, 1957

106 Sandwich overlay lamp
Kern, William E. "Reminiscences of the Boston and Sandwich Glass Company," in *American Association of Flint and Lime Glass Manufacturers Inc. . . ., Papers Read . . . at the Annual Meeting . . .*, July 20, 1906
Lee. *Sandwich Glass*, pl. 195

107 New England Glass Co. covered vase
The Toledo Museum of Art. *American Glass*, by Millard F. Rogers, Jr., [n.p.], [n.d.], pl. 55, no. 5
Libbey Glass, A Tradition of 150 Years 1818-1968, exhib. cat., [n.p.], [n.d.], no. 182, illustration p. 33

108 United States Pottery Co. water cooler
Spargo, John. *The Potters and Potteries of Bennington*, Boston, 1926, pp. 103-133
Schwartz, Marvin D. *Collectors' Guide to Antique American Ceramics*, Garden City, New York, 1969, pp. 64-68, pl. 41

109 American Pottery Co. Canova plate
Clement, Arthur W. *Our Pioneer Potters*, New York, 1947, pl. 10
Schwartz, Marvin D. *Collectors' Guide to Antique American Ceramics*, Garden City, New York, 1969, pl. 42

110 Harker, Taylor & Co. pitcher
Barber. *Pottery and Porcelain of The United States*, 1893 ed., p. 199

111 Cornelius & Co. mantel set
Butler, Joseph T. *Candleholders in America 1650-1900 . . .*, New York, 1967, pp. 136-137

112 Baltimore gas lamp
Watkins, C. Malcolm. "Artificial Lighting in America 1830-1860," in *Annual Report Smithsonian Institution* (1951), pp. 385-407

114 Solar lamp
Webster, Thomas. *An Encyclopaedia of Domestic Economy . . .*, New York, 1845, pp. 185, 186
Thwing, Leroy. *Flickering Flames*, p. 75

115 Cast-iron fountain
Ackermann, Rudolph, ed. *A Series, Containing Forty-four Engravings in Colours, of Fashionable Furniture*, London, 1823, p. 49
[J. W. Fiske]. *Fountains, Vases, Iron and Wire Railings of all kinds . . .*, (manufacturer's catalogue), New York, [1864-1870], p. 11

116 Cast-iron "rustic" settee and chair
Bigelow, David. *History of Prominent Mercantile and Manufacturing Firms in the United States, with . . . Truthful Illustrations*, vol. 6, Boston, 1857, p. 215
[J. W. Fiske]. *Fountains, Vases, Iron and Wire Railings of all kinds . . .*, (manufacturer's catalogue), New York, [1864-1870], p. 31
[Samuel S. Bent & Son]. *Illustrated Catalogue and Price List of Settees, Chairs, Vases, Summer-house, Crestings, Tree-Boxes, Manufactured by Samuel S. Bent & Son . . .*, New York, [1890-1894], pp. 2, 5

117 Van Dorn Iron Works urn
[Van Dorn Iron Works]. *Van Dorn Iron Works sole manufacturers of the Cleveland Wrought Iron Fence . . .*, (manufacturer's catalogue), Cleveland, 1884, p. 7

119 Cast-iron bench
Drepperd, Carl W. *Victorian The Cinderella of Antiques*, New York, 1950, p. 54
Aslin, Elizabeth. *Nineteenth Century English Furniture*, Faber Monographs on Furniture, New York, 1962, pls. 47, 48
Offer of Gift Letter, Mr. and Mrs. James B. Tracy to the Museum (Apr. 29, 1966), in The Metropolitan Museum of Art Archives

120 Roux Elizabethan slipper chair
Eberlein, Harold Donaldson, and Hubbard, Cortlandt Van Dyke. *Historic Houses of The Hudson Valley*, New York, 1942, pp. 89, 93
Hauserman, Dianne D. "Alexander Roux and his 'Plain and Artistic Furniture'," *Antiques*, vol. 93, no. 2 (Feb. 1968), pp. 210-217

121 Brooks Jenny Lind cabinet
Gaines, Edith, ed. "Collectors' Notes," *Antiques*, vol. 88, no. 4 (Oct. 1965), pp. 526-527
Silliman, Benjamin, Jr. and Goodrich, C. R., eds. *The World of Science, Art, and Industry Illustrated from Examples in The New-York Exhibition, 1853-54*, New York, 1854, pp. 12-13

124 Belter center table
Vincent, Clare. "John Henry Belter's Patent Parlour Furniture," *Furniture History*, vol. 3 (1967), pp. 92-99

125 New York tête-à-tête
Ingerman, Elizabeth A. "Personal experiences of an old New York cabinetmaker," *Antiques*, vol. 84, no. 5 (Nov. 1963), pp. 576-580
Vincent, Clare. "John Henry Belter's Patent Parlour Furniture," *Furniture History*, vol. 3 (1967), pp. 92-99, no. 124

126 New York rococo sofa
J. H. Belter and Co., New York. Invoice of Sept. 5, 1855 to Col. B. L. Gordon of Georgia, ms. in private collection, New York, copy in the American Wing Archives, The Metropolitan Museum of Art

127 New York rococo armchair
Freedley, Edwin J. *Philadelphia and its Manufactures*, Philadelphia, 1858, p. 273
Ingerman, Elizabeth A. "Personal experiences of an old New York cabinetmaker," *Antiques*, vol. 84, no. 5 (Nov. 1963), pp. 576-580
Vincent, Clare. *John Henry Belter—Manufacturer of all Kinds of Fine Furniture*, unpublished M.A. thesis, Institute of Fine Arts, New York University, 1963, 2 vols.

130 New York rococo table and garniture
"A Visit to Henkel's Warerooms," *Godey's Magazine and Lady's Book*, vol. 40-41 (Aug. 1850), p. 123

132 New York rococo center table
Watson, John Fanning. *Annals of Philadelphia and Pennsylvania*, 2 vols., Philadelphia, 1856-1857, vol. 2, 1857, appendix, p. 607

133 Baudouine card table
Bill of sale of card table to J. Watson Williams of Utica, dated May 26, 1852, ms. in the Proctor Family papers, Munson-Williams-Proctor Institute, Utica, New York, copy in the American Wing Archives, The Metropolitan Museum of Art
[Strong, George Templeton]. *The Diary of George Templeton Strong, Young Man in New York, 1835-1875*, 4 vols., New York, 1952, vol. 1, p. 347
Ingerman, Elizabeth A. "Personal experiences of an old New York cabinetmaker," *Antiques*, vol. 84, no. 5 (Nov. 1963), pp. 576-580

136 Meeks sofa and chair
Pearce, John N. "The Meeks family of Cabinetmakers," *Antiques*, vol. 85, no. 4 (Apr. 1964), pp. 414-420

137 Boch porcelain pitcher
Barber. *Pottery and Porcelain of The United States*, 1893 ed., p. 162

Schwartz, Marvin D. *Collectors' Guide to Antique American Ceramics*, Garden City, New York, 1969, p. 106

138 United States Pottery Co. "Niagara Falls" pitcher
Barber. *Pottery and Porcelain of The United States*, 1893 ed., pp. 165-176
Spargo, John. *The Potters and Potteries of Bennington*, Boston, 1926
Barret, Richard Carter. *Bennington Pottery and Porcelain . . .*, New York, 1958, pls. 50-51

139 Cartlidge cup and saucer
Barber. *Pottery and Porcelain of The United States*, 1893 ed., pp. 163-164

140 Cartlidge New York Assembly pitcher
Barber. *Pottery and Porcelain of The United States*, 1893 ed., pp. 163-164
Schwartz, Marvin D. *Collectors' Guide to Antique American Ceramics*, Garden City, New York, 1969, pp. 101-103, illustration 78

141 Ball, Tompkins and Black tea kettle and stand
Silliman, Benjamin, Jr. and Goodrich, C.R., eds. *The World of Science, Art, and Industry Illustrated from Examples in The New-York Exhibition, 1853-54*, New York, 1854, p. 107
Heydt, Geo[rge] Frederic. *Charles L. Tiffany and the House of Tiffany & Co.*, New York, 1893, p. 21

143 Caldwell pitcher
"Disasters and Gales &c.," New York *Shipping and Commercial List*, (Nov. 14, 1857)
"Arrivals," New York *Shipping and Commercial List*, (Nov. 25, 1857)

144 Roux cabinet
Silliman, Benjamin, Jr. and Goodrich, C.R., eds. *The World of Science, Art, and Industry Illustrated from Examples in The New-York Exhibition, 1853-54*, New York, 1854, pp. 162, 191
Ingerman, Elizabeth A. "Personal experiences of an old New York cabinetmaker," *Antiques*, vol. 84, no. 5 (Nov. 1963), pp. 576-580
Hauserman, Dianne D. "Alexander Roux and his 'Plain and Artistic Furniture'," *Antiques*, vol. 93, no. 2 (Feb. 1968), pp. 210-217

145 Nunns and Clark piano
Official Descriptive and Illustrated Catalogue of the Great Exhibition of the Works of Industry of all Nations, 1851, vol. III, *Foreign States*, London, 1851, pp. 1459-1460. Exhibitor's number 374 of the United States collection
Letter, George Lowther to the Museum, (New York, Mar. 6, 1906), in The Metropolitan Museum of Art Archives
"Principal Accessions," *The Metropolitan Museum of Art Bulletin*, vol. 1, no. 11, (Oct. 1906), pp. 154-155

146 Mitchell and Rammelsberg dressing bureau
Weale, J., ed. *Chippendale's One Hundred and Thirty Three Designs of Interior Decoration . . .*, London, 1834 (reprint of Johnson, Thomas. *New Book of Ornament*, London, 1758, and *One Hundred & Fifty New Designs . . .*, London, 1761), pl. 22 in Weale ed.
Bishop, J. Leander. *A History of American Manufactures from 1608 to 1860; exhibiting . . .*, 3rd ed., rev. and enl. 3 vols., Philadelphia and London, 1868, vol. 3, p. 465

147 Tiffany pitcher
Jones, Owen. *The Grammar of Ornament*, London, 1856, pl. 82

148 Dessoir étagère
Silliman, Benjamin, Jr. and Goodrich, C.R., eds. *The World of Science, Art, and Industry Illustrated From Examples in The New York Exhibition, 1853-54*, New York, 1854, pp. 173, 175, 191, illustrations

149 Roux child's bed
Hauserman, Dianne D. "Alexander Roux and his 'Plain and Artistic Furniture'," *Antiques*, vol. 93, no. 2 (Feb. 1968), pp. 210-217

150 Tiffany and Company sword
[Tiffany and Co.]. *Presentation Swords, Made by Tiffany & Co.*, New York, [n.d., after 1862], nos. 550, 552

152 LePrince-Marcotte chair and table
Downing, Andrew Jackson. *The Architecture of Country Houses . . .*, New York, 1850, pp. 411-412
Silliman, Benjamin, Jr. and Goodrich, C.R., eds. *The World of Science, Art, and Industry Illustrated from Examples in The New-York Exhibition, 1853-54*, New York, 1854, p. 47
de Forest, Emily Johnston. *John Johnston of New York, Merchant*, New York, 1909
de Forest, Emily Johnston. *James Colles 1788-1883 Life & Letters*, New York, 1926

153 Marcotte suite
Davis, Felice. "Victorian Cabinetmakers in America," *Antiques*, vol. 44, no. 3 (Sept. 1943), pp. 111-115, p. 113, quotation from *The New York Evening Post* (1860), advertisement
The Lockwood-Mathews Mansion Museum, Stamford, Connecticut, [1966]
The Lockwood-Mathews Museum of Norwalk, Inc. *The Lockwood-Mathews Mansion*, Norwalk, 1969

154 Marcotte armchair
Ingerman, Elizabeth A. "Personal experiences of an old New York cabinetmaker," *Antiques*, vol. 84, no. 5 (Nov. 1963), pp. 576-580

157 Dorflinger vase
Everhart Museum, Scranton, Pennsylvania. *An Exhibition of Dorflinger Glass from the Collection of Mr. and Mrs. John C. Dorflinger*, by Carl E. Ellis, (June 1-July 31, 1960), [n.d.], [n.p.]
Schwartz, Marvin D. *Collectors' Guide to Antique American Glass*, Garden City, New York, 1969, pp. 92-94

158 Paperweight
Hollister, Paul, Jr. *The Encyclopedia of Glass Paperweights*, New York, 1969, pp. 223-232

159 Sandwich decanter
Kern, William E. "Reminiscences of the Boston and Sandwich Glass Company," in *American Association of Flint and Lime Glass Manufacturers Inc. . . ., Papers Read . . . at the Annual Meeting . . ., July 20, 1906*
The Sandwich Glass Museum, Sandwich, Massachusetts. *. . . Glass Exhibited in The Sandwich Glass Museum*, Sandwich, 1969, pp. 26-27

160 Vaupel goblet
Watkins, Lura Woodside. *Cambridge Glass 1818 to 1888, The Story of The New England Glass Company*, Boston, 1930, pp. 114, 116

162 Dorflinger claret jug
Daniel, Dorothy. *Cut and Engraved Glass 1771-1905 . . .*, New York, 1950, pp. 166-168, pl. 146

163 Dorflinger (?) wine glass and bowl, Sandwich sugar bowl and decanter
Daniel, Dorothy. *Cut and Engraved Glass 1771-1905 . . .*, New York, 1950
The Sandwich Glass Museum, Sandwich, Massachusetts. *. . . Glass Exhibited in The Sandwich Glass Museum*, Sandwich, 1969, pp. 26-27

164 Roux cabinet
Holt, J. Lovegrove. *Modern Furniture Original and Select*, London, [n.d.], pp. 280-282
Carroll, G. Danielson. *New York City Directory*, 1859, p. 114
Symonds, R. W. and Whineray, B. B. *Victorian Furniture*, London, 1962, pl. 34, entry quotes J. B. Waring, *Masterpieces of Industrial Art and Sculpture*
Hauserman, Dianne D. "Alexander Roux and his 'Plain and Artistic Furniture'," *Antiques*, vol. 93, no. 2 (Feb. 1968), pp. 210-217

166 Egyptian center table
Ingerman, Elizabeth A. "Personal experiences of an old New York cabinetmaker," *Antiques*, vol. 84, no. 5 (Nov. 1963), pp. 576-580

169 Statue, "Autumn"
[J. L. Mott Iron Works]. *"M" Illustrated Catalogue and Price List of Statuary and Animals, Manufactured by The J. L. Mott Iron Works . . .*, [New York], 1890, p. 15

170 Cast-iron vase
Downing, Andrew Jackson. *A Treatise on The Theory and Practice of Landscape Gardening, Adapted to North America . . .*, London, 1841, pp. 354-355

173 Renaissance revival pedestal
Cook. *The House Beautiful*, p. 107

174, 178 Jelliff armchair, Jelliff (?) parlor table
The Newark Museum, Newark, New Jersey. *Early Furniture Made in New Jersey, 1690 to 1870*, by Margaret E. White, (Oct. 1958-Jan. 1959), Newark, 1958
White, Margaret E. "Some Early Furniture Makers of New Jersey," *Antiques*, vol. 74, no. 4 (Oct. 1958), pp. 322-325

175 Renaissance revival easy chair
Ackermann, Rudolph, ed. *The Repository of Arts, Literature, Commerce, Manufacture, Fashions and Politics*, London, 1809-1828, pl. 51 (plate originally published March 1813)
Cook. *The House Beautiful*, pp. 72-73

176 Renaissance revival armchair
"A Princely Residence," in "Matters About Home," *Meriden Daily Republican*, Meriden, Connecticut, (Nov. 28, 1870)
The Lockwood-Mathews Mansion House, Stamford, Connecticut, [1966]
Ward, Bradley. "90 Days to Live?" *Yankee*, (Oct. 1967), pp. 79-82, 142, 144

177, 179 Mitchell, Vance & Co. chandelier, Renaissance revival sofa and side chair
"A Princely Residence," in "Matters About Home," *Meriden Daily Republican*, Meriden, Connecticut (Nov. 28, 1870)

180 Gorham cheese scoop, Tiffany fish server
McClinton. *Collecting American 19th Century Silver*, pp. 59-60, 67

185 Berkey and Gay table
Sironen, M. *A History of American Furniture*, East Stroudsburg, Pennsylvania, and New York, 1936, p. 43

186 Hunzinger side chair
Subject Matter Index of Patents for Inventions Issued by the United States Patent Office from 1790 to 1873 Inclusive, comp. by M. D. Leggett, 3 vols., Washington, 1874, vol. 1, p. 58
Kimball, J. Wayland. *Book of Designs, Furniture and Drapery*, Boston, 1876, p. 9, pls. 2, 4, 6, 7, 17, 23

189 New England Glass Co. candlestick and sugar bowl
Watkins, Lura Woodside. *Cambridge Glass 1818 to 1888, The Story of The New England Glass Company*, Boston, 1930, p. 99, pl. 42
Revi, Albert Christian. *American Pressed Glass and Figure Bottles*, New York, 1964, p. 256
Boston and Sandwich Glass Company, factory catalogue for 1874, facsimile ed., Wellesley Hills, Massachusetts, 1968

190 Bakewell, Pears & Co. bowl
Revi, Albert Christian. *Nineteenth Century Glass, its Genesis and Development*, New York, 1959, p. 154
Innes, Lowell. "Pittsburgh white and clear and the Bakewell patent," *Antiques*, vol. 79, no. 6 (June 1961), pp. 557-559

191 Boston & Sandwich Glass Co.(?) pressed-glass pitchers
Lee. *Sandwich Glass*, pp. 537, 539
Revi, Albert Christian. *American Pressed Glass and Figure Bottles*, New York, 1964

192 Gillinder compote
Revi, Albert Christian. *American Pressed Glass and Figure Bottles*, New York, 1964

193 Bakewell, Pears & Co. compote
Lee, Ruth Webb. *Early American Pressed Glass*, 12th ed., Framingham Centre, Massachusetts, 1933, pp. 187-188
McKearin. *American Glass*, pp. 138-141

194 La Farge stained-glass window
Marquand, Henry G. *Illustrated Catalogue of the Art and Literary Property collected by the late Henry G. Marquand*, sales cat., American Art Association, New York, (Jan. 23-31, 1903), no. 947A
Cortissoz, Royal. *John La Farge, A Memoir and a Study*, Boston and New York, 1911
Remington, Preston. "A Gift of a Window by John La Farge," *The Metropolitan Museum of Art Bulletin*, vol. 25, no. 5 (May 1930), pp. 119-121
James, Henry. *The American Scene*, introd. by Irving Howe, New York, 1967, p. 94
Lloyd, John Gilbert. *Stained Glass in America*, Jenkintown, Pennsylvania, 1963

195 Price cabinet
Sturgis, Russell. "The Works of Bruce Price," *The Architectural Record*, supplement, Great American Architects Series, no. 5 (June 1899), pp. 1-64

196 Mueller pedestal
Barber. *Pottery and Porcelain of The United States*, 1893 ed., pp. 252-259

197 Chelsea Keramic Art Works vase
Barber. *Pottery and Porcelain of The United States*, 1893 ed., pl. 117, pp. 260-267
Hawes, Lloyd, et al. *Dedham Pottery*, Dedham, Massachusetts, 1968

198 Broome bust of Cleopatra
Barber. *Pottery and Porcelain of The United States*, 1893 ed., pp. 211-213, pl. 96
Schwartz, Marvin D. *Collectors' Guide to Antique American Ceramics*, Garden City, New York, 1969, p. 114

199 Mueller, The Finding of Moses
Barber. *Pottery and Porcelain of The United States*, 1893 ed., pp. 252-259

200 Mueller "Century Vase"
Barber. *Pottery and Porcelain of The United States*, 1893 ed., pp. 252-259
Schwartz, Marvin D. *Collectors' Guide to Antique American Ceramics*, Garden City, New York, 1969, pp. 111-114, fig. 83

201 Union Porcelain Works Liberty cup
Barber. *Pottery and Porcelain of The United States*, 1893 ed., pp. 252-259, pl. 113

202 Dorflinger decanter and wine glasses
Zieber, Eugene. *Heraldry in America*, Philadelphia, 1895, pp. 141-146
Daniel, Dorothy. *Cut and Engraved Glass 1771-1905 . . .*, New York, 1950, pl. 59
Schwartz, Marvin D. *Collectors' Guide to Antique American Glass*, Garden City, New York, 1969, p. 94

203 Mueller "tête-à-tête set"
Barber. *Pottery and Porcelain of The United States*, 1893 ed., pp. 252-259, pl. 115
Schwartz, Marvin D. *Collectors' Guide to Antique American Ceramics*, Garden City, New York, 1969, pp. 111-114, fig. 84

204 Mueller porcelain pitcher
Barber. *Pottery and Porcelain of The United States*, 1893 ed., pp. 252-259
Schwartz, Marvin D. *Collectors' Guide to Antique American Ceramics*, Garden City, New York, 1969

205 New York City Pottery, General Grant
Barber. *Pottery and Porcelain of The United States*, 1893 ed., pp. 179-180

206 Broome baseball vase
Barber. *Pottery and Porcelain of The United States*, 1893 ed., fig. 94

207 Pottier and Stymus chairs
Letter, Auguste Pottier to the Museum, (New York, May 22, 1888), in The Metropolitan Museum of Art Archives
Ingerman, Elizabeth A. "Personal experiences of an old New York cabinetmaker," *Antiques*, vol. 84, no. 5 (Nov. 1963), pp. 576-580

208 Firescreen
Aitchison, G. "Colored Glass, II," *American Architect and Building News*, vol. 15, no. 433 (Apr. 12, 1884), pp. 175-178

210 Herter Brothers desk
Eastlake, Charles L[ock]. *Hints on Household Taste in Furniture, Upholstery and Other Details*, ed. by Charles C. Perkins, 1st American, from the rev. London, edition, Boston, 1872, pp. 162-163
Herter Brothers, New York, invoice to Jay Gould, Mar. 7, 1882, Ms. dept., The New-York Historical Society
Pevsner, Nikolaus. *Studies in Art, Architecture and Design*, 2 vols., London, 1968, vol. 2, *Victorian and After*, "William Morris and Architecture," pp. 108-117, quotation from William Morris, p. 109

211 Herter Brothers bed and other pieces
[Obituary of Christian Herter]. *New York Daily Tribune* (Nov. 3, 1883)
"Christian Herter," in *Dictionary of American Biography*, ed. by Allen Johnson and Dumas Malone, New York, 1928-1964

212 Herter Brothers maple bedroom suite
Cook. *The House Beautiful*, p. 226

213 New York pedestal
Cook. *The House Beautiful*, pp. 223-224

214 New York table
[Godwin, E. W.]. *Art Furniture . . . Designed by Edward W. Godwin F. S. A. and Manufactured by William Watt*, London, 1877
Cook. *The House Beautiful*, pp. 72, 108

215 Herter Brothers side chair
Cook. *The House Beautiful*, p. 322
Artistic Houses . . ., 2 vols. in 4 folios, New York, 1884, vol. 2, pt. 2, pl., Jacob Ruppert's Drawing-room, p. 101

216 Cast-iron "Woodbury" vase
[Chase Brothers & Co, Boston Ornamental Iron Works]. *Illustrated Catalogue, of Plain and Ornamental Iron Furniture, Iron Railing, and Bronzed Iron Goods*, Boston, [1850s?], p. 21
[J. W. Fiske]. *Fountains, Vases, Iron and Wire Railings of all kinds . . .*, (manufacturer's catalogue), New York, [1864-1870], p. 17

218 Cast-iron fern chair
[A.B.&W.T. Westervelt]. *Illustrated Catalogue and Price List of Settees, Chairs, Tables, Archways, Etc., Manufactured by A.B. & W.T. Westervelt . . .*, New York, [n.d., after 1879], pp. 10, 12
[Samuel S. Bent & Son]. *Illustrated Catalogue and Price List of Settees, Chairs, Vases, Summer-house, Crestings, Tree-Boxes, Manufactured by Samuel S. Bent & Son . . .*, New York, [1890-1894], pp. 3, 6

219 Cast-iron stag
[J. W. Fiske Iron Works]. *Illustrated Catalogue and Price List of Zinc Animals, Deer, Dogs, Lions, Etc. Manufactured by J. W. Fiske Iron Works*, New York, [n.d.], p. 5
[J. L. Mott Iron Works]. *"M" Illustrated Catalogue and Price List of Statuary and Animals, Manufactured by the J. L. Mott Iron Works . . .*, [New York], 1890, p. 52

220 Tiffany & Co. Bryant vase
"The Bryant Testimonial Vase," *The Art Journal*, [New York], n.s., vol. 1 (1875), pp. 145-149
Smith, Walter. *The Masterpieces of the Centennial International Exhibition, Vol. II: Industrial Art*, Philadelphia, 1875, pp. 275-276
Osgood, Samuel. "The Bryant Vase," *Harper's New Monthly Magazine*, vol. 53 (July 1876), pp. 245-252
McClinton. *Collecting American 19th Century Silver*, pp. 139-143

221 Tiffany & Co. kettle
Heydt, Geo[rge] Frederic. *Charles L. Tiffany and the House of Tiffany & Co.*, New York, 1893, p. 19
New York, Tiffany & Co., ledgers, for date of piece

222, 223 Tiffany & Co. sugar bowl and creamer, peppers
New York, Tiffany & Co., ledgers, for dates of pieces

224 Tisch cabinet
Eastlake, Charles L[ock]. *Hints on Household Taste in Furniture, Upholstery, and Other Details*, Boston, 1872, pp. 136-137
Smith, Walter. *The Masterpieces of the Centennial International Exhibition, Vol. II: Industrial Art*, Philadelphia, 1875, pp. 167-169
Cook. *The House Beautiful*, pp. 96-97, 101
Letter, Charles Tisch to the Museum (New York, Apr. 22, 1889), in The Metropolitan Museum of Art Archives

225 Eastlake-style table
[Godwin, E. W.]. *Art Furniture . . . Designed by Edward W. Godwin F. S. A. and Manufactured by William Watt*, London, 1877

226 New York chandelier
[I. P. Frink]. *Frink's Patent Reflectors For Gas, Kerosene, Electric or Day Light . . .* (manufacturer's catalogue), New York, 1882, 1883, pp. 2, 14

227 Chelsea Keramic Art Works vases
Barber. *Pottery and Porcelain of The United States*, 1893 ed.
Hawes, Lloyd, et al. *Dedham Pottery*, Dedham, Massachusetts, 1968

228 Imitation bamboo bedroom set
Kimball, J. Wayland. *Book of Designs, Furniture and Drapery*, Boston, 1876, pl. 5, illustration of bamboo chair made by Kilian Brothers, ref. p. 7
Cook. *The House Beautiful*, p. 74
The Decorator and Furnisher, vol. 8, no. 3 (June 1886), p. 83

229 Tiffany & Co. clock
de Forest, Lockwood. *Indian Domestic Architecture*, [n.p.], 1885
Indian Architecture and Ornament, introd. by Lockwood de Forest, Boston, 1887
Desmond, Harry W. and Croly, Herbert. *Stately Homes in America from Colonial times to the Present Day*, New York, 1903
Letter, Mary J. Kingsland to Henry Watson Kent, (Scarborough, New York, Oct. 17, 1906), in The Metropolitan Museum of Art Archives
de Forest, Lockwood. *Illustrations of Design Based on notes of line as used by the Craftsmen of India*, Boston, 1912
Koch, Robert. *Louis C. Tiffany, Rebel in Glass*, 2nd ed., New York, 1966

230 Tiffany & Co. tête-à-tête set
New York, Tiffany & Co., ledgers, for date of piece
Heydt, Geo[rge] Frederic. *Charles L. Tiffany and the House of Tiffany & Co.*, New York, 1893
Letter, Tiffany & Co. to the Museum, (New York, Feb. 18, 1898), in The Metropolitan Museum of Art Archives

231 Tiffany & Co. tea set
New York, Tiffany & Co., ledgers, for date of piece
Bouilhet, André. "L'Exposition de Chicago: Notes de Voyage d'un Orfèvre," *Revue des Arts Décoratifs*, vol. 14 (1893-94), pp. 65-79

232 Tiffany & Co. mantel set
Smith, Walter. *The Masterpieces of The Centennial International Exhibition, Vol. II: Industrial Art*, Philadelphia, 1875, pp. 97-98
Lamb, Martha J. *History of The City of New York, Its Origin, Rise and Progress*, 3 vols., New York, 1877, 1880, 1896; reprinted, New York, 1921, vol. 3, p. 810

233 Greenpoint Faience Manufacturing Co. vase
Barber. *Pottery and Porcelain of The United States*, 1893 ed., p. 317, pl. 157

234 Whiting Manufacturing Co. trophy
Typescript, Inventory of Trophies . . . , (May 1965), no. 8, in The New York Yacht Club archives
McClinton. *Collecting American 19th Century Silver*

236 Richardson furniture
[Boito, Camillo, ed.]. *La Basilica di San Marco in Venezia Illustrata nella Storia e nell'Arte da Scrittori Veneziani . . .*, 14 vols. Venice, 1888; vols. 1-3, Venice, 1881
Van Rensselaer, M. G. *Henry Hobson Richardson and His Works*, Cambridge, Massachusetts, 1888
Hitchcock, Henry-Russell. *The Architecture of H. H. Richardson and His Times*, 2nd ed. rev., Hamden, Connecticut, 1961
Museum of Fine Arts, Boston. *The Furniture of H. H. Richardson*, exhibition notes by Richard H. Randall, Jr., (Jan. 9-Feb. 18, 1962)
Roseberry, Cecil R. *Capitol Story*, Albany, New York, 1964

237 Timmes cast-iron settee
[Chase Brothers & Co., Boston Ornamental Iron Works]. *Illustrated Catalogue, of Plain and Ornamental Iron Furniture, Iron Railing, and Bronzed Iron goods . . .*, Boston [1850s?], p. 20
[Samuel S. Bent & Son]. *Illustrated Catalogue and Price List of Settees, Chairs, Vases, Summer-house, Crestings, Tree-Boxes, Manufactured by Samuel S. Bent & Son . . .*, New York, [1890-1894], p. 1

238 North American Iron Works chair
[Samuel S. Bent & Son]. *Illustrated Catalogue and Price List of Settees, Chairs, Vases, Summer-house, Crestings, Tree-Boxes, Manufactured by Samuel S. Bent & Son . . .*, New York, [1890-1894], p. 6

240 Union Porcelain Works dinner set
Barber. *Pottery and Porcelain of The United States*, 1893 ed., pp. 252-259

242 Tobey Furniture Company dining set
Marquardt, Mary Oona. Sources of Capital of Early Illinois Manufacturers, 1840-1880, unpublished Ph.D. thesis, University of Illinois, Urbana, Illinois, pp. 387-393
Letter, Frank Wells McCabe to the American Wing, (New York, Oct. 7, 1969), in the American Wing Archives, The Metropolitan Museum of Art

243, 245 Rookwood vase, Rookwood ewer, vase, bowl
Koch, Robert. "Rookwood pottery," *Antiques*, vol. 77, no. 3 (Mar. 1960), pp. 288-289
Peck, Herbert. *The Book of Rookwood Pottery*, New York, 1968

244 Owens umbrella stand
Barber, Edwin Atlee. *Marks of American Potters*, Philadelphia, 1904, p. 132

246 Mt. Washington Glass Co. lamp
Revi, Albert Christian. *Nineteenth Century Glass, its Genesis and Development*, New York, 1959, pp. 36-45

247 New England Glass Co. vase
Revi, Albert Christian. *Nineteenth Century Glass, its Genesis and Development*, New York, 1959, pp. 46-51

248 Hobbs, Brockunier & Co. vase, ewer, pitcher
[Morgan, Mrs. Mary J.] *Catalogue of the art collection formed by . . . Mrs. M. J. Morgan . . . sold . . . Mar. 3d . . . 5th, [1886] . . . at Chickering hall . . . Mar. 8th, and ff. days at the American Art Galleries . . .*, New York, 1886, no. 341
Revi, Albert Christian. *Nineteenth Century Glass, its Genesis and Development*, New York, 1959, p. 46
Grover, Ray and Lee. *Art Glass Nouveau*, Rutland, Vermont, 1967, p. 41

249 New England Glass Co. pitcher
Revi, Albert Christian. *Nineteenth Century Glass, its Genesis and Development*, New York, 1959, pp. 60-64
Grover, Ray and Lee. *Art Glass Nouveau*, Rutland, Vermont, 1967, p. 54

250 Mt. Washington Glass Co. vase
Revi, Albert Christian. *Nineteenth Century Glass, its Genesis and Development*, New York, 1959, pp. 76-83
Grover, Ray and Lee. *Art Glass Nouveau*, Rutland, Vermont, 1967, pp. 46-47

251 New England Glass Co. cracker jar, bowl, Mt. Washington Glass Co. sugar bowl, creamer
Watkins, Lura Woodside. *Cambridge Glass 1818-1888, The Story of the New England Glass Company*, Boston, 1930, pp. 149-153
Revi, Albert Christian. *Nineteenth Century Glass, its Genesis and Development*, New York, 1959, pp. 17-20

252 Knowles, Taylor & Knowles vase
Barber. *Pottery and Porcelain of The United States*, 1893 ed., pp. 201-207

253 Ott & Brewer vase
Barber. *Pottery and Porcelain of The United States*, 1893 ed., pp. 214-223

254 Ott & Brewer pitcher
Barber. *Pottery and Porcelain of The United States*, 1893 ed., pp. 232-237
The Newark Museum, Newark, New Jersey. *The Pottery and Porcelain of New Jersey 1688-1900*, preface by Arthur W. Clement, (Apr. 8-May 11, 1947), Newark, 1947, no. 233

255 T. G. Hawkes candelabra
Daniel, Dorothy. *Cut and Engraved Glass 1771-1905 . . .*, New York, 1950, pp. 184-188

256 Pairpoint Manufacturing Co. pitcher, cut-glass bowl and clear bowl
Pearson, J. Michael and Dorothy T. *American Cut Glass*, New York, 1965, p. 69

257 Libbey Glass Co. punch bowl
Revi, Albert Christian. *American Cut and Engraved Glass*, New York, 1965, p. 26
The Toledo Museum of Art. *Libbey Glass, a Tradition of 150 Years 1818-1968*, Toledo, 1968, no. 83, illustration p. 42

258 Tiffany & Co. magnolia vase
Heydt, Geo[rge] Frederic. *A Glimpse of the Tiffany Exhibit at the Columbian Exposition, Chicago* (reprint from *Godey's Magazine*, Aug. 1893), pp. 6, 9-10
Wheeler, Candace. *Yesterdays in a Busy Life*, New York and London, 1918
Stern, Madeleine B. "An American Woman First in Textiles & Interior Decoration: Candace Wheeler," in *We the Women, Career Firsts of Nineteenth-Century America*, New York, 1963, pp. 273-303
Rainwater, Dorothy T. *American Silver Manufacturers*, Hanover, Pennsylvania, 1966, p. 181
McClinton. *Collecting American 19th Century Silver*, p. 83, illustration p. 85

259 Tiffany & Co. Viking punch bowl
Heydt, Geo[rge] Frederic. *A Glimpse of the Tiffany Exhibit at the Columbian Exposition, Chicago* (reprint from *Godey's Magazine*, Aug. 1893), p. 7

260 Tiffany (?) horn chair
Artistic Houses . . ., 2 vols. in 4 folios, New York, 1884, vol. 2, pt. 2, pl. opp. p. 168, p. 169
Butler, Joseph T. *American Antiques 1800-1900 A Collector's History and Guide*, New York, 1965, pp. 82, 88-89
Koch, Robert. *Louis C. Tiffany, Rebel in Glass*, 2nd ed., New York, 1966

261 Tiffany andirons
de Forest, Emily Johnston. The House, 7 Washington Square, and an Inventory of its contents, New York, 1928, unpublished ms. in the collection of Mrs. Douglas Williams, New York, copy in the American Wing Archives, The Metropolitan Museum of Art
Koch, Robert. *Louis C. Tiffany, Rebel in Glass*, 2nd ed., New York, 1966

262 Tiffany chairs, table, lamp
Spofford, Harriet Prescott. *Art Decoration Applied to Furniture*, New York, 1878, pp. 78, 161

[Tiffany Glass & Decorating Co.]. *A Synopsis of the Exhibit of the Tiffany Glass and Decorating Co. in the American Section of the Manufacturers and Liberal Arts Building at the World's Fair*, Chicago, 1893, p. 7
Koch, Robert. *Louis C. Tiffany, Rebel in Glass*, 2nd ed., New York, 1966, p. 134

263 Tiffany peony lamp
Koch, Robert. *Louis C. Tiffany, Rebel in Glass*, 2nd ed., New York, 1966

264 Tiffany column
[Tiffany Glass & Decorating Co.]. *Tiffany Glass Mosaics for Walls, Ceilings, Inlays, and Other Ornamental Work; Unrestricted in Color, Impervious to Moisture and Absolutely Permanent*, New York, 1896, quotation p. 9
Koch, Robert. *Louis C. Tiffany, Rebel in Glass*, 2nd ed., New York, 1966

266 Tiffany wisteria window
The Museum of Modern Art, New York (June 6-Sept. 6, 1960), Carnegie Institute, Pittsburgh (Oct. 13-Dec. 12, 1960), Los Angeles County Museum (Jan. 17-Mar. 5, 1961), Baltimore Museum of Art (Apr. 1-May 15, 1961). *Art Nouveau, Art and Design at the Turn of the Century*, Peter Selz and Mildred Constantine, eds., with articles by Greta Daniel, Alan M. Fern, Henry-Russell Hitchcock and Peter Selz, New York, 1960, no. 266

267 Tiffany enamels
Howe, Samuel. "Enamel As a Decorative Agent," *The Craftsman*, vol. 2, no. 2 (May 1902), pp. 61-88
Koch, Robert. *Louis C. Tiffany, Rebel in Glass*, 2nd ed., New York, 1966

268 Tiffany vase, inkwells
Koch, Robert. *Louis C. Tiffany, Rebel in Glass*, 2nd ed., New York, 1966

269 Tiffany vases, bowl
[Bing, Siegfried]. *Salon de l'Art Nouveau, Catalogue premier*, Paris, 1895
[Tiffany Glass & Decorating Company]. *Tiffany Favrile Glass . . .*, 5th ed., New York, 1899
deKay, Charles. *The Art Work of Louis C. Tiffany*, New York, 1914
Feld, Stuart P. "'Nature in her most seductive aspects': Louis Comfort Tiffany's Favrile Glass," *The Metropolitan Museum of Art Bulletin*, n.s., vol. 21, no. 3 (Nov. 1962), pp. 101-112
Koch, Robert. *Louis C. Tiffany, Rebel in Glass*, 2nd ed., New York, 1966
Letter, Heinz Spielmann, Museum für Kunst und Gewerbe, Hamburg, Germany, to the American Wing, (Hamburg, Oct. 2, 1969), the American Wing Archives, The Metropolitan Museum of Art (verifying the first name of Bing as Siegfried)

270 Tiffany cameo vase
[Bing, Siegfried]. *Salon de l'Art Nouveau, Catalogue premier*, Paris, 1895
Koch, Robert. *Louis C. Tiffany, Rebel in Glass*, 2nd ed., New York, 1966

271 Tiffany punch bowl
[United States Commission, Paris Exposition of 1900, Department of Fine Arts]. "Applied Arts at the Paris Exposition," *American Art Annual III* (1900), pp. 21-22

272 Tiffany daffodil lamp
Koch, Robert. *Louis C. Tiffany, Rebel in Glass*, 2nd ed., New York, 1966

273 George C. Flint & Co. cabinet
Soulier, Gustave. "L'Ameublement à l'Exposition," *Art et Décoration*, vol. 8 (1900), pp. 33-45
Catalogue Général Officiel Première Exposition Internationale d'Art Décoratif Moderne (May-Nov. 1902), Turin [n.d.], section on France, 11th entry, p. 136
Rais, Jules. "L'Ecole de Nancy et Son Exposition au Musée des Arts Décoratifs," *Art et Décoration*, vol. 13 (1903), pp. 129-138
Genuys, Ch. "L'Exposition de la Société des Artistes Décorateurs," *Art et Décoration*, vol. 15 (1904), pp. 78-92
Saunier, Ch. "L'Exposition de la Société des Artistes Décorateurs au Musée des Arts Décoratifs," *Art et Décoration*, vol. 20 (1906), pp. 191, 205
Sedeyn, Emile. "L'Art Appliqué au Salon d'Automne," *Art et Décoration*, vol. 22 (1907), pp. 154-155

275 Gorham Martelé punch bowl
McClinton. *Collecting American 19th Century Silver*, pp. 102-121

276 Unger Brothers letter opener, brooch, buckle
Johnson, J. Stewart. "Silver in Newark," *The Museum* [published by The Newark Museum], n.s., vol. 18, nos. 3 & 4, (Summer-Fall 1966), pp. 32-33, 44-45
McClinton. *Collecting American 19th Century Silver*, pp. 117-120

277 Alvin Manufacturing Co.(?) vase
Revi, Albert Christian. *Nineteenth Century Glass, Its Genesis and Development*, New York, 1959, pp. 198-201
McClinton. *Collecting American 19th Century Silver*, pp. 121-126

278 Honesdale vase
Revi, Albert Christian. *American Cut and Engraved Glass*, New York, 1965, pp. 269-270
Revi, Albert Christian. *American Art Nouveau Glass*, Camden, New Jersey, 1968, pp. 221-230

279 S.A. Weller vase
Barber. *Pottery and Porcelain of The United States*, 1909 ed., pp. 563-564

280 Steuben Glass Works vase
Revi, Albert Christian. *American Art Nouveau Glass*, Camden, New Jersey, 1968, pp. 128-142

281 Tiffany & Co. Adams vase
[Tiffany & Company]. *The Adams Gold Vase*, New York, 1896
McClinton. *Collecting 19th Century American Silver*, p. 71

282 Bitter cup
The Metropolitan Museum of Art. *American Sculpture, A Catalogue of the Collection of The Metropolitan Museum of Art*, by Albert TenEyck Gardner, New York, 1965, p. 99
Dennis, James M. *Karl Bitter, Architectural Sculptor 1867-1915*, Madison, Milwaukee, and London, 1967

283 Tiffany & Co. candelabrum
McClinton. *Collecting American 19th Century Silver*, pp. 67, 87

284 Tiffany & Co. thistle goblet
[The Engineers' Club]. *Golden Anniversary of the Present Headquarters of the Engineers' Club . . .*, New York, 1957

285 Tiffany & Co. Belmont tray
Brown, H. C. *The New Subway in Manhattan*, New York, 1904
[Chamber of Commerce of The State of New York]. *Rapid Transit in New York City and in Other Great Cities*, New York, 1906

286 Grueby vase
The Craftsman, vol. 1, no. 2 (Nov. 1901), illustrations pp. 50-51
Koch, Robert. *Louis C. Tiffany, Rebel in Glass*, 2nd ed., New York, 1966
Schwartz, Marvin D. *Collectors' Guide to Antique American Ceramics*, Garden City, New York, 1969, p. 130

287, 288 Newcomb vases
Stiles, Helen E. *Pottery in the United States*, New York, 1941, pp. 187-190
Blasberg, Robert W. "Newcomb pottery," *Antiques*, vol. 94, no. 1 (July 1968), pp. 73-77

289 Maher chairs
[Passe, Crispin de, ed.] *Oficina Arcularia*, Amsterdam, 1642, 14th page, chair 7, design by Hans Vredeman de Vries, originally published in *Different pourtraicts de menuiserie*, [ca. 1583]
Maher, George W. "Originality in American Architecture," *The Prairie School Review*, vol. 1, no. 1 (1st quarter 1964), pp. 12, 14-15; originally published in the *Inland Architect* (Oct. 1887)

Rudd, J. William. "George W. Maher, Architect of the Prairie School," *The Prairie School Review*, vol. 1, no. 1 (1st quarter 1964), pp. 5-7, 9-10

290 Tiffany hanging lamp
de Forest, Emily Johnston. The House, Wawapek Farm, and an Inventory of its Contents, Cold Spring Harbor, New York, 1928, unpublished ms., in the collection of Mrs. Douglas Williams, New York

292 Wright vase
"The Work of Frank Lloyd Wright," *Chicago Architectural Annual* (1902)
Manson, Grant. *Frank Lloyd Wright*, New York, 1958, pp. 135-136

293 Wright chairs
Wright, Frank Lloyd. "In the Cause of Architecture," *The Architectural Record*, vol. 23, no. 3 (Mar. 1908), pp. 155-221
Manson, Grant. *Frank Lloyd Wright*, New York, 1958, pp. 115-117

294 Stickley armchair
[Stickley, Gustav]. "Foreword," *The Craftsman*, vol. 1, no. 1 (Oct. 1901), p. i
The Craftsman, vols. 1-31 (1901-1916), ed. by Gustav Stickley
Koch, Robert. "Elbert Hubbard's Roycrofters as Artist-Craftsmen," *Winterthur Portfolio III* (1967), pp. 67-82

295 Stickley suite, Dirk van Erp lamps
Stickley, Gustav. "Craftsman Furniture," in *Catalogue of Craftsman Furniture Made by Gustav Stickley . . .*, Eastwood, New York, 1909, p. 3
Craftsman Homes, New York, 1909
"What Craftsman Furniture Stands For," in *Craftsman Furniture Made by Gustav Stickley*, (manufacturer's catalogue), New York, 1913, p. 3
Freeman, John Crosby. *The Forgotten Rebel*, Watkins Glen, New York, 1966
Typescript (1969), Terence and Ethel Leichti to the American Wing, American Wing Archives, The Metropolitan Museum of Art

296, 297, 298 Greene and Greene suite, chandelier, table, Tiffany lamps, bowl
McCoy, Esther. *Five California Architects*, New York, 1960
Makinson, Randell L. "Greene and Greene: The Gamble House," *The Prairie School Review*, vol. 5, no. 4 (4th quarter 1968), pp. 5-26
Typescript (1969), Randell L. Makinson to the American Wing, American Wing Archives, The Metropolitan Museum of Art